Missiological Hermeneutics

American Society of Missiology
Monograph Series

The ASM Monograph Series provides a forum for publishing quality dissertations and studies in the field of missiology. Collaborating with Pickwick Publications—a division of Wipf and Stock Publishers of Eugene, Oregon—the American Society of Missiology selects high quality dissertations and other monographic studies that offer research materials in mission studies for scholars, mission and church leaders, and the academic community at large. The ASM seeks scholarly work for publication in the Series that throws light on issues confronting Christian world mission in its cultural, social, historical, biblical, and theological dimensions.

Missiology is an academic field that brings together scholars whose professional training ranges from doctoral-level preparation in areas such as scripture, history and sociology of religions, anthropology, theology, international relations, interreligious interchange, mission history, inculturation, and church law. The American Society of Missiology, which sponsors this series, is an ecumenical body drawing members from Independent and Ecumenical Protestant, Catholic, Orthodox, and other traditions. Members of the ASM are united by their commitment to reflect on and do scholarly work relating to both mission history and the present-day mission of the church. The ASM Monograph Series aims to publish works of exceptional merit on specialized topics, with particular attention given to work by younger scholars, the dissemination and publication of which is difficult under the economic pressures of standard publishing models.

Persons seeking information about the ASM or the guidelines for having their dissertations considered for publication in the ASM Monograph Series should consult the Society's website—www.asmweb.org.

Members of the ASM Monograph Committee who approved this book are:

James R. Krabill
Mennonite Mission

Judith Lingenfelter
Biola University

Bonnie Sue Lewis
University of Dubuque Theological Seminary

Missiological Hermeneutics
Biblical Interpretation for the Global Church

Shawn Barrett Redford

American Society of Missiology
Monograph Series

11

☙PICKWICK *Publications* • Eugene, Oregon

MISSIOLOGICAL HERMENEUTICS
Biblical Interpretation for the Global Church

American Society of Missiology Monograph Series 11

Copyright © 2012 Shawn Barrett Redford. All rights reserved. Except for brief quotations in critical publications or reviews, no part of this book may be reproduced in any manner without prior written permission from the publisher. Write: Permissions, Wipf and Stock Publishers, 199 W. 8th Ave., Suite 3, Eugene, OR 97401.

Pickwick Publications
An Imprint of Wipf and Stock Publishers
199 W. 8th Ave., Suite 3
Eugene, OR 97401

www.wipfandstock.com

ISBN 13: 978-1-60899-402-1

Cataloging-in-Publication data:

Redford, Shawn Barrett.

    Missiological hermeneutics : biblical interpretation for the global church / Shawn Barrett Redford.

    xx + 364 p. ; 23 cm. — Includes bibliographical references and indexes.

    American Society of Missiology Monograph Series 11

    ISBN 13: 978-1-60899-402-1

    1. Bible—Hermeneutics. 2. Missions—Theory—Biblical teaching. I. Title. II. Series.

BV2073 R3 2012

Manufactured in the U.S.A.

*To Kristin,
whose beautiful nature is an
ever present witness of
Jesus' love, care, and patience*

Contents

List of Tables · ix

List of Figures · x

Foreword · xi

Acknowledgments · xviii

List of Abbreviations · xx

ONE   Introduction · 1

TWO   Biblically Informed Missional Hermeneutics · 8

THREE   A Missional Critique of Current Hermeneutical Theory · 85

FOUR   A Missional Critique of the Hermeneutics Used in a Difficult Missional Issue: A Case Study · 133

FIVE   The Role of Mission Praxis upon Missiological Hermeneutics: A Case Study · 232

SIX   Conclusion · 290

Appendix A The Promise to Bless All Nations · 301

Appendix B Chart of All Known Polygamists in Scripture · 314

Appendix C Comparison of Acts 10 and Acts 11 · 319

Glossary · 325

Bibliography · 327

Author and Subject Index · 341

Scripture Index · 353

Tables

Table 1	The Promise Revealed and Interpreted · 14
Table 2	Continuity and Discontinuity of the Promise · 20
Table 3	Original Language Comparison of Genesis 12:3a and Numbers 24:9 · 47
Table 4	Original Language Comparison of Genesis 12:3a and Psalm 72:17 · 51
Table 5	Comparing Acts 3:25 and Galatians 3:8 with LXX · 55
Table 6	Five Theological Interpretations on Polygamy · 140
Table 7	Comparison of NLT with du Preez and Kaiser · 143
Table 8	Leviticus 18:18 translation of "Her Sister" · 146
Table 9	The Quotations of Genesis 2:24 in the New Testament · 157
Table 10	Likelihood of Various Meanings for 1 Timothy 3:2, 12; 5:9 · 178
Table 11	Comparing Peter in Acts 10 with Jonah · 239
Table 12	Outline of Themes in Genesis · 302
Table 13	Occurrences of the Promise with respect to Land, Growth, and Blessing the Nations · 306
Table 14	Detailed Summary of the God-Given Promises in the Old Testament · 309
Table 15	Detailed Summary of the Re-Statement or Interpretation of the Promises · 312
Table 16	All Known Polygamists in the Bible · 315

Figures

Figure 1	Overview of the Promise in Genesis to Bless All the Nations of the Earth · 15	
Figure 2	Missional Impact in Genesis · 29	
Figure 3	The Indirect Meaning of the Sign of Jonah · 78	
Figure 4	Improving Perceptions of Intertextuality and Mission · 83	
Figure 5	Liberal Method in Hermeneutics · 88	
Figure 6	Evangelical Method in Hermeneutics · 90	
Figure 7	Examining the Western Lens · 93	
Figure 8	Current Hermeneutics of Theology of Mission · 95	
Figure 9	Tapestry of Scripture · 98	
Figure 10	Current Theology of Mission Lens · 109	
Figure 11	Spiritual Dimensions in Hermeneutics · 121	
Figure 12	The Role of Prayer · 124	
Figure 13	A Priority Lens Based in Humility · 130	
Figure 14	Holistic Hermeneutics · 131	
Figure 15	A Hermeneutic of Proof-Texting · 152	
Figure 16	The Thread of Genesis 2:24 in the New Testament · 161	
Figure 17	Supposed Fading of Polygamy throughout Scripture · 174	
Figure 18	Hermeneutical Building Blocks · 249	
Figure 19	Cultures Change at Different Rates · 253	
Figure 20	Hermeneutical Commitment · 284	
Figure 21	A Commonly-Held Perception of Scripture · 291	
Figure 22	A Balanced Perception of Scripture · 293	

Foreword

THE RELATION OF BIBLICAL studies to missiological reflection is one of the most neglected fields of investigation in missiology. Intuitively, we might think it obvious that one of the most basic aspects of mission theology would have to do with the relation of the Bible to mission theory and practice. Sadly, such is not the case. Determining the scriptural understanding of mission is not as simple as we might think. According to the South African missiologist, David Bosch, "We usually assume far too easily that we can employ the Bible as a kind of objective arbitrator in the case of theological differences, not realizing that [all] of us approach the Bible with [our] own set of preconceived ideas about what it says. . . . This means that it is of little avail to embark upon a discussion of the biblical foundations of mission unless we have first clarified some of the hermeneutical principles involved."[1]

In a similar vein, Roman Catholic biblical scholars, Donald Senior and Carroll Stuhlmueller, end their magnificent work in this field with the statement that they have not meant to "imply that the biblical style of mission is absolutely normative for mission today. There is no definite biblical recipe for proclaiming the Word of God. . . . Nevertheless there is a value in reflecting on the biblical patterns of evangelization."[2] Interestingly, as late as 1993, David Bosch stated that the work of Senior and Stuhlmueller was "still the best study in the entire field."[3]

Both biblical scholars and mission practitioners have contributed to the confusion by ignoring each other. To a large extent prior to the 1970s, biblical scholars focused on questions of origin, form, the faith community, and surrounding human civilizations to examine how these shaped the biblical text. These are important considerations. Unfortunately, with notable exceptions, their analysis of Scripture seldom asked the

---

1. Bosch, "Hermeneutical Principles," 437–38.
2. Senior and Stuhlmueller, *Biblical Foundations for Mission*, 332.
3. Bosch, "Reflections on Biblical Models," 178.

Foreword

missiological questions regarding purpose, design, and God's intentions as presented in the Bible. Meanwhile, the practitioners of mission, and the missiologist scholars, essentially continued to superimpose their particular agendas on Scripture, or ignore the Bible altogether.

The disconnect between biblical studies and missiological reflection can be appreciated in a report by Stanley Skreslet. Between 2001 and 2003, Skreslet examined 925 English-language doctoral dissertations on mission that had been published around the globe from 1992 to 2001. He found that a mere 43 of those dissertations, or 4.6% of them, had to do with Bible and mission. And of the 43, only 2 focused on the Old Testament.[4]

So as late as 2001, Köstenberger and O'Brien observed, "Mission has thus far been one of the step-children of New Testament theology [for example]. Rarely has this significant biblical theme been given its due in the overall discipline." Thus, with reference to their own endeavor, they write, "The present study, while also concerned to deal with larger missiological issues, represents a modest effort to help fill this gap. . . . The present work seeks to [combine] a commitment to a biblical-theological method and a salvation-historical approach with an openness to examine the various portions of Scripture regarding their respective contributions to the biblical theme of 'mission'. . . . In claiming that our approach is biblical-theological we recognize that it is neither a systematic-theological nor a missiological examination."[5]

At the risk of oversimplification, a brief look back might help us understand how we got here and in what way this work by Shawn Redford represents a major step forward in bridging the gap between biblical studies and missiological reflection.

THE BIBLE BASIS OF MISSION SHOWS HOW THE BIBLE SUPPORTS AND JUSTIFIES CHRISTIAN MISSION PRACTICE.

Prior to the 1970s, mission theorists and practitioners drew from the Bible mostly as a way to justify the mission agendas they had already adopted. And the missions-folks did this in the context of biblical scholarship that mostly ignored mission as an uninteresting and unnecessary theme in biblical exegesis and hermeneutics.

---

4. Skreslet, "Doctoral Dissertations on Mission," 100–101.
5. Köstenberger and O'Brien, *Salvation to the Ends*, 19–20.

Foreword

As David Bosch explained it, "At least since the days of William Carey, two centuries ago, Protestant missionary advocates have argued that they were defending and propagating an enterprise that had its roots in Scripture. And indeed, much trouble was taken to find biblical authorization for the missionary enterprise. Unfortunately, this was frequently done by gleaning so-called 'missionary texts' from the Bible to undergird the contemporary missionary enterprise. . . . Behind this entire approach lay the assumption that one already knew what 'mission' was and now only had to prove that it was mandated by Scripture. And, of course, in the modern era mission meant (and by and large still means) the geographical movement from a Christian locality to a pagan locality for the purpose of winning converts and planting churches in that area."[6]

A brief look at some of the most well-known Protestant works associating Bible and mission from 1920 to the 1970s would bear out Bosch's observations. One could examine the following, for example, to see that the primary (though not always the only) question being asked of Scripture is whether Scripture supports, commands, and motivates—that is, justifies—the missionary practices of the day.[7]

MISSION IS A THEME THAT COURSES ITS WAY THROUGH THE ENTIRE BIBLE AND A THUS A FULL-ORBED READING OF THE BIBLE SHOULD INCLUDE THE QUESTION OF GOD'S MISSION.

During the 1970s through the 1990s a new approach to the question began to be offered. Arguably the deep, soul-searching questions being asked about mission during the 1960s, especially by mainline Protestant scholars associated with the World Council of Churches, may have stimulated folks to begin to approach the issue of the relationship of the Bible to Christian mission from a different angle.

In 1961, Gerald Anderson and his colleagues pointed the way for this new direction by describing the basic contours of a broader hermeneutic in part 1 of *The Theology of the Christian Mission*.[8] Here G. Ernest

---

6. Bosch, "Reflections on Biblical Models," 175–76.

7. See, for example, Montgomery, *Bible and Missions*; Glover, *Bible Basis of Missions*; Rowley, *Missionary Message of OT*; de Groot, *Bible on the Salvation*; Peters, *Biblical Theology of Missions*.

8. Anderson, *The Theology of the Christian Mission*, 17–94.

Foreword

Wright, Johannes Blauw, Oscar Cullmann, Karl Barth, Donald Miller, and F. N. Davey surveyed a wide range of biblical material, deriving from the Bible what the church's mission ought to be.

At about the same time the missiological reflection of the Second Vatican Council on the role of Scripture also called for a new approach.[9] Subsequent papal encyclicals like *Evangelii nuntiandi* and *Redemptoris missio* have also appealed to Scripture.

Thus Arthur Glasser called for a deeper missiological reflection on the biblical message: "All Scripture makes its contribution in one way or another to our understanding of mission. . . . In our day evangelicals are finding that the biblical base for mission is far broader and more complex than any previous generation of missiologists appears to have envisioned. . . . In our day there is a growing impatience with all individualistic and pragmatic approaches to the missionary task that arise out of a proof-text use of Scripture, despite their popularity among the present generation of activistic evangelicals."[10]

And Johannes Verkuyl advocated a similar change in hermeneutical approach. "In the past the usual method was to pull a series of prooftexts out of the Old and New Testaments and then to consider the task accomplished. But more recently, biblical scholars have taught us the importance of reading these texts in context and paying due regard to the various nuances. . . . [O]ne must consider the very structure of the whole biblical message."[11]

Along the same line, David Bosch wrote, "[I]f we wish to reflect on 'biblical foundations for mission,' our point of departure should not be the contemporary enterprise we seek to justify, but the biblical sense of what being sent into the world signifies. It also means that, however important single biblical texts may (seem to) be, the validity of mission should not be deduced from isolated sayings but from the thrust of the central message of Scripture. . . . We may now proceed to draw the contours of a 'biblical theology of mission.' Such a project seeks answers . . . to three basic questions: . . . Why mission? . . . How mission? . . . What is mission? . . . In light of the exposition above it should be clear

---

9. For example, *Lumen Gentium: Costituzione Dogmatica Sulla Chiesa, Promulgata Dal Concilio Ecumenico Vaticano II*; *Ad Gentes*; *Decreto Conciliare Sull'attivita Missionaria Della Chiesa*, in Flannery, *Documents of Vatican II*, 350–440, 813–62.

10. Glasser, *Kingdom and Mission*, 26–27.

11. Verkuyl, *Contemporary Missiology*, 90.

Foreword

that it would not do to build a biblical theology of mission on isolated proof-texts."[12] During this time, a large number of publications appeared on the subject. Some of the more well-known that follow the perspective outlined above would include the following (placed in the order in which they appeared).[13]

THE BIBLE'S VIEW OF MISSION IS A HERMENEUTICAL LENS THROUGH WHICH WE CAN SEE MORE CLEARLY GOD'S MISSION IN GOD'S WORLD.

Over the last several decades a significant global consensus has emerged with regard to the Bible and mission. Yet in each generation there is a need to reflect again on the way the church uses or abuses the scriptural understanding of mission. Thus David Bosch summarized the matter saying, "Our conclusion is that both Old and New Testament are permeated with the idea of mission. . . . [But] not everything we call mission is indeed mission. . . . It is the perennial temptation of the Church to become . . . 'a club of religious folklore.' . . . The only remedy for this mortal danger lies in challenging herself unceasingly with the true biblical foundation of mission."[14]

Drawing from the seminal ideas found in "B" above, a number of biblical scholars and missiologists in this new century have begun to develop a new approach to relating Bible and mission. This new endeavor seeks to allow the Bible itself to question, reshape, and transform the missiological assumptions, the hermeneutic, with which the Church approaches the Scriptures so that the Scriptures themselves are allowed to portray God's mission. This present work is part of that new movement

---

12. Bosch, "Reflections on Biblical Models," 177, 79.

13. De Ridder, *Discipling the Nations*; Stott, *Christian Mission*; Verkuyl, *Contemporary Missiology*; Bosch, "True Biblical Foundation,"; Bosch, *Witness to the World*; Gilliland, *Pauline Theology & Mission Practice*; Senior and Stuhlmueller, *Biblical Foundations for Mission*; Ro and Eshenaur, *Bible & Theology in Asian Contexts*; Gnanakan, *Kingdom Concerns*; Bosch, *Transforming Mission*; Carriker, *Missão Integral*; Bosch, "Reflections on Biblical Models,"; Hedlund, *God and the Nations*; Nuñez, *Hacia Una Misionología*; Padilla, *Bases Bíblicas de La Misión*; Terry et al., *Missiology*; Nissen, *NT and Mission*; Kaiser, *Mission in the OT*; Zabatiero, *Liberdade E Paixão*; Loewen, *Bible in Cross-Cultural Perspective*; Carriker, *Caminho Missionário de Deus*; Köstenberger and O'Brien, *Salvation to the Ends*; Glasser, *Announcing the Kingdom*; Gallagher and Hertig, *Mission in Acts*; Carriker, *Visão Missionária da Bíblia*; Wright, *Mission of God*; Okoye, *Israel and the Nations*.

14. Bosch, "Hermeneutical Principles," 451.

Foreword

that seeks to allow the missional lenses of the Bible to offer us a new set of assumptions, new "paradigms," a new hermeneutic from which to read the Bible itself. This new approach seeks to explore the Bible's view of God's mission as a key to unlocking the meaning of the Bible itself. In this work, Redford seeks ways to allow the Bible itself to guide him. He wants to see the Bible itself set the parameters of the hermeneutical process in reflection-action in mission theology.

This work seeks to build a new bridge across the great divide between biblical studies and missiological reflection. Here, Redford breaks new ground in pointing the way forward toward the creation of a missiological hermeneutic, a missional lens that, like a microscope, shows us aspects of God's nature and God's mission that other lenses have not demonstrated. Redford then takes a step further. He experiments with the new missiological hermeneutic. He tries out this new hermeneutical lens by looking through it to examine two difficult, sensitive and problematic issues that have plagued missiology for decades: polygamy and Christian conversation with followers of Islam. The application of a missiological hermeneutic to these two issues helps the reader grasp how important it is for the Bible itself to define the center, the parameters, and the meaning for understanding God's mission.

Further, the unique contribution of this work is that it incorporates the presence and illumination of the Holy Spirit coupled with careful culturally-appropriate contextualization as factors in constructing a new missiological hermeneutic. The author is at once committed to proclaiming in word and deed the coming of the Kingdom of God in Jesus Christ, committed to world evangelization, and committed to grace-filled, grace-full, contextual sensitivity.

Dr. Redford is well-qualified to write this book. Some of what is written here he worked out during team-teaching in biblical theology of mission at Fuller. Now living in Nairobi, Kenya, Dr. Redford is developing his missiological hermeneutic even further, as that relates to the African context. And the theological tradition that has shaped him is one that strongly affirms the "sola Scriptura" perspectives of the Reformation, emphasizing the role of the Bible for understanding God's mission in God's world.

This work represents a profound exploration in search of a biblically-grounded, Holy Spirit anointed, grace-filled, contextually-sensitive re-reading of the Bible in order to understand and participate in God's mission, in this new century, in a lost and hurting world so loved by God. This work offers us a way forward. It gives us hope that the Church of Jesus Christ, spread around the globe, can bring together that which should never have been separated: reading the Bible in context and participating in God's mission in a grace-full manner.

Charles E. Van Engen
Glendora, California
March 21, 2011

Acknowledgments

I GIVE GREAT THANKS to God for the journey into this field that has inspired and solidified my understanding of Scripture. I thank my family and friends for sustaining and encouraging me.

Thank you Kristin for your overwhelming contribution in this journey. You are an amazing wife and companion, mother extraordinaire, fellow missiologist, missionary, colleague, and an amazing therapist. Thank you for the thousands of meals, clean clothes, washed dishes, proofread words, talks, ideas, hours of childcare, and steps hiking together. Thank you for three amazing children. Thank you Grace for your excitement and joy in life. Thank you Peyton for your sweet laughter and hugs. Thank you Carter for your confident spirit in all things.

Thank you to my mother, Prudence Thayer. Your parental support and encouragement are only exceeded by your consistent prayers for the nations. Thank you Thomas Redford, my brother, for your encouragement and love in the midst of an often uphill journey. Thank you Ray and Phyllis Lindquist for your proof-reading, persistent joy, and your witness of Christ's nature.

I give great thanks to dear friends Dr. Charles and Jean Van Engen. You have opened your hearts, shared your lives with ours, and we have been blessed. As my mentor Chuck, you have empowered me in ways that I never knew existed and I will always treasure the confidence you have placed in me, not to mention your willingness to share the classroom. You are the greatest story-teller I have ever known, and I thank God that you use your gifts sharing the greatest story ever told!

Thank you Dr. Wilbert Shenk. Your encyclopedic knowledge of the broad field of missiology is a mark that challenges us all. Your devotion to God's mission is as persistently evident as your humility. Thank you Dr. Dan Shaw. Your passion as an educator is an inspiration to all. Thank you Dr. Paul Hertig for your devotion to this topic, your feedback, and

Acknowledgments

your critique. Thank you Dr. Dean Gilliland for your astute editorial and missiological direction.

Thank you Dr. J. Dudley Woodberry for your gentile nature, your leadership, and your passion for God's mission. Thank you Dr. Charles Kraft and Dr. Robert Gallagher for the influence that each of you have had on my learning and growth as a missiologist. Thank you for the prayers and encouragement from so many friends including Larry, Jeff, Peter, Darin, and Jerry.

Abbreviations

Afer	*African Ecclesial Review*
AMP	Amplified Bible
ASV	American Standard Version
ATJ	*Africa Theological Journal*
CEV	Contemporary English Version
CMF	Christian Missionary Fellowship
Darby	1890 Darby Bible
ESV	English Standard Version
GNT	Good News Translation
HCSB	Holman Christian Standard Bible
KJ21	21st Century King James Version
KJV	King James Version
Living	The Living Bible
MSG	The Message
NA27	Nestle Aland Greek New Testament, 27th Edition
NAB	New American Bible
NASB	New American Standard Bible
NCV	New Century Version
NIRV	New International Reader's Version
NIV	New International Version
NIVUK	New International Version—UK
NJB	New Jerusalem Bible
NKJV	New King James Version
NLT	New Living Translation
NLV	New Life Version
NRSV	New Revised Standard Version
RSV	Revised Standard Version
SDA	Seventh-Day Adventist
Tanakh	Tanakh, The Holy Scriptures
TNIV	Today's New International Version
YLT	Young's Literal Translation

ONE

Introduction

Thesis: Within Scripture, the biblical figures demonstrate their own use of an over-arching hermeneutic infused with both missional assumptions and spiritual vitality as they engage in the act of interpreting Scripture in their time. This over-arching hermeneutic is most apparent when these same biblical figures demonstrate a high allegiance to God's mission and a genuine response to influential spiritual activity. This same over-arching hermeneutic must be the starting point for the assumptions and direction held by the worldwide missional community who foremost has the missional skills and background to further refine the true nature of a missional hermeneutic.

WESTERN HERMENEUTICS IN THE modern era have been guided predominantly by scientific reason. This has not only secularized the hermeneutical process, but it has opened the doors for secular biblical interpretation. While this is not necessarily a problem, it is an issue if the missiological communities adhere to these standards without adequate biblical and missional critique.

The field of Biblical Theology of Mission exists in many ways as a response to a basic hermeneutical failure. For the most part, Western theologians trained in traditional hermeneutical methods fail to perceive mission in Scripture and this failure has generated greater attention to the field within missiology. However, many missiologists and missionaries who have been trained in traditional hermeneutics have simply applied traditional hermeneutics to the field of Biblical Theology of Mission. In this sense, the missiological community has, in many ways, followed the trends of the theological community with respect to hermeneutics.

However, the theological community, for the most part, has not only accepted Western scientific standards in hermeneutics but they have unwittingly become dogmatic proponents of a historical-critical hermeneutic methodology. Only in rare cases do authors challenge these standards, and it is even more rare to find those who challenge the reigning hermeneutical standards from a biblical standpoint.[1]

BACKGROUND IN THE FIELD

One way to determine if there is such a thing as biblical hermeneutics is through intertextual hermeneutics. Through this approach scholars consider the ways in which New Testament figures have interpreted the Old Testament. While there are notable works in this field, the field of intertextual hermeneutics has been relatively small and is dominated by theologians who have little or no perception of mission in Scripture.[2] This bias has hindered their efforts.

There has been a great deal of interest in trying to determine if biblical figures made use of "valid" hermeneutics but these efforts have not generally been fruitful because the authors have judged biblical figures by modern-day hermeneutical standards, and, as mentioned, they generally lack a perception of mission in Scripture. Additionally, those who have integrated intertextual hermeneutics with a biblical understanding of mission are few. Only a handful have offered glimpses that recognize an original author's missionally oriented understanding of the Old Testament.[3]

Likewise, some missiologists and even a few theologians have tried to define missiological hermeneutics. Many scholars call for a missiological hermeneutic in the most general sense.[4] By this I mean that these authors are advocating that the Bible be read with enough openness to allow for God's missionary activity while avoiding the tendency to in-

---

1. DeYoung and Hurty, *Beyond the Obvious*; Maier, *Biblical Hermeneutics*.

2. Beale, *Right Doctrine*; Dodd, *OT in the New*; Evans and Sanders, *Paul and the Scriptures*; Evans and Sanders, *Early Christian Interpretation*; Harrison et al., *Scripture, Tradition, and Interpretation*; Hays, *Echoes of Scripture*; Lindars et al., *Scripture Citing Scripture*.

3. Bosch, "Hermeneutical Principles," 448; Kaiser, *Mission in the OT*, 75–82; Okoye, *Israel and the Nations*, 49–54; Wagner, *Heralds of Good News*; Wright, *Mission of God*, 191–94, 247–49.

4. Guder and Barrett, *Missional Church*, 227–28.

Introduction

terject missional activity where it does not exist. For those trained in theology, this likewise requires that they avoid forcing the existing biblical missionary activity into unintended theological dogma. While this is a very basic missiological hermeneutic, these authors do little to help define our understanding of the hermeneutic itself.

However, there are a few works that are completely devoted to missional hermeneutics. These include theologian James V. Brownson, who suggests the adoption of a complex hermeneutical matrix centered around the biblical writers' range of meanings associated with "the gospel." Brownson seems to think that "multicultural dialogue" can fulfill Western mission today.[5] Likewise, theologians and missiologists in D. A. Carson's multi-authored volume focus heavily in ecclesiology while covering many pitfalls in missional hermeneutics.[6] Missiologists R. Daniel Shaw and Charles E. Van Engen suggest a model of interpretation based on four horizons that builds partially upon Thiselton's work and demonstrates the strong influence of anthropological factors in hermeneutical understanding.[7]

Though not communicated by as many written pages, Van Engen's hermeneutical model has been consistently taught to thousands of students taking Fuller Seminary's introductory course in Biblical Theology of Mission (MT520), and as such this model, more than likely, is having the strongest impact of any missional hermeneutic in existence. Van Engen's tapestry model is a hermeneutic that naturally avoids prooftexting as the hermeneutic calls for integrated and holistic missional themes found throughout Scripture. It likewise allows for a wider latitude of adoption by avoiding the Western tendency to be overly rigid.[8] Other than these, the only other significant piece is the article by Bosch, which has strong underlying hermeneutical implications calling for holistic biblical interpretation with respect to mission. This is primarily an excellent article for demonstrating the validity of assuming a general

---

5. Brownson, *Speaking the Truth*.
6. Carson, *Biblical Interpretation*.
7. Shaw and Van Engen, *Communicating God's Word*. In terms of the "four horizons," Shaw and Van Engen draw from Thiselton's original two horizons and Carson's three horizon adaptation of Thiselton (Carson, *Biblical Interpretation*, 16; Thiselton, *Two Horizons*).
8. Van Engen, "Relation of Bible," 27–36; Van Engen, *Mission on the Way*, 35–43.

missiological hermeneutic amidst those who have ignored mission in Scripture.[9]

Other authors have likewise tried to define missional hermeneutics in a variety of unique ways. Richard Bauckham advocates a basic missional hermeneutic in the midst of reading Scripture that additionally follows the Bible's movement from the particular to the universal.[10] H. Daniel Beeby argues that a missional hermeneutic must not be exclusive and should be given the highest priority of all hermeneutics.[11] Larry W. Caldwell questions the supremacy of the historical-critical method and suggests an ethnohermeneutical model that allows for culturally appropriate hermeneutical relativism.[12] Francis M. DuBose outlines and demonstrates a thematic missional hermeneutic related to "sending."[13] David J. Hesselgrave, similar to Beeby, argues that a missionary framework is the "proper teleological pre-understanding" for biblical interpretation.[14] Larkin uncritically advocates the use of the historical-critical method.[15] Johannes Nissen calls for a hermeneutic that is founded upon dialogue and co-learning between the missiological and theological communities.[16] Charles R. Taber questions whether or not a single hermeneutical approach can have validity for all societies and suggests that the poor and disenfranchised may have the least biased hermeneutic.[17] Tite Tiénou and Paul G. Hiebert suggest a case-law model in which mission theology offers a multiplicity of cases to stretch and test existing biblical and

---

9. The original book chapter is extremely difficult to find (Bosch, "True Biblical Foundation,"). However, this work was reprinted with some editing as an article and again as a book chapter (Bosch, "Hermeneutical Principles,"; Phillips and Coote, *Toward the Twenty-First Century*, 175–92). I have chosen to use the 1993 article in *Evangelical Review of Theology* because of the later editing and the title, "Hermeneutical Principles in the Biblical Foundation for Mission," which is most likely to surface in computerized searches related to this topic.

10. Bauckham, *Bible and Mission*, 11.

11. Beeby, *Canon and Mission*, 100–115; Beeby, "Missional Approach to Renewed Interpretation."

12. Caldwell, "Towards Ethnohermeneutics," 21–43.

13. DuBose, *God Who Sends*, 22–29.

14. Hesselgrave, "Missionary Hermeneutic."

15. Larkin, "Methods in Missiological Research."

16. Nissen, *NT and Mission*, 13–18.

17. Taber, "Missiology and the Bible," 239–44.

systematic theology that make up the "law."[18] Robert L. Thomas gives an overview of hermeneutics in evangelical missiology that includes relative newcomers such as Caldwell. However, while failing to include the more significant writings of Bosch and Van Engen, he takes up ideas and authors that have no background in missiology.[19] Christopher J. H. Wright suggests a thematic model that is very similar in practice to that of Van Engen.[20]

A related yet different field is that of ethnohermeneutics (sometimes called "contextual hermeneutics" or "indigenous hermeneutics") which attempts to portray the value of hermeneutical approaches taken by a particular society.[21] Ethnohermeneutics has great value in examining the way in which worldview assumptions affect biblical interpretation.[22] Exposure to a variety of ethnohermeneutical interpretations encourages every interpreter to examine their own worldview assumptions and calls into question our more obvious ethnocentric tendencies.

However, the field of ethnohermeneutics, while valuable, is a hermeneutic that is primarily defined by worldview values rather than biblical guidance. As such, the hermeneutic itself may be biblically guided, but this is most often coincidental rather than an intentional focus to discover biblically informed hermeneutics. Likewise, there is a strong likelihood that a given culture will perceive their ethnohermeneutic as normative rather than infused with their own worldview assumptions, as has been the case in the West. Nevertheless, ethnohermeneutic principles provide a very helpful lens for understanding ethnohermeneutic tendencies found throughout Scripture.

THE RESEARCH PROBLEM

In the prior literature there has not been any concerted attempt to consider the interplay between the following: (1) the factors that most influence biblical interpretation within Scripture; (2) the reason for adopting

18. Tiénou and Hiebert, "Missional Theology."

19. Thomas, *Evangelical Hermeneutics*, 407–50.

20. Wright, "Mission as a Matrix," 102–43; Wright, *Mission of God*, 33–69.

21. Dietrich and Luz, *Bible in World Context*; Gnanakan, *Biblical Theology in Asia*; Oleka, "Bible in African Context," 104–25; Sugirtharajah, *Voices from the Margin*, 306–18 is exemplary.

22. Blomberg, "Globalization of Hermeneutics,"; Shaw and Van Engen, *Communicating God's Word*.

a particular hermeneutic within Scripture, (3) the measure of God's grace allotted for understanding God's revelation, and (4) the role of the hermeneutical process in God's mission. It is to this multifaceted connection that this study is devoted.

The Central Research Question for this book is:

1. How does the Bible and mission inform missiologists and missionaries in our hermeneutical practice today?

Related to that central question, it is necessary to answer:

2. Does Scripture itself demonstrate the need for a missiological hermeneutic?
3. What are the barriers, if any, to a biblically informed missional hermeneutic?

CHAPTER OVERVIEW

In terms of this book's structure, Chapters 2 through 5 are the major chapters. Chapters 2 and 3 address hermeneutical theory, while Chapters 4 and 5 deal with field practice issues related to missional hermeneutics.

Chapter 2 is focused on biblical studies that investigate some of the most influential hermeneutics that are found within Scripture, as well as distorted hermeneutics that anger God. A significant portion of this chapter is devoted to the way in which Old and New Testament figures interpreted God's promise to bless all the nations of the earth (Gen 12:3). Likewise, the interpretational models found in Daniel 9–12 and Matthew 8–12 are considered. Although Acts 10–11 could easily have been included here, it is dealt with in Chapter 5 due to its relevance with respect to that case study.

Chapter 3 offers guidance for future direction in hermeneutics as well as a critique of the current hermeneutical trends in the West and the present state of missiological hermeneutics. This chapter attempts to integrate the existing biblical data and the thoughts of other missiologists in order to provide direction for the future of missiological hermeneutics.

Chapter 4 is a historical case study looking at the underlying hermeneutics employed over a wide range of authors who address the theological implications and missiological responses to issues in African polygamy. The primary focus of this chapter is to offer a practical critique with respect to theological and missiological hermeneutical assumptions.

Chapter 5 is the final case study in which the role of mission experience is examined as a significant hermeneutical lens. This particular hermeneutic is not only beneficial for biblical understanding but is essential for developing missiological insights in Scripture while avoiding the tendency to relegate valid mission insights in Scripture to the realm of theology.

Finally, chapter 6 is a summary conclusion drawing together all of the insights and offering recommendations for the future of missiological hermeneutics.

TWO

Biblically Informed Missional Hermeneutics

Thesis of this chapter: When biblical figures demonstrate breakthrough accounts in their own interpretation of Scripture, these most often take place through intense spiritual events, such as appearances of God (Gen 12:3; 18:18; 26:4; 28:14; Acts 10:19–20; 11:12), dreams, and visions (Gen 28:14, Dan 9:23; 10:1–2; Acts 10:3–6, 10–16; 11:5–10), interpretation by angels (Gen 22:18, Dan 9:21–27; Acts 10:4–6, 22, 30–33; 11:13–14) and understanding through prayer (Dan 9:3–20; 10:12; Acts 10:9; 11:5). Furthermore, correct interpretations of Scripture are most often surrounded by correct understandings and practices of God's mission (Gen 41–50; Dan 3–7; Acts 10:44–48; 11:15–18), while obscured interpretation occurs precisely when mission is obscured (Jonah 1–4; Matt 8–12). An equally relevant thesis is that the New Testament writers' interpretation of the Old Testament consistently demonstrates an ever growing missional hermeneutic with respect to Scripture, and this yields far more concern for developing an understanding of God's mission than today's historical-critical analysis that focuses on the historical setting and grammatical accuracy.

THE ANTITHESIS OF THIS chapter is that correct biblical interpretation within Scripture never took place solely through historical-critical hermeneutics and likewise did not lead to a unified or systematic theology. Rather, correct biblical interpretation took place gracefully through a complex and unpredictable set of events that were most often influenced by existing mission practice and these events likewise influenced the mission practice that would follow. From a practical standpoint, this type of study should cause missionaries to be very humble in terms of our own hermeneutical methods and open to considering the

Biblically Informed Missional Hermeneutics

ways that God chooses to influence us in order to understand Scripture. Furthermore, it should cause scholars to see some of the major faults present in historical-critical hermeneutics.

For those involved in missionary action, there are unique and distinctive times in which a transformation takes shape in our missionary experience that uniquely reforms our understanding regarding God's intent in mission. When this experience is potent, it will deeply transform missionary practice. Typically, this happens in the midst of missionary practice, but these occurrences are not common even though they have lasting effects in the life and practice of missionaries.

One of the telltale signs of these experiences is a renewed understanding of Scripture that aligns more closely with God's missional intentions. Those who have no involvement in God's mission rarely experience these transformational paradigms primarily because they lack "eyes to see and ears to hear" what God is doing in mission. For those who struggle in their allegiance to God, these instances are almost entirely elusive except as they are experienced through others.

As in the modern day, there are accounts throughout Scripture when the biblical figures undergo this same sort of transformational shift in understanding Scripture and their role in God's mission (as will be shown in the lives of Abraham, Jacob, Joseph, Balaam, Daniel, Peter, and Paul). This nearly always transforms their understanding of God's missionary practice and calls for adjustments in the ways that they have carried out God's mission. Likewise, there is often transformation in terms of the biblical writers' understanding of the Scripture, while keeping in mind that often the Old Testament, or some portion of the Old Testament, was their only Scripture. Unfortunately, the biblical figures struggle in the same way that the church does today in terms of their allegiance to God's mission and even in terms of their basic allegiance to God. As a result, the record of Scripture contains only a select number of instances in which the people of God understand Scripture in new ways that transform their ministry and mission practice.

However, there are enough accounts in Scripture to teach us something about the way in which the biblical figures reread Scripture and understood it in new ways that substantially affected their role in the mission of God. The most obvious accounts of this are in Acts, in the conversion of Paul (Acts 9) and Peter (Acts 10–11) since both accounts have a very dramatic effect in terms of the expansion of mission from the Jewish to the Gentile world. Accounts similar to these are the focus of this chapter, and the major concern is to understand how the biblical writers interpreted Scripture and to learn from the hermeneutical lenses that influenced their understanding. Therefore, the purpose of this chapter is to find those places in Scripture in which Old or New Testament figures demonstrate some renewed understanding of Scripture that relates to God's mission and to learn from their hermeneutic. One of the predominant inquiries of this study is to consider the major influences that affected the biblical figures' re-reading of Scripture which ultimately lead to a transformation in the way they understood their role as co-laborers in God's mission.

To put it in simple terms, I would say that the initial focus of this chapter is to search for those instances in Scripture where the people of God "got it," meaning that they put aside their own misconceived theological and missiological baggage and understood God's missional concerns. The real crux is to discover what made the difference in their renewed understanding of Scripture that ultimately improved their mission practice. Furthermore, this chapter is focused upon learning the ways in which valid biblical interpretation (hermeneutics) takes place within Scripture, specifically when these instances of renewed understanding take place.

Sometimes this renewed understanding begins through personal study, such as in Daniel 9–12, while in other cases the understanding takes place after a frenzy of efforts on the part of God, such as Acts 10–11. Yet in other cases, it takes hundreds or thousands of years before a complete understanding takes place, such as God's promise to bless all families/nations through Abraham and his descendants (as we look at Gen 12–50; Num 22–24; Ps 72; Gal 3–4; Acts 3 and Rom 4). Finally, we will consider one case in Matthew 8–12 in which Jesus reinterprets Scripture for Israel in the first century with a message that is predominantly negative with respect to their understanding of God and mission.

BIBLICAL FIGURES INTERPRETING THE PROMISE TO BLESS ALL THE NATIONS OF THE EARTH

How did the patriarchs understand the blessing declared by God in Genesis 12 and repeated by God at least four more times in Genesis (Gen 12:3; 18:18; 22:18; 26:4; 28:14)? How did later biblical figures understand this promise (Num 24; Ps 72; Acts 3; Rom 4; Gal 3–4)?

Answering these questions is the main focus of this section. The concern here is not to ask what the promise means to us today. Rather, the focus is to look for clues to understand the ways in which they interpreted or misinterpreted the promise that God had given to bless all the nations (or families) of the earth.

The Promise Interpreted by the Patriarchs
(Gen 12:3; 18:18; 22:18; 26:4; 28:14)

The repetition of the promise to Abraham, Isaac and Jacob is enough in itself to draw our attention.[1] Very few verses have been repeated as often in the Old Testament as the promise to Abraham in Genesis 12 which is that, "In you all the families/nations of the earth will be blessed (or shall bless themselves)."[2,3] This passage is frequently repeated and the

---

1. Tracing the theme of the promise in this work is an attempt to see how the biblical figures interpret the promise. These passages alone do not in themselves validate mission in the Old Testament. Bosch is correct that, "As far as the Old Testament is concerned, it is vital to recognize that a missionary mandate cannot be derived from a few isolated universalistic passages. . . . A careful reading of the Old Testament thus reveals the enormous missionary significance of Yahweh's dealing with Israel. This already becomes apparent in the call of Abraham (Gen. 12:1–3). . . . What Babel has lost, is promised and guaranteed in the history of Abraham's election. Genesis 12 follows Genesis 11: The entire history of Israel is nothing but the continuation of God's dealings with the nations. Yahweh alone can make history by breaking out of the circle of the eternal return and by journeying into the future with his people, with Abraham out of Ur, with Israel out of Egypt, moving to the nations. Only a historical religion can be truly missionary" (Bosch, "Hermeneutical Principles," 442, 444).

2. "I will be your/their God and you/they will be my people" is one of the most frequently repeated phrases in the Old Testament with at least 17 Old Testament and 2 New Testament occurrences, (Exod 6:7; Lev 26:12; Jer 7:23; 11:4; 24:7; 30:22; 31:1, 33; 32:38; Ezek 11:20; 14:11; 36:28; 37:23, 27; Zech 8:8; 2 Cor 6:16; Heb 8:10). The promise to Abraham originating in Genesis 12:3 is one of the next most frequently repeated passages with 7 to 9 Old Testament occurrences and 2 New Testament occurrences (Gen 12:3; 18:18; 22:18; 26:4; 27:29; 28:14; Num 24:9; probably Ps 72:17 and Isa 61:9; Acts 3:25; Gal 3:8). Even the Sh'ma (Shema)—"Hear O Israel, the Lord our God is one God" is only repeated once in the New Testament (originally in Deut 6:4 and again in Mark 12:29).

3. Scholars, in trying to translate the verb (will bless themselves), have missed the missiological significance of what's happening, and this is largely the reason they're having trouble with the translation. Note that nearly all of the scholars translate the verb based on the exegetical implications that they wish to follow (compare Filbeck, *God of the Gentiles*, 62–63; Martin-Achard, *Light to the Nations*, 33; Okoye, *Israel and the Nations*, 46–47; Rowley, *Missionary Message of OT*, 26; Schnabel, *Early Christian Mission*, 62–63; Tait, *Christ and the Nations*, 27–28; Wisdom, *Blessing for the Nations*,

Missiological Hermeneutics

promise is communicated entirely through God's direct intervention as it is shared with Abraham, Isaac and Jacob.

As if the repetitions in the Old Testament were not enough, we find that the passage is likewise repeated (or recounted) in the New Testament by Paul and Peter, using missional hermeneutics that draw attention to the importance of the promise with respect to God's mission. The biblical figures, however, are not the only ones who have commented on the passage. A vast number of modern day missiologists have followed the apostles' thinking and these make up an even larger group who have repeatedly cited this passage as a text of key importance revealing some aspect of God's missional purpose in the Old Testament.[4]

28–29). The blessing takes place as the nations join in with Israel and become part of Abraham's seed (the father of many nations). In this sense the nations both bless Abraham and they are blessed since they learn to follow God within the community of Israel. They are further blessed as they now reach out to the nations to show the way of God in the Old Testament. Therefore, the blessing is further manifest in the fact that they become a missional part of Israel. It is helpful here to realize that in the grand scheme, many modern day missionaries often feel that the inner transformation of their lives as a missionary has been a greater blessing than that which they were able to provide in service. Wright offers a similar discussion along different lines (Wright, *Mission of God*, 218).

4. A large number of missiologists who have written works in Biblical Theology of Mission cite Genesis 12:3 and its similar passages (Gen 18:18; 22:18; 26:4; 28:14; etc.) as an indication of Old Testament mission (Bauckham, *Bible and Mission*, 3–5; Blackman, *Biblical Basis*, 13; Blauw, *Missionary Nature of Church*, 19–22; Burnett, *Healing of the Nations*, 48–54; Carver, *Bible a Missionary Message*, 28; Carver, *Missions in the Plan*, 159, 266; Cook, *Missionary Message of Bible*, 22–24; De Ridder, *Discipling the Nations*, 22–30; Filbeck, *God of the Gentiles*, 60–64; Gilliland, *Pauline Theology & Mission Practice*, 51, 53, 164; Gilliland, *The Word among Us*, 69–71; Glasser, *Announcing the Kingdom*, 57–68; Gnanakan, *Kingdom Concerns*, 52; Goerner, *All Nations*, 22–31; Guder, *Incarnation and Church's Witness*, 22; Hedlund, *Mission of the Church*, 32–38, 66–67, 215; Hedlund, *God and the Nations*, 18–27, 48, 61–62, 168; Howard, *Student Power*, 16–20; Kaiser, *Mission in the OT*, 15–21, 39–40; Kane, *Missions in Biblical Perspective*, 22–23; Lapham, *Bible as Missionary Handbook*, 5–7; Martin-Achard, *Light to the Nations*, 33–37; McLean, *Hand-Book of Missions*, 28–33; McLean, *Where the Book Speaks*, 22–31; Montgomery, *Bible and Missions*, 20; Moreau et al., *Introducing World Missions*, 31–32; Ober, *Bible Studies in Missions*; Okoye, *Israel and the Nations*, 46–49; Peskett and Ramachandra, *Message of Mission*, 89–101; Peters, *Biblical Theology of Missions*, 99–100, 109–10; Piper, *Nations Be Glad*, 167–69; Schnabel, *Early Christian Mission*, 60–66; Sjogren, *Unveiled at Last*, 44–46; Storr, *Missionary Genius*, 65, 77–78; Shenk, *Transfiguration of Mission*, 161–62, 170; Shipp, *Fire in My Bones*, 20–30; Senior and Stuhlmueller, *Biblical Foundations for Mission*, 17–18, 83–84, 95; Sundkler, *World of Mission*, 11–17; Van Engen and Redford, "Syllabus," 47 originally Van Engen; Warren, *Calling of God*, 4–6; Wright, *Mission of God*, 194–221; Zwemer, *Into All the World*, 8–11). A smaller number cite only Genesis 12:3, but still relate this passage to Old Testament mission (Ådna and Kvalbein, *Mission*

Biblically Informed Missional Hermeneutics

Though the giving of the land plays a large role in the Pentateuch, I would suggest that the unifying theme of Genesis 12–50 is the blessing of the nations, and through this blessing the growth of Israel as the fulfillment of Abraham's name begins to take prominence within the book of Genesis. I begin with the assumption that Abraham's existing revelation, or body of Scripture, is based primarily on what God had spoken to Abraham, and possibly included Genesis 1–11 in oral tradition. In the same way that New Testament writers saw the Old Testament as their Scripture, Abraham, Isaac, and Jacob would have necessarily had a more limited scope of God's revelation. I likewise assume that the patriarchs perceived God's direct appearances as being equal in stature to any existing "Scripture" that they might have known. Moreover, God's revelation must have had impact on their lives since God's promises (especially the promise of land) were consistently repeated by the Old Testament patriarchs in the face of great turmoil. Likewise, I assume that the patriarchs passed on their most treasured blessings as they blessed their own offspring or shared the story with others. It is the blessing given by the patriarchs to their offspring that gives us a good indication of how they interpreted God's promise to bless all the nations of the earth.

Throughout this investigation of the patriarchs' interpretation of the promise, I will compare what the patriarchs heard from God with their own repetition of the promise as they pass on their own relevant

---

of Early Church, 57, 147; Bashford, *God's Missionary Plan*, 44; Bosch, *Witness to the World*, 61; Brownson, *Speaking the Truth*, 19; Culver, *Greater Commission*, 124; Driver, *Understanding the Atonement*, 24; DuBose, *God Who Sends*, 55; Hahn, *Mission in the NT*, 18–19; Horton, *Bible: A Missionary Book*, 110; Jordan, *Song and the Soil*, 24; Kaiser, "Israel's Missionary Call," 27–29; Kavunkal and Hrangkhuma, *Bible and Mission*, 40, 56, 309; Love, *Missionary Message of Bible*, 21; Newbigin, *Open Secret*, 32, 72; O'Donnell, *Doing Member Care Well*, 9–10; Park, *Mission Discourse*, 7–8; Power, *Mission Theology Today*, 67; Wilkins, *Bible and God's Mission*, 8–10; Willis, *Biblical Basis of Missions*, 31–32). Only a few authors address Old Testament mission in some way but do not cite Genesis 12:3 (Bosch, *Transforming Mission*; Martin, *Kingdom without Frontiers*; Van Engen et al., *Good News of Kingdom*; Van Rheenen, *Missions*). However, Bosch and Van Engen both cite this passage in other works (as shown above) and none of the authors in this last group reject the missional implications of Genesis 12:2–3. Only H. H. Rowley and G. Ernest Wright (following Rowley) seem to have some reservation in the development of Genesis 12:3, but I cannot understand how that can cause them to think that "Moses was the first missionary" (Rowley, *Missionary Message of OT*, 15, 24–26; Wright, "OT Basis for Mission," 17–18). Kane, uniquely quotes Rowley regarding Moses, but cites the Genesis passages as having missional focus (Kane, *Missions in Biblical Perspective*, 17, 22–23).

understanding of the message. Furthermore, following the patriarchs I will look into later Old Testament passages that appear to be a repetition of the God-given blessing as well as New Testament restatements and interpretations. Table 1 outlines the accounts in which God repeatedly reveals the promise to bless all the nations of earth (second column) and the passages in which the biblical figures repeat the promise to others (third column). (Table 13 in Appendix A comprehensively lists the occurrences of the promise with respect to land, growth, and blessing the nations.)

Table 1: The Promise Revealed and Interpreted

Biblical Figure:	God Promise to Bless All Nations:	Repetition and Interpretation of the Promise:
Abraham	Gen 12:1–3 Gen 18:18–19 Gen 22:16–18	Gen 24:7 (Abraham calls his chief servant)
Isaac	Gen 22:16–18* Gen 26:3–5	Gen 27:29 (Isaac blesses Jacob) Gen 28:4 (Isaac helps Jacob flee)
Jacob	Gen 28:14	Gen 32:12; 48:4 (Jacob recounts God's message) Gen 49:8–10, 22–26 (Jacob blesses Judah, Joseph)
Joseph	Gen 41–50**	Gen 45:5–8; 50:20 (Joseph speaks to his brothers)
Balak	Num 24:9	Num 23–24 (*Gen 12:3a verbally repeated*)
David		Ps 72:17
Peter	Acts 2**	Acts 3:25 (Peter's restatement and interpretation)
Paul		Gal 3:8–10 (Paul's restatement and interpretation)

*Isaac is present and most likely hears God speaking the promise

**This will be further developed in the section on Joseph and Peter, as the propositional and narrative aspects are discussed.

There are at least two ways to approach a discussion of the patriarchs' interpretation of the promise. One is to cover the topic in a typical chronological fashion, looking at Abraham, Isaac, Jacob, and Joseph.

Biblically Informed Missional Hermeneutics

Another way is to look at the themes that flow through Genesis (and the rest of Scripture) and discuss this on a thematic basis. Though I have struggled in deciding which approach to use, I have chosen the latter because I think it offers greater synthesis and cohesion. This is because the missional themes that course their way through Genesis have such strong cohesion themselves. Depending on the readers learning style, one of the approaches may feel more comfortable.

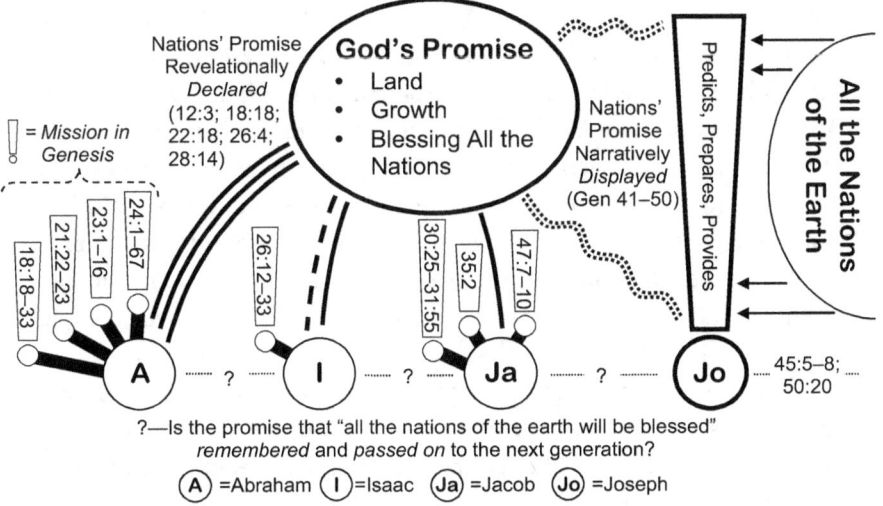

Figure 1: Overview of the Promise in Genesis to Bless All the Nations of the Earth

Additionally, for those who prefer a right brain learning style, I have included a graphical summary in Figure 1 that is explained in the present footnote and again in footnotes throughout this section.[5] If the figure seems confusing, then please refer to it again after a complete reading.

---

5. Explanation of symbols in Figure 1: The focus of the figure is God's promise (large oval), and the curved lines underneath "God's promise" represent God's declarations of the promise. The dotted curve moving toward Isaac is a likely but uncertain account. The circles at the bottom represent Abraham, Isaac, Jacob, and Joseph respectively. The question marks between adjacent circles represent the absence of passing on the promise to "bless all nations" to succeeding generations (though the promise of land and numerical growth were often passed on). Acts of mission by each patriarch are graphically illustrated by individual exclamation marks near their names. The right side of the diagram portrays a change in God's announcement of the promise—from declaration to a display through Joseph's life. Consequently, the large exclamation mark over Joseph

15

MISSIOLOGICAL HERMENEUTICS

Fear in the Background

As we consider the five occurrences of God declaring the promise that all nations of the earth will be blessed (Gen 12:3; 18:18; 22:18; 26:4; 28:14), it is important to keep the background of each of these accounts in mind.[6] More than anything, I would like to focus on the psychological background of the patriarchs in terms of the fears they have that affect the relationship with the nations. I suggest that it is nothing less than "the fear of death" that is the common psychological backdrop for each of the instances in which God repeats the promise to the patriarchs.[7] The exposure of being a foreigner leads to fears of violence and theft, while famine is a constant problem throughout Genesis 12–50. Abraham, Isaac and Jacob share fears that are similar to those that many missionaries encounter when living as foreigners in a new land even though few missionaries fear death in the way that Jacob did from Esau—Genesis 27:41-44. Furthermore, many missionaries today enjoy greater civil protection than the patriarchs often had, though there are cases in which the nations provided civil protection for them (compare Gen 20:16; 26:11).

Beginning with God's original promises in Genesis 12:2-3, Abraham is still in Haran. There is a great journey that takes place in Genesis 12:5-6. It would be natural for Abraham's fears to be amplified when he arrives in Canaan as he feels the impact of being a stranger in a foreign land. Abraham's fragile state is exposed soon after his arrival. Abraham's fear is not only over the possibility of being killed due to his wife's beauty. In Haran, Abraham might have been able to suffer through a famine, but his lack of adequate provisions in Canaan meant

---

is due to the missional impact that is narratively portrayed through his life that likewise draws the attention of quite possibly all the nations of the earth. For a survey of other themes within Genesis see Table 12 in Appendix A.

6. Legrand, *Bible on Culture*, 64.

7. I was introduced to Abraham's missional fear by Dr. Charles Van Engen in the Fall 1992 course titled Biblical Foundations of Mission, MT520. Since 2000, I have co-taught this same course with Van Engen and extensively edited a joint syllabus. Therefore, I will add "originally Van Engen" to any footnote from that resource in which the ideas were originally from Van Engen. Van Engen notes Abraham's fear, focused on self-preservation in both accounts in which Abraham asks Sarah to lie about her status as his wife and how these accounts are debilitating toward mission (Gen 12:10-20; 20:1-18) (Van Engen and Redford, "Syllabus," 47 originally Van Engen). In terms of "fear" being a part of Abraham's emotions, this is ultimately speculation, but it is a quite reasonable speculation given the events and concerns of Abraham.

that he must travel to Egypt (Gen 12:10–20). Abraham's fear of death as it related to Sarah's beauty might have been lessened or eliminated if he had either sufficient agricultural or military strength while in Egypt. However a very powerful theme surfaces as Abraham is consistently placed in situations where he must live from a position of weakness, and this has a tremendous missional impact.

The context of the second occurrence of the promise (Gen 18:18) is quite different but the same fears are present, though not quite as personal. There is a fear of death in the background of this situation, but it is once removed. Abraham's outward concern is a fear of the destruction (or death) of the righteous, and this is likely intertwined with a genuine concern for his nearby relatives—Lot and his family. The loss of Lot means both a loss of family and the loss of a military ally.

Finally, in the most dramatic instance of all, the promise is repeated following the near-death of Isaac (Gen 22:18). The fear over the loss of Isaac represents a fear of death on multiple levels—the death of the loved son, the death of his being a father (since Ishmael was no longer with him—Gen 21), the death of a visionary promise, that of becoming a unique nation (which could only be resurrected through faith—Heb 11:18–19), and it could possibly mean even an early death for Abraham if there was no one to care for him in his elderly years.

As dramatic as this account would have been for Abraham, it must have had an even more acute effect on Isaac. In all probability, Isaac heard the promise twice in his life, once as a boy (Gen 22:18) and once as a man (Gen 26:4). As a boy in Genesis 22, he clearly notices that there is no sacrifice, and would likely have experienced extreme levels of fear as his father bound him and laid him over the altar (22:7–9). There is no way of knowing if Isaac also heard the halting command of the angel of the Lord, but since Isaac and Abraham are close enough to touch each other, this seems most likely. If Isaac heard the decree that saved his life, he would likewise have heard God's promise to bless all the nations of the earth (22:16–18). From an emotional and psychological standpoint, it would most likely benefit Isaac to have heard the angel of the Lord commanding Abraham to halt, so that he would also understand the seemingly preposterous actions of his father. Isaac's experience of God's promise as a boy would have undoubtedly made an indelible imprint on his mind for life—one that must have been overwhelming, confusing and a great relief at the same time. How could Isaac ever forget being saved at the last minute by the angel of YHWH?

As a man, there is no question that Isaac heard God's promise to bless all the nations of the earth (Gen 26:4). Like his father before him, Isaac hears the promise in a time of needed reassurance. In the same way that God spoke the promise to Abraham in times of great fear, Isaac was called and reassured by God in the midst of nearly identical fears. Isaac, like Abraham, was facing the fear of famine, and death due to Rebecca's beauty, as well as the fear of living as a foreigner in a new land. Moreover, Isaac planned to deal with these issues in ways identical to those of his father. He too would travel to Egypt to deal with the famine, and claim that his wife was his sister to avoid attack. The positive side of Abraham and Isaac's response is that they share a pattern in terms of obedience. Just as God clearly links the giving of the promise with Abraham's obedience, Scripture subtly notes that Isaac likewise obeyed God by staying in Gerar (26:5–6).

Jacob clearly experiences a fear of death, and while the fear itself matches the fears of Abraham and Isaac, Jacob experiences this fear from his brother Esau over the repercussions of stolen blessings (Gen 27). As a result, Jacob also experiences the fear of living as a foreigner in a new land as he flees to Haran. God's promise to bless all the nations of the earth comes in the midst of these deep-seated fears (Gen 28:14). God's promise also occurs in a different form much later in Jacob's life, as Jacob likewise faces fear of death over famine (Gen 42:2). This uniquely occurs in the midst of God's providential missionary activity through Joseph's life. Therefore, Jacob's timely entry into Joseph's adult life occurs in the midst of a far larger and more encompassing narrative declaration of the promise to bless all the nations of the earth.

Interestingly enough, the famine that occurs within Canaan in the midst of each of the patriarchs' lives (Gen 12, 26, 42) drives each of them outside of the land and into contact with the surrounding nations. Whether intentional or not, the famine itself is a driving force for missionary contact. Although there is nothing definitive to show if the famines in Genesis 12 and 26 are intentional manifestations of God's will (versus natural occurrences), there can be little doubt that God chose to bring about the famine predicted through Pharaoh's dream (Gen 41:30–32).

The background of exposure and fear play a consistent role in each case in which the promise is revealed. As will be seen, the giving of the promise in each account is a very graceful reminder of God's presence, protection and provision for each of the patriarchs. Uniquely, however, God's promise includes the focus to bless all the nations of the earth which extends beyond the personal concerns of the patriarchs. This leads me to think that God means to instill in the patriarchs a combined understanding of provision that addresses their fears while simultaneously teaching them about God's capacity to move beyond their fears and involve them in the blessing of the nations.

However, the key to understanding the fear of death in Genesis is a much deeper fear that is rooted in a mistrust of the nations (compare Gen 12:12; 19:30, 20:11–13; 26:7; 27:46; 28:16–17). Abraham and Isaac openly declare this mistrust in asking their wives to lie about their status, and Jacob embodies mistrust through his consistent conniving. There is even a mistrust of the Canaanite women that is unrelated to Jacob's flight, and so Jacob is subtly taught mistrust and prejudice by having to go elsewhere to find a wife.[8] This defensive and distrusting posture constantly threatens the exposure and vulnerability needed for the patriarchs to function as part of God's providential mission to bless all the nations of the earth.

The Promise Declared

Having looked at the continuity of the background in which the promises were given, it is helpful to consider the continuity and discontinuity within the promises themselves. Within the giving of the promise, there are three major areas that subtly shift as the promises given. There is a subtle change in tense with respect to the verb "to bless," as well as a more obvious change with respect to the object of the blessing, which becomes either, "all the families of the land" or "all the nations of the earth." Finally, there are variations in terms of the instrument or agent by which the blessing is accomplished. Three major variations occur here, which are, "in you" (Gen 12:3) and the very similar, "in him" (Gen 18:18), "in your seed" (Gen 22:18; 26:4) and a combination of the two

8. One of the greatest signs of missionary adaptation in a culture is whether or not their children are allowed to intermingle with nationals. While I know of no conclusive studies on this, it becomes very obvious when missionaries continue to have cultural reservations or prejudices that prevent their children from having romantic or marital relationships with nationals.

(Gen 28:14).[9] Additionally, Peter and Paul quote these passages and include their own variations as part of their own Greek renderings (Acts 3:25; Gal 3:8). Table 2 shows the major changes in the wording of the promise within Genesis:

Table 2: Continuity and Discontinuity of the Promise

vv.	Speaker	Means (verb)	Agent	Focus (impacting)
Gen 12:3	יְהוָה (YHWH)	וְנִבְרְכוּ ('to bless' niphal)	בְּךָ (through you)	כֹּל מִשְׁפְּחֹת הָאֲדָמָה (all families of the land)
Gen 18:18	יְהוָה (YHWH)	וְנִבְרְכוּ ('to bless' niphal)	בוֹ (through him)	כֹּל גּוֹיֵי הָאָרֶץ (all nations of the earth)
Gen 22:18	מַלְאַךְ יְהוָה (Angel of YHWH)	וְהִתְבָּרֲכוּ ('to bless' hithpael)	בְזַרְעֲךָ (through your seed)	כֹּל גּוֹיֵי הָאָרֶץ (all nations of the earth)
Gen 26:4	יְהוָה (YHWH)	וְהִתְבָּרֲכוּ ('to bless' hithpael)	בְזַרְעֲךָ (through your seed)	כֹּל גּוֹיֵי הָאָרֶץ (all nations of the earth)
Gen 28:14	יְהוָה (YHWH)	וְנִבְרְכוּ ('to bless' niphal)	בְּךָ ... וּבְזַרְעֶךָ (through you ... and your seed)	כָּל־מִשְׁפְּחֹת הָאֲדָמָה (all families of the land)

Cook suggests that the change from "families" (in Gen 12:3) to "nations" (in Gen 18:18; 22:18) takes place in order for Abraham to "realize the bigness of the scheme."[10] God's recount to Isaac also uses the term "nations" (in Gen 26:14). Also, he most likely heard the same term in Genesis 22:18 as a boy. However, the sole account in which Jacob hears God propositionally reveal the blessing through his visions uses the term "families." Furthermore, Jacob is the only one to learn that the promise to the nations will be fulfilled "in you" (Gen 28:14 is similar to Gen 12:3 or "in him" Gen 18:18) and "in your seed" (similar to Gen 22:18; 26:4). This will be discussed further in Jacob's interpretation of the promise, but the surrounding context has tremendous implications.

The account of Genesis 35:1–15 is a strong echo of Jacob's hearing of the promise in Genesis 28:14. Similar to Abraham and Isaac's obedience, Jacob obediently commands that all foreign idols be put away, and

9. Referring back to Figure 1: The curved lines underneath "God's promise" represent God's declarations of the promise, and the dotted curve moving toward Isaac is a likely but uncertain account.

10. Cook, *Missionary Message of Bible*, 22.

Jacob worships God in the same place where God appeared to him as he was fleeing Esau. In a climactic ending, God once again promises Jacob growth as a nation, and as many nations, as well as the land. This account of Jacob's being renamed as "Israel," as well as Jacob's prior wrestling with God, has extremely strong parallels with Abraham's renaming (Gen 32:22–32—compare 17:5).

Foremost, the divine means of revealing the promises illustrates shocking levels of continuity and importance. In four of the five accounts in which the promises to bless the nations is declared, YHWH (MT: יְהוָה LXX: κύριος) appears and declares the promise (Gen 12:3; 18:18; 26:4; 28:14). The account in Genesis 28 takes place within a dream or a vision, but is nonetheless very real to Jacob. In the account of Isaac's sacrifice in Genesis 22, the sacrifice is commanded by God (MT: אֱלֹהִים LXX: θεὸς) and the command to save Isaac's life is given by an angel or messenger of YHWH (MT: מַלְאַךְ יְהוָה LXX: ἄγγελος κυρίου). [11]

11. The way in which the translation of the passages affects the interpretation may be shown from the following translations of Genesis 12:2–3:

2 I will make you a great nation, and I will bless you. I will make you famous, *and you will be a blessing to others.* 3 I will bless those who bless you, and I will place a curse on those who harm you. And all the people on earth will be blessed through you (NCV).

2 And I will make you a great nation, And I will bless you, And make your name great; *And so you shall be a blessing;* 3 And I will bless those who bless you, And the one who curses you I will curse. And in you all the families of the earth will be blessed (NAS).

2 I will make of you a great nation, and I will bless you, and make your name great, *so that you will be a blessing.* 3 I will bless those who bless you, and the one who curses you I will curse; and in you all the families of the earth shall be blessed (NRSV compare NAB, ESV, GNT).

2 And I will make you into a great nation; and I will bless you; and I will make your name great. *And be a blessing.* 3 And I will bless those who bless you; whereas the one who belittles you, I will curse; and in you will be blessed all kinship groups on the earth (Wright, *Mission of God*, 200).

Wright translates the ending of the second verse as an imperative. Walter Kaiser has one of the most unique translations of Genesis 12:2–3 that exists, primarily because he translates the promise to all nations as a purpose ("so that") clause.

2 I will make you into a great nation and I will bless you; I will make your name great, *So that all the people on earth may be blessed through you.* 3 *In order that* you may be a blessing; I will bless those who bless you, And whoever curses you I will curse. *So that all the people on earth may be blessed through you* (Kaiser, *Mission in the OT*, 18).

Even though Walter Kaiser is skilled in his understanding of Hebrew, he demonstrates a less than objective way of translating the Scriptures. For example, Walter Kaiser translates Leviticus 18:18 (the prohibition against marrying two sisters), as a prohibition for any form of polygamy (Kaiser, *Toward Old Testament Ethics*, 185–86). Kaiser is among a small minority who would like to translate the phrase as a figure of

The point is that the initial giving of the promise is surrounded by the miraculous appearance of God, and the repetition of the promise continues through miraculous means and agents. This keeps the promise in the forefront of their minds and allows for the possibility that the patriarchs may interpret the meaning of the promise within their time. There is tremendous emphasis in YHWH personally repeating the promise four times within the span of three generations, and the angel of YHWH being involved at the center of the five accounts. God's grace can be seen in God's patience and consistent reminders that place "the promise to bless all the nations" as the missional climax of the earlier promises of land and growth.

Mission within Genesis

Despite the miraculous giving of the promise, there are no explicit indications that the patriarchs interpreted the promise as a command to bless the nations. However, there are impressive accounts within Genesis of mission taking place through the patriarchs.[12] As already mentioned, the impact of famine consistently drives the patriarchs to the nations (most notably Philistia and Egypt), while other calamities such as Jacob's fleeing from Esau allow for continuing witness to Laban. More than any other, Joseph works almost entirely from a position of weakness as he grows to a position of influence that has a missional impact on the entire world. The impact of these tragedies, the patriarchs as an alien-nation, and the fears already discussed, leaves the patriarchs in a position of weakness that causes mission to surge forth in Genesis. As we will see, following this section, it is only when wealth, strength, and power set in

---

speech pertaining to all Israelite women claiming that the term "sister" is idiomatic for any two women. It seems that in this particular case, Kaiser's desire to refute polygamy has overly biased his translation. Kaiser may stand on better ground, however, when it comes to Genesis 12:1–3, primarily because he is assigning a purpose clause (a specific syntactical function) to the phrase that some translate as "and" by rendering it "so that." The NRSV and other translations follow Kaiser's thinking at least in Genesis 12:2 (for example, "so that you will be a blessing").

12. A great deal of whether or not a scholar perceives mission in Genesis depends on his or her definition of mission. Kane writes, "Some biblical scholars claim they find missionary purpose, message, and activity in the Old Testament. Other scholars fail to find any of these. Much depends on one's definition of 'mission.' If by 'mission' is meant the crossing of political or cultural boundaries to take the message of the one true God to those who know nothing about him, then, with the exception of Jonah, we will not find much about 'mission' in the Old Testament. This does not mean the *idea* is not there" (Kane, *Missions in Biblical Perspective*, 17).

Biblically Informed Missional Hermeneutics

that the nations are intimidated by the patriarchs and mission quickly suffers. First, however, let us turn to some of the more impressive missionary acts carried out by the patriarchs.[13]

The fact that Abraham leaves his homeland at God's request and comes to a new region is foundational for providing some existing witness. What links Abraham's actions with modern-day missionary activity is not his cross-cultural travel or departure from family, even though these two elements are commonplace in present-day missionary activity. Rather, it is the obedience of Abraham to live for God in the midst of the nations. Whether or not Abraham perceives his role missionally is irrelevant. What is relevant is that Abraham's obedience in the midst of God's encompassing vision of mission (the *missio Dei*) allows for this human being to be part of God's providential missionary activity. There are certainly times when Abraham fails to act as a witness for God (for example, Gen 12:10–20), and engages in activities that seem to be at odds with missionary practice today (for example, Gen 14). However, few pioneer missionaries have spotless records and here we likely have the first pioneer missionary ever.

Interestingly enough in Genesis 18, God asks the unique question, "Should I hide my plan from Abraham?" before repeating (or reminding) Abraham of the promise to bless all the nations of the earth. And, in the next breath, God details the purpose and expectations surrounding Abraham's election (Gen 18:18–19). Given that Abraham is somehow involved as a means to bless all the nations of the earth, God may not have initially wanted Abraham to see the destruction of Sodom and Gomorrah, since it appears to be an extreme and rare situation. God may simply not have wanted Abraham to think that this was common practice, especially since this occurs relatively early in the election of Abraham. However, it may likewise be that God sees this as an opportunity to determine if Abraham has concern for the nations.

Regardless of what is intended, this account provokes a petition from Abraham that stands head and shoulders above any concerns for the nations seen so far.[14] The extremely powerful result of Abraham's petition before God is that Lot and his daughter's lives were spared.[15]

---

13. Referring back to Figure 1: Acts of mission by each patriarch are graphically illustrated by individual exclamation marks near their names.

14. Van Engen and Redford, "Syllabus," 47 originally Van Engen.

15. Lot's wife was rescued as well, but died for other reasons.

Scripture takes note of this, saying that, "God had listened to Abraham's request and kept Lot safe, removing him from the disaster that engulfed the cities on the plain" (Gen 19:29). Like most missionary activity, the impact of Abraham's petition before God transforms the lives of both the missionary and those who benefit from the missionary.

However, transformation for Abraham is a slow process (as it is for most of us) and the lie that Abraham propagates in Genesis 12 is committed again in Genesis 20 as Abraham deceitfully avoids telling the Philistines that Sarah is his wife. The impact of the lie and Genesis 20, however, is radically different than the former account. Rather than being escorted out of the country and thereby having no opportunity for further witness (Gen 12:20), Abimelech blesses Abraham by allowing him to stay in the region and giving him any land he chooses (Gen 20:15). Abraham's subsequent prayer is a prayer that blesses Abimelech's household even though Abraham's lie is the cause of all the mishap.

What occurs here are narrative echoes of Genesis 12:3a ("I will bless those who bless you . . .") and 12:7 (the promise of land). In a fascinating twist of events, the leader of this nation is giving up land and blessing Abraham. However, the real impact in terms of godly witness takes place through Abraham's longevity in this region as Abimelech notices God's blessing upon Abraham's life (Gen 21:22–23).[16] Interestingly enough, Abimelech simply requests a mutual level of trust and loyalty that Abraham should have displayed in Genesis 20. It is unclear if Abraham had missional intentions, but God's providential mission and grace shines through the ambiguity Abraham may have had.

Likewise, Abraham's life shows tremendous impact in the midst of Sarah's death (Gen 23:1–16).[17] Notably, this is a situation in which

---

16. Abraham lived for an extended length of time in the following places: (1) in the hill country between Bethel on the west and Ai on the east (Gen 12:8) and returned there again after Egypt (13:3). (2) Separated from Lot and moved to *Hebron* (13:18; 14:13; 18:1—Abraham's family is always camped in the same area, giving the impression of a semi-nomadic society) (3) Camps in Gerar (near Philistia) (20:1) and in *Beersheba* (21:30–34) and stayed there sometime (22:19) (4) Sarah dies in *Hebron* (23:1, 19). Isaac follows the same path moving to Gerar (26:1) and then to *Beersheba* (26:23). Likewise, alters or places of worship were setup by Abraham in Shechem (12:7); the hill country (between Bethel on the west and Ai on the east, (12:8); and in Hebron (13:18). Isaac also sets up an alter in Beersheba (26:25), as does Jacob at Bethel (or Luz) (28:18–19; 35:1, 7).

17. One very interesting dynamic in Abraham's life is that nearly all of his children become nations. Despite the early prophecy, God promises that Ishmael will become

Abraham is in a place of weakness as he mourns Sarah and lacks a proper burial place. In a somewhat surprising statement, Abraham refers to himself as an alien in a strange land (Gen 23:4). The reason this statement is strange is that Abraham has been in the land for at least 25 years (compare Gen 12:4; 21:5), and the Hittite people clearly know him well enough to feel quite differently—"The Hittites replied to Abraham, 'Certainly, for you are an honored prince among us. It will be a privilege to have you choose the finest of our tombs so you can bury her there'" (Gen 23:5).

There are two impressive missional issues apparent in the Hittite response. First, Abraham has won the respect of the Hittite people and with this respect comes missionary witness. Second, the Hittite people are willing to bless Abraham with land. Here again, we find a most unlikely source echoing the promise of land (Gen 12:7 and other following passages). Remarkably, we have a second account in which the nations are blessing Abraham with land.

The surprising segue between Abraham's missional involvement and that of Isaac comes through Abraham's chief servant (Gen 24:2; compare 15:2).[18] Aside from the sheer loyalty this servant has toward Abraham, there are a number of spiritual disciplines displayed by this servant. Foremost, Abraham's servant prays and understands God through God's response to his prayer (Gen 24:12–15, 26–27). How did this chief servant learn to pray to God (compare Gen 24:7b, 40)? The effect of Abraham's discipleship cannot be overlooked as the servant prays to "the God of my master Abraham" and worships God when his prayer is answered and when Laban agrees that this is from God (Gen 24:12, 26, 48, 52).

Furthermore, Scripture uniquely emphasizes not only the prayer, but the witness taking place by twice repeating the experience of the chief servant with God (Gen 24:34–48). The result ultimately is that Laban understands and believes they are part of God's answer to prayer and cooperates (or follows) God in the matter. It is certainly possible that Laban is motivated by the gifts sent by Abraham, (given the later

---

a great nation and God's presence is with Ishmael as he grows up (Gen 21:13, 18, 20—compare 16:10–12). Furthermore, after Sarah's death Abraham marries Keturah and the children are representative of many nations, which is a very strong echo of the growth promises in Genesis. Achtemeier believes that this is a partial fulfillment of Genesis 15 (Achtemeier et al., *Harper's Bible Dictionary*, 524).

18. The chief servant may have been Eliezer of Damascus (Gen 15:2).

greed that Laban displays with Jacob), but this account seems to validate the spiritual side of Laban rather than attest to his greed.

The missional overview of Genesis 24 is astounding. Abraham's servant (most likely from Damascus) has understood enough about the God of Abraham to begin praying, worshiping and witnessing for God. The fruit of the chief servant's allegiance to God must be credited in a large part to Abraham's witness. Though Jacob will have greater duration in terms of witness to Laban, the initial witness to Laban comes as an extension of Abraham's witness in the servant's life.

Of all the patriarchs, we are only given a short glimpse into Isaac's life. Scripture tells us that Isaac is blessed by God and that he amasses a great amount of wealth and power through this. However, the power that Isaac amasses is, in many ways, a roadblock for mission, even though those around him eventually realize that this blessing is from God (Gen 26:16, 28). In the midst of the tension, the most notable missional trait of Isaac is that he is willing to commit to peace (Gen 26:26–31).

By all accounts, Isaac probably would have felt justified if he had retaliated over the destruction of his father's wells. The wells seem to be central for sustained living in the region, since they are the foremost concern for settling in the land (compare Gen 26:22, 32). However, rather than choose aggression, Isaac peacefully relocates again and again (Gen 26:14–22), and is willing to make an oath of peace even when it appears that he possesses the capacity to fight those who wronged him. Isaac's actions in this account narratively illustrate forgiveness and offer a blessing to this nation (through his oath—Gen 26:31) in spite of the grievances inflicted upon him (Gen 26:16).

Jacob's life and missional impact occurs in two phases of his life in Genesis—as a young man and as an elderly patriarch. In this brief look at mission in Jacob's life, I will focus on his missional impact as a young man, and later consider the missional impact in his elderly years when looking at Joseph. Like Abraham and Isaac, the blessing of God in Jacob's life was observed by those around him, specifically Laban (Gen 30:25–35 compare Gen 21:22–23; 26:28–29). Despite all the conniving between Laban and Jacob, the most powerful testimony to Jacob's missional witness is that Laban knows God at the point when Jacob is commanded by God to leave Haran (Gen 31:2, 21, 24, 52–53). Throughout the account of Jacob's stay with Laban, Jacob works from a position of weakness, much like an indentured servant, but has tremendous impact on Laban's life.

Once Jacob leaves Haran, he and his family encounter a very difficult situation in which Dinah (Jacob's daughter through Leah) is sexually attacked by Shechem the Hivite (Gen 34:2–3). However, Scripture tells us that Shechem loved Dinah and that he was insistent on marrying her (Gen 34:3–4, 11–12). What is most remarkable, however, is that all the men of the town agree to Jacob's sons' demand to undergo circumcision in order for Shechem to marry Dinah.

If we were to list the golden opportunities for mission in Genesis, this instance would have to be at the top of a very short list. If forgiveness over Shechem's actions could have taken place, this might have meant that the entire town would have developed some relationship with God. However, this is an instance of spiritual abuse leading to vengeance rather than anything remotely close to mission (Gen 34:13–17). The spiritual abuse is most notable in the fact that Simeon and Levi quote directly from God's account with Abraham asserting that "Each male among you must be circumcised" (Gen 17:10b NLT; 34:15).[19] Though Simeon and Levi attack the town while the men are still in pain and kill Shechem, they also proceed to kill the rest of the men in the town (Gen 34:25–29). Therefore, an entire town of Hivite men die over Shechem's sin, while the Hivite women and children are taken as slaves along with all the town's livestock and possessions—all because Jacob's sons held such a deep-seated revenge despite potential reconciliation with Shechem.

Though the situation with Dinah was clearly a tragedy in which she should not be forced to marry her attacker, Shechem indicates esteem for her in his limited ways (Gen 34:11–12). This ensuing violence could seem like grievous actions fueled by temporary madness, but Jacob's "blessing" at the end of his life informs us that Simeon and Levi had a pattern of violence in their lives (Gen 49:5–7). Furthermore, it is unclear what role Jacob played as he condemns these actions because of his own focus on self-preservation rather than concern for witness (compare Gen 34:30 and 48:22 especially NCV).[20] In any case, this vindictive bloodbath could have been an opportunity for great forgiveness and missional redemption.

---

19. Cp. Wenham, *Genesis 16-50*, 308.
20. Ibid., 466.

Another challenging aspect of this whole account is Jacob's call for the elimination of idolatry in his household (Gen 35:2). It is difficult to tell in this instance if Jacob is addressing idolatry within his family, such as Rachel's theft of Laban's idols (Gen 31:19, 34–35) or if this is a pronouncement to the Hivite women and children who have just been taken captive (Gen 34:29). From a missional perspective, Jacob's motivation is good, but this is problematic since it represents a forced allegiance to God, especially if it is focused on the latter group who are subjugated. In all likelihood, this is directed toward the Hivite women and children, given that Jacob was never aware of Rachel's theft (Gen 31:32). There is a possibility, however, that this was directed toward both the Hivites and Rachel, and that Jacob saw this as an opportune time to indirectly confront his beloved Rachel without singling her out.

A final and very interesting consideration is the geographical locations where the patriarchs lived, as shown in Figure 2. Many of these locations placed them right in the midst of the nations. Nearly all effective witness begins with a physical presence, and Abraham, Isaac, Jacob, and Joseph all had impact simply through their daily living. Only Abraham and Isaac had a great deal of continuity in where they lived. However, in the midst of the promise to Isaac there is an important and unique phrase in the promise spoken by God. When God speaks to Abraham in Genesis 12:1 and asks Abraham to leave his homeland, it is natural to assume that Abraham is a stranger or an alien in a new land.

Biblically Informed Missional Hermeneutics

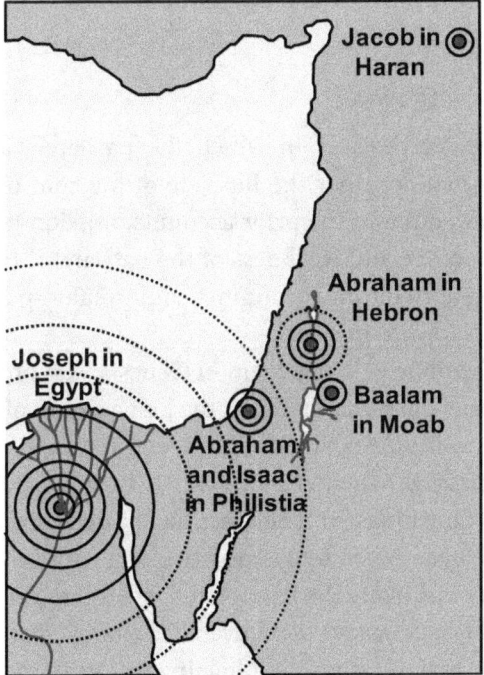

Figure 2: Missional Impact in Genesis

However, when God speaks to Isaac, God uses a verb that specifically means "to dwell as an alien" or "sojourner" (גּוּר) in the land, even though Isaac lives in the same locations as Abraham (Gen 26:3).[21] In contrast, Abraham, Jacob (for most of his adult life) and Joseph all lived in lands that were unique locations where their ancestors had not had any presence as a witness for God. The only exception to this is Abraham's initial move (Gen 12) and Isaac in Philistia and Hebron, which makes God's request for Isaac to be an alien even more relevant since Isaac would have had history in the area. Figure 2 shows the major missional impact on areas through the expanding circular rings. Abraham lived in Hebron and Beersheba (Philistia). Isaac lived in Beersheba and later in Hebron. Jacob fled to Haran and lived their 20 years, and Joseph lived his adult life in Egypt. Joseph's missional impact will be discussed in relationship to the interpretation of the promise but of all the patriarchs,

---

21. Koehler et al., *HALOT*, 185.

Joseph has overwhelming impact on not only his family but all the nations of the earth.

Mission Ceases with Power

Before we consider the way in which the patriarchs interpreted the promise, let us first consider the flip side of the coin of what we have just discussed. So often in the prior accounts, mission flourished in the midst of the exposure and weakness of the patriarchs. However, the effect of amassing agricultural, economic, and military power most often acted as barriers toward mission.

Abraham's military involvement in Genesis 14 is probably the most difficult to discern missionally. This is the first account of extensive military power, following Abraham's call in Genesis 12:1–3. It is difficult to tell from this passage whether Abraham is taking an offensive stance toward the invading kings, or if he is acting in a defensive manner to free those who have been taken into captivity along with Lot (compare Gen 14:14–15). It is most likely the latter, but a few things are notable.

If it is purely a defensive maneuver, it is strange that Abraham waits until after the invasion rather than helping to fortify the existing towns or helping Lot's household prior to the attack. However, the reason for this is most likely that the news of the attack simply reached Abraham after it had taken place (Gen 14:13). In either case mission flowing from this account is difficult to see.

The king of Sodom is very appreciative of the return of the people of his city (Gen 14:21–23). The brief appearance of Melchizedek adds a great deal of mystery to the passage (Gen 14:18–20).[22] In Melchizedek, there is a very powerful missional contrast that takes place. Abraham comes into this scene as someone of great power while Melchizedek has no obvious military power. However, Melchizedek blesses Abraham in such a way that Melchizedek quickly becomes the spiritual leader of this entire account. By contrast, the king of Sodom is very tentative and cautious as he directs Abraham to return his people. This is not too unexpected since Abraham apparently holds the military capacity to overcome even the strongest kings in the land.

Essentially, Abraham's military involvement obscures his capacity to act as a witness to the king of Sodom. However, Melchizedek comes onto the scene and takes on a missional role of indirect witness as the

---

22. Cp. Wenham, *Genesis 1-15*, 315–17.

king of Sodom observes Melchizedek blessing Abraham. This is very likely an echo of Genesis 12:3, as the outsider blesses God's chosen people.[23] About the only thing related to mission that takes place through Abraham in this account is Abraham's response to the king of Sodom, which seems to indicate that Abraham has a vested interest in being able to demonstrate God's blessing upon his life (Gen 14:23b). In short, this account shows a breakdown of Abraham's ability to witness to the king of Sodom due to his military leadership, while Melchizedek acts as a witness and has no apparent power.

Similarly, Isaac is driven from the land solely because he gained so much power and is perceived as a military threat. This is the case despite the fact that Abimelech recognizes that God is blessing Isaac's situation. Once again mission breaks down in the midst of power. The account of Jacob and his sons involved in the slaughter of Shechem (already mentioned in Genesis 34) is one of the most vivid accounts of the way in which military power and even spiritual abuse are jointly used for awful purposes.

Finally, Joseph is not someone who commands vast military power, but he does operate from a position of daunting economic and agricultural power during the peak of the famine in his time. Overall, Joseph's missional emphasis is astounding (as will be mentioned), and his allegiance to God in the midst of the nations is the testimony that stands head and shoulders above those before him.

However, Joseph's missional vision may have suffered at the peak of the famine which was likewise the point of greatest need among the Egyptians and the Canaanites (Gen 47:13–26). It is at this point that Joseph obtains everything that the people own, their cattle and their land, and eventually they all become servants of Pharaoh. The response of the people is positive because they can live through the famine (Gen 47:25), but they obviously had no other choices.

Joseph's implementation of a system to gain one-fifth of the food produced was likely the sort of agricultural engineering needed to survive the remaining years of the famine. However, it may not have been necessary to enslave all the people since they had such a great need and no means to live except by agreeing to what Joseph asked. In this case, it is difficult to understand how this could not hinder mission. If essential mission retains the idea that "Evangelization is humanization," then the

23. Ibid., 317.

people must retain their dignity, and it is hard to see how slavery helps in that purpose.[24] However, a seven-year drought encompassing the entire known world is an exceptional situation which may have required extraordinary requests, even though these requests are questionable from a missional perspective.

The Patriarchs' Interpretation of the Promise

Though there are clearly missional surprises and demises within Genesis, the burning question is really whether or not the patriarchs had any sense of missional calling in their election and whether their motivation was to work with God in mission. I will suggest that one of our predominant means of understanding the patriarchs' interpretation of God's promises is to examine their retelling or reiterations of God's promises throughout Genesis, and, specifically, to consider how they repeated God's promise "to bless all the nations of the earth." With the exception of Abraham, the main means of transferring or retelling the promises occurred at the end of their lives as they blessed their sons with a spiritual and physical inheritance.[25]

Beginning with Abraham, the repetition of God's promise to bless all the nations of the earth is awe-inspiring since he is not only the first one to hear the promise but the only one to hear the promise three times, all of which are directly from God (YHWH) or the angel of YHWH. Furthermore, there are similar echoes in the Abrahamic covenant and the renaming of Abraham.[26] However, in spite of the repetitions of the promise, Abraham is the only patriarch for which we have no detailed account of his conferring this promise upon Isaac (or any other for that matter). All we are told is that Abraham gave all that he owned to Isaac (Gen 25:5). The only account we have of Abraham repeating God's promises takes place as he commissions his most faithful servant to find a wife for Isaac (Gen 24:5–7). Therefore, it is through this short account that we gain some insight regarding Abraham's interpretation of God's promises.

---

24. Neill et al., *Concise Dictionary of Mission*, 594.

25. Referring back to Figure 1: The question marks between adjacent circles represent the absence of passing on the promise to "bless all nations" to succeeding generations. For greater detail, see Table 14 and Table 15 in Appendix A.

26. Lapham counts four repetitions of the promise by including the covenant in Genesis 15, 17 as essentially the same (Lapham, *Bible as Missionary Handbook*, 7).

When the servant suggests a contingency plan, in the event that Isaac's future wife will not leave her homeland and venture off to distant Canaan, Abraham makes it very clear that this is not an option because God promised the land to his offspring. There is no record of Abraham focusing upon the promise of growth nor any indication that he conveyed to the servant God's promise to bless all the nations of the earth. The missing promise to the nations is notable in this case, because the servant is being sent to a distant region. Since the servant is clearly willing to pray, follow, and worship God, the one promise that would have given him greater security and purpose would be to know that he was fulfilling God's promise to bless all the nations of the earth. However, this promise is nowhere discussed even though the servant does become a blessing in the region where he travels, largely due to Abraham's influence. In other words, the servant by extension of his faith, becomes part of the people of God and has missional impact but is never told the promise of God because either Abraham did not remember this promise or possibly did not feel it important enough to share with the servant.[27]

Moving from Abraham to Isaac, there is comparatively little written on the life of Isaac. However, Jacob's deception and the ensuing pleading of Esau actually provide us with the most definitive understanding of Isaac's interpretation of God's promises and, specifically, Isaac's interpretation of the promise to bless all the nations of the earth. As already mentioned, Isaac most likely heard the blessing twice in his life.

However, of all the misunderstandings related to mission in Genesis, Isaac's interpretation is the most antithetical to God's promise for the nations. Isaac literally blesses Jacob with the hope that the nations will "serve" Jacob and "bow down" to Jacob (Gen 27:29 NIV). Interestingly, the Hebrew verb "to bless" (בָּרַךְ) means "to kneel" when used in the

---

27. The other possibility is that Abraham told the servant and it was not recorded. This is a very unlikely possibility given the number of times that the promise to bless all the nations of the earth is repeated in Genesis. Some may want to accuse me of making arguments from the silence of Scripture. If it were this sole account of silence, I could accept the validity of these accusations. However, as I will demonstrate there are multiple accounts in which the patriarchs simply do not pass on this message. It is highly unlikely that the patriarchs repetition of the promise would go unrecorded given that the original promise was delivered directly from God in at least five instances within Genesis (more if you include Gen 15 and 17 as echoes of Gen 12:3). When there is a pervasive silence on a particular topic in Scripture, I simply find it unreasonable to reject the idea that the consistent silence does not substantively communicate to the modern-day reader.

active sense (similar to "bow down"). In the Hebrew mindset, the verb carries the connotation that blessing and kneeling correlate with one another.[28] It seems that Isaac reversed God's intention and adjusted the verb to take it to further extremes.[29]

Though Isaac did play the role of a peacemaker in his time, this account gives the impression that he grudgingly agreed to peace and inwardly wanted to subjugate the nations throughout his life. In Isaac's defense, he does give a veiled transfer of the promise of land, but there is no mention of the promise to the nations (Gen 28:4). Furthermore, Isaac refers to the "blessing of Abraham" in the singular (בִּרְכַּת אַבְרָהָם) which may indicate that he perceived only one blessing promised to Abraham rather than three. To say that Isaac misinterpreted or misrepresented the promise to bless the nations would be an understatement.

However, what is so definitive about Isaac's interpretation of the promise is that we do not have to speculate over the possibility that Isaac simply did not reveal part of the promise as he blessed Jacob (thinking it was Esau). Why is this? It is because we have an account of Isaac bestowing the blessing to Jacob, which is quickly followed by Esau's entrance, and a very helpful question is asked that relates to our concern—"Oh, haven't you saved even one blessing for me?" Esau asks a second time "Not one blessing left for me?" (Gen 27:36, 38). This is extremely helpful because it gives us confidence that we have a full account of Isaac's understanding of the promise.

We know that Isaac did not pass on God's promise to bless the nations when he blessed Jacob. So, there actually is a blessing left to be

---

28. As in Hebrew, the two ideas of kneel and bless are in this word. The usage is very like Hebrew in that "kneel" is restricted to the active participle . . . with bless in the infinitive and passive participle . . . The word is used of blessing or praising God. It is not used of blessing men . . . Harris et al., *Theological Wordbook of OT*, 996

29. It is interesting to note that the accounts in which Isaac hears the blessing are likewise the accounts in which the Hebrew verb "to bless" is used in the hithpael form. Scholars have spent a fair amount of effort considering the reasons for the niphal form of בָּרַךְ (in Gen 12:3; 18:18 and 28:14) compared to the hithpael form (in Gen 22:18 and 26:4). What seems to have gone unnoticed is that the latter passages are those in which Isaac is hearing God's promise (even though Gen 22:18 is addressing Abraham). More work needs to be done, but I would not be surprised to find that this subtle shift in the verb is God's way of biasing the message to deal with Isaac's heart (which only God would know), especially since Isaac demonstrates the strongest tendency toward subjugating the nations. It seems quite possible that God adjusted the verb to compensate for the manner in which Isaac wanted to relate to the nations.

given, but this blessing is not remembered by Isaac. As a result, Esau remains void of a blessing even though there is much to be given. The irony of the story is that it really is not Jacob's deception that leaves Esau without a blessing. Rather, it is Isaac's ethnocentrism and lack of missional vision that leaves Esau void of the pinnacle of all blessings.

As we move to the last two principal figures in Genesis, we find far more of Jacob's life revealed and even more in the case of Joseph. One of the most powerful things about Jacob's dream is that it takes place in a land that Jacob feels is void of God's presence (Gen 28:10–22). As Jacob fears for his life, alone in an unknown place, he is comforted by God's repetition of the Abrahamic covenant. The surprise in Jacob's response gives us greater confidence that he had never before heard the promise. However, it is unclear whether Jacob understands the full meaning of this covenant. It is deeply meaningful that God repeats this covenant in this "foreign place" where Jacob is surprised to find God's presence.

Jacob's response is not only one of joy in knowing that he is protected. Rather, Jacob believes he has found the gateway to heaven and this gateway touches earth in a foreign land.[30] The fact that God repeats Genesis 12 in the midst of this dream is fascinating. First of all there is the means by which Genesis 12 is repeated—it is in the midst of a spiritual vision and Yahweh is speaking to Jacob. This is a far cry from an academic study of the passage, despite the fact that this revelation has already been communicated multiple times to Jacob's father and grandfather.

Furthermore, there are important corrective differences countering the final wishes that Isaac gave to Jacob. Amidst the backdrop of Isaac's promise of prosperity, military rule and subjugation of the nations, Jacob learns that he and his descendents will be a blessing to all nations (Gen 28:14). This is an interesting expansion of earlier passages. In the original (Gen 12:3), we are told that, "all the families of the earth will be blessed through *you*," and Genesis 18:18 and 22:18 convey that this will take place "*through your descendents.*" Without reading further, this shift might leave the impression that God was refining the promise to the

---

30. Jacob's response is filled with modern-day mission principles, the most obvious of which is that God goes far ahead of us in mission and resides in places that we may believe are void of godly character. Just like Jacob, many modern-day missionaries feel tremendous fear and God's message to Jacob is one of protection and care and oversight *in the midst of a missional vision.*

Missiological Hermeneutics

nations in a purely futuristic manner, being fulfilled only at the time of Christ (compare Gal 3:6–16).

However, both are agents of the promise in Jacob's account (for example, "All the families of the earth will be blessed through *you . . . and your seed, or your descendents*"—Gen 28:14 italics mine: וּבְזַרְעֶךָ . . . בְּךָ). We have to ask how Jacob might have interpreted this phrase. Much of the answer lies in Genesis 28:13.

There is little question that Jacob would interpret "you . . . and your seed" in verse 14 in the same way as in verse 13. In verse 13, God tells Jacob that the land is promised to "you . . . and your seed" (לְךָ וּלְזַרְעֶךָ . . .) and then, in verse 14, an identical construction is used (וּבְזַרְעֶךָ . . . בְּךָ) differing only in the preposition "to" (ל) versus "through" (ב). It is highly unlikely that Jacob would interpret the promise to the nations in a purely futuristic manner. Just as he would see the land as a present reality, the promise to the nations would also be seen as a present missional reality ("through you"), and possibly as a future messianic prophecy ("your seed"). It is more likely, however, that he would have interpreted this as something carried out through his immediate descendents.

From a purely linguistic perspective, collective nouns (like "seed") are rarely ever used in plural form, even though this is part of Paul's argument in Galatians as he notes the importance of "seed" verses "seeds" (Gal 3:16).[31] How is it then that scholars have suggested that the promise "to bless all the nations of the earth" essentially jumps over the entire Old Testament and refers solely to Christ? There is certainly no evidence to suggest that Jacob could possibly have interpreted the blessing in this way. It is only through a reductionistic interpretation of Paul's argument that this leap can be made, but this is not Paul's intent as will be shown later.

Just as Jacob saw the blessing of the land as an immediate promise for him and his children, he would likewise have had to consider himself and his children the immediate agents for the blessing of the nations. Opponents of a missiological reading of the promise may claim that the phrase "you . . . and your descendants" is idiomatic, but it simply represents a missional expansion of the wording in Genesis 12:3.

---

31. Genesis 9:9 uses "seed" in the singular (זֶרַע—m,s,c) to denote more than one descendant. 1 Samuel 8:15 is the only passage in the Bible to use "seed" (זֶרַע) in the plural form.

This expansion is taking place because the blossoming people of Israel are not fully interpreting their missional purpose in their election. As we have seen, there are times when the patriarchs step (or stumble) into mission, but it remains questionable if they perceive this as part of God's purpose in their election. This can be seen most profoundly in Jacob's response to God's promise. Jacob's surprising response is a mere promise of allegiance to God while in a foreign land, and Jacob is very clear that this is conditional upon receiving God's protection. Jacob's response is entirely self-focused, and as such it is unlikely that he realizes the expansive and broader impact of God's promise for the nations.[32] Any committed Christian today who repeats Jacob's response would probably be questioned for wavering in his or her commitment to God.

However, there are some promising points at which Jacob gives echoes similar to Genesis 12:3. Many missiologists have pointed out that Genesis 49:10 is a continuation of the promise to bless all nations due to the messianic overtones.[33] Some have further noted the correlation between Genesis 49:10 and Numbers 24:17.[34] While the messianic overtones seem credible in both of these passages, I am not fully convinced that Jacob (or Balaam) understood this deeper meaning of his own words.[35]

However, Teng's thoughts over Jacob's concept of mission, as expressed in his blessing of Joseph, has far more credibility; "This line of thought does not stop here. Through the mouth of Jacob, a great blessing was given to Joseph, who was the next link in the line of this mission: 'Joseph is a fruitful bough . . . whose branches run over the wall' (Gen. 49:22). What a beautiful metaphor for a vessel of blessing!"[36]

---

32. In Genesis 32:22–32, Jacob wrestles with God. This is more than likely God's highly contextual form of communication for someone who has operated this way his entire life. Jacob never received anything normally. He always tricked or fought or was prepared to fight. It is quite interesting that he wrestles with God and "wins!" What does Jacob win? He wins the name Israel—the elected nation prepared to minister to all the nations of the earth. He wins a missionary calling! But, he probably doesn't realize it.

33. Carver, *Missions in the Plan*, 160; Kaiser, *Mission in the OT*, 47; McLean, *Hand-Book of Missions*, 30; McLean, *Where the Book Speaks*, 24; Montgomery, *Bible and Missions*, 20; Zwemer, *Into All the World*, 11.

34. Kaiser, *Mission in the OT*, 47; Zwemer, *Into All the World*, 11.

35. In this sense, I am arguing that there is some type of "sensus plenior" taking place through God's authoring of Scripture.

36. Teng, "Biblical Basis of Missions," Web Page 1 of 4 quoting from NRSV, ellipsis in original quote.

Teng merely mentions this metaphor, but does not spend any time to expand on its meaning. This metaphor of mission is compelling because Joseph is represented as a main branch bearing fruit (or a fruitful bough), that is drawing its life from a nearby spring while Joseph's branches reach over a wall (or boundary).

Permit me to speculate for a moment, since the metaphorical interpretation of this blessing nearly jumps from the page. Joseph is a main branch because he has been so faithful to God throughout his life. This main branch bears fruit, which is a sign of mission that has taken place. This branch draws its life from a spring. At first glance, a spring might not seem overly impressive. Yet, consider the need for water throughout Genesis, the squabbles over the wells that plagued Isaac, and the drought and famine experienced by all the patriarchs. Drought and famine were most poignant in Joseph's life, but a "spring" is a metaphor for a source of life, which is God in this case.

Finally, there is the image of branches that offer shade. After water, shade is one of the most sought after places of rest in semi-arid regions.[37] Shade attracts the weary and gives them rest. Interestingly enough, the shade that this tree offers reaches beyond the wall or the barrier that separates one people from another—suggesting a spiritual barrier between the people of God and those who do not know God. The shade is an image of life-giving blessing to the nations.

Though this verse focuses on Joseph, I believe that Jacob understood the meaning of his words because he lived through this missional dimension as he reunited with Joseph and saw the impact that Joseph's life had on Egypt and the world. There are echoes of mission in Jacob's blessing of his son. Even though it does not appear that there is a direct or intentional attempt to pass the promise of blessing the nations onto his children, Jacob does seem to reiterate the promise of growth and the land (Gen 48:15–16; 49:13).

In moving from Jacob into Joseph's life, I would like to begin by suggesting that God chose to modify the way in which the promise for the nations was declared. Up to this point, God had verbally proclaimed

---

37. A modern-day example of this in nature is the fact that kangaroos in the Australian outback fight over shade due to the 140° peak temperatures occurring in January. After water, shade is the most sought after resource to reducing the heat by up to 80%. See PBS, *Nature: Big Red Roos* (26:45—28:00).

Biblically Informed Missional Hermeneutics

the promise of blessing to the nations.³⁸ As we have seen, the response of the patriarchs is either absent or was at best an echo of the original promise. The patriarchs had a minimal response in terms of assuming ownership and responsibility in mission, and this failure becomes a predominant paradigm throughout the Old Testament.

However, God's grace is fully evident in this with respect to both the patient waiting upon the people of God and a continued concern to reformulate the message of mission. This reformulation takes shape as God communicates the message of mission again to the elected missionary nation (Israel) in subtly new and creative ways. This, in turn, allows the next generation to break free of their ancestors' pattern and take ownership of their role in God's mission. This over-arching change is most powerfully seen in the life of Joseph and the way in which God's providential missionary efforts are ordained in the joys and sorrows of Joseph's life journey.

In Joseph's life, God's message of mission takes on new proclamational shape through the use of narrative communication.³⁹ Similar to Jacob's blessing in Genesis 49:22, God's plans carried out through Joseph become a living metaphor of mission (Gen 41–50) that replaces the verbal promise given to Abraham, Isaac and Jacob (Gen 12:3; 18:18; 22:18; 26:4; 28:14). This shift and Joseph's obedience result in a vast increase in the magnitude and fulfillment of the blessing of the nations, as Joseph's life becomes a noticeable blessing to any nation he serves.⁴⁰

---

38. In four of the five accounts, YHWH proclaimed the promise to the nations personally (Gen 12:3; 18:18; 26:4; 28:14). In Jacob's account, the message comes through a vision, but nevertheless is very real to Jacob. In Genesis 22:18, God works through a messenger or an angel.

39. I would suggest that one of the reasons scholars have missed this shift is due to the modern concern to look solely for "evidence" in the form of direct proclamation. Narrative meaning, by contrast, does not hold the same level of validity in the mind of modern scholars, even though the use of narrative held more validity in the Old Testament. While it is true that narrative has a range of interpretations, it also provides greater consistency than proclamation because the meaning in narrative flows through the entire story rather than in just a few words.

40. Referring back to Figure 1: The right side of the diagram portrays a change in God's announcement of the promise—from declaration to a display through Joseph's life. Consequently, the large exclamation mark over Joseph is due to the missional impact that is narratively portrayed through his life that likewise draws the attention of quite possibly all the nations of the earth.

Joseph blesses Potiphar (Gen 39:5), and he is a tremendous blessing to Egypt and eventually the entire known world. In a very powerful narrative statement, Joseph even leads Jacob to bless the Pharaoh in a remarkable instance of Joseph helping his father to carry out the Abrahamic promise to all nations (Gen 47:7). Therefore, I consider Joseph's life to be a genre that is a "living image" of promise in that his real life reflects a larger missional fulfillment and acts as a reminder of God's plan, orchestrated by God's direction.[41]

The entirety of the Old Testament, however, is filled with so much failure in developing allegiance to God (and allegiance to God's mission) that the success cases of mission in the Old Testament can often be overlooked.[42] Bauckham, for example, struggles to see the fulfillment of the promise that takes place within Genesis; "For the canonical reader Genesis creates a strong expectation that the blessing of the nations through Abraham's descendents is to be the goal of the rest of the biblical story. But in fact for the rest of the Old Testament story it remains no more than a promise."[43]

Bauckham's generalization does not hold up in the life of Joseph. The main difference in Joseph's life is that the promise that was previously declared propositionally is now orchestrated in vivid living imagery by God through Joseph's life. Furthermore, even though Joseph's life embodies the promise of a blessing to all nations of the earth, it is more important to realize that it is God's providence behind the scenes that "proclaims" the promise to all nations.

Consider the many steps set in motion by God: (1) Joseph is in the royal prison which creates a bridge to the king's wine server who (2) has a God-given dream which (3) Joseph can interpret through God's gifting, setting the stage for (4) the time when God gives the king of Egypt

---

41. Compare Hosea and Jonah. One similar example in Exodus is suggested by Sjogren, noting that the 70 palms and 12 springs of Exodus 15:27 may be a physical example or living reminder of Israel's mission with the 70 palms representing the 70 known nations of Genesis 11 and the 12 springs representing the life-giving ability of the 12 tribes of Israel (Sjogren, *Unveiled at Last*, 46). There are very similar "living images" in the New Testament such as "living water" in John 4 and the "Bread of Life" as a living image in John 6.

42. Though beyond the scope of this study there are many other examples of the ways in which Israel blesses the nations in the Old Testament (compare Bauckham, *Bible and Mission*, 30–32).

43. Ibid., 30.

a dream to serve as a call for Joseph, which (5) Joseph can once again interpret through God's gifting. This unlikely set of events occurs in the overall canvas of Joseph's life, as he suffers tremendous calamities that consistently place him in a state of weakness and are even worse than those of his forefathers.

Unlike his forefathers who were displaced wanderers, aliens in a foreign land, Joseph is a slave and a criminal in a foreign land. Joseph is someone who operates with absolutely no power except for his personal integrity and God-given abilities in dream interpretation. The result is blessings that come from Joseph's acquaintances and, ultimately, the entire nation of Egypt blesses Joseph in remarkable ways (Gen 47:5–12). The blessings bestowed upon Egypt for trusting in Joseph who demonstrated consistent God-ordained leadership result in further blessing that literally saves the life of Egypt. Moreover, the positive repercussions of Egypt recognizing God's gifting in Joseph means that Egypt becomes "a blessing to all the nations of the earth" and likewise echoes "I will bless those who bless you" (Gen 12:3). As such, *Joseph does not hear the promise. Joseph lives it.* Through God's providence, Joseph is carried by God's hand from calamity to caretaker three times in his life.

Three times, Joseph moves from a position of weakness to a means of blessing successively larger groups. Early in Joseph's life he experiences the calamity of his own family selling him into slavery, and yet Potipher makes him caretaker of the entire household (Gen 37:28; 39:4). Then Joseph experiences the calamity of being falsely thrown in jail after a false accusation of rape, only to be entrusted as the caretaker of all the prisoners (who may have just as easily been as innocent as Joseph—Gen 39:14–23). Last of all, Joseph experiences the calamity of being forgotten and left confined by an absent-minded wine server, only to be remembered years later, after which he quickly rises to become the caretaker of Egypt (Gen 40–41).

In the midst of God's missional providence, Joseph's life again and again touches ever increasing spheres of influence. As Joseph is put in trust of the national food storage and distribution in Egypt, he is lifted into a position of influence over the entire world of his day by providing for so many during the seven-year drought. Up to this point, none of Jacob's ancestors have had this massive level of influence. There is no question that Joseph's life was "a blessing to all the nations of the (then-known) earth." "When we think of Joseph, the descendant of Abraham who brought deliverance from famine and social distress to the greatest nation of the ancient world, we see anticipatory fulfillment of the promise of Abraham's seed blessing the nations (Gen 12:3)."[44]

Now, we must take a step backward and consider Jacob's interpretation of Joseph's life. It would not have been too surprising if Jacob had stood up when he arrived in Egypt and exuberantly proclaimed that God has now fulfilled the promise "to bless all the nations of the earth" through Joseph's life! Had Jacob made such a claim, it might have been premature on Jacob's part to think that the promise had been entirely fulfilled, but this would be a reasonable claim given Jacob's limited scope of God's redemptive plan.

However, Jacob does not appear to correlate Joseph's life-ministry with the promise given to Jacob in Genesis 28:14.[45] How can it be that Jacob's blessing upon his sons does not relate the promise to the obvious blessing that Joseph had been for the nations? Two reasons come to mind. One is that it took place but simply was never recorded. Another could be that Jacob simply missed the connection between Joseph's life and the promise. Given the track-record of the patriarchs and Jacob's self-focused conniving nature, I would speculate that the latter is much more likely.

Did God fail to create a missional vision within Genesis? No. God tried again and again. God's often repeated promises certainly instilled confidence in this fledgling missionary force who were heavily exposed to the threats of violence, famine, and displacement. Any missionary living in the same context today would consistently need to hear God's reaffirmation of this promise. However, the principal reason for God's repetition was to gracefully remind the elected people that their failed ownership in God's mission and their failure to pass on missional concern to their descendants needed to be reassessed.

Only in the life and actions of Joseph do the nations begin to see a living image of God's promise. Joseph's life becomes a means of interpretation (a missional hermeneutic) of God's promise.[46] But, does this hermeneutic embody God's grace? It certainly does since three generations of God's elected representatives seem to selectively exclude any

---

44. Glasser, *Announcing the Kingdom*, 67–68.

45. Again, there is the possibility that this took place and was not recorded, but that is a remote possibility given the importance of this concept throughout Genesis.

46. Cp. Newbigin, *Gospel in Pluralist Society*, 232–33; Newbigin, *Truth to Tell*, 35.

aspect of the promise that did not benefit them directly.[47] Furthermore, God's providential mission is still carried out through Abraham, Isaac and Jacob in limited ways, as a graceful reminder that even these absent-minded and at times conniving "missionaries" can be used by God.

However, the most dynamic display of mission to the nations takes place through forced slavery, false imprisonment and national exile—the frailty of missional direction in Joseph's life. In fact, the message is so powerful that Joseph is able to correctly interpret his purpose in God's plan of outreach even though he is standing before the same brothers who took "pity" on him by selling him as a slave rather than taking his life (Gen 45:5–8; 50:20).

Joseph's brothers, like Jacob, miss the significance of God's providential missionary activity because they are so concerned over their own self-preservation. No one could blame Joseph for being flustered in such company, but *he alone utilizes a missionary hermeneutic that gracefully interprets and declares an early fulfillment of the promise spoken to his father, grandfather and great-grandfather—a promise which he in all likelihood never heard.*

The overall missional journey of Genesis is that of God orchestrating Joseph's life as a display of blessings, following five earlier attempts to communicate the blessing directly to Abraham, Isaac and Joseph. In light of this, I would contend that the promise to bless all nations was something that God actively intended to carry out in the Old Testament provided that the people of God would faithfully display allegiance to God (compare Gen 12:4; 18:19; 22:18b; 26:5–6; 28:16–22).[48]

The call and responsibility set before the people of God was one of allegiance through which God's providential mission would flow. One of the main reasons that mission flows so mightily through Joseph is be-

47. I am not suggesting here that the promise was a explicit command that the patriarchs needed to follow. I am simply pointing out that recounting the promise to the generations that follow would have been the least they could have done in being responsible with God's revelation given in the midst of their lives, as the mere remembrance and sharing of the phrase would have allowed succeeding generations to reflect on its meaning.

48. It is for these reasons that I would have to disagree with Rowley and others who believe that the verb in the promise to Abraham should be translated "will bless themselves" due to their thinking that the nations will merely observe Abraham's blessing and wish for a similar blessing. Even though this is a form of mission, it is not what God carries out through Joseph's life. Rather, the promise as shown through Joseph is a blessing that reaches out to the nations in the midst of their need.

cause he holds such high allegiance to God in the midst of dire circumstances. By contrast, Jacob's allegiance-response is the weakest in that Jacob merely claims that "YHWH will be my God if . . ." the conditions of God's protection and provision are afforded to Jacob (Gen 28:16–22).[49]

Finally, there is one other remarkably helpful interpreter beyond that of Abraham, Isaac, Jacob, and Joseph. The nations are one of the most impressive interpreters in Genesis! The nations consistently observe the patriarchs' lives and interpret that God is with them and blessing them. Beginning in Genesis 12:17–20, we learn that Pharaoh interprets the signs of God and is able to connect this with Abraham. In Melchizedek, we find this mysterious figure emerge from the nations solely to bless Abraham (Gen 24:19–20).

Abimelech, similar to Pharaoh in Genesis 12, speaks with God and learns that Abraham is a prophet (Gen 20:1–18). Furthermore, the narrative of Abimelech is the first account of the nations blessing the patriarchs with land. He furthermore becomes a part of the means by which the Philistines are impacted through Abraham's life and witness (Gen 20:15; 21:22–23, 32–34).

A second account in which the nations bless the patriarchs with land is the Hittite offer to give Abraham the burial cave owned by Ephron (Gen 23:5–11). Following this same theme, Isaac's family is protected by Abimelech despite the same deception of both father and son (Gen 26:11), and Isaac lives among Abraham's wells as is therefore blessed by the continuation of the giving of land (which is now a third account of land being given—until Isaac becomes so powerful that the nations ask him to leave—Gen 26:16, 19–22).

Lastly, the giving of land occurs as the king of Egypt offers the very best land to Joseph's family (Gen 47:5–6). The surprise is that those whom the patriarchs perceived as untrustworthy enemies demonstrate repeated concern for their security and survival. The shock is that the nations become one of the most unlikely sources to echo the promise of land for the patriarchs and their descendants (Gen 12:7, etc.)!

---

49. Jacob also appears surprised that God exists in a foreign land, as it seems that Jacob has a territorial perspective of God. However, Joseph has no difficulty calling upon God in the even more distant land of Egypt.

Overview of the Promise in Genesis

What can we learn then from this extensive study of mission that takes place in Genesis? The dominant theme that shows up in Genesis is God's continued interest in mission despite the fact that the patriarchs did not perceive God's missional promises important enough to pass on to the next generation.

Some may say that since mission in Genesis is not a command, there is no reason to pass it on. It is true that God's promises in Genesis are not explicit commands. However, this does not diminish the idea that mission held great importance as an integral aspect of God's plan within Genesis.[50] Nor does it explain why the patriarchs would fail to bless their sons with this promise even if the meaning was confounding for them.

Furthermore, what we learn from this is that God is creative in communicating God's missional intentions in a number of resourceful ways—propositionally, narratively, and even as a living metaphor. Why did God choose this type of approach rather than making an explicit command? Mission based upon "command" rarely has an impact. The great commissions of the Gospels and Acts are really more inspirational than commanding. If there is a command for mission in Scripture, it is based on the continuity and longevity of the message of mission in Scripture. Therefore, I would suggest that God is using something similar to the discovery principle to help this fledgling missional nation take ownership in God's missionary agenda.[51]

Ultimately, the appropriate question with respect to the missional implications of the promise in Genesis should be, "Was the promise to 'bless all the nations of the earth' important enough to remember and pass along?" The nature of the promise (for example, a command, a blessing), does not diminish its importance. The mere fact that God repeated this five times and that it stood as the final clause in each account should have caught the attention of the patriarchs. If it did, we have no

---

50. Cp. Wright, *Mission of God*, 51–61, 194–221.

51. By the "discovery principle," I mean the idea that personal discovery provides infused ownership and personal attachment toward missionary activity. In my opinion, it is the discovery principle that most likely explains the passive or middle force of the Hebrew verb "to bless" (ברך), in that there is a collect great blessing perceived by those involved in mission as their lives take on a very powerful partnership with God and in infused meaning that relates directly to God's election of Abraham and his descendents.

record of it. There is no mistaking, however, the core of the covenant which is a call to allegiance and obedience to God, even as strangers in an alien land (Gen 17:7–8; 18:19; 22:16–18; 26:5; 35:1–12; compare 49:10).

Therefore, the patriarchs did not actively consider the blessing to all nations as something to pass on. At times they do show a vision for mission and they are at their best when they are likewise at their weakest points. It is then that they are most dependent on God. The main difference between the patriarchs versus Peter and Paul's interpretation of the promise to "bless all the nations of the earth," is that both Peter and Paul actively reread the passage with a missiological hermeneutic. The result is that the patriarchs' lack of missional emphasis leaves the Old Testament in similar deficit, while Peter and Paul's interpretations are infused with mission.

The Promise among Later Old Testament Biblical Figures (Num 24:9; Ps 72:17)

Throughout the remainder of the Old Testament, there are narratives and a number of passages that have strong echoes of Genesis 12:3. For example, Ruth blesses Naomi through her profound loyalty and Ruth's integrity is likewise blessed through Boaz (Ruth 1:16–17; 3:10–13; 4:9–15). As such, the narrative echoes "I will bless those who bless you . . . and all peoples on earth will be blessed through you" (Gen 12:3 NIV). In terms of passages re-stating the promise, the vast majority of these occur in the Psalms and in Isaiah (Ps 22:27; 47:1; 49:1; 67:2; 72:11; 72:17 "all nations will be blessed through him"; 86:9; 96:3–5; 102:15; 113:4; 117; Isa 2:2; 25:7; 29:7–8 effectively those who curse you will be cursed; 52:10; 56:7; 61:8b–9 "all the nations are blessed", 61:11; 66:18–20). In addition to these, there are the prophetic words of Balaam in Numbers 24:9.

Among these, the closest parallels are found foremost in Numbers 24:9 while Psalm 72:17 is a more distant echo, and Isaiah 61:8b–9 is even more distant. In this section, we will investigate Balaam's prophetic proclaim of a promise that is nearly identical to the original, and then consider David's prayer for Solomon and Psalm 72 which is an account that has strong thematic similarities despite linguistic differences.

Balaam and the Promise to the King of Moab (Num 22–24; 24:9)

One of the most unique repetitions of Genesis 12:3a occurs in Numbers 22–24, where the very questionable prophet Baalam eventually understands something of God's plan for mission. He is used by God to warn Balak even while Balak attempts to curse Israel. Balaam is a an unusual witness in helping Balak to understand God's power.

Before venturing further, let us consider if we are dealing with a repetition of Gen 12:3a from a linguistic standpoint. Table 3 compares the two clauses in both their original form and the root words.

Table 3: Original Language Comparison of Genesis 12:3a and Numbers 24:9

Passage	Hebrew Clause	Hebrew Roots
Gen 12:3a	וַאֲבָרְכָה מְבָרְכֶיךָ וּמְקַלֶּלְךָ אָאֹר	(ו ברך ברך ו קלל ארר)
	I will bless those who bless you, and whoever curses you I will curse (NIV).	
Num 24:9	מְבָרְכֶיךָ בָרוּךְ וְאֹרְרֶיךָ אָרוּר	(ברך ברך ו ארר ארר)
	May those who bless you be blessed and those who curse you be cursed! (NIV)	

The construction is almost identical with the exception of the participle for "the one who curses you" (וּמְקַלֶּלְךָ root verb קלל) in Genesis 12:3 being replaced with a stronger participle meaning "those who curse you" (וְאֹרְרֶיךָ root verb ארר) in Numbers 24:9. Most likely the former indicates the rarity with which a curse was expected to be leveled in Genesis, while the latter is indicative (in this instance) of Balak's repeated attempts to curse the massive nation of Israel. The verb in this verse is issued in response to Balak's third failed attempt to curse Israel. Therefore, it seems likely that this is the same clause with an appropriate contextual modification, given Balak's repeated attempts to cause harm through a curse.

The barrier of dealing with Balak's animistic intention of trying to wield God against Israel makes for an unusually high missional barrier (Num 23:23). Furthermore, the curses issued by Balak in Numbers 22–24 are a clear spiritual attack that would require God to engage in the promise of protection (Gen 12:3a). Likewise, the barriers that God has to deal with in Balaam are significant barriers even though they are common missional problems found throughout the Old Testament.[52] As such, this less-than-ideal missionary and the curse-casting king of Moab are a missiologist's nightmare.[53]

Yet, how does God initiate change in Balaam's attitude? God begins by using dreams, a talking donkey, a confrontational angel, and direct prophetic utterances.[54] God deals with Balaam's misdirection by a flood of spiritual agents and methods. Yet, to our shock Balaam still has some doubt regarding God's true intentions until the near-end of this account (compare Num 24:1). Nevertheless, God works through Balaam in order to overcome the barriers in Balak.

As we read through the story of Balaam and Balak, one of the more obvious questions is, "why would God use Balaam as a witness to Balak, especially when Israel is present in force and any one of the faithful Israelites could be used as a missionary to Balak?" Had God used a witness from Israel, Balak would most likely have assumed that someone from Israel was simply unwilling to curse their own people, or lacked the proper prophetic power.

However, God does use a questionable witness with no allegiance to Israel. In this way, God demonstrates that even a false prophet who is known to trade his prophetic gifting for financial reward, is unable to overcome plans that God has for this nation. Balaam would not have known that Israel will bear witness of God's nature throughout the region. God's involvement, juxtaposed against Balaam, gives God the opportunity to demonstrate true spirituality, in contrast to the spiritual power that Balak sought in Balaam. Notably, Balak wrote Balaam saying "I know that blessings fall on any people you bless, and curses fall on

---

52. The biblical record records Balaam's vices, which includes that of often resorting to divination as well as greed, but Balaam is so notorious that he appears in the New Testament as well (Num 24:1; 2 Pet 2:15; Jude 11).

53. Van Engen summarizes McGavran's principles stating that "The higher the barriers the more intentional, complex and costly is the crossing of them" and this can be seen in Numbers 22–24 (Van Engen and Redford, "Syllabus," 103 originally Van Engen; compare McGavran and Wagner, *Understanding Church Growth*, 47–53).

54. Interestingly, the miraculous aspects of Balaam and Jonah has in many cases caused scholars to assume a unique genre for these works due to its spiritually infused aspects, but this is an obvious example of a bias against the spiritual. If God were to have used a means other than a large fish and hungry worm to deal with Jonah, these works might be assigned more real-world missiological implications. Likewise, the role of the talking donkey in Numbers 22 may obscure the larger missiological significance of this passage.

Biblically Informed Missional Hermeneutics

people you curse" (Num 22:6 NLT). Though Numbers 22:6 is a close match to Genesis 12:3a, the primary difference is that Balak has ascribed God's power to Balaam. Therefore, from a contextual standpoint Balak genuinely believes that Balaam has real spiritual power. As such, when God uses this tainted and deceptive prophet in order to witness to Balak, the missional impact is authoritative. God's rule is demonstrated over the spiritual territory of Balaam's will, the spiritual territory of the land of Moab, and even the high places that Balak consistently sought.[55]

Balak is forced to witness the power of God as a greedy false prophet, with no allegiance to Israel and a painfully low allegiance to God. He is not only blocked in his ability to curse Israel but is forced to bless them. Balaam's actions repeatedly demonstrate that God has far more authority than Balaam himself. Therefore it is likely that God used Balaam as a missionary witness because Balak considered Balaam to be one of the most prevailing spiritual forces in the land, and God is consistently demonstrating that he has far more authority than that of Balaam. In fact, throughout the narrative, it is clear from Balaam's response that Balaam is likewise in the process of realizing that he is subjugated entirely to God. Balaam sees that God demonstrates authority over nature through the donkey, authority over Israel in protecting them, and consistent authority over the spiritual territories already mentioned.

In spite of this subjugation, there is tremendous grace given to the false prophet Balaam as God uses him to act as a witness. Grace and mercy are offered to Balaam through the spiritual capacity of his donkey. The humor of this passage often obscures an act of grace. The donkey is Balaam's only true ally during their journey and this same donkey is allowed to see into the spiritual realm (Num 22:23, 25, 27). God not only opens the donkey's mouth, but also the donkey's spiritual eyes and intellect in order to challenge Balaam's mindset and prophetic capacity. Ultimately, the donkey outsmarts Balaam and acts as a true prophet in order to save Balaam's life. More importantly, grace is given as Balaam is permitted to be a messenger in God's mission and to learn about God's ways, despite his extremely slow realization that he must serve God wholeheartedly (Num 24:1).

---

55. Balak may have sought high places for his own animistic reasons or this may have been a misconception on Balak's part regarding the name El-Shaddai (El šadday: God Almighty) which can literally mean "God of the Mountain" or "God the mountainous One."

However, the most notable aspect of this entire account is that we are offered a glimpse into God's missional response to someone who is actively trying to harm Israel. This follows the grace-infused aspects of Genesis 12:1–3 to a fault. By all accounts, Balak certainly is deserving of a curse, given his active attempts to curse Israel (Gen 12:3a). Therefore, it would come as no surprise if an immediate curse fell upon Balak or possibly on all of the Moabites. This is not the path taken by the missionary God of the Old Testament despite the fact that Balak demonstrates consistent rage as God replaces curses with blessings.

Grace is given to Balak in that he receives a witness while trying to curse Israel. Instead of a curse for a curse, Balak is allowed to learn of God through Balaam's prophecy and that Israel holds a special authority in God's redemptive plan (Gen 12:1–3). Moreover, Balak has the Scriptures explained to him in the prophesy as Balaam repeats the Abrahamic covenant at the end of the third blessing (Num 24:9). As curses are changed to blessings, God repeatedly re-interprets Genesis 12:1–3 for Balak to hear through Balaam. In this regard, the repetition of Genesis 12:3 in Numbers 24:9 stands in stark contrast to Balak's earlier claim, for Scripture reveals that it is God who has the true spiritual authority to curse or bless (compare Num 22:6).

Likewise, contained within the blessings for Israel are warnings, that are specifically directed toward those who might try to oppose or curse Israel. Balak is acting upon his fears since he believes his own nation will starve to death if Israel is allowed to consume their food (Num 22:3–4). As such, the account of Numbers 23–24 is full of warnings that indirectly offer protection to the Moabites by addressing Balak's fears. Furthermore, through each occurrence of creating altars and giving sacrifices, Balak is learning to worship God. Ultimately there is no escaping the fact that a corrupt prophet from among the nations is actively witnessing for God.[56]

In spite of all these missional attempts, Balak is unyielding in his conviction to bring harm to Israel. Likewise, the family history between the Moabites (through Lot) and Israel is unknown or of no concern to Balak, even though this linkage will eventually afford the Moabites and the Ammonites special protection (compare Gen 19:36–37; Deut 2:9, 19). By contrast, Israel stands off in the distance unaware (at this point in

---

56. Interestingly enough, one meanings of the term prophet (προφήτης) is that of an *interpreter* of God's word or God's will.

time) of the spiritual calamity that surrounds them. They receive God's protection and even though unknown to them, they receive three blessings from the king of Moab and a frustrated prophet who realizes that he will be working for free on this day.

More importantly, God repeatedly warns, informs, and witnesses to those intending harm to the people of God while protecting the elected nation of Israel. Even though tragedy is an ultimate reality, God's missional heart to bless the nations is openly displayed. As such, we find that the repetition of Genesis 12:3a is spoken while the repetition of Genesis 12:3b is carried out in God's attempt to gracefully bless Balak through a missional witness. In connection with the thesis of this chapter, we see that God uses a plethora of spiritual agents and means to repeat and reinterpret Scripture even for the nations, and even for those who have no missional concern. Furthermore, God actively witnesses through misguided hearts while changing curses to blessings so that the nations will know God.

David Prays for Solomon (Ps 72:17)—A Possible Echo of the Promise

Psalm 72:17 is a more distant passage from a linguistic standpoint, but a possible echo of the Genesis 12:3 promise in terms of meaning. In considering whether or not this is a repetition of Gen 12:3, Table 4 compares the two clauses in both their original form and the root words. Clearly only the beginning of the two passages are similar, but it is the conceptual similarities that capture our focus.

Table 4: Original Language Comparison of Genesis 12:3a and Psalm 72:17

Passage	Hebrew Clause	Hebrew Roots
Gen 12:3a	וַאֲבָרֲכָה מְבָרְכֶיךָ וּמְקַלֶּלְךָ אָאֹר	(ו ברך ברך ו קלל ארר)
	I will bless those who bless you, and whoever curses you I will curse (NIV).	
Ps 72:17	וְיִתְבָּרְכוּ בוֹ כָּל־גּוֹיִם יְאַשְּׁרוּהוּ	(ו ברך ב הוא כל גוי אשר הוא)
	All nations will be blessed through him, and they will call him blessed (NIV).	

In relation to Gen 12:3, John L. Amstutz asks, "Can you think of any illustrations in Scripture showing that the way a people/nation re-

Missiological Hermeneutics

sponded to God's people determined how God responded to them?"⁵⁷ One of the more startling biblical examples of a "response" occurs in the Gibeonite motive for deceiving the Israelites, as the Gibeonites claim they are from a distant land, though it is later discovered that they are nearby relatives (Josh 9–10). What initially captures our attention is the fact that the Bible expressly states that the Israelites did not pray before signing the Gibeonite treaty. Yet, there was no similar tragedy inflicted upon Israel like that which ensued as a result of Achin's failure and the subsequent battle losses at Ai (compare Josh 6:17–18; 7:25; 9:9–15). Instead, when others in the region attempt to kill the Gibeonites due to their newfound alliance, the Israelites come to their aid rather than allowing the Gibeonite's enemies to "end" the treaty with no blood on Israel's hands.

The startling portion of the account is that this "unique" response on the part of God and Israel includes not only the military aid of Israel but God likewise performs one of the greatest miracles in Scripture to aid in defeating the Gibeonite's enemies (Josh 10:1–13). This account makes sense only when seen through a missional hermeneutic that perceives God's underlying missional heart for any in the region who show the slightest allegiance to God. Here God gives aid even to those who work through means of a deceptive treaty with Israel, despite pre-existing commands to destroy all those in the region (compare Deut 31:3–4; Josh 2:8–21; 6:17; 9:24).⁵⁸

As we consider, Psalm 72, it is helpful to keep the Gibeonite account in mind since this occurs in the midst of the overwhelming violence of Joshua. Even this account includes God's express missional concerns alongside missional narratives that illustrate God's priority for mission (Josh 4:24; 24:17–18). Secondarily, if the missional impact in Joshua is

---

57. Amstutz, "Humanitarianism," 40.

58. Van Engen and Redford, "Syllabus," 55 originally Redford. Many perceive Joshua as exemplary in terms of his military obedience to God. I affirm this but point out that he lacked a missional vision. Other Old Testament leaders humbly begged God for mercy upon their own and other peoples, but nothing similar can be found in Joshua's leadership. After giving this lecture and expanding my thoughts, an unknown female student succinctly stated that this was "the rewards of a tenacious faith." Certainly beseeching God for the salvation of a people in the midst of God's judgment is dangerous, but it does demonstrate a genuine care within humanity that has biblical precedence (Gen 18:16ff; Exod 32:11ff.).

even loosely related to Genesis 12:2–3, how much more impact might Solomon's reign have in times of relative peace?

The temple is a hallmark in Israel's history that is synonymous with Solomon. However, Van Engen suggests that the tabernacle was an earlier form of a God-derived means of centripetal mission. As God dwells or tabernacles with Israel, the nations witness the ongoing relationship of God and Israel (Lev 26:11–12). As Israel worshiped God, centered around the tabernacle, this allowed the nations to observe Israel's allegiance to God (Num 10:29–32).[59] Van Engen claims that the heart of the exodus is the worship of an unseen God amidst nations with physical idols. Therefore, the tabernacle is a contextualized form of experiencing God. Israel is not worshipping the tabernacle but the tabernacle offers a means to experience and know God.[60] Interestingly, Stephen's speech alludes to the Israelite misconceptions of the tabernacle and the temple. This is likely related to Israel's failure in misinterpreting the missional versus nationalistic intentions behind these structures (Acts 7:44–48). Likewise, the tabernacle is referred to as the "Tent of the Testimony" (Num 9:15; 17:7–8 NIV) which alludes to the declaration of God in the midst of God's people while in the midst of the nations.

However, Scripture declares even greater missional implications when referring to Solomon's temple that likewise was intended to proclaim to the nations that it was God who made Israel holy (Isa 56:7; Jer 7:1; Ezek 37:26–28; Mark 11:17). The temple was even built in part by the nations (1 Chr 28:21). Therefore, given David's prayer for Solomon in Psalm 72:17 and the linkage to Solomon's building of the temple, it is easy to see how this becomes a fairly strong echo of Genesis 12:3.

Psalm 72 as a whole has unique missional implications that address both mission to the oppressed as well as mission to the political nations; nations that need to follow God in order to provide true justice to the disenfranchised. It is for this reason that the Psalm begins with a call for righteousness and mission to the poor requesting that the king might provide this sort of care and protection (72:1–7). However the focus

59. Ibid., 50–51 originally Van Engen.

60. This is not included in the Van Engen and Redford MT520 syllabus but it is a point that we consistently teach related to the tabernacle or holy place. The basic ideas originated with Van Engen. Beale has done extensive work on this theme and likewise claimed that the foci of Isaiah 42:5–7; 49:1–6 are indicative of the missional aspect of the temple (Beale, "Eden, the Temple, and the Church's Mission in the New Creation," 19).

quickly moves toward the allegiance of the nations with God (72:8–11). As the focus once again moves back toward the deliverance of the disenfranchised, the nations are clearly watching the king's actions, and even praying to God for the king of Israel to have wisdom (72:15). The implication is that the nations are looking to the king of Israel as a witness of proper conduct and rule before God and men, and this witness results in peace throughout their kingdoms and the whole earth. Therefore, the nations are not only blessed but they recognize the blessing that Israel's witness has bestowed and they wish to reciprocate by blessing the king (72:17).[61] As such, this prayer is a request for the fulfillment of Genesis 12:3 and is fulfilled as Solomon's temple centripetally gathers the nations and ultimately stands as a monument of God's missional intentions, just as the tabernacle once did (compare Matt 12:42).

The Promise in the New Testament (Acts 2–3; Rom 4; Gal 3–4)[62]

The final aspect to consider with relationship to the promise are the New Testament interpretations of Genesis 12:3 and its corollaries. We must begin by noting that the promise is shared with three extremely different audiences—devout Jews from many different regions, Jewish and Gentile believers in the heart of Gentile territory, and Judaizers (Acts 2; Rom 4; Gal 3–4 respectively). These respective backgrounds meant that the Christian message would be shared uniquely in each context. However, their backgrounds also meant that they may have developed certain pre-existing expectations for the most pertinent questions and answers brought to the Scriptures, all of which were conditioned by a perception of the proper approach (or hermeneutic) for interpretation.

---

61. Cp. Okoye, *Israel and the Nations*, 50.

62. Though it is difficult to explain, any useful insights in this section seem to have come through the Holy Spirit's leading as an answer to repeated prayer. Any mistaken perceptions in this section would certainly be a result of my inability to listen to the Holy Spirit's guidance.

Biblically Informed Missional Hermeneutics

Table 5: Comparing Acts 3:25 and Galatians 3:8 with LXX

vv.	LXX	MT
Gen 12:3	καὶ ἐνευλογηθήσονται ἐν σοί (*in you*) πᾶσαι αἱ φυλαὶ τῆς γῆς (*all the families of the earth*)	וְנִבְרְכוּ בְךָ כֹּל מִשְׁפְּחֹת הָאֲדָמָה
Gen 18:18	καὶ ἐνευλογηθήσονται ἐν αὐτῷ (*in him*) πάντα τὰ ἔθνη τῆς γῆς (*all the nations of the earth*) and continues "I have singled him out so that he will direct his sons and their families to keep the way of the Lord and do what is right and just. Then I will do for him all that I have promised."	וְנִבְרְכוּ בוֹ כֹּל גּוֹיֵי הָאָרֶץ
Gen 22:18	καὶ ἐνευλογηθήσονται ἐν τῷ σπέρματί σου (*in your seed*) πάντα τὰ ἔθνη τῆς γῆς (*all the nations of the earth*) and continues "all because you have obeyed me."	וְהִתְבָּרְכוּ בְזַרְעֲךָ כֹּל גּוֹיֵי הָאָרֶץ
Gen 26:4	καὶ ἐνευλογηθήσονται ἐν τῷ σπέρματί σου (*in your seed*) πάντα τὰ ἔθνη τῆς γῆς (*all the nations of the earth*) and continues "I will do this because Abraham listened to me and obeyed all my requirements, commands, regulations, and laws."	וְהִתְבָּרְכוּ בְזַרְעֲךָ כֹּל גּוֹיֵי הָאָרֶץ
Gen 28:14	καὶ ἐνευλογηθήσονται ἐν σοί (*in you*) πᾶσαι αἱ φυλαὶ τῆς γῆς (*all the families of the earth*) καὶ ἐν τῷ σπέρματί σου (*in your seed*)	וְנִבְרְכוּ בְךָ כָּל־מִשְׁפְּחֹת הָאֲדָמָה וּבְזַרְעֶךָ
Acts 3:25	καὶ ἐν τῷ σπέρματι σου (*in your seed*) ἐνευλογηθήσονται πᾶσαι αἱ πατριαὶ τῆς γῆς (*all the families of the earth*) Peter's version shows the singular "in your seed," which follows the beginning of Genesis 22:18; 26:4, but Peter follows the ending of Genesis 12:3; 28:14. Genesis 28:14 is the closest match since Peter uses "families" and "in your seed."[63]	
Gal 3:8	ἐνευλογηθήσονται ἐν σοί (*in you*) πάντα τὰ ἔθνη (*all the nations*). Paul's includes προευηγγελίσατο ("pre-good news") but Paul uses "in you," and he ends with "all the nations." Paul follows the beginning and ending of Genesis 18:18 ("in him" versus "in you") and Genesis 28:14. Genesis 28:14 also includes "in your seed" but it is not addressing Abraham (as in Gal 3:16).	

---

63. Lindars et al., *Scripture Citing Scripture*, 238.

Though it is possible that Peter and Paul both had the Septuagint in front of them when they quoted the Old Testament, it is more likely that they were working from memory. However, their particular recall of the wording may give us some idea of the particular biblical passage(s) in Genesis that they were referencing. In order to look at these accounts, Table 5 will serve as an attempt to compare Luke's record of Peter's wording in Acts 3:25 and Paul's wording in Galatians 3:8 with the Septuagint (LXX). The Masoretic text is provided for reference.

Peter's Interpretation—Israel Fulfills a Missional Promise (Acts 2–3)

The immediate background of Peter's account is especially relevant given the strong missional significance of Acts 2. Pentecost has just taken place, and literally all the nations have heard the gospel in their own tongue. Peter and the other disciples have, in their pronouncement given the greatest blessing of all time—salvation through Jesus Christ. The fulfillment of "the covenant God promised" has been manifested through tongues of fire that speak the languages of the world (Acts 3:24)! All of this activity is nothing less than an initial fulfillment by Jewish believers toward blessing all the nations of the earth!

The audience is not made up of Gentiles from other regions. Rather, we are told that the listeners were "*devout Jews from every nation* living in Jerusalem" (Acts 2:5 NLT, italics mine). Likewise, we can be reasonably certain that the mother tongue of these Jewish sojourners was not Hebrew or Aramaic, for they were "bewildered to hear *their own languages* being spoken" (Acts 2:6 NLT, italics mine). They also exclaimed, "These people are all from Galilee, and yet we hear them speaking in *our own native languages!*" (Acts 2:7 NLT, italics mine).

In essence, Peter and the other disciples proclaim Christ's salvation to devout or God-fearing Jews who most likely have more in common culturally with their home country than they do with one another (Acts 2:36). In terms of the multicultural gathering that has taken place, this account has much in common with Joseph in the Old Testament, except for the highly centrifugal expectations. The world gathers as they did then, but this time they hear about the Messiah, and the Jews come to understand a significantly new missional direction regarding the true nature of Jesus. Just as Joseph demonstrated a capacity to understand God's future famine and provide for the world, the apostles and the many devout Jews who commit their lives to Jesus are beginning to understand that they will be taking living bread to the nations (compare John 6).

In light of the miraculous background, Peter's statement in Acts 2:38–39 takes on additional missiological significance. When Peter refers to the promise in Acts 2:39, he is undoubtedly referring to the gift of the Holy Spirit (2:38). However, the claim that the "promise is to you, and to your children, and even to the Gentiles—all who have been called by the Lord our God" combined with the immediate context indicates that this promise has missional implications (2:39 NLT). The missional continuity with respect to the Holy Spirit's role in Acts 1–3 is unmistakable. Peter's claim is not simply an isolated text that stands apart from the preceding events. Peter's claim is missionally significant because it maintains such continuity with the recently witnessed out-pouring of the Holy Spirit so that the nations of the earth will hear the proclamation of Christ.

The proclamation, the context and the foreseeable future is entirely centered around God's mission and God's promise to cause the Jews to take the message of Jesus Christ to foreign lands. As such, the 3000 mentioned in Acts 2:41 are not simply believers. Rather, they are a fledgling missionary force that God is preparing to send to the nations! Nevertheless, Peter has not yet made a direct linkage back to the Genesis 12 promise in this first speech of the day.

This is remedied later in the same day as Peter embraces another opportunity to share further details of the Christian message. In this instance, Peter draws deeply upon Jewish history (contextually appropriate for this audience) and informs the Jews that mission is part of their history. Peter does this by reinterpreting the Genesis 12 promise. As Peter works through the history of the people of God, he ultimately claims that the faithful Jews, who listen to the prophets, are indeed those who will inherit "the covenant God promised to your ancestors" (Acts 3:25a NLT). What is this covenant? It is that which "God said to Abraham, 'Through your descendants all the families on earth will be blessed'" (Acts 3:25b NLT). And notably, Peter's final words are that Jesus came first to the Jews to bless them. After Peter has just quoted Genesis 12:3, his final words are a strong echo of Genesis 12:2—"I will make you into a great nation. I will bless you and make you famous, and you will be a blessing to others" (NLT).

The main point that Peter and the Acts 2 account affirms is that this interpretation of the promise includes the people of God as a dispersed missional nation, rather than as a monolithic political force. *Peter's interpretation creates a very strong linkage that mission to the nations is to take place through the Jews and that Christ recognized this was based originally on the Abrahamic covenant.*

Paul's Interpretation—Contextualized Hermeneutics for Mission (Gal 3–4)

Given the overall dynamics of Acts 2–3, Peter's interpretation of Genesis 12:3 is an impressive confirmation to the early church that they were always called to be a missional community and that they can now take hold of their destiny in Christ. However, Paul's interpretation of the promise in Galatians 3:8, "All nations will be blessed through you," seems to suggest, on the surface at least, that the passage was intended to skip the entire Old Testament and point solely to Christ. Like Peter, the audience that Paul is addressing is of great importance.

Consider for a moment the type of hermeneutic that a missionary might adopt if the missionary knew that his or her audience held highly dogmatic views regarding a particular interpretational approach. What hermeneutic might a missionary utilize among Western seminary-trained Christians today? I suggest that if Paul were to interpret Scripture for the West today, he would likely adopt a purely historical and spiritually vacant approach because this would be the only (flawed) method that exegetes would respect.[64] Paul would not likely be using his preferred hermeneutic, but he would be using one that communicates to an audience who holds highly dogmatic views regarding the proper way to interpret Scripture.[65] In essence, Paul's missional hermeneutic would be an example of a contextually appropriate hermeneutic.

Might Paul have chosen to introduce a contextually appropriate hermeneutic when dealing with a similarly dogmatic Judaizing audi-

---

64. Cp. Newbigin, *Foolishness to the Greeks*.

65. When teaching introductory courses in Biblical Theology of Mission, a missional hermeneutic is predominantly taught through inductive means precisely because a dedicated Christian audience often holds dogmatic views regarding the proper way to interpret Scripture, and the proper interpretations associated with specific biblical passages. Few other fields in missiological training face this challenge because it is very rare for an entire class of students to arrive with dogmatic perceptions of history, leadership, anthropology (and so on) versus their perception of Scripture.

Biblically Informed Missional Hermeneutics

ence? Given that the Galatian Judaizers had separated themselves from Gentile Christians, Paul is most likely facing an audience that holds rigid views regarding their own "proper" hermeneutic. Accordingly, we should expect that the Judaizers' hermeneutic would differ markedly from the Western hermeneutic employed today. In short, it would seem foreign to the Westerner.

Should we then assume that Paul was putting his best hermeneutic on display, or might Paul have been offering a hermeneutic that would be acceptable, such as midrashic hermeneutics, especially since Paul had been trained specifically in this field as a Pharisee? For, "In the Greek world of the New Testament period there was a widely recognized method of interpreting an ancient literature which was venerated as an authority . . . There are a few outstanding examples. Paul's treatment of the story of Hagar and Ishmael, in Galatians 4:21–31, is (as he expressly says) allegorical; and in fact it observes the strictest rules of the game."[66] It seems highly likely, therefore, that Paul is using a less-than-ideal hermeneutic in this case because it conforms to the expectations of the Judaizers. Furthermore, this is a missional hermeneutic because it is based on contextual understandings.

Prior to Galatians 4, Paul seems to be using this contextual hermeneutic in Galatians 3:16. Paul claims that the singular nature of the collective noun "seed" is indicative of Christ, and this likely refers back to Genesis 12:7. However, the use of "your seed/descendant(s)" (זַרְעֶךָ) in Gen 12:7 is identical to Gen 13:15–16 (with the exception of the prepositions). All three verses include singular nouns (they are common, masculine, singular and therefore both would be "seed" rather than "seeds"). Likewise, they include a suffixed second person, masculine, singular pronoun (for example, "*your* seed"), but the nature of the passages are quite differently understood. While Gen 12:7 could be interpreted in accordance with Paul's unique claim in Galatians 3:16, Genesis 13:15–16 cannot. In this light, Paul's claim over the singular nature of term "seed" would be nonsense for the literalist or Western scholar, but Paul's claim would make a great deal of sense to those who value midrashic hermeneutics.

> Paul, early Christianity's apostle to the Gentiles, gives evidence of his Jewish training in Scripture in many places in his epistles. His appeal to the singular form of "seed" (*sperma/zeraʿ*) in Gal.

66. Dodd, *OT in the New*, 5–6.

> 3:16 is a classic example of rabbinic exegesis. In Gen. 12:7 God promised Abraham a "seed," not "seeds." Surely the singularity of the word implies prophecy of a particular coming one, the Messiah. Paul, of course, would readily allow that the promise to Abraham also envisions a multitude of people (the *peshat*, or plain meaning of the text), but the singularity of the word "seed" also implies a special, singular fulfillment (the *midrash*, or "searching" for less obvious meaning). Arguments of this nature are plentiful in rabbinic literature.[67]

Again, Paul's argument in Galatians 3:16 is a good indicator that a midrashic interpretation has begun long before the allegory found in Galatians 4. This is likewise evidenced in the fact that Paul's use of the Old Testament is a combined reference that blends Genesis 12:3; 18:18; and 22:18 into a composite verse.[68]

Though there are a number of astute Western scholars who eloquently perceive Paul's midrashic tendencies, their main downfall is their notion that Paul is foremost a theologian and secondarily a missionary (if a missionary at all). If Paul is understood foremost as a missionary and secondarily as a theologian, his arguments take on a different focus. Paul, the missionary, wants the Galatians to refocus their spiritual energy toward a relationship with Jesus Christ through the Holy Spirit (compare Gal 3:2, 5:16).

Based on Paul's exclusion of Israel's history, it likewise appears that Paul has intentionally biased away from the history of Israel in order to correct the ethnocentric tendencies of the Judaizers. For example, in opposition to Paul's claim in Galatians 3:16, there are specific Old

---

67. Evans, *Interpretation of Scripture*, 20.

68. While most Bibles have a reference to Genesis 12:7 as the verse that Paul is citing in Galatians 3:16, it is more likely that Paul is referring to a combination of the promise passages. Referring back to Table 5, Paul's quotation includes "in you," and "all the nations." This follows the beginning and ending of both Genesis 18:18 and 28:14. However, in Galatians 3:16 Paul states that the promise is to Abraham and to his "seed" (or "in your seed," implying Gen 12:3; 18:18; 22:18). However, Genesis 22:18 is the only account of the promise spoken to Abraham that also includes "in your seed", but this verse does not include the phrase "in you" that Paul mentions in Galatians 3:8. Since the clear focus of the "promise" in Galatians 3:6–16 is the promise to bless the nations or Gentiles through faith (rather than only "the land" mentioned in Gen 12:7), Paul must be working with a composite reference that combines Genesis 12:3; 18:18 and 22:18. The likely reason that numerous Bibles reference Genesis 12:7 is because we are subconsciously forcing Paul to adopt the same hermeneutical standards that we follow today—that of proper direct quotations.

Testament claims demonstrating that the promise to Abraham's seed was fulfilled long before Christ (Josh 24:3; Isa 51:2). However, Paul does not draw upon these accounts due to the misguided audience he is addressing.

Therefore, it is likely that Paul has adopted a contextual hermeneutic with biases added to deal with religious ethnocentrism, but Paul still holds to an underlying missional hermeneutic. In quoting Genesis 12:3, he makes use of the missional agent "in you" (ἐν σοὶ) denoting Abraham's personal active involvement that comes through faith rather than ethnic lineage (Gal 3:2–5; 23–25). Additionally, Paul's focus upon Abraham's active faith-involvement suggests that there are "hear and now" missional implications of the promise. However, Paul also moves to the Christological aspect of the promise shortly after that. Paul demonstrates; (1) a missional hermeneutic for both the gospel preached to Abraham (Gal 3:8), and (2) Christ's fulfillment of the passage (Gal 3:14–16).

Paul, like the more skilled modern-day missionaries, realized that the guidance of the Holy Spirit is essential for proper theology, and, as such, his arguments were not attempts to introduce a systematic or integrated theology.[69] Unlike most Western spirituality, Paul did not intentionally introduce theology, because it was not Paul's underlying assumption that proper theology would restore the believers. Rather, Paul's intentionality rested in his use of midrashic hermeneutics as a proper contextual hermeneutic. This would hopefully capture the Galatians' spiritual attention and spiritually restore them to faith in Christ through the Holy Spirit—all of which is consistent with missionary practice. Certainly Paul included theological ideas to develop his arguments but those were necessarily constrained by the highly contextual midrashic hermeneutics that were already in play. Furthermore, the central theo-

---

69. For example, extensive effort has been expended to show that the majority of scholars assume that Paul has a missing premise, which is that the entirety of the law must be obeyed (Wakefield, *Where to Live*, 66–74). Paul is simply supplying his argument in the reverse order from what some scholars are expecting, because Paul explicitly states in Galatians 3:10 that all of the law must be obeyed (regardless of whether this quote agrees with an Old Testament passage). Therefore, for Paul this "premise" is not "missing"—rather, it is explicitly stated. The scholarly debate on this issue is an example of dealing with minutia that ultimately avoids the major issues. Paul's concern here is to talk about salvation through faith versus the law, and issues such as the "missing premise" obscure the larger focus.

logical ideas of Galatians 3–4 served a missional purpose and yielded to Paul's missional concerns.

Most importantly, while Paul did maintain an underlying missional hermeneutic, he was not so rigid that he could not adopt an entirely different and comparatively poor hermeneutic for the sake of sharing the gospel. In this way, Paul appropriately demonstrates that unwavering allegiance to a particular hermeneutic (such as, for example, the historical-critical method) is an unnecessary barrier when guiding others into a valid understanding of faith in Christ.

Paul's Interpretation—The Promise Recorded for Jew and Gentile (Rom 4)

How does Paul's claim in Romans 4 differ from that of Galatians 3–4? The underlying theme that Paul wants to communicate regarding faith in the risen Christ and the lack of power in the law is nearly identical in both accounts. However, the way in which Paul goes about sharing that message differs markedly. In Romans 4, we find a much more direct form of communication and a comparatively less difficult hermeneutic to follow.[70]

Why is this? Paul may have known that the Roman Church was a mixture of Jews and Gentiles, or Paul may simply have been unaware of Judaizing tendencies in Rome. In either case, the message of Romans 4 is comparatively straightforward for both the Jew and the Gentile. On the one hand, the Gentiles would hear that Abraham is the spiritual father of the uncircumcised who live by faith (Rom 4:11). On the other hand, the Jews would hear that Abraham is the spiritual father of the circumcised, but only if they have faith as Abraham did (Rom 4:12). Remarkably, Paul is centrifugally sharing the news of Christ to the Jew and Gentile, but Abraham's faith reaches forward from the Genesis account to act as a highly centripetal example for the Jew (Rom 4:12) as well as the Gentile (Rom 4:11) and ultimately for all who will believe (Rom 4:16).

By consistently referring to Abraham as a spiritual father, Paul appears to have, on the surface, made a claim that is entirely opposite of Galatians 3:16. Whereas in Galatians, Paul is explicitly clear that the term "seed" (σπέρμα) refers only to Christ, he now uses the exact same

---

70. A similar intertextual account occurs in Romans 9:6–7 in which Genesis 21:12 is referenced, as well as numerous other Old Testament passages (Wagner, *Heralds of Good News*, 49–51).

word (σπέρματι) and makes the claim that the "descendents" (or seed) are those who live by faith (Rom 4:13). Likewise, Paul freely refers to Abraham as the spiritual father of Jew and Gentile in Romans 4:11–12, but there is only a hint of this possibility in Galatians (compare Paul's use of "seed" (σπέρμα) in Gal 3:16, 19, 29).

On the surface, Paul's arguments in Romans 4 and Galatians 3–4 appear to be polar opposites. Why would Paul make seemingly opposite claims? It is most likely because Paul does not perceive the church in Rome to have the same level of negative bias toward Gentiles when compared to the church in Galatia. Given that the church in Rome was in the heart of Gentile territory, it would not be too surprising if the Jewish believers in Rome had developed greater cultural sensitivity than those who manifested Judaizing tendencies in Galatia.

In any case, when comparing Romans 4 and Galatians 3–4, we can see that Paul is highly contextual in the manner in which he interprets the Old Testament. Paul's intentional bias in the discussion toward the Galatian Judaizers is clearly evident. Furthermore, if we were to assume that Paul is foremost attempting to create theological statements, we would misinterpret Paul's real thought and force missionally significant contextual actions into a theological mold that was never intended by the author.

Therefore, the meaning is found in the broader brush strokes of Paul's thought. In both accounts, Paul interprets the promise to Abraham with missional significance, continuing to manifest an ever growing Pauline missional hermeneutic. Likewise, Paul demonstrates that he was willing to modify his communication (often seen as theological statements) for the sake of introducing others to Christ. Moreover, Paul even felt comfortable modifying his very hermeneutic as a legitimate means of introducing others to Christ. How radically different is Paul's missional willingness to adjust his hermeneutic for the sake of others, when contrasted to the Western tendency to claim that only one valid hermeneutic exists.

It may be claimed that Paul may not have met the standard that Western ethicists would require by adopting a less "truthful" hermeneutic, but Paul was not bound by Western ethical perceptions. Paul was bound by an immense passion to share the gospel of Jesus Christ and his boundaries for communicating this message would not likely match the Western values that ethicists assign to him.[71]

More importantly, God's missional vision was much larger than that of Paul. For in the final verses of the chapter, Paul makes it very clear that the scriptural record of Abraham's faith is without a doubt for missional purposes so that all might have faith as Abraham did (Rom 4:23–24). Therefore even if Abraham himself or his descendents lacked a full understanding of God's missional plan, God had planned to use the biblical record of Abraham's faith for the purpose of missional witness![72]

The Promise Is Ultimately Understood through Christ and Mission

"In this early promise of Genesis 12:1–3 the essential features basic to the missionary task are to be found. Although, as many have correctly observed, there is here no command to evangelize the nations in the way the New Testament expressed this, Yahweh asserts his lordship over the nations and will guide their destiny and accomplish his purpose."[73]

Israel's witness in the Old Testament is essentially providential mission (rather than simply centripetal mission) because it seems that God providentially intends to display a people's unwavering allegiance to God in the crossroads of the ancient world. God is calling upon Abraham, Isaac and Jacob to faithfully follow God as they sojourn and live in the

---

71. The pinnacle concern of Scripture is a restored relationship between God and humanity and this is foremost missionary in nature. Theology takes a much lesser role when seen in this light, and the missionary statements and actions of biblical figures can often make more sense. For instance, in modern-day theology there is a consistent focus on ethics. I doubt that Paul ever held the same level of ethical concern that theologians do today. Paul's primary concern was to bring people into relationship with Jesus Christ. I would not go so far as to say that in Paul's mind, "the end justifies the means." However, I do think Paul was willing to use standards that would be considered less-than-ideal in modern-day practice. Therefore, Paul likely had a certain set of standards that he held, but his concern for someone genuinely coming to Christ was his primary interest and this alone gave him greater freedom to trust the Holy Spirit to correct unforeseeable mistakes that Paul may have introduced and this likewise gave Paul the freedom to focus foremost on God's mission.

72. What scholars have failed to notice is that the gap between this phrase's revelation in Genesis and its missional reinterpretation in the New Testament does not correspond solely to the coming of Christ (note that Christ does not cite this passage himself), but rather it corresponds to the development of a broader missional hermeneutic that was infused by renewed understanding that came through mission practice.

73. De Ridder, "OT Roots of Mission," 176; cp. De Ridder, *Discipling the Nations*, 22ff.

midst of surrounding nations. A consistent and unwavering allegiance to God in the midst of concerns over security, agriculture, livestock, fertility, and drought would speak volumes to nations who animistically worship a wealth of idols in order to appease their like-minded fears. I believe that God realized the strong centripetal attraction this would create with those who witnessed Israel's display of faith.

As such, God's providential mission plan in the Old Testament seems to simply call upon Israel to follow God, and mission would follow. Israel may have not been called into an identical missional paradigm as that of the New Testament church, but Israel was consistently called to demonstrate their allegiance to God, and this type of presence and visibility is a principal requirement in order for witness to take shape.

"Whereas Israel was called on to *display* the wonderful deeds of God, the New Testament church is called on to *declare* that message to the people."[74] As the New Testament church witnesses, it becomes a manifest presence of Jesus Christ here on earth, so that the physical existence of Christ takes place through the body of the church. And yet Christ leads the church in a mysterious and joined union that even the apostle Paul had trouble understanding (Eph 5).

It is likely that the Abrahamic covenant in Genesis 12 was depicting a similar paradigm in the Old Testament. Israel as a nation was called to be the manifest presence of faith in God that would give witness to all people of the earth (Rom 4). Just as the church and Christ coexist today in mystical union, Israel was being called to live the life of faith that would manifest the presence of the Messiah to come. The nations of the Old Testament would be blessed through this faith, and likewise the faithful within Israel would become those that missionally point to the Messiah (Ps 72). Therefore, the blessing is one that takes place during Israel's allegiance to God, one that is confirmed in Jesus Christ, and one that continues to be actively manifest in the church today.

When engaged with the nations in their weakness, the patriarchs demonstrated a missional vision, and certainly a stronger receptivity to dealing with the nations.[75] However, the exclusion of "blessing all the na-

74. Sandmel, *Anti-Semitism in NT*, 33.

75. The opposite of mission practice that is intended to bless the nations seems to be a predetermined opinion that the nations are to be feared and treated as a threat. Van Engen has referred to this as self-preservation (Van Engen and Redford, "Syllabus," 47 originally Van Engen). This attitude is intensely destructive toward not only mission, but also toward a proper hermeneutic of Scripture. The way that self-preservation influ-

tions of the earth" transferred to the patriarchs' posterity demonstrates a lack of vision in understanding God's missional intentions. Although it is reasonable to argue that the focus of blessing all nations was not an explicit command issued to the patriarchs, this does not excuse the fact that they truncated the message that God had consistently given to them. In their re-interpretation they reduced the word of God to something significantly less than was intended. Furthermore, other Old Testament writings, such as Jonah, demonstrate an expectation that Israel should have at least a basic missional vision.

Likewise, it cannot reasonably be argued that the patriarchs could have interpreted the passage in a sole messianic fashion. This is because the literary construction of "you and your seed," referring to the land and the future growth into a nation, is identical to that of the "blessing of all nations." Moreover, even if the blessing to all nations referred only to Christ, the mere mention of this phrase, while engaged with the nations, would have undoubtedly caused Israel and the nations to try to interpret this passage's meaning. This course, in turn, would have manifest a missional hermeneutic that would cause the very act of biblical interpretation to become a type of witness as Israel encountered the nations.

As such, the "blessing of all nations" seems to be one of God's early attempts to instill a missional vision in the hearts of this fledgling nation. The frequency with which God appeared and repeated this to the patriarchs reveals the importance of this promise. This cannot go unnoticed. Furthermore, the passage is consistently found in the broader context of mission, such as in Abraham's petition to God over Sodom and Gomorrah, Jacob's observance of Joseph's influence and respect in Egypt, or Joseph's actual mission practice through his faithfulness in his walk with God.

However, the lack of repetition of this by the patriarchs especially as they blessed succeeding generations with only a portion of the prom-

---

ences hermeneutics is that it shows up in both the revelation remembered (for example, "these thoughts of God will help my life") while subtly or subconsciously forgetting those passages that involve the people of God's role in mission. This simple culling of Scripture is the hermeneutical equivalent of the psychological concept of "selective memory." As a result, the passages that would have stretched the would-be missionary into greater service are silenced and they lack the experiences that would have allowed them to move a step deeper in interpreting God's missionary grace and elegance flowing through Scripture. In the end, self-preservation has a deafening impact on mission that is rescued only by God's repeated encouragement.

ise suggests that God began to use additional means to instill a missional vision within Israel.[76] Though there are other times in the Old Testament when writers echo this early missional watchword, it is only when we come to the New Testament that this passage is properly reinterpreted with infused missional meaning by Peter and Paul.

As we step into the New Testament and begin to further understand the hermeneutics involved, it becomes even clearer that the Old Testament passages are understood only in the light of Jesus Christ and mission. The common elements in Paul and Peter's interpretation are threefold. First of all, Paul and Peter both interpret the meaning of the blessing itself, but in uniquely different ways. Peter notes that the blessing is one of repentance for sins in the midst of Christ's ministry to the Jews (Acts 3:12–26). Paul, by contrast, notes that the blessing is one in which the Gentiles are now allowed to be grafted into the people of God (Gal 3, Rom 4). The common element in both cases is that the blessings deal with reconciliation to God, which means that the blessings have active redemptive focus (despite the passive nature of the verb).[77]

Secondarily, Paul and Peter both demonstrate that the interpretation of this passage has missiological implications flowing on multiple levels. Paul makes it clear that the gospel was preached before hand to Abraham (Gal 3:8 "pre-good news" προευηγγελίσατο). Peter, likewise is demonstrating the role of personal evangelism as he and John heal the paralytic (Acts 3:1–11). However, they also point out that the passage has messianic significance that many had missed. Peter is the strongest in this as he boldly speaks to a Jewish audience informing them of their past mistakes (Acts 3:12–26). Paul, likewise moves in his argument from Abraham, who existed prior to the law, to Christ, who is above the law, and shows the way that this passage reflects the former reality, while other Old Testament passages from Genesis help build the focus upon Christ (Gal 3:6–16).

Thirdly, Paul and Peter do not interpret the Old Testament apart from mission. Rather, everything they interpret from Genesis has mis-

---

76. compare Sjogren, *Unveiled at Last*, 46.

77. This should assist those needing some guidance in the translation of the Hebrew verb. Since there is no active form of the verb "to bless" (for example, the active form of this same verb means "to kneel") (Koehler et al., *HALOT*, 159–60). There is an obvious limitation in the Hebrew language if someone wants to express an active intent in blessing. It seems that God worked within the limitations of human language in order to convey a message that had a much fuller meaning.

sional significance which means that this intertextual biblical interpretation is decidedly missional, and that the Old Testament has significant missional implications. Both interpret Genesis 12:3 with a missional hermeneutic. Therefore, a theology or Christology that is void of missional significance would be inadequate for either of them. What Paul and Peter are doing with the Old Testament should cause those interested in intertextual hermeneutics to take notice. Foremost, *Paul and Peter consistently make use of missional hermeneutics in their own interpretation of the Old Testament! As such, Scripture itself demonstrates an underlying and expanding missional hermeneutic!*

Furthermore, Paul and Peter are joined by other biblical authors who perceive and build upon a missional hermeneutic even in an eschatological sense, as the promise to bless the nations literally stretches from Genesis to Revelation.

> In the Book of Revelation there is one more reference to God's promise to Abraham (7:9 ff.). John sees in a vision "a great multitude which no man could number." It is an international throng, drawn "from every nation, from all tribes and people and tongues." And they are "standing before the throne," the symbol of God's kingly reign. That is, his Kingdom has finally come, and they are enjoying all the blessings of his gracious rule. He shelters them with his presence. Their wilderness days of hunger, thirst and scorching heat are over. They have entered the promised land at last, described now not as "a land flowing with milk and honey" but as a land irrigated from "springs of living water" which never dry up. . . . All the essential elements of the promise may be detected. For here are the spiritual descendants of Abraham, a "great multitude which no man could number," as countless as the sand on the seashore and as the stars in the night sky. Here too are "all the families of the earth" being blessed, for the numberless multitude is composed of people from every nation. Here also is the promised land, namely all the rich blessings which flow from God's gracious rule. And here above all is Jesus Christ, the seed of Abraham, who shed his blood for our redemption and who bestows his blessings on all those who call on him to be saved.[78]

The primary hermeneutical difference in the Old Testament is that occasional acts of mission are not enough to remove the hermeneutical blinders of ethnocentrism and the fear of crossing barriers for the

78. Stott, "Biblical Basis of Missions," Web Page 1 of 4.

Biblically Informed Missional Hermeneutics

sake of the nations. Through faith in Christ, this is overcome in the New Testament and the overarching theme of the promise in Scripture is that it is only understood properly with a missional hermeneutic that is likewise open to God's miraculous interventions.

DANIEL'S MISSION LEADS TO FAITHFUL INTERPRETATION (DAN 9–12)

Daniel's consistent allegiance to God counts him among the minority of Old Testament figures who definitely understood God's mission as well as deep biblical insights. Few others in the Old Testament demonstrate the type of consistent witness to the nations, that results in the conversion of major leaders such as Nebuchadnezzar. The witness of Daniel, Shadrack, Mischak, and Abendigo are outstanding examples of missionary witness in the face of martyrdom. They also demonstrate an unwavering commitment to God in the midst of other gods that would have provided far more short term comfort and peace for these exiled Jews. As such, the book of Daniel is one of the more helpful Old Testament books from a missional perspective.

However, the attitude of Daniel and his peers is what stands out all the more. In spite of Israel's centuries (if not millennia) of ethnocentrism, Daniel and his fellow Jews do not hold triumphalistic or militaristic attitudes. Furthermore, these faithful ones are not absolutely confident if God will save their lives even though their witness begins with a refusal to worship Nebuchadnezzar's statue (Dan 3:17–18). It would be hard to fault these believers if they felt that God would not save them, since God has already given Israel over to the Babylonians and they were part of the exile.

In Daniel 9–12, we encounter a hermeneutic that combines human study, prayer, and an angelic exegete! These chapters together make up one of the most outstanding examples of Old Testament biblical interpretation. Within this account, we see a variety of ways in which Scripture is interpreted and developed. These chapters are unique, because the interpretation itself is written down as Scripture.

In Daniel 9:2, we are told that Daniel is studying the writings of the prophets. While we are not told from Daniel what passage is under review, the content reveals that Jerusalem would be desolate for 70 years. This information provides some solid linkage to Jeremiah. Most likely, Daniel is studying Jeremiah 25:11–12 or 29:10. Daniel seems to be unaware of the decree in this passage prior to this point. Here Daniel enters into a potent and pious time of prayer and repentance on behalf of his people.

It would be a mistake to think that Daniel only understood that Jerusalem would be desolate for an extended period. It is clear that Daniel recognizes much more, as his prayer reveals an understanding of the misguided complaints of the Israelites toward God. Likewise, his prayer reveals that God intends to redeem Israel if they were to repent. Finally, it is clear that Daniel realizes Israel must repent before God which is the very heart of Daniel's prayer. It is for this reason that James M. Scott includes Daniel's prayer in a "penitential prayer tradition" that flows from earlier Old Testament prayers of remorse.[79]

Daniel's prayer is quite moving, because in his fervor and desire to follow God, Daniel assumes the sins of his people in a communal manner that negates any individualistic qualities. This is more than just humility before God. Daniel appears to genuinely accept that he is part of a larger community and likewise feels responsible for the actions of this community.[80]

As the account continues in Daniel 9:20–23, we encounter what might be one of the most impressive hermeneutical responses in the Old Testament. Daniel is visited by Gabriel and we are specifically told that Gabriel has come to give Daniel, "insight and understanding" (Dan 9:22 NLT).

However, if it is not enough that an angel has come to provide biblical insight and understanding for Daniel, we are told that the entire reason for this wisdom to be dispersed is because Daniel began praying (Dan 9:23). What is even more profound is that Daniel never makes a request in his prayers regarding the interpretation of Scripture. The simple fact that Daniel is praying in the midst of exile is enough reason to send out an Archangel for the purpose of interpreting Daniel's vision, and the interpretation itself becomes Scripture.

Almost all of Daniel 11 and 12, represent a hermeneutical interpretation of a prophetic vision. This is one of the most difficult textual genres to interpret due to the highly symbolic nature. The angel did not

---

79. Scott compares the role the impact that Deut 27–32 may have had on later traditions (Scott, "For as Many," 204). It is likewise notable that Deut 28:1—30:3 is indicative of the covenantal witness that Israel is to have with God before the nations.

80. As such, it is noted that "Daniel's petition sounds quite Pauline" (ibid., 199).

come foremost because Daniel was studying Scripture, nor did the angel appear because Daniel correctly interpreted portions of Jeremiah. The angel came because a command was issued in response to Daniel's prayer of repentance. Another surprising aspect of the angel's appearance is the backdrop of the spiritual battle that is taking place in Daniel. The impression gained from reading this passage is that time is of the essence for the angel. Therefore, the very act of taking time to interpret Daniel's vision demonstrates how important the act of interpretation is in the spiritual realm.

Did Daniel understand Scripture in new ways? Certainly he did! While this passage does affirm the importance of human study and correct biblical interpretation, it demonstrates that these disciplines alone are not adequate for the hermeneutical process. Daniel understands a small portion of Scripture using his own capacity, but the floodgates are opened in the interpretational process as Daniel prays.

Few accounts in Scripture illustrate the impact of prayer upon the hermeneutical process as clearly as Daniel 9–12. If Daniel's vision alone were to have been recorded, we might expect to find scholars spending years understanding this vision and many schools of thought committed to this or that interpretation. However the simple act of Daniel's prayer brings us closer to seeing how important it is to God that proper understanding takes place and to appreciate the resources God allocates for this to take place.

JESUS CITES A FAILED MISSIONAL HERMENEUTIC IN THE PEOPLE OF GOD

In studying the promise to bless all the nations of the earth, we have seen that there are various levels of missional understanding, but it has required millennia for a strong missional hermeneutic to develop. By contrast, Daniel's understanding follows intense missionary witness and occurs in a relatively short period of time, though the backdrop of the exile was certainly a motivating factor for biblical study and prayer.

We now turn our attention to Jesus' use of the Old Testament in Matthew 8–12. While the former accounts have been positive for the most part, this account is an admonishment over the Jewish failure to develop a basic missional hermeneutic.

The Nations Will Rise Up! (Matt 8–12)

Indirect presentations of the truth are often the only way to address the most stubborn audiences (as shown in Chapter 5).[81] For example, Matthew's genealogy begins with Abraham, while Luke begins with Adam (Matt 1:1–2; compare Luke 3:38). Why is this? It has been suggested that Matthew, in a very subtle and highly contextual manner, is using his opening genealogy to communicate a message of God's universal mission to the Jews and Gentiles. In essence, this is Matthew's subtle way of indirectly communicating Genesis 12:1–3 compared to that of Peter and Paul's direct propositional style.[82]

Throughout Matthew 8–12, Matthew includes a number of indirect or interpretationally difficult statements in which Jesus' consistent eschatological remarks claim that the Gentiles and other nations have greater faith and allegiance to God than that of Israel. For example, in Matthew 8 the faith-filled Roman centurion recognizes Jesus' power without seeing, but the disciples do not recognize the Christ while experiencing his power (Matt 8:10–13; 27). The demonized are healed and witness regarding Christ's nature, but the "healthy" in a nearby town want nothing to do with Jesus (Matt 8:28–33).

Likewise, when the man with leprosy is healed, his missional fervor is quenched. Why, then, is the leper asked to remain silent (Matt 8:1–4)? More than likely, Jesus makes this request in order to avoid the persecution that would have followed if the Jewish religious leaders were aware of the healing. In essence, Jesus knows that the opposition of the Jews will impede his mission. Likewise, both Jesus and the leper could face martyrdom, which would be a premature end in Jesus case.[83] The underlying reason for this silence is due to a consistent Jewish failure to properly interpret Christ's mission and the mission of God found throughout Scripture.

The ensuing chapters demonstrate that Jesus' ministry is impeded over similar issues. A ray of hope is encountered as the Jews bring a paralytic on the mat, but the religious leaders' theology dampens their missional quest until Jesus restores hope by healing of the paralytic (Matt 9:1–8). Those bringing the sick to Jesus were most likely unclean

---

81. Glasser, *Announcing the Kingdom*, 189.

82. Bauckham, *Bible and Mission*, 33; Park, *Mission Discourse*, 7–8; compare Blomberg, "Globalization of Hermeneutics," 587.

83. Cp. Woodberry, "Evangelicals, Stereotypes and Diversities," 11.

Jews (*'am ha-'arets*) since they were willing to come in contact with a paralytic, while the religious leaders (*haberim*) who should have the best skills in interpreting God's presence in their midst are unable, due to their pre-existing interpretational bias.[84]

This bias has its roots in a mission-less hermeneutic, which is made explicitly clear in Matthew 9:9–13. Jesus is in the very act of engaging in mission, most likely with unclean Jews, and this is without question an unclean audience (Matt 9:10–11). Yet, the Pharisees lacked the interpretational ability to recognize mission in their midst (Matt 9:12)! However, this offers the perfect opportunity for Jesus to demonstrate grace combined with a missional hermeneutic (Matt 9:13).

In Matthew 9:12–13, Jesus surrounds his primary question with two indirect claims that illustrate his mission by depicting himself as a doctor and a healer. However, the central question is one in which he asks the reigning authorities of the day to once again look at Scripture in order to understand their own shortcomings. Jesus makes a grace-filled response when he asks these leaders to be involved in the hermeneutical process for at least two purposes.

First, the religious authorities are not prepared to admit how wrong their understanding of Scripture had been, and, more importantly, how wrong their actions had been. By asking them to reinterpret Scripture, Jesus gives them a chance to dig into Scripture and also gives them time to accept a message that would have been too difficult to accept in a short period of time. More importantly, it would only be through a missiological hermeneutic that these leaders could arrive at an interpretation of Scripture that affirms Jesus' actions. Therefore, Jesus is countering their mission-less hermeneutic with a mission-filled hermeneutic!

Second, Jesus is using this hermeneutical request as an indirect means of communication. Given that the Pharisees are so focused upon keeping up public appearances, Jesus gracefully gives them a chance to understand their errors and inadequacies in a private setting where they can reflect upon Scripture without fear of public embarrassment. Though we typically do not think of Jesus as someone who gracefully addresses the Jewish leaders, we find Jesus doing just that in this instance as he gives the rulers an opportunity to save face, despite the fact that they are attacking Jesus' ministry.

---

84. See chapter 5 for more details on the *haberim* and *'am ha-'arets*.

Had Jesus publicly scolded the Pharisees, we can rest assured that they would most likely remain entrenched in their current theological and missiological errors. This passage is very interesting because it combines some level of trust by Jesus with respect to the Pharisees' potential to interpret Scripture correctly, while Jesus was likewise aware of the deep syncretism that existed in the Pharisees' views.

Rarely within modern-day mission practice do we find this kind of response to syncretism. Rather, we most often assume that those who have already misinterpreted Scripture will continue to misinterpret Scripture if they are given the chance. I have little doubt that many of the Pharisees continued to misinterpret Scripture. However, who might have been standing in this group of Pharisees that was listening to Jesus? Was Nicodemus among them? Might there have been a close friend of Paul among this group? Were there other Pharisees who were still unsure if this healer who stood among them might be the Messiah?

Likewise, who among us today is without theological or missiological error? At what point in the history of missions did we understand the *missio Dei* so well that we did not need to re-read Scripture in order to re-understand our directive? The challenge that Jesus sets before the Pharisees is a challenge that is likewise put before the people of God today. For today God continues to offer that same level of graceful trust to those who have so often relegated God's mission to be a minor or even optional role for the church.[85] As such, grace continues as God waits upon the church for a missional reinterpretation of Scripture.

In Matthew 10, Jesus calls the disciples and sends them into mission. However, Christ's declaration to go only to the Jews (Matt 10:5) must be coupled with the claim that the Jews are lost (Matt 10:6) and this matches the broader context of the surrounding chapters. Rather than perceiving Christ's command as an exclusion of the nations, it should be perceived as a missional declaration to go into the regions of greatest spiritual darkness. The dire need to address the extreme spiritual iniquity of the people of God is the real force behind the direction given by Christ. Yet, in the midst of such a difficult context, Jesus' message to John the Baptist is that of a flourishing witness (Matt 11:4–6).

Nevertheless, Jesus' message to the Jews is that the wicked Gentile towns of Tyre and Sidon would have responded (Matt 10:21), and in fact will respond (Matt 10:22), far sooner than the Jewish towns of Korazin

---

85. Cp. Shenk, *Write the Vision*.

Biblically Informed Missional Hermeneutics

and Bethsaida. Likewise, ancient Sodom will be better off spiritually than Capernaum, and Sodom would have repented had they encountered Jesus' same witness (Matt 10:23–24). Once again in Matthew 12, the Pharisees are asked again to re-interpret Scripture, but Jesus continues to challenge their paradigms that are rooted in a wrong hermeneutic (Matt 12:3, 7).

As Jesus engages with one miracle after the next, Jesus' actions are consistently misinterpreted and Jesus' mission is halted through a consistent failure due to the entrenched hermeneutics of the day (Matt 12:9–17, 22–37). Moreover, Jesus fulfills a highly missional prophesy in their midst that likewise has implications for the nations and the world, but there is little, if any, response by the Jews (Isa 42:1–4; Matt 12:17–21). As such, Jesus again claims that the outsider, the queen of Sheba, will also rise up and condemn the first-century Jews (Matt 12:42). In comparing himself to Solomon, Jesus has certainly picked a heroic figure in Jewish history that likewise has echoes of the temple's witness (Matt 26:61; 27:40; Mark 14:58; 15:29; John 2:19–20). Yet, no figure in Jewish history could compare with Jesus' witness, but the Jews simply cannot correctly interpret Christ in their midst due to the blinding effects of their deeply entrenched and misguided hermeneutic.

The Sign of Jonah (Matt 12:40)

Furthermore, as we near the end of Matthew 12, Jesus begins to share the very challenging interpretation of Jonah and the Ninevites, as well as Solomon and the queen of Sheba. Jesus is informing the Jews that the nations will condemn the supposed missionaries. He is telling them that the dreaded oppressive Assyrians, who were masters in torture and death, will rise up and condemn their lack of missional fervor.

If they really understood the implications of this, they would realize that Jonah was an unwilling missionary whose main concern was not over the fear of a tortuous Assyrian death, but over the fear that God would give grace to the nations. And yet, Jesus is informing them that they are standing with the living God in their midst, whose love is far greater than Jonah's angry heart, and they still will not turn to God.

One of the major threads in the Old Testament is: "I will be your God and you will be my people, (and I will dwell in your midst)" (Exod 6:7; Lev 26:12; Jer 7:23; 11:4; 24:7; 30:22; 31:1, 33; 32:38; Ezek 11:20; 14:11; 36:28; 37:23, 27; Zech 8:8; 2 Cor 6:16; Heb 8:10). However, Hosea is the exact opposite of this covenant—just look at the names of Hosea's children: Lo-Ruhamah "Not loved" and Lo-Ammi "Not my people" (Hos 1:6, 9). Therefore, Hosea may be seen as an Old Testament anti-type of the major thread above which is the "type." The term anti-type does not mean "against the grain" or "opposite to" the first type—anti-type is a more general term that means "counterpart." Whether anti-type is "aligned with" or "in contrast to" the original type is a secondary but important matter.

A great deal of the missional analysis of the book of Jonah has already been done and I have no desire to repeat that work. However, few missiologists have looked at Jonah as an allegory to understand God's mission in the Old Testament. One main reason for this seems to be that missiologists feel defensive over the historical issues related to Jonah and therefore feel that they must defend the historical at the expense of an allegorical interpretation. This may also be related to the intense scholarly critique of the miraculous in Jonah.[86]

I think it is quite possible to believe that Jonah is both historical and allegorical. There is enough valid historical information in Jonah to affirm its historical side, but scholars have been skeptical in claiming that Jonah is historical due to the miraculous events that take place in Jonah's life. By contrast, I believe that the actual events took place historically and some of the most intentional missional statements are contained in the miraculous events, events that, in fact, have a larger and fuller allegorical meaning. In essence, I am claiming that there is a deeper meaning or technically a *sensus plenior* ("fuller sense") that flows beneath the surface events of this account to reveal a "type" of mission.[87] Furthermore, I believe that Jesus is demonstrating in Matthew 12 that the historical and allegorical perspectives can be properly interpreted only in light of a missional hermeneutic, as Jesus is showing himself to be the anti-type to Jonah (or vice-versa).

Clearly, this sort of genre is not outside of God's capacity as shown in Hosea. One of the reasons that scholars think that Jonah is purely fable is because it is quite an orchestration of surprising events such as the repentance of Ninevites, and miracles such as the great fish and the worm that are needed to make this happen. However, when considered from an Old Testament missiological perspective, God could choose

---

86. Cp. Mills, *Jonah*.
87. LaSor, "*Sensus Plenior* and Interpretation," 270–75.

Biblically Informed Missional Hermeneutics

nearly any Jew and obtain a similar response to what we see in Jonah, solely because the Israelites were so consistent in their hardheartedness toward the nations and God's missional efforts in the Old Testament.

In short, I believe that the book of Jonah is very similar to the book of Hosea, in that Hosea's actions take place historically and yet have a larger allegorical meaning that Israel is to understand. The main difference that I see between Hosea and Jonah is that Hosea is focused on issues of allegiance to God in the midst of the nations, while Jonah is focused on issues of allegiance to God's mission to the nations. The ground that I will not try to cover is the historical and literal side of Jonah.

However, if Jonah is likewise representative allegorically of mission in the Old Testament, then it must be seen as the chastisement of Israel's consistent ethnocentrism throughout the ages. In using an allegorical approach, I assume with Bosch, that Jonah is representative of Israel throughout the story;

> What is being castigated is Jonah's—and Israel's—appropriation of God's favour and compassion exclusively for themselves. The irony of the story is that Jonah knows that God is "gracious and compassionate, long-suffering . . . and always willing to repent of the disaster" (Jonah 4:2), but that it never dawned upon him that all this could be applicable to peoples other than Israel. The missionary significance of this midrash does not therefore lie in the physical journeying of a prophet of Yahweh to a pagan country but in the fact that Yahweh is compassionate and that this compassion knows no boundaries.[88]

The feelings that flow through this allegory are those of sadness and satire, shame and scorn, as well as grace and love. The satire in Jonah gives the intended audience some chance to laugh if only for a moment, for Jonah is bursting with unlikely situations,—virtuous and moral sailors, a great fish who must vomit his "missionary meal," repentant cattle who wear sackcloth and ashes, a worm that willingly obeys God while the missionary does not, and one of the fiercest and most terrifying military forces in the ancient world quickly turns to God in the face of little or no hope at the word of a single Jew from a distant land most likely suffering from sunburned skin that exists only because it was so recently exposed and bleached by the stomach acid of a great fish.[89] The message

---

88. Bosch, "Hermeneutical Principles," 443–44.

89. Peskett and Ramachandra, *Message of Mission*, 126; compare Briscoe, *Jonah and the Worm*.

in the satire, however, is one of sadness; that common sailors have more integrity than Israel; that the Assyrians will quickly turn to God if given the chance in contrast to Israel's hardheartedness; that even the Assyrian cattle show signs of repentance; and the great and powerful predator of the sea chooses to vomit rather than stomach the bitter-tasting Israel.

On a larger scale, the allegory of Jonah is telling us that it takes miracle upon miracle to get Israel involved in mission. To put it in modern-day English, it's like hell getting Israel to carry out mission to the nations, and even when they do, their attitude is so poor that even an obedient and spineless worm is more capable of being used by God to address Israel than Israel is to address the nations (Jonah 4:7).[90] The overall message of Jonah is that God deeply cares for the nations and the nations are willing to hear God's message, but Israel has no heart for the nations. In many ways, this seems to be an Old Testament narrative of the phrase echoed by Jesus—"the harvest is plentiful but the workers are few" (Matt 9:37; Luke 10:2).

A final and most troubling aspect of Jonah from this allegorical perspective, is that Jonah has an excellent "theological" understanding of God's nature and grace (Jonah 4:2). This seems to be indicative of the fact that Israel was well aware of God's grace and mercy, but was unwilling to share this with the nations. Though many have searched for the meaning of blaspheming against the Holy Spirit, it may be that this unforgivable sin is knowing God's grace and not only refusing to share God's grace but actively trying to impede the *missio Dei* as empowered by the Holy Spirit (Matt 12:22–37)?

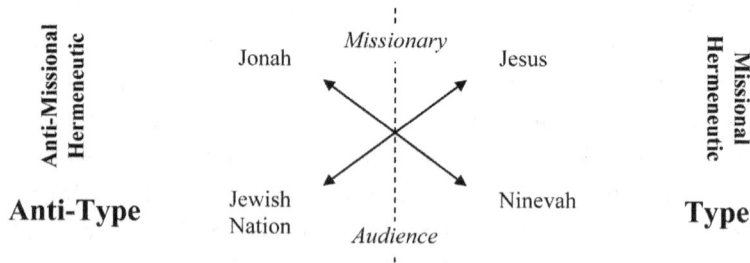

Figure 3: The Indirect Meaning of the Sign of Jonah

90. Cp. Briscoe, *Jonah and the Worm*.

Biblically Informed Missional Hermeneutics

Figure 3 offers a graphical depiction of the meaning that Jesus likely intended when referring to the sign of Jonah. Jesus depicts himself as the counterpart to Jonah, and likewise depicts the Jewish nation throughout Matthew 8–12 as the counterpart to Nineveh. Effectively, Jesus is indirectly claiming that the first-century Jews are the least receptive from among the Gentiles and the worst in history, despite the fact that they have the greatest missionary of all time, God in the flesh, witnessing directly to them. Likewise, Jesus is pointing out that the nations have been repentant even when Jonah, the worst missionary of all time, was their only witness.

While Jesus and Nineveh represent a type that follows a missional hermeneutic, Jonah and the first-century Jews encountering Jesus are an anti-type that is anti-missional. Though the diagram illustrates a chiastic tendency, it is unclear if Jesus is intending this much infused structure from indirect statements. However, the type/anti-type structure is consistent with the claims of Matthew 8–12 and Jonah.

Since Jesus is using a missional hermeneutic to condemn the Jewish failure in mission, this may cause us to wonder how the Jews could possibly understand what Jesus was saying. Certainly Jesus was communicating to the Jews using the very hermeneutic that they had failed to grasp. Two important issues must be kept in mind however. First, a deep allegiance to God was the foremost concern and this would lead to allegiance in mission and a resulting missional hermeneutic. Secondarily, Jesus faced intense persecution (discussed further in Chapter 5). As a result, Jesus offered grace through the parables and indirect statements that provided opportunity for the spiritually hungry to grow as well as a softening of Jesus' critique against the spiritually wayward. It is for this reason that Jesus quotes Isaiah 6:9–10 in Matthew 13 claiming that his audience "will be ever seeing but never perceiving, ever hearing but never understanding" (Matt 13:14–15 NIV, compare Mark 4:12, 30–32).

In relation to the thesis of this chapter, we can see that those unwilling to appreciate Jesus' spiritual activity, such as healing or deliverance, were likewise blinded from a proper missional interpretation of the Old Testament, such as Isa 42:1–4 or Jonah. In contrast, Jesus' claim is that receptivity and involvement in God's mission are critical for developing a proper biblical hermeneutic.

THE CONSEQUENCES OF WILLFUL MISINTERPRETATION
(JER 8:8-9; MAL 2:9; LUKE 4:1-13)

The biblical accounts that we have considered up to this point demonstrate that the most significant understanding of biblical intentions takes place within God's missionary endeavors. However, Scripture briefly mentions cases of intentional misinterpretation. God delivers a strong admonishment for leaders who willfully misinterpret. Briefly, in Jeremiah it is mentioned that the "teachers have twisted" the Scriptures badly (Jer 8:8, NIV). However, God's response toward these teachers will cause them to be shamed, thrown into exile, separated from their wives and destroyed because "they have rejected the word of the Lord" (Jer 8:9-13, NLT). Likewise, the ramification for demonstrating partiality or favoritism in matters of the law is that these leaders will be humbled and despised before multitudes (Mal 2:9). Jesus similarly points out that the Jews' pre-existing motivations are their main failure in understanding the real emphasis of Scripture (John 5:39-40).

Proof-texting is also found within Scripture, and no account is more obvious than Satan's attempts to trick Jesus in Luke 4:1-13. This is one of the most helpful examples to contrast proof-texting versus a healthy hermeneutic. In each case we see Satan using a proof-text model for Scripture in order to trap Jesus. Jesus' response, however, gives an expanded view of Scripture that demonstrates an underlying knowledge of the working themes that flow through Scripture. Jesus does not develop an entire theme in each case, most likely because he doesn't care to assist Satan in becoming more skilled as a deceptive exegete, but Jesus' response does demonstrate major thematic understandings of Scripture that are likewise ingrained in Christ's heart.

OTHER IMPORTANT ACCOUNTS

The transformation that takes place in Peter's understanding of mission in Acts 10-11 is a significant account illustrating the integration of biblical interpretation, spirituality and mission. The combined role of the Holy Spirit, prayer, meditation, visions, and the Gentile missionary community demonstrates numerous themes that have been discussed in this chapter. However, this transformation in re-interpreting God's mission to Gentiles is dealt with in Chapter 5 due to the significant influence of mission experience.

Similarly, there are even accounts of the resurrected Christ interpreting the Bible. In Luke 24:13–34, Jesus suddenly appears and explains the Scriptures, and those on the Emmaus road understand Jesus' nature through his interpretation. If the risen Christ can explain Scripture to correct misunderstandings in the first-century, we should expect Christ to similarly work through the Holy Spirit today. Furthermore, given Paul's extensive background with Scripture and his encounter with Jesus in Acts 9, a hermeneutic that dispenses with the supernatural is inadequate. Paul was trained in Scripture but needed the miracle of Jesus' confrontation to reinterpret the role of the Messiah and understand that Israel's mission existed beyond its own borders—to the Gentiles. Yet, hermeneutical problems were the larger context throughout the gospels and Acts. For example, the disciples "still did not understand from Scripture that Jesus had to rise from the dead" (John 20:9 NIV). Likewise, Peter struggles to grasp God's mission to the Gentiles despite his own speeches in Acts 2–3.

Finally, there are numerous accounts in which the nations correctly interpreted God's concerns based on supernatural occurrences. Abimelech interprets God's dream and understands God's will in the face of Abraham's lie (Gen 20:3–7). Joseph and Daniel both interpret dreams for their leaders and through this the leader correctly interpreted the nature of God (Gen 40–41; Dan 2:47). The Philistines treat the ark with proper reverence and correctly interpret God's affliction through scientific steps designed to determine if the calamity is a natural event or evidence of God's power (1 Sam 5–6).[91] Namaan's healing leads to faith and monotheism in spite of the spiritual weakness of Israel's king and the greed of Elisha's servant (2 Kgs 5). The Ninevite king repents and takes a proper stance of repentance in the face of Jonah's proclamation of impending doom (Jonah 3:4–10).

CONCLUSION

Darrell Guder claims that many of our "missionary methods and strategies have contradicted both the teaching and actions of Jesus as he trained his disciples to continue his ministry. The message may have been the gospel, but the way the message was known was often not congruent with the gospel."[92] There are accounts in the history of mission in which

---

91. Van Engen and Redford, "Syllabus," 53 originally Van Engen.
92. Guder, *Incarnation and Church's Witness*, xii.

skewed mission practice and even skewed messages were properly understood by others, but more than likely this took place through the Holy Spirit's intervention to correct such problems.[93] However, missionaries should not assume that an accurate gospel message can be developed in the midst of missionary practice that is significantly skewed from God's intent. Scripture indicates that a well developed missional hermeneutic is integrated with good missionary practice. As such, we must break through the misconception that missionaries can understand the gospel apart from appropriate mission practice. The two are intertwined.

Likewise, there exists a great deal of biblical teaching that is divorced from mission, and most of that is, metaphorically speaking, far too proud of its inherent hermeneutical superiority. Modern-day scholars often assume that the truth must be presented in a pure form through the best hermeneutical methods possible and only then can that understanding be used to reach those who do not know Christ. This prevailing attitude means that mission can only take place when "truth" is fully known, and this has an underlying effect regarding the discipleship of new Christians today.

New Christians are removed from their cultural environment, brought into a church environment, taught a particular understanding of truth for years, and only then are they ready to go out and share Christ with the world. However, Scripture does not employ this Western discipleship model, and the most compelling case for this is Jesus with his disciples. During Jesus' ministry, his disciples often misunderstood the role and mission of the Messiah, but they nevertheless walked with Jesus on a daily basis and were entrusted to participate in the mission of the Master. Though the disciples were missing a great deal of understanding regarding Christ's mission, hermeneutical correctives were addressed while engaged in mission practice rather than serving as a pre-requisite for candidacy in mission.

As scholars likewise fail to see the missional implications of the supernatural within Scripture, their biases have redefined the supernatural in creatively intellectual ways that significantly reduce God's in-breaking presence.[94] This process not only removes the spiritual from the hermeneutical, but likewise promotes a hermeneutic that is doubtful and unexpectant regarding God's role as an active agent and refiner of

---

93. Taylor, *Growth of Church in Buganda*, 252–54.
94. Cp. Blomberg, "NT Miracles."

missional hermeneutics. We must learn from the hermeneutical failures of Matthew 8–12.

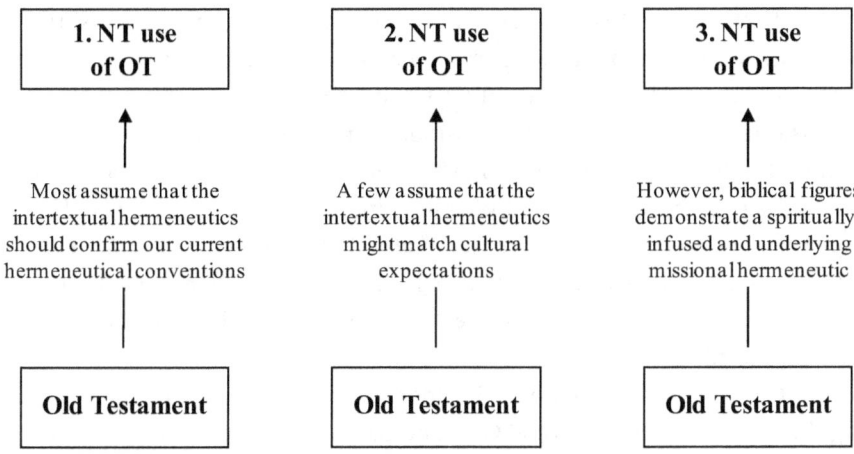

Figure 4: Improving Perceptions of Intertextuality and Mission

In terms of our own hermeneutical mindset, we must draw upon common elements found in the intertextual interpretations within Scripture. Figure 4 is a simple depiction of improving perceptions of intertextuality. (1) The concern for absolute truth has been investigated but fails because this does not match the missional mindset of biblical figures. (2) Anthropological insights add another helpful layer, but these still fall short because cultural insights are not on par with mission. (3) As the biblical figures experience God's grace in understanding mission, they likewise model God's grace by allowing others to recognize the same missional hermeneutic they have adopted through God's spiritual correction.

Therefore, missional hermeneutics must develop eyes to perceive the interpretation of God's mission within Scripture. Since a great deal of the New Testament is engaged in the flow of mission, it is rare to find accounts in which mission is not the backdrop for the writer. In the far more lengthy Old Testament record, the level of mission is complicated by the issue of Israel's allegiance.[95] As such, a missional hermeneutic

95. The missional gaps in the Old Testament occur as a common failure on the part of the people of God to maintain allegiance to God's mission, and this was rare because Israel most often struggled in simply maintaining a basic allegiance to God. As such, there are examples of mission in the Old Testament, such as Joseph and Daniel, but we

must begin by perceiving Scripture in terms of increased missional practice or reduced missional practice and then we must learn from those instances in which missionaries in Scripture are transformed.[96]

Throughout this chapter, I have shown that the major missional breakthroughs of biblical figures take place through active spiritual engagement and this has resulted in the development of a persistent missional hermeneutic. Some missional hermeneutics took millennia in their development (Gen 12:3 and its repetitions). Other transformations in missional hermeneutics took place in much shorter periods (Dan 9–12; Acts 10–11), and some never adopted a missional hermeneutic (Matt 8–12; Jon). As such, Scripture indicates that the strongest hermeneutic is one that above all is open to spiritual direction and missional understanding.

Consequently, a biblical hermeneutic seeks the leadership and guidance of a risen missional God and Savior, with the expectation that the Holy Spirit will aid and inform the interpretational community that seeks missional insight for the sake of sharing the gospel. Given that the biblical record demonstrates God's involvement, which is by nature spiritual, we must likewise allow Scripture to transform us by a renewed expectation of God's involvement in the hermeneutical process. However, to begin the transformation we must allow Scripture to critique the spiritual biases present in Western hermeneutics as well as biases that have been adopted in missiological hermeneutics. Furthermore, we must allow Scripture to likewise inform the hermeneutical process through a proper integration of spiritual disciplines. To this task we now turn.

---

likewise can learn from the accounts of ethnocentrism, apathy, and antagonism toward mission.

96. My thinking regarding "increased missional practice or reduced missional practice" is inspired through Kraft's concept of hi-context and low-context (Kraft, *Christianity in Culture*, 139–40).

THREE

A Missional Critique of Current Hermeneutical Theory[1]

Thesis of this chapter: Hermeneutics in Biblical Theology of Mission must properly critique the cultural polarization in Western hermeneutical method by validating and developing new openness to spiritual dimensions as an equally esteemed part of the total hermeneutical process. The field of Biblical Theology of Mission must gracefully address the pitfalls of Western hermeneutics, while simultaneously validating its strengths, so that a more holistic hermeneutic can be offered to students, missiologists, missionaries and most importantly new Christian believers.

SCHOLARS OF BIBLICAL THEOLOGY of Mission have carried the difficult burden of missiologically critiquing the underlying cultural assumptions inherent in Western theology. This effort has resulted in new hermeneutical understandings in theology of mission that have played a crucial role in interpreting the missionary nature of the Bible.

While in the process of writing this chapter, I was called upon by missionaries from a unique background—those of the Latter Day Saints of the Church of Jesus Christ (LDS). The young LDS missionaries began by asking me the two most common questions asked to those outside the LDS tradition; "Have you read the Book of Mormon?" and, "Have you prayed to know if the Book of Mormon is true?" As we were talking, it dawned upon me that perhaps only LDS missionaries utilize prayer as a litmus test to discern the validity of Scripture.

---

1. When I originally wrote this chapter, I had in mind that it would be part of this book. However, a prior version of this chapter has been published and edited by Charles H. Kraft in *Appropriate Christianity* (Redford, "Appropriate Hermeneutics,").

However, it was not the LDS missionaries who ultimately brought about the concerns of this chapter. It was the task-master of Western academia that "offers" a hermeneutical process filled with the splendor of human reasoning, but with little room for the Creator of the universe to speak, clarify, or guide in understanding the very Scripture that God has created.

THEOLOGICAL CIRCLES

The focus of this chapter is not a historical look at hermeneutics, yet some background must be considered in order for missiologists to perceive the "air that we breathe."[2] Three hermeneutical traditions come to mind when looking at the cultural assumptions of the Western hermeneutical process: (1) liberal scholars, sometimes referred to as conciliar theology or German rationalism, (2) evangelical scholars who have adopted a great deal from the former, including the highly esteemed historical-critical method, and (3) Protestant fundamentalists which has primarily been a reaction to the former groups.[3]

In looking at these traditions, my main concern is to address underlying hermeneutical and spiritual assumptions that are made by adherents to these traditions. I should add that proponents of these traditions would very likely claim they make no assumptions at all, and that their perceptions are absent of bias. As Newbigin pointed out, "What came to be known as the 'historical-critical method' grew to eventually be accepted as the only proper method for interpreting these ancient writings. . . . [T]his move is misunderstood if it is seen as a move to a more objective understanding of the Bible. It is a move from one confessional stance to another, a move from one creed to another. *But it is very hard to persuade the practitioners of the historical-critical method to recognize the creedal character of their approach.*"[4]

Insightful theologians and missiologists alike have consistently recognized that no one comes to Scripture without assumptions.[5] In the words of Gordon Fee, "neither does the exegete come to the text with a

---

2. I owe this phrase to Wilbert Shenk.

3. The official name for the historical-critical method would be the historical-grammatical method. These two terms will be used synonymously throughout this chapter.

4. Newbigin, *Proper Confidence*, 79–80 italics mine.

5. Kirk, *Mission of Theology*, 9–10, 25; Kraft, *Confronting Powerless Christianity*, 30–32; Newbigin, *Truth to Tell*, 44.

clean slate, but also brings his or her agendas to the text, not to mention a whole train load of cultural baggage and biases."[6]

Liberal Method

Liberal methodology has most often assumed that all of the accounts in Scripture should be explained through natural means. The leading assumption is that Scripture is strictly a historical record. Historically, critics attacked this chiefly horizontal approach. "What made liberalism 'another religion' was, above all, its disbelief in the supernatural Christ-events. . . . Liberalism negated historic Christianity by minimizing human estrangement from God. It denied the unique authority of the scriptures. It viewed Christ as an example rather than as a supernatural person and the Savior of mankind."[7] The unstated assumption that followed is that God is not involved with humanity in Scripture.[8] It could be characterized as an agnostic hermeneutical approach because God is not part of the process and indeed God need not necessarily exist.[9] The burden of proof for any account in Scripture rests solely upon humanity (whether good or bad) because an a priori decision has been made that God is not at work in human history, including the history set forth in the Bible.[10] These assumptions are, of course, validated in the name of "scientific integrity."[11] Since it is assumed that God is not at work in Scripture, all of God's in-breaking in Scripture must be explained "rationally."[12] Newbigin puts this overall focus in perspective: "They practice rather the 'hermeneutic of suspicion' which leads the student of an ancient record to ask not What is the truth which is here articulated? but What is the interest which is here being advanced? The biblical material is thus interpreted in terms of the various power struggles in Israel and in the church."[13]

---

6. Fee, *Listening to the Spirit*, 9.
7. Hutchison, *Modernist Impulse*, 265.
8. Kirk, *Mission of Theology*, 18–19.
9. Newbigin, *Proper Confidence*, 69, 100.
10. Cp. ibid., 95–96.
11. Hutchison, *Modernist Impulse*, 89–92; compare Barth, *Credo*, 187–90.
12. Marshall, "Developing a Biblical Hermeneutic," 12; Gasque, "Nineteenth-Century Roots of Contemporary New Testament Criticism," 148.
13. Newbigin, *Proper Confidence*, 83.

Figure 5 is an attempt to illustrate this concept and the main areas that liberal theologians draw upon when involved in the hermeneutical process. The large eye on the left of this figure (and all diagrams in this chapter) represents the perspective or vision of the one involved in the hermeneutical process—in this case the liberal theologian. The lines drawn from the eye toward the Bible illustrate the hermeneutical focus upon Scripture that ultimately offers some sort of meaningful interpretation.

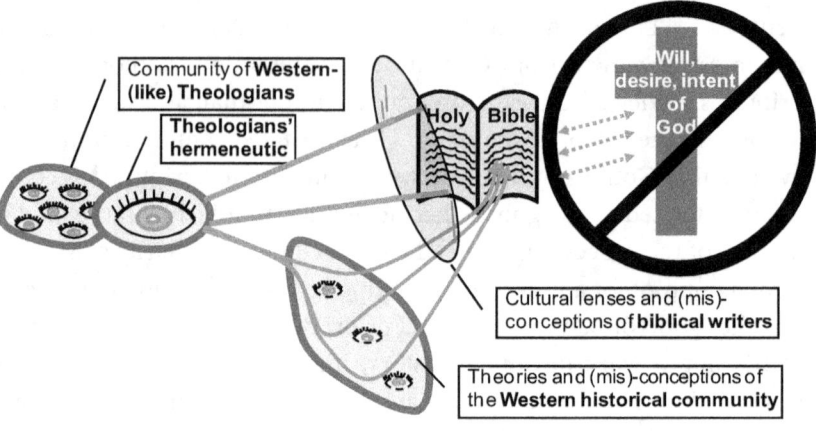

Figure 5: Liberal Method in Hermeneutics

The lens that covers a portion of the Bible illustrates the cultural values of the biblical writers and biblical contexts. Liberal and evangelical theologians alike have made many astute observations in understanding the perceptions and values of the biblical writers and this contribution is something that should not be overlooked.

The smaller eyes represent the perspectives of others who influence and work with the theologian. Like most Western theologians, they work with a community of theologians who most often value the same hermeneutical process, even though theological dogma may differ as a result of using the same hermeneutic. Also among these perspectives are those of the historical community who continue to speak to the theologians through their writings.

The main point of the diagram is illustrated in the cross with arrows pointing to Scripture, all of which are crossed out. Liberal theologians have limited their understanding of Scripture because they have chosen to severely limit the role of God in Scripture and God's continuity in the development of Scripture.[14] The main thrust of this God-less process places humanity in control of nearly every facet of Scripture, as expressed by Newbigin: "The gospel challenges liberals' thinking in the sharpest possible way, and perhaps this is the hardest thing for them to accept. It exposes as illusion the liberal picture—the picture of ourselves as sovereign explorers who formulate the real questions in a search for a yet-to-be-discovered reality. The gospel . . . exposes our false pretensions. We are *not* honest and open-minded explorers of reality; we are alienated from reality because we have made ourselves the center of the universe."[15]

Evangelical Theologians

The dividing line between liberal and evangelical hermeneutics is blurred largely because evangelical scholars have so faithfully adopted the historical-critical method from the liberals. However, evangelical scholars have, for the most part, held their conviction that Scripture is the word of God. Therefore, the Bible is not seen solely as a historical record, but evangelical scholars have virtually treated it this way because their methodology rarely stretches beyond the confines of the historical-critical process.[16]

---

14. Frei, *Eclipse of Biblical Narrative*, 64.

15. Newbigin, *Proper Confidence*, 104.

16. Some scholars with strong backgrounds in theology likewise write in the field of Biblical Theology of Mission, but they seem to either support historical-critical methods entirely, as in Larkin's case, or, in the case of Köstenberger and O'Brien, they so exclusively utilize historical-critical methods that they implicitly provide no critique (Köstenberger and O'Brien, *Salvation to the Ends*; Larkin, "Methods in Missiological Research").

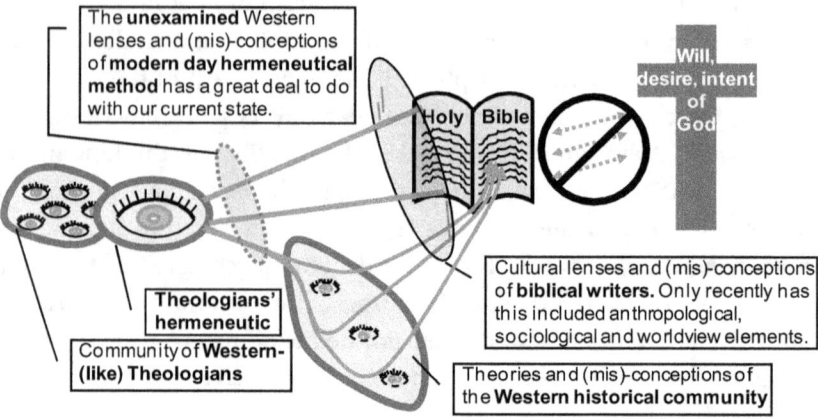

Figure 6: Evangelical Method in Hermeneutics

Figure 6 is an attempt to illustrate the perception of God in the evangelical method of hermeneutics. This diagram is very similar to that of the liberals except that God is part of the overall conception. However, God is given little capacity to influence the hermeneutical process among evangelicals (represented by the crossed-out arrows between God and Scripture) because they feel that assumptions cannot be made regarding God's involvement in the development of Scripture (which is in itself an assumption). Andrew Kirk notes the paradox that this creates for the scholar who believes in the inspiration of Scripture and is confined to historical-critical methodology that has drawn too heavily from the liberals:

> [T]heology has relied so heavily on the renowned historical-critical method. Even where new approaches have arisen that concentrate on the finished text . . . [this] method remains pervasive. . . . The interpreter cannot remain detached from the message of the text, in a kind of cocoon of suspended judgment. For the attempt to remain free from any interaction with the text as communication *is already a judgment about one's method and one's relation to the particular configuration of words*. As a consequence, I have never understood how it is possible to study the text of the Bible as if it were just another piece of literature from the Ancient Near East, for it manifestly is not. . . .[17]

---

17. Kirk, *Mission of Theology*, 9–10 italics mine.

As a result, God is excluded from the hermeneutical process even though evangelical scholars most often profess profound faith in God and inspiration of the Scriptures. Additionally, few observations are made over the continuity in Scripture since this exists precisely due to God's involvement in developing Scripture. As a result, historical-critical analysis is prone to fragmentation, and comparatively little work has been done in discourse-level analysis. Themes coursing through Scripture are seen as coincidental to God's nature, but not intended by God, which has made meta-narratives suspect in Scripture. Kirk validly claims that "the dominant approach to theology in the West has been rooted in skepticism, rather than in a properly self-critical critical method."[18]

Additionally, the lack of missionary experience among evangelical theologians (whether at home or abroad) has most often forced Scripture into a pattern of ideas about truth (even when the historical-critical method avoids being reductionistic). The hermeneutical ideas that then guide the very Scripture that consistently demonstrates the missionary tragedies and triumphs between God and his people, are most often void of missional questions and categories.

Figure 6 also illustrates a Western lens, representing Western cultural values that for the most part have gone unexamined by theologians. This lens is expanded in the following diagram, which is the starting point for addressing our current crisis in hermeneutics. Therefore, Figure 7 attempts to make greater sense of the impact that Western assumptions have had on our perceptions of Scripture and God in relation to hermeneutics.

Protestant Fundamentalism

Given the liberal and evangelical scholars' claims of supposed "objectivity" and "neutrality" in their "assumption-less" methods of interpreting Scripture, a reactionary force grew that attempted to force Scripture into another mold of modernity typified by a "fundamentalism which seeks to affirm the factual, objective truth of every statement in the Bible and which thinks that if any single factual error were to be admitted, biblical authority would collapse."[19] Protestant fundamentalism seemed quite different from its liberal "enemy" but it likewise was built upon a modern worldview that uses reason as the principle method for interpreting

---

18. Ibid., 48–49.
19. Newbigin, *Proper Confidence*, 85.

Scripture. Gordon Fee illustrates this reactionary tension by taking on the perspective of the Church:

> Taking Scripture away from the believing community, the exegete made it an object of historical investigation. Armed with the so-called historical-critical method, he thus engaged in an exercise in history, pure and simple, an exercise that appeared all too often to begin from a stance of doubt—indeed, sometimes of historical skepticism with an anti-supernatural bias. Using professional jargon about form, redaction, and rhetorical criticism, the exegete, full of arrogance and assuming a stance of mastery over the text, often seemed to turn the text on its head so that it no longer spoke to the believing community as the powerful word of the living God.[20]

As a result of these uneasy tensions, Christians from all three above traditions perceived their only choice was to choose some position along a continuum of "reason," all of which imprisoned Scripture by Western concerns over reason, truth, and inerrancy. Furthermore, missional concerns were given little or no consideration at all. Historically, "the dispensationalists were responding to some of the very same problems in Biblical interpretation that were troubling theological liberals in the nineteenth century. If Biblical statements were taken at face value and subjected to scientific analysis, major anomalies seemed to appear."[21] The greater irony in all of this is that the lack of vision in understanding mission in Scripture among all of these groups has left them in the predicament that they now face.

Examining the Western Lens

All of the above groups suffer from equally deficient perceptions of Scripture because they are all swept up in the values of modernity. In order to understand the overall focus of the Western worldview as it relates to Scripture, I have diagrammed the assumptions that flow from Western worldview into the historical-critical method as shown in Figure 7. This figure illustrates the Western "eye" and the filtering that takes place as the Western lenses influence one's perception of Scripture, which I have characterized as polarization.

---

20. Fee, *Listening to the Spirit*, 8.
21. Marsden, *Fundamentalism and American Culture*, 54.

A Missional Critique of Current Hermeneutical Theory

In this illustration, the Bible itself is in the very center of the illustration since it is the focus of the hermeneutical process. Surrounding the Bible are numerous disciplines that represent various ways of knowing, interpreting, and relating to God's message in Scripture. However, among the disciplines, rational thought has been placed at the top to illustrate its perceived superior status over other means of understanding Scripture.

By contrast, spiritual "disciplines" (for lack of a better term) have been placed at the very bottom of the diagram to illustrate that these disciplines have been given the least credibility as a means of understanding Scripture. Narrative and experiential ways of knowing hold a higher position, but nothing holds the same level of esteem as rational thought.

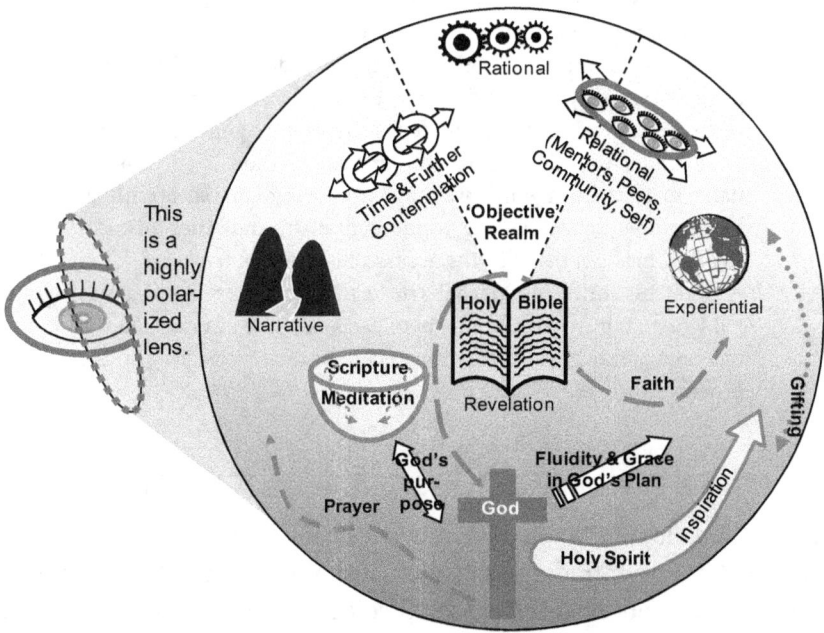

Figure 7: Examining the Western Lens

Superimposed over all of these areas is a polarized lens showing the additional bias in terms of the attention and stigma that each discipline has been assigned. Rational thought is illustrated as an "objective realm" because Western theologians, until recently, have presented the rational hermeneutical process of the historical-critical method as a discipline that was un-biased and objective in its vision of Scripture. This is clearly a fallacy that will be addressed later. Other disciplines, and especially those related to spiritual areas, have the greatest polarization because of the severely limited way in which these have been perceived in the West. Andrew Kirk keenly notes the dichotomy of Western hermeneutical thought as it relates to itself, others, and spiritual matters:

> Academic theology's pretensions to being a genuinely critical method are suspect. In traditional academic theology, the historical-critical method has been the bedrock of any work able to claim intellectual rigor and credibility. In accordance with certain Enlightenment emphases, out of which it grew, the method begins with a first principle of doubt (or suspicion). Thus the historical accounts of the biblical narrative are assumed to be guilty of exaggeration or of reconstructing stories to fit a predetermined theological stance, until proved innocent. . . .
>
> In my estimation, in this whole procedure skepticism has been disastrously confused with criticism. For two hundred years or so theological faculties and departments have gone about their work under the illusion that the critical method is an impregnable fortress from which we may sally forth to do battle with all kinds of theological naïveté, fundamentalism, and other forms of strong Christian belief in the accessibility of final truth. . . .
>
> It is this confusion, perhaps more than anything else, that has led to a certain schizophrenia between academic pursuits, on the one hand, and spirituality, mission, and pastoral concerns, on the other.[22]

CURRENT HERMENEUTICS IN THEOLOGY OF MISSION

Biblical Theology of Mission has moved beyond the cultural assumptions and restrictions of traditional hermeneutical limitations (see Figure 7). Missiologists and mission-focused theologians have addressed some of the deficiencies that were so limiting. Among these developments have been the recognition of assumptions regarding Scripture, historical understanding, cultural perspectives, narrative and community-based theology in mission. As a result, it is important to consider the significant contributions to the hermeneutical process that have taken place. I would certainly not claim that this is a comprehensive overview, but the areas that follow do represent major shifts from traditional hermeneu-

---

22. Kirk, *Mission of Theology*, 15–16.

A Missional Critique of Current Hermeneutical Theory

tics that have come about largely due to natural dialogue between the Bible and mission that has allowed new hermeneutical understanding to emerge.[23]

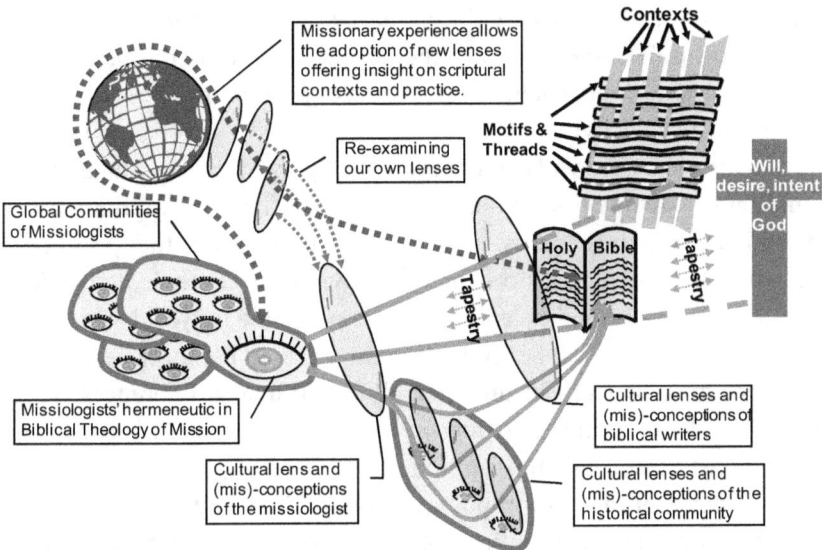

Figure 8: Current Hermeneutics of Theology of Mission

Figure 8 illustrates the overall hermeneutical picture and this diagram will be the focus of this section. Although this diagram appears somewhat complex, it is actually a combination of disciplines that define the current state of hermeneutics in Biblical Theology of Mission.

Cultural Lenses of the Missiologist

The cultural lens of the missiologist is illustrated as the oval lens closest to the "eye" in Figure 8. One of the strengths of missiology has been the tremendous development that has gone on in terms of Christian anthropology. Missiologists have actively sought to understand the ways in which worldview assumptions affect mission theory and practice. Among Western missiologists, the study of modernity and postmodernity has provided even greater depth in owning Western values ingrained at the worldview level such as individualism, technique/strategy,

23. Nissen, *NT and Mission*, 13–15.

specialization/fragmentation, time-space separation, rationalism, and working from strength and power.[24]

This development has helped missiologists and missionaries to realize that they do not operate from an "objective" position, most often corroborated by cross-cultural clashes when missionaries do not address or understand their own tendencies. As a result of this development, missionaries actively attempt to recognize their practical tendencies toward subjectivity.

Missiologists do place assumptions upon Scripture but they are simultaneously involved in becoming aware of their assumptions. Since missiologists actively study their own cultural lenses, they are better prepared to understand how their worldview affects their perceptions of Scripture. Missiologists are likewise responsible to world-wide communities who approach Scripture from a variety of perspectives and this provides greater depth in understanding worldview differences. These understandings motivate us toward views that validate a broader and more holistic hermeneutical approach.

Understanding anthropology, modernity, and postmodernity has therefore helped those in Biblical Theology of Mission to become more aware of their own assumptions when approaching Scripture. Tendencies toward an overarching rationalism and individualism are obviously negative assumptions that have to be addressed in the life of any missiologist coming to Scripture, but there can be positive assumptions as well.

The Tapestry of Scripture

It is important to note that we all make certain assumptions about the nature of Scripture (most of which we probably do not realize). One positive assumption, drawn from Biblical Theology of Mission, is that God is involved in the development of Scripture over the course of human history and that God's agenda in mission is left on the pages of Scripture through time.

A model of Scripture developed by Charles Van Engen carries this positive assumption. This model is known as the "Tapestry of Scripture," and the model assumes that God has woven (revealed through time)

---

24. Shenk, *Write the Vision*, 56, 62; Shenk, *Changing Frontiers of Mission*, 135–37.

various threads (themes or motifs) in the many cultural contexts (books or contexts within a book) of Scripture.[25]

Figure 8 illustrates the role of the tapestry in relation to God, Scripture, and the context of the missiologist. Figure 9 expands the tapestry itself, showing "the Bible as a tapestry, with the woof (horizontal threads) of various themes and motifs interwoven in the warp (vertical) of each historical context."[26] The tapestry was originally developed to avoid the tendency of proof-texting Scripture in missiology in order to support human agendas. Van Engen notes, "Such a critical hermeneutic helps us get away from finding a few proof-texts or isolated nuggets in the Bible to buttress our missional agendas."[27] In this sense the model provides a measure of check and balance upon how far an interpretation can vary from Scripture. David Bosch points out how subtle this tendency can be: "[I]t can easily happen that, consciously or unconsciously, *the reader refers only to the biblical data which particularly appeal to him or provide the 'answers' he is looking for. . . . As a result, it inevitably happens that a canon develops within the canon*; what is not to the liking of a particular group is simply ignored."[28]

Van Engen has created a practical application for Kraft's concept of a "tethered distance for proper interpretation."[29] Although the tapestry was not based upon Kraft's concept, the tapestry does offer one of the most effective ways for the missiologist to understand God's mission biblically and likewise address highly suspect interpretation. Van Engen does not stand alone with this concept.[30] Larry Caldwell points out that, "the final authority will not be the individual culture's particular hermeneutical method but the Bible itself and *how each new meaning is consistent with the overall thrust of Scripture*. The Bible must always take

---

25. Van Engen and Redford, "Syllabus," 35 originally Van Engen, illustration by Redford.
26. Van Engen, *Mission on the Way*, 41.
27. Ibid., 42.
28. Bosch, *Witness to the World*, 45 italics mine.
29. Kraft, *Christianity in Culture*, 191–92.
30. Allen, *Spiritual Theology*, 134–35; Bauckham, *Bible and Mission*, 12; Beeby, *Canon and Mission*, 32–38, 75, 113; McCartney, "Should We Employ," 3; McCartney and Clayton, *Let the Reader Understand*, 200–06; Wright, "Mission as a Matrix," 102–43; Wright, *Mission of God*, 33–69.

precedence over any culture and that culture's particular interpretation, no matter how relevant or receptor-oriented it may be."[31]

The tapestry is a model based on the assumption that God has actively and consistently revealed himself throughout the ages. This assumption, that God has been involved in the development of Scriptural themes, is no more or less of an assumption than the idea that God has not been involved in the development of Scripture. To those who value reason above all else, this is a most reasonable assumption for the nature of Scripture.[32] If God is not revealed in the Bible then where is God revealed?

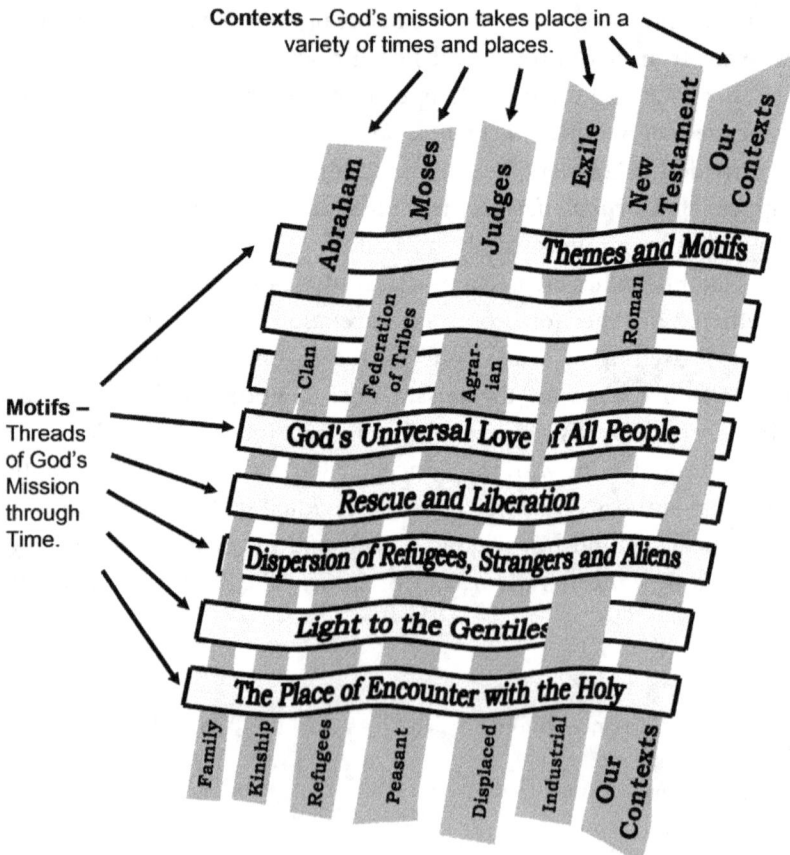

Figure 9: Tapestry of Scripture

31. Caldwell, "Ethnohermenutics," 144 italics mine.
32. Brunner, *Word and the World*, 93–94.

A Missional Critique of Current Hermeneutical Theory

To those who cry "foul" due to the historical-critical and faithless assumption that God has not been involved in revealing himself in Scripture through the ages, I would simply point out that they do come to Scripture with assumptions. More often than not, these are negative assumptions that oppose the claims of Scripture regarding God's consistent nature and God's repetitive work in trying to involve the people of God in mission. Furthermore, the idea that God is absent in Scripture or the idea that God's will is absent in Scripture (a perspective most often built upon scientific agendas that are exclusive of faith) is just as clearly an assumption as the idea that God and God's will are involved and existent in Scripture.[33] The assumptions in the tapestry model are rooted in faith in God and faith in God's concern for humanity. As early as 1908, Robert Horton recognized this same tendency especially as the Bible relates to mission: "It is the strange characteristic of the Bible that *a unity pervades it which makes its several parts interpret one another*, and displays the same truths with more or less completeness under differing forms. Thus, when the *principles of interpretation* which have occupied our attention are sufficiently understood, and we have learnt to trace the lines of historical and spiritual development *through the whole*, arranging the parts chronologically, in order to illustrate it we can take up the Bible where we will, *and read on every page from Genesis to Revelation the missionary purpose*."[34]

A final point regarding the tapestry is that it is designed to allow biblical themes to flow into the missionary contexts of today (see the far right vertical thread in Figure 9). Therefore, the tapestry supports integration between Scriptural interpretation and missionary application. Those new to Biblical Theology of Mission have perceived this as a simple model to follow, but nothing could be further from the truth.[35] This model requires tremendous integration of biblical concepts and contexts that ultimately require a much broader knowledge of Scripture.

---

33. Cp. Newbigin, *Proper Confidence*, 101–2.

34. Horton, *Bible: A Missionary Book*, 183–84 italics mine.

35. It has been my personal observation when teaching Biblical Foundations of Mission (MT520), that many students readily agree and understand the conceptual ideas of the tapestry, but then struggle when trying to put this model into practice primarily because they are not prepared for the complexity of integrative and cohesive understandings within Scripture (McCartney and Clayton, *Let the Reader Understand*, 200). This lack of integration stems from a consistent perception that one passage can be isolated from another when learning to interpret Scripture.

Additionally, the tapestry avoids the Western tendency to isolate biblical texts and atomize the overall nature of Scripture.

Cultural Lenses in History and Historical Hermeneutics in Mission

The greatest contribution provided by those in the history of mission has been to demonstrate the way in which modern thought has taken missions captive in the present-day missionary movement. Those who come to this discussion primarily as theologians, epistemologists, such as Lesslie Newbigin and David Bosch, and those who come as historians, such as Andrew Walls and Wilbert Shenk have written extensively on the influence that modernity has played upon mission practice.[36] The ability to see the deficiencies in our understanding have come largely from investigating the cultural values infused in Western theology through the lenses of mission history. The small lenses in the historical community of Figure 9 illustrate these insights.

As a result, historical perspectives illustrating the missionary use of Scripture are one of the most helpful taskmasters in avoiding the tendency to force Scripture to fit the missionary's agenda. David Bosch notes the underlying danger of missionaries cutoff from missions' history:

> A study of mission through the ages may, for instance, teach us a lesson in reserve. Churches and missionaries expose themselves to grave danger *whenever they isolate their own missionary activities from the current of nineteen centuries of Church history*. A lack of historical perspective all too easily causes people to draw direct lines from the Bible to their own missionary practice, *oblivious of the degree to which their interpretation of the Bible might be conditioned by their situation*. They then remain blissfully ignorant of the deficiencies of their own enterprise and tend to regard it as the only correct one, perfectly in harmony with what the Bible teaches.[37]

Mission historians have also recognized the contextual factors that influence the particular choices of the missiologist in his or her own time. Much of the critique of hermeneutics offered in this chapter also applies

---

36. Bosch, *Witness to the World*; Bosch, *Transforming Mission*; Bosch, *Believing in the Future*; Newbigin, *Truth to Tell*; Newbigin, *Word in Season*; Newbigin, *Proper Confidence*; Shenk, *Transfiguration of Mission*; Shenk, *Write the Vision*; Shenk, *Changing Frontiers of Mission*; Walls, *Missionary Movement*.

37. Bosch, *Witness to the World*, 87 italics mine.

A Missional Critique of Current Hermeneutical Theory

to the missionary practice of Western missionaries in the modern missions era. From a hermeneutical standpoint, we need a great deal more historical research to understand the theological assumptions made by various missionaries and the role that these assumptions have played in their understanding of mission.

Missionary Experience

Experience has been excluded from the hermeneutical process for the most part because the "reaction against extreme emotionalism has led many, especially academics, to discount the value of experience in the interpretive process."[38] This issue has left missiologists timid in defining the role of experience in hermeneutics. However, missionary experience is critical for the missiologist to relate to the Bible. "Knowing cannot be severed from living and acting, for we cannot know the truth unless we seek it with love and unless our love commits us to action."[39]

While introductory texts on hermeneutical method have recognized that various genre's require genre-specific insights (i.e. a good understanding of Hebrew poetry will benefit the interpreter when analyzing poetic passages of the Old Testament), few of these works recognize that missionary activity as its own unique genre despite the abundance of mission in the Bible.[40] This is critical because Scripture is filled with narratives that include missionary applications such as contextualization (for example, Matt 5:46–47 and Luke 6:33–34), the translation of Christianity (for example, Acts 9, 22, 26), cross-cultural tensions (for example, Acts 15), and missionary training (for example, 1 Timothy) to name a few.[41] The reason for this is at least two-fold: There is a lack of experience in mission among theologians, and an assumption that the impact of experience is necessarily negative. However, the Gospels and the book of Acts consistently integrate missionary experience to transform the understanding of the apostles (this will be discussed in more

---

38. Kraft, *Confronting Powerless Christianity*, 32; compare Allen, *Spiritual Theology*, 31.

39. Newbigin, *Proper Confidence*, 105.

40. Cp. Klein et al., *Introduction to Biblical Interpretation*, 322–448; McCartney and Clayton, *Let the Reader Understand*, 223–42; Osborne, *Hermeneutical Spiral*, 149–258; Tate, *Biblical Interpretation*, 71–77.

41. Redford, "Contextualization in Acts,"; Van Engen and Redford, "Syllabus," 106–7; Walls, *Missionary Movement*, 25–27, 32–36.

detail on the "Holy Spirit"). "Theologians today are afraid of the word 'experience'.... But... the New Testament writers are free from this fear. They recount happenings which we would subsume under the head of religious experience, and do not hesitate to ascribe them to the mighty power of God and to give them right of way in theological argument over long-cherished convictions."[42]

Missionary experience has been one of the most valuable bridges for modern day missionaries and the Bible, and this has a two-fold benefit. On the one hand, understanding the nature of God's mission in the Bible manifestly guides Christians in application toward missionary practice, which declares our understanding of Scripture. "There are no more reliable grounds than what are given to us in God's revelation. The proper answer to the charge of subjectivity is world mission, but it is world mission not as proselytism but as exegesis... The missionary action of the Church is the exegesis of the gospel."[43]

On the other hand, missionary experience provides new categories of understanding that allow the biblical interpreter to perceive Scripture in new ways that were previously hidden or misunderstood.[44] The implication of this latter concept is that missionary practice is continually needed in order to gain a proper historical understanding to the strongly missional contexts of the Bible. The dynamic interplay between experience and re-developing our missional understanding of Scripture is what I have referred to as a reflexive hermeneutic: "Scripture is needed to know God's mission; mission is needed to know God's Scripture."[45]

Narrative and Mission

Narrative theology has been a topic of great discussion among theologians and missiologists. This brief look at narrative will not attempt to cover that ground.[46] However, missionary experience does provide a unique understanding on the use of narrative in Scripture. Narrative approaches are of great benefit in contexts that are not receptive to the Christian message or in contexts of extreme persecution. In the case of

---

42. Newbigin, *Household of God*, 117–18.
43. Newbigin, *Truth to Tell*, 33, 35.
44. Brownson, *Speaking the Truth*, 80.
45. Van Engen and Redford, "Syllabus," 25.
46. For a missiological overview see Van Engen, *Mission on the Way*, 44–68; Van Engen et al., *Footprints of God*, xvii-xxv.

A Missional Critique of Current Hermeneutical Theory

Jesus' missionary activity in the gospels, he was addressing a context that was both non-receptive and persecutory.

In non-receptive contexts, narrative teaching such as the parables forces the faithful listeners to take on greater responsibility in interpreting the message (Matt 13:2, 11, 12). In Jesus' own ministry, he realized "that when the heart of a people grows dull–that is, unreceptive–direct presentations of truth evoke little or no positive response (compare Isa 6:9–10 and Zech 7:11 with Matt 13:13–17). The only alternative then is to use the language of metaphor, narrative and parable."[47]

Additionally, since narrative is an indirect form of communication, it has the ability to act as a filter for the listeners in various ways. It can provide pace for those needing slow change. For example, the mystery of Jesus' person and the spiritual nature of his kingdom were so new and revolutionary that he could only disclose these realities gradually, since the Jews were so convinced that the Messiah would be an earthly ruler.

Narrative can also provide delayed meaning when the ideas are very difficult. For example, some hearers, including the disciples, would have great difficulty initially but would eventually follow Christ and later grasp a more complete understanding of earlier ideas (cp. John 6:60; Matt 26:26–28).

Finally, narrative can provide no meaning for listeners of hostile intent. Some hostile hearers had no intention of following Jesus, but were searching for ideas to bring about accusations. For hostile listeners, the parables would be no more than "hard sayings" that were thought to be devoid of significance, while faithful believers could interpret and grow from these ideas. As Jesus nears the last week of his ministry, his communication becomes much more direct and hostile hearers attack Jesus based on these direct statements.[48]

Narrative then has the overall benefit of forcing its readers to engage in the hermeneutical process themselves, allowing them to succeed or fail, but at least they are involved.[49] It illustrates that Scripture may have been missionally intended for everyone to interpret (rather than having professional interpreters carry out the task). Narrative listen-

---

47. Glasser, *Announcing the Kingdom*, 189.

48. I owe my thoughts in this paragraph to insights from Dudley Woodberry. These concepts are further discussed in ch. 5.

49. Frei, *Eclipse of Biblical Narrative*, 18–19; McCartney and Clayton, *Let the Reader Understand*, 178; Van Engen, *Mission on the Way*, 60.

ers of the New Testament were not trained in hermeneutical method. They inductively learned hermeneutical method based on their interest. Therefore, one reason why narrative forms of communication may be so abundant in Scripture is that believers become relational rather than process-oriented. Narrative is powerful because it develops relationship and ownership in the process of understanding God!

Process-oriented hermeneutical methods have the danger of allowing the exegete to feel that interpretation is finished when the process is correctly followed. This can result in a divorce between theology and knowing God, which inevitably results in a divorce between theology and mission. Narrative helps the believer to interpret God's actions in Scripture from a standpoint of knowing and discovering the nature of God. This, in turn, inevitably results in a discovery of God's love for all humanity and greater appreciation for God's missionary activity in Scripture.

From a missional perspective, it is more important to involve the listeners in the role of hermeneutical discovery that aids their interest in relating to God, rather than providing the correct interpretation based on correct hermeneutical procedure. "The apostle asked the converts of Apollos one question: 'Did ye receive the Holy Spirit when you believed?' and got a plain answer. His modern successors are more inclined to ask either 'Did you believe exactly what we teach?'"[50]

Communities of Missiologists

Missionary activity, by its very nature, has always had to deal with a worldwide community and its many ways of understanding the Christian faith. Missiologists have likewise been forced to face this challenge in realizing that there are many ways of perceiving mission. However, alternate perceptions are crushed at the point when paternalism and cultural hegemony silences the voices of those who stand outside the reigning power structures.

Much of what Kirk and Newbigin have done over the 1990s was to lead the theological struggle in breaking free from Western hermeneutical control while Van Engen offered new direction in the hermeneutical process.[51] No other decade has focused so heavily on addressing the is-

---

50. Newbigin, *Household of God*, 122–23.

51. Kirk, *Mission of Theology*; Kirk, *What Is Mission*; Newbigin, *Proper Confidence*; Van Engen, "Relation of Bible,"; Van Engen, *Mission on the Way*.

sues that deeply affect the way that Western missiologists perceive and understand Scripture. However, Shenk appropriately claims that "the control center [is] still in the West."[52] Newbigin's ideas, although broad sweeping, are focused upon the community of Western faith. "[T]he confessional reader stands within the tradition of the Christian church. . . . It is that community that has put the Bible into their hands and has taught them how to understand it. They read as believers. The difference between this way of reading the Bible and the historical-critical way is not that the latter is neutral or scientific whereas the former is confessional or sectarian; rather, it is the difference between two confessions, two traditions of interpretation developed in two different human communities."[53]

Shenk is addressing a fundamental problem in that Western domination in missiology has not given proper attention to non-Western concepts. I do not believe that this has taken place consciously, but it has taken place. Shenk is calling for a level of "affirmative action" in missiology by asking missiologists to intentionally give a voice to the non-Western world.

> While the churches of the Two Thirds World are eager to have interlocutors representing the church universal, they want conversation partners who truly understand their situation. These they find readily in the first three centuries of Christian history, not in modern Western theology.
> This methodological suggestion has important implications. It encourages the theologian of mission to range over the whole of Christian history rather than being tied to an institutional or ecclesiastical tradition or a particular historical period.[54]

Although missiology has only begun to heed this call, this will have sweeping impact on hermeneutics.[55] The real challenge for Western missiologists in approaching the non-Western world is to take a stance as learners and listeners.[56] Otherwise, missiologists will subconsciously impose their assumptions and thoughts in the process and leave this issue unchanged. "[T]here is an urgent need to discover an approach to

---

52. Shenk, "Theology of Mission since 1990," 1.
53. Newbigin, *Proper Confidence*, 101–2.
54. Shenk, "Theology of Mission since 1990," 5–6.
55. Brownson, *Speaking the Truth*, 81.
56. Shenk, "Theology of Mission since 1990," 2.

theology which is a dynamic process of confronting the community of faith with the full range of meaning of the biblical faith without resort to theological systems which become self-regulating. If a church is robbed of this experience in the first generation, by virtue of needing to accept a second-hand theological system from an alien people and culture, it may be very difficult to change course later on."[57]

Just as Newbigin called the churches in mission toward repentance over issues of disunity, Shenk is calling for a similar attitude among missiologists to address academic barriers.[58] Since missiology is typically not well understood beyond the community of missiologists and trained missionaries of the world, few others will call attention to this problem. Consequently, missiologists must pay attention and address this concern.

Figure 8 represents this hermeneutical influence by illustrating multiple communities that guide the overall hermeneutic of the missiologist. The intent is to illustrate that the many cross-cultural communities of missiology must have impact and that together we form the entire believing community of God, avoiding the tendency toward cultural isolation. "[O]ur exegesis, therefore, must be kept in the context of the believing community. We must learn to hear the text together, to let the exegetical expert work hard on the text, but to insist that what he or she has learned in the privacy of one's study must be tested in the believing community."[59]

Missional hermeneutics can benefit a great deal from understanding the hermeneutical tendencies of cultures that have worldview characteristics similar to those of the Bible. These societies have greater "natural" ability to correctly interpret biblical concepts that are quite distant from 21st Century Western thinking. Caldwell illustrates a case in which the Cotobato Manobo society have a more natural means of interpreting the parables in Scripture.[60] It is for these same reasons that many missionaries from the West, who have experience working in traditional cultures, have offered unique insights into biblical complexities

---

57. Shenk, "Theology and Missionary Task," 307.
58. Newbigin, *Is Christ Divided*, 22, 25.
59. Fee, *Listening to the Spirit*, 15.
60. Caldwell, "Towards Ethnohermeneutics," 35–36.

that have sometimes confounded Western theologians.⁶¹ Chapter 5 will investigate this trend in much greater detail.

However, much of what needs to happen among groups of missiologists is a discussion over the parameters or boundaries that will assist missional hermeneutics in moving forward. This needs to take place among missionaries and missiologists from a variety of cultural backgrounds so that insights from all perspectives can be understood and critiqued. Using the existing example of Western historical-critical hermeneutics, it is important that we understand the assumptions of this western method and that we are prepared to critique it appropriately. Notably, proponents of this hermeneutic are for the most part uninvolved in mission and therefore lack a central basis for understanding missional hermeneutics. Likewise, they seem unaware that they have elevated this hermeneutic to become the self-proclaimed standard. "For any one of these to claim that their theology is normative is ethnocentric."⁶² As such, missional hermeneutics must always be cautious when giving significant attention to those uninvolved in God's mission and keenly aware of unconscious culturally-based hermeneutical imperialism.

Furthermore, "Exegesis and hermeneutics are not the rights of individuals but of the church as an exegetical and hermeneutical

---

61. In a very real sense, the *genuine* (and not skeptically focused) need for the historical-critical model of hermeneutics arises in part from the vast cultural chasm between the Biblical writers and those of 21st Century Western Society (Shenk, "Theology of Mission since 1990," 5). From the start of modernity, "change" has been a core value resulting in exponential cultural change in the West. Prior to modernity traditional cultures valued stability rather than change. As a result of the influence of technology and drastic shifts in Western cultural values, Westerners have much greater need for the historical-critical method when addressing the Old Testament than the Maasai of East Africa, for instance (Kraft, *Christianity in Culture*, 132–34). An interesting validation of cultural change in the United States was the PBS documentary *Frontier House* in which 21st century families attempted to live as Montana homesteaders in 1883 for a period of six months (not including the winter), using only what was available in 1883. They all had great difficulty with the experiment and some "cheated" in order to cope with their circumstances. However, if the Maasai were required to live as their ancestors 120 years earlier, I doubt they would have the same difficulty because cultural change among the Maasai over the last 120 years has not been as drastic. My point is that societies that have greater cultural similarity to their ancestors, and to the Bible, do not share the same need for the Western historical-critical method. As such, Caldwell's focus calls missionaries to critically access the real need for introducing specific hermeneutical models into non-Western societies.

62. Hiebert, "Critical Contextualization," 108.

community."⁶³ Cross-cultural communities are generally more adept at perceiving Western syncretism. It is for this reason that Hiebert states, "We need each other to see our sins, for we more readily see the sins of others than our own. Similarly, we see the ways others misinterpret Scriptures before we see our own misinterpretations. Along the same line, we need Christians from other cultures, for they often see how our cultural biases have distorted our interpretations of the Scriptures."⁶⁴

Missiologists, therefore, must draw upon their strengths as cross-cultural communities, and avoid the Western tendency that has largely ignored the repeated hermeneutical concerns of non-Western Christians.

Examining the Theology of Mission Lens

Following this brief look at the current state of Biblical Theology of Mission, it is helpful to re-consider the traditional theological lens (Figure 7) in light of missiological contributions. Missiologists have opened up important fields that have reduced the polarization of the former.

Figure 10 illustrates the changes that have taken place in the struggle to break free from the bias of Western rationalism. As illustrated, missiologists have given clearer understanding to the validation of narrative, experience, and have called for broadened boundaries in the role of community (due in part to the very nature of cross-cultural mission activity). However, a dark cloud remains over the use of spiritual disciplines in relation to biblical interpretation. The reason for our lack of spiritual understanding is that missiologists have likewise been succumbed by the research approaches from the hard sciences without fully considering what has been discarded in that process.

---

63. Ibid.
64. Ibid., 110.

A Missional Critique of Current Hermeneutical Theory

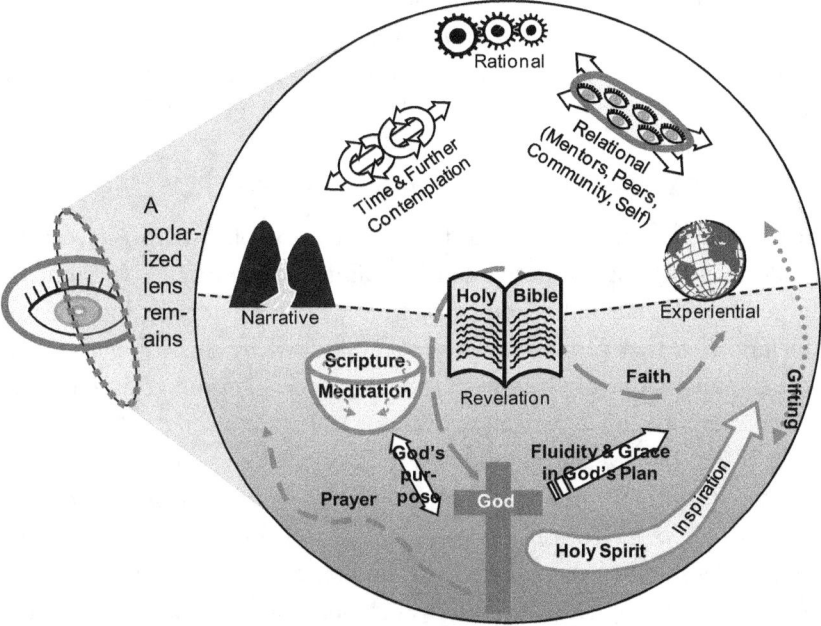

Figure 10: Current Theology of Mission Lens

The methods of science are ultimately inappropriate for the much more complex relationship found in Scripture between God and humanity. Modern day hermeneutics in Biblical Theology of Mission have existed for the most part as a faithless process because the very source of our understanding, God, has been left out due to a lack of critical assessment of the methods of modern hermeneutics. As missiologists, we need to recognize how true Kirk's statement is for ourselves; "To take seriously and to be rigorously honest about every kind of bias is the first step toward helping theology in general to be more widely self-critical than it is at present."[65] The underlying problem in our hermeneutical understanding stems from an inability to see our own blind spots. "Missiologists have sometimes raised the cry of syncretism when they have seen churches in Asia or Africa trying to express the gospel in their own cultural forms. The most obvious examples of syncretism, however, are to be found in our Western churches, which have worked so hard to tailor the gospel to fit the so-called requirements of modern thought."[66] The real implication for missiology today is that we have adopted a

65. Kirk, *Mission of Theology*, 25.
66. Newbigin, *Word in Season*, 130.

hermeneutic that has little room for faith and God, and even less room for areas that seek interaction with God for understanding. Moreover, this hermeneutic has been exported to foreign contexts by missiologists, some of whom recognize and struggle with the severity of the problem.[67]

HERMENEUTICS—FOREMOST A SPIRITUAL ACT

Looking forward, I would like to suggest areas of growth that can be made in missiological hermeneutics. Biblical Theology of Mission has forged formidable and needed direction into hermeneutics, but one important area that remains relatively untouched by missiologists is the role of spiritual disciplines in hermeneutics. Westerners, trained in rational methods, have typically not made this their strength. "One thing clear is that our Western worldview greatly interferes with our attempts to gain insight into the spiritual realities lying behind biblical events. From the perspective of our Western evangelicalism, we can read the descriptions and easily pick up the human factors. Given our worldview blindness in the spiritual area, however, our instincts are untrustworthy when we try to understand what is going on in that area."[68]

The one thing that is certain regarding hermeneutics is that there is little, if anything, to be said about the role of the Holy Spirit, prayer, meditation, giftedness, and faithfulness. Spiritual disciplines simply are not recommended as part of the hermeneutical process, and this is largely due to the extreme skepticism built into the historical-critical method.[69] "Indeed, in most theological seminaries, one can take courses in exegesis, but 'spirituality,' that most slippery of words to pin down, is pretty much left to the individual—and there is seldom any suggestion that the latter has very much to do with the former."[70]

Despite Western weakness in this field, there has been repeated recognition in the biblical validity of the sovereign role of the Holy Spirit in mission.[71] Mission fails without the Holy Spirit and for this reason God's missionary activity is often changing throughout Scripture to pro-

---

67. Caldwell, "Towards Ethnohermeneutics," 24–27.
68. Kraft, *Confronting Powerless Christianity*, 34–35.
69. Allen, *Spiritual Theology*, 5–6; Kirk, *Mission of Theology*, 15.
70. Fee, *Listening to the Spirit*, 4; compare Kirk, *Mission of Theology*, 16.
71. Allen, *Spontaneous Expansion*; Bevans, "God inside Out"; Gordon, *Holy Spirit in Missions*; Stronstad, *Charismatic Theology of Luke*.

A Missional Critique of Current Hermeneutical Theory

duce relational dependence between God and the missionary.[72] When the people of God uniquely understand their role as God's missionary people, God's leadership is followed in order to understand God's direction in mission.[73]

Sadly, formulaic understandings of mission result in human independence that becomes misguided and loses sight of the fact that "there is no absolute and mechanical uniformity of the Spirit's working in these matters [Acts 8:14–17; 10:44–48]."[74] Therefore, God's missionary people must interpret their role in God's mission by constantly seeking God's will.

Missiologists must incorporate these same principles in hermeneutics. Western hermeneutics have attempted to define hermeneutics in rigid ways so that there is no place for spiritual insight. Formulaic hermeneutics also suffer from a lack of spiritual guidance, because the process assumes some level of self-actualization that exceeds even God's capacity to communicate with us in our hermeneutical quest for meaning. Some type of balance must be achieved.

> Let us admit that it is part of the fallen human nature . . . to desire always criteria of judgment which can be used without making too heavy demands upon the delicate faculty of spiritual discernment, clear-cut rules by which we may hope to be saved from making mistakes, or rather from being obviously and personally responsible for the mistakes. We are uncomfortable without definite principles by which we may guide our steps. We fear uncharted country, and the fanatics of all kinds who, upon the alleged authority of the Holy Spirit, summon us with strident cries in all directions simultaneously. . . . But on the other hand let us admit that according to the New Testament we are summoned precisely to the task of "discerning the spirits"; that it is there taken for granted *both* that the Holy Spirit is free and sovereign, able to work in ways that demand re-thinking of our traditional categories, *and* that He Himself gives to the Church the necessary gifts by which He may be known (e.g., I Cor. 12.10). . . .[75]

---

72. Burrows, "Seventh Paradigm," 128.
73. Van Engen, *God's Missionary People*, 187–88.
74. Newbigin, *Household of God*, 129.
75. Ibid., 125–26.

Proper hermeneutics must avoid the tendency to eliminate God's involvement since our quest is ultimately one of understanding God's intentions for our lives.[76] "Only relatively recently have doctrinal and spiritual theology been pursued in isolation from each other; for most of the history of theology, they interacted richly."[77]

Furthermore, if God is involved as an author in Scripture, then the author's own intent must be sought out by the very criteria of the historical-critical method.[78] Missiologists cannot consistently call upon the leadership of the Holy Spirit in mission and then adopt hermeneutical methods that reverse this tendency, especially when mission has become known as "the mother of theology."[79]

Scientific methods do have their place in hermeneutics, but the Bible is not a scientific book and missionaries/missiologists are not first of all scientists.[80] We are believers in Jesus Christ. As such, we should approach the Scripture with methods beyond science, beyond even "method!" "[Lastly] . . . and most important, hermeneutics when utilized to interpret Scripture is a spiritual act, depending upon the leading of the Holy Spirit. Modern scholars too often ignore the sacred dimension and approach the Bible purely as literature, considering the sacral aspect to be almost a genre."[81]

I cannot imagine how surprised New Testament writers would have been if they were informed that prayer and the Holy Spirit were not acceptable means of interpreting God's message. Most likely, we would be charged as "false teachers." I cannot imagine how it pains God for us to request help in so many areas of life, but to absolutely avoid asking God in prayer for the meaning of ideas that God revealed throughout human history. Considering how often missionaries through the ages have requested prayer for God's guidance in their endeavors, it seems preposterous that we should adhere to a hermeneutical construct that is any less spiritual.

---

76. Allen, *Spiritual Theology*, 3–4, 152–53.

77. Ibid., 19.

78. LaSor, "*Sensus Plenior* and Interpretation," 270.

79. Kähler, *Schriften Zur Christologie*, 190; translated in Bosch, *Witness to the World*, 24, 138.

80. Kirk, *Mission of Theology*, 14–15; LaSor, "*Sensus Plenior* and Interpretation," 265.

81. Osborne, *Hermeneutical Spiral*, 5.

A Missional Critique of Current Hermeneutical Theory

The interpretation of Scripture is ultimately a process of seeking God's will by understanding God's intentions in the Bible. *Hermeneutic method is foremost a spiritual exercise in relationship with God as the author of Scripture.* It requires spiritually committed women and men to enter into the process of interpreting and understanding God's message in Scripture.[82] This spiritual act of interpreting God's message through Scripture must be done using spiritual means.

I should note as I continue that I am not advocating a moratorium on reason or the historical-critical method. I am not advocating, as Origen did, that the text should be interpreted purely in a "spiritual" way without any regard for the "literal" meaning of the text.[83] I am advocating that spiritual disciplines be given equal credibility to the many hermeneutical areas already discussed. I am advocating that spiritual disciplines be given equal attention and development, as have others. In the end, I would hope that multiple hermeneutical avenues lead to similar understandings of Scripture and actually help to build a more integrative and cohesive hermeneutical development.[84] Certainly any of these areas can be abused and contorted for the benefit of the interpreter, including reason-based approaches. No solitary method or discipline should stand on its own as the sure-fire hermeneutical pillar, nor should any single discipline have to bear that burden. We must move away from hermeneutical foundationalism and toward mutual integration of multiple means of understanding Scripture.[85]

Spiritual disciplines must be hermeneutically validated and included if we are to adequately validate the spiritual activity that is hermeneutics. Concerns over the way in which spiritual disciplines might be used is not an adequate reason to avoid dealing with this issue. Growing pains over the use of spiritual disciplines will exist along with their benefits over time. Rational thought was refined and given direction (whether rightly or wrongly) for its role in hermeneutics, which gave rise to a certain type of thinking in hermeneutical method that produced greater

---

82. Fee, *Listening to the Spirit*; Wallace, "Holy Spirit and Hermeneutics," 4.

83. Cp. McCartney and Clayton, *Let the Reader Understand*, 85–89; Fuller, "Holy Spirit's Role," 189.

84. McCartney and Clayton, *Let the Reader Understand*, 178.

85. Hiebert, *Missiological Implications of Epistemological*, 3–14. This could also be termed naïve hermeneutics in keeping with Hiebert's description of positivists/naïve realists.

trust and cohesion in the process (i.e., historical-critical method, exegetical method, authorial intent of the writer, use of original languages, redaction criticism, etc.)

Spiritual disciplines must be given this same opportunity to be refined, offered proper attention, and placed in practice to bring about a holistic understanding unencumbered by the fear or ridicule from self-perceived elitist advocates of traditional methods and hard-science approaches. Spiritual disciplines must be part and parcel to the hermeneutical process because "our concern in coming to the text is to hear from God. No other stance is exegetically in keeping with the text itself."[86] *Hermeneutics is foremost a spiritual act!*

What are the spiritual disciplines that should be included in our hermeneutical process? How do we carry out spiritual disciplines in the hermeneutical process? This chapter will not adequately answer those questions, but the suggestions that follow are the start of an attempt to consider the practical implications of spiritual disciplines within the hermeneutical process.

I would agree with Fee in claiming that the end-result of the hermeneutical process should result in a deepening of Christian spirituality.[87] However, I am making a different claim. I am stating that spirituality should be part of our hermeneutic.

Hermeneutics Guided by Scripture

Related to the issue of spiritual disciplines is the issue of allowing the Bible to guide believers in the hermeneutical process. Does the Bible offer insights and even examples for its own interpretation? Caldwell, whose focus is ethnohermeneutics, advocates that "no one hermeneutical method is inspired; each and every method simply emerges from its own unique hermeneutical milieu [including those in the Bible]."[88] Caldwell is correct in pointing out that there is no way to avoid the hermeneutical tendencies of a particular society, because societies have no other starting point than their own worldview. However, left to their own, this presents the same danger as found in the West—that the society may subconsciously develop a narrow and highly ethnocentric

---

86. Fee, *Listening to the Spirit*, 14.
87. Ibid., 4.
88. Caldwell, "Towards Ethnohermeneutics," 32.

hermeneutical approach that is erroneously propagated as a norm in cross-cultural missionary endeavors.

At the same time, the Bible does not teach a single hermeneutical method that emerges from Scripture.[89] Specialists dealing with intertextuality, the exegetical use of Old Testament Scripture by New Testament writers, consistently demonstrate multiple hermeneutical understandings within the Bible.[90] Since cultural and worldview values do play an important role in the hermeneutical process, we cannot in a wholesale manner claim that hermeneutics in the Bible are normative since there are a multiplicity of cultures, worldviews, and hermeneutical models presented in Scripture. If all the hermeneutical models contained within Scripture were adopted together, it would take a lifetime of adopting biblical worldviews just to begin the process of Bible interpretation. However, students in Caldwell's ethnohermeneutics course were certainly in agreement that the Holy Spirit is paramount and universal in the interpretative process.[91]

As shown in the previous chapter, I start with the assumption that the Bible does teach us ways of interpreting and understanding God's message, and many of those are spiritual ways. The Bible demonstrates a multiplicity of hermeneutical insights that can synergistically integrate and provide holistic understanding.[92] For example, the Bible demonstrates a slow (often grudging) process in which Israel, as the people of God, learned to respect the ethnic perceptions and epistemologies of other ethnic groups (for example, Acts 10, 15, 26). It has likewise been a slow process for Western hermeneutical method, but this biblical motif is one way that hermeneutics can be informed and shaped.

A great deal of the problem dealing with hermeneutics is similar to that of missionary practice. Missionaries have to be capable of understanding their own cultural values as they relate to God's message so that the Christian message can be properly translated to the cultural context where the missionary is serving.[93] It is critical then that the Bible inform our hermeneutics, and likewise our hermeneutics must be a translated-

89. Brownson, *Speaking the Truth*, 44.

90. Beale, *Right Doctrine*; LaSor, "*Sensus Plenior* and Interpretation," 274–75; McCartney, "Should We Employ," 8.

91. Caldwell, "Syllabus."

92. Marshall, "Developing a Biblical Hermeneutic," 12.

93. for example Walls, *Missionary Movement*, 112 n. 2.

hermeneutics infused with biblical integrity. There are principles that can be taken from Scripture that should be helpful to guide Christians hermeneutically.[94]

The Holy Spirit

Throughout the New Testament, missionaries misunderstood God's grace extended to the Gentiles because of predetermined assumptions. These assumptions were most often addressed by God through the work of the Holy Spirit. Nicodemus in John 3 demonstrates ignorance of the Spirit, but likewise illustrates that no one can predict the ways in which the Spirit will work. Acts 10, often referred to as Peter's conversion, primarily demonstrates the tremendous difficulty in changing the prescribed notions of the missionary.

We should likewise heed this caution in our own time. To assume that the Holy Spirit will only act in a certain capacity is to undermine the capacity of the Holy Spirit.[95] This assumption quenches the role of the Holy Spirit in leading God's people into mission. To force the Holy Spirit into any prescribed mode of operation is to limit the Spirit. While it may be helpful to understand how the Spirit has worked, we should avoid the tendency toward generalizing the Spirit's activity and be observant of the many instances in Scripture where God's missionary people missed or even acted as barriers to the role of the Holy Spirit in mission. At the same time, we must clearly understand the role of the Spirit in mission. "[T]he active agent of mission is a power that rules, guides, and goes before the church: the free, sovereign, living power of the Spirit of God. Mission is not just something that the church does; it is something that is done by the Spirit, who is himself the witness, who changes both the world and the church, who always goes before the church in its missionary journey."[96] While many would agree that the Holy Spirit has a predominant role in mission, how is it that we can think of hermeneutics apart from this same guidance?

---

94. Allen, *Spiritual Theology*, 135–36; McCartney and Clayton, *Let the Reader Understand*, 61–69.

95. Cp. Allen, *Spiritual Theology*, 10; Fuller, "Holy Spirit's Role," 192; McCartney and Clayton, *Let the Reader Understand*, 75–77; Osborne, *Hermeneutical Spiral*, 340–41; Wallace, "Holy Spirit and Hermeneutics," 3–4.

96. Newbigin, *Open Secret*, 56.

A Missional Critique of Current Hermeneutical Theory

Exegetical work on the role of the Holy Spirit in hermeneutics has focused on specific texts (predominantly 1 Cor 2:12–14; 1 John 2:20, 27), but this is only a small portion of the biblical witness.[97] Acts 1:2 points out that instructions were given by the Holy Spirit to the apostolic missionaries. Furthermore, the famous account of the Holy Spirit in Acts 2 comes as a watershed to provide an understanding of God's missionary intentions for the Gentile world.

It was not through the scientific historical-grammatical method in Acts 10 that Peter developed a new understanding of mission through Cornelius' receiving the Holy Spirit. It was through revelation given in a dream on the roof of a tannery, coupled with the unmistakable direction of the Holy Spirit (Acts 10:19) and the timing of the Holy Spirit coming upon the Gentiles (Acts 10:44). This was the hermeneutical path, despite ample Old Testament accounts that consistently demonstrated what Peter (and most Jews) had missed—Israel was to be a missionary nation to the Gentiles! The role of the Holy Spirit was more than a conviction of sin, dealing with prejudice, or mere illumination. The Holy Spirit gave Peter a means of interpreting Scripture. New "data" was imparted to Peter and validated by his missionary experience of the Holy Spirit's interaction with Cornelius. This resulted in Peter's ability to correctly interpret the existing body of Scripture (Acts 10:34–36) and share this new understanding with fellow believers (Acts 11:15–18; 15:7–19). This missional re-interpretation of Scripture was something that the larger community of Jewish "exegetes" had consistently misinterpreted. God did provide a new means of understanding what had already been revealed and written; that running throughout Scripture was the backbone of mission to the nations.[98]

It was not the scientific historical-grammatical method in Acts 9 that led to Paul's radical change in understanding God and mission. It was through Jesus' appearance on the Damascus road that Paul was transformed in his understanding and thereby given a new theology of mission in his time. However, Paul was highly trained in the method of his day and one of the most knowledgeable of Scripture. While one could argue that the Holy Spirit is not prevalent in this instance (compare 9:17), my main point is that it was decisively through spiritual

---

97. Cp. Fuller, "Holy Spirit's Role"; Wallace, "Holy Spirit and Hermeneutics."

98. Cp. Bevans, "God inside Out," 103; Kaiser, "The Great Commission in the Old Testament"; Kaiser, *Mission in the OT*.

Missiological Hermeneutics

means that Paul was forced to transform his interpretation of existing Scripture. This lead to new insights in Paul's understanding of God and God's will.

Certainly this sort of query could continue with the Holy Spirit interceding so that Scripture might be understood and interpreted for the Ethiopian eunuch (Acts 8:30–31) and for the leading of Philip in mission (Acts 8:29). It was through the leading of the Holy Spirit that Paul and Barnabas were sent out to proclaim God's message in the synagogues (Acts 13:2–5). "The Holy Spirit is party to the decisions of a Church Council" (Acts 15:8, 28) appropriately interpreting the Old Testament for the Gentiles.[99] Paul even cites the role of the Holy Spirit in noting that Israel was unwilling to correctly interpret Scripture (Acts 28:25–28), which is very similar to Stephen's use of Israel's stubbornness in mission history (Acts 7). Both passages demonstrate that continued resistance to the Holy Spirit was coupled with resistance to God's mission, showing that the scholars of the day had misinterpreted Scripture (Acts 7:51; 28:25).

> The gift of the Spirit was a visible, recognisable, unquestionable sign that God had accepted these Gentiles as His own people, and before that fact the most massive and fundamental theological convictions simply had to give way. The Holy Spirit may be the last article of the Creed but in the New Testament it is the first fact of experience. We are accustomed to discuss the Holy Spirit as a doctrine after we have dealt with creation, incarnation, atonement and so on. In the New Testament the Holy Spirit appears rather as a sheer fact, God's recognisable witness (e.g. Acts 15.8) to His own presence, and therefore entitled to right of way before all arguments based on an *a priori* reasoning. The repeated use of the word "witness" in relation to the Spirit is a reminder of just this point: the Holy Spirit's presence is the plain fact by which we know God's mind towards us.[100]

The Holy Spirit also provided leadership in mission stating that Paul was not to enter Asia (Acts 16:6–7), as well as offering the prophesy of Agabus (given by the Holy Spirit) regarding Paul's capture (Acts 21:10–11). We cannot assume that the Holy Spirit so easily provides "data" for missionary direction and understanding while offering pre-

---

99. Newbigin, *Household of God*, 115.
100. Ibid., 114.

A Missional Critique of Current Hermeneutical Theory

cious little when it comes to direction in the interpretation of Scripture. A dichotomy in these two areas is unacceptable because it is simply not biblically defensible.

Regardless of how one might evaluate the activity of the New Testament that leads to a proper missional hermeneutic of the Old Testament, it is clear that spiritual activity did exist and that human understanding was guided by spiritual activity. Human reasoning was not an independent and predominant means of interpretation within Scripture—it was the problem of the day, much like our own dilemma. "Jesus promised his disciples that they would receive the gift of the Holy Spirit, the Spirit of the Father and of the Son, and that the Spirit would interpret to them the meaning of his words and deeds and lead them into the truth as a whole. That promise was fulfilled. This gift of the Spirit, however, did not make the disciples infallible any more than the same gift given to the prophetic writers of the Old Testament made them infallible."[101]

The plain and simple fact is that there is an abundance of instances in the New Testament in which missionaries were given "new data" in order to understand the nature of God's mission, despite background, knowledge, and the existence of the Scripture of the day. Therefore, missiologists must avoid the trap of claiming boundaries over the role of the Holy Spirit in hermeneutics.

For those who want to thrust upon Scripture the idea that monumental themes, such as God's mission or the leading of the Holy Spirit, are for "that day only," I would respond by noting that the ability to eliminate mission and the Holy Spirit on such an unfounded basis will allow anything, even Christ's atonement, to be antiquated and relativized in the same way. Virtually anything sacred in Scripture can be eliminated at will.

Admittedly, the Holy Spirit is most often self-effacing in Scripture, constantly giving glory to the Son in mission, which makes it very difficult to see all of the ways the Holy Spirit works. However, formulaic conceptions of the Holy Spirit will only diminish our capacity to follow the leading of the Holy Spirit, resulting in a spiritual blindness that continues to misunderstand the Holy Spirit (compare John 3). Those who

---

101. Newbigin, *Proper Confidence*, 90.

address formulaic misconceptions often develop a renewed perspective in following the lead of the Holy Spirit.[102]

This is quite evident in three modern day missionaries who have had different ways of seeing the Holy Spirit work in their missionary activity. Roland Allen began his career as an Anglican Missionary in China but eventually wrote the mission classic *The Spontaneous Expansion of the Church* addressing the way in which paternalism and control in mission had crushed any opportunity for the Holy Spirit to move freely among the newly developing churches.[103] C. Peter Wagner began as a sociologist and church growth expert but was consistently moved toward healing and prayer as a means of missionary activity.[104] Charles Kraft began as an anthropologist and communications expert but has consistently moved toward deliverance ministry as an effort toward missional freedom.[105] The Holy Spirit simply could not be contained or rigidly defined for these missiologists, but the Holy Spirit changed the course of their lives. Realistically the Holy Spirit cannot be diagrammed or dissected for study, but the influence of the Holy Spirit is evident by the transformation and new understanding given in the midst of God's missionary activity.

Prayer

Figure 11 is a diagram of different spiritual dimensions loosely illustrating the way that these interact with God and Scripture. This diagram will be referenced repeatedly in this section.

---

102. Archer, "Pentecostal Hermeneutics."
103. Allen, *Spontaneous Expansion*.
104. Wagner, *Have a Healing Ministry*.
105. Kraft, *Christianity with Power*.

A Missional Critique of Current Hermeneutical Theory

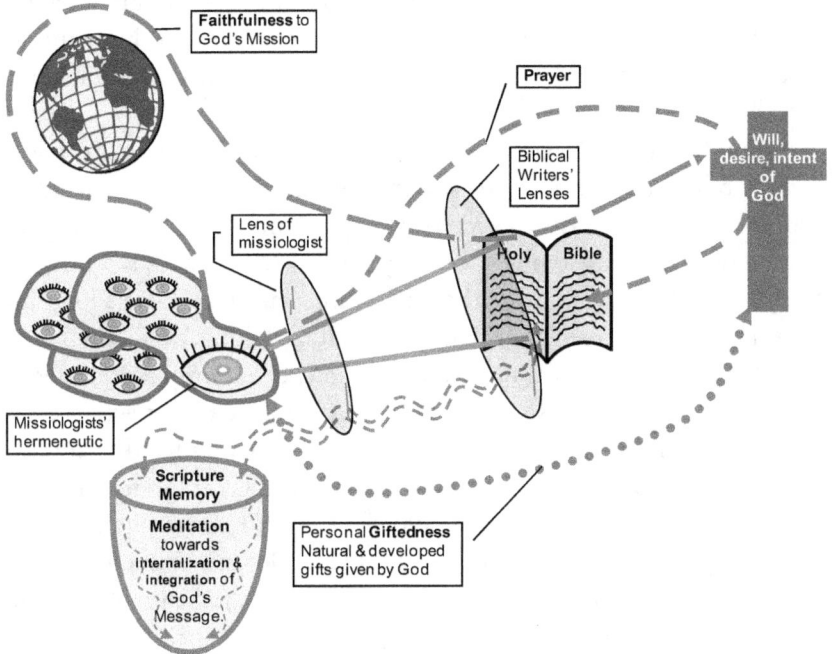

Figure 11: Spiritual Dimensions in Hermeneutics

If missiology assumes that God is the ultimate source for understanding God's intentions, then prayer has the unique role of allowing missiologists to petition for understanding in Scripture. As shown in Figure 11, prayer has the advantage of circumventing the biblical lens since God is the focus of our petition.[106] Prayer likewise benefits from God's ability to skillfully speak into our own cultural context (or lens). Simply put, God is aware of our cultural background and has the ability to offer insight into biblical contexts through prayer. Without prayer we may never otherwise discern portions of Scripture.

Related to prayer, Newbigin suggested that science is actually a closed system of thought because it relies on itself to validate its own

---

106. Figure 14 (at the end of this chapter) does attempt to illustrate the Holy Spirit as part of our overall hermeneutical understanding, but the illustration is intentionally meant to have broad characteristics showing that the Spirit can work in many ways through many methods. The illustration primarily serves as a reminder of the Holy Spirit's involvement and is not intended to be definitive.

Missiological Hermeneutics

hypotheses.[107] Conversely, Newbigin claimed that Christianity is not a closed system because Christianity seeks a source beyond humanity—God—to lead and guide Christians in the process of understanding our faith.[108]

Building upon Newbigin's insight, prayer then allows us to reach beyond our own understanding and engage with God for spiritual understanding. Without prayer, hermeneutics is doomed to become a circular system of human reasoning. Certainly human reasoning has a place in the process, but it cannot be the only place that missiologists look for meaning. We must recognize that "practically speaking, a Christian does need to ask God to reveal the meaning of a text to him, not in order to avoid the labor of exegesis or to get some guarantee of correctness, but in recognition that all genuine insight comes by God's hand."[109] Prayer is not a means of avoiding the research and struggle to understand the nature of Scripture, but prayer should be central to that struggle.[110]

Biblical examples of prayerful hermeneutics are abundant, as already shown in Daniel 9. In Jesus' famous prayer in John 17, pleading to the Father for the care of missionaries, Jesus' prayer includes a request for the Father to teach them words of truth (17:17). The account of Acts 10 that we have already discussed begins with Peter praying (10:9) and this opens the doors for the Holy Spirit and the cross-cultural community of Jews and Gentiles (10:19; compare 11:4), allowing Peter to understand the implications of his visions. Hermeneutical insight takes place through the interaction of multiple disciplines that cannot be splintered in real practice. The narrative of Luke 11:5–13 likewise illustrates the integration of prayer, the Holy Spirit and gifting in understanding. This passage practically cries out for believers to repeatedly pray for understanding. Paul likewise prayed for believers to grow in their understanding and wisdom (Eph 1:16–19; Phil 1:9–11) and interestingly enough, Paul prayed that this would take place through spiritual wisdom and understanding (Col 1:9–13).[111]

---

107. Newbigin, *Gospel in Pluralist Society*, 48.
108. Newbigin, *Truth to Tell*, 63.
109. McCartney and Clayton, *Let the Reader Understand*, 178.
110. Allen, *Spiritual Theology*, 51–52.
111. Osborne, *Hermeneutical Spiral*, 340.

A Missional Critique of Current Hermeneutical Theory

In the Orthodox Church, decisions of biblical interpretation are collaborative and reflected in councils through the ages.[112] Given the radical individualism of our day, we must learn from this and integrate community with prayer. "Christianity's appeal to the understanding has to be balanced by a reaching out to God in prayer. However natural it is to seek to enlarge our understanding of God through our mind, Christianity is not merely an intellectual option."[113] There are rare cases in Scripture where group decisions were wrong, but these decisions were not rooted in prayer (for example, Sodom and Gomorrah—Gen 19, Moses and the golden calf—Exod 32, Isaiah and Jeremiah addressing Israel and Judah, the Corinthian Church and the man of sin—1 Cor 5, Lystra and Derbe's response to Paul and Barnabus—Acts 14). Missiology should advocate praying together as a means of understanding God's meaning in Scripture.

In the Fall 2002 class of Biblical Foundations of Mission, I informed over eighty students in the class that I expected them to pray together in small groups in order to understand the meaning of the themes that flow through Scripture. I even went so far as to encourage them to cite their understanding from prayer as validly as any footnote they might find from other authors (I was intentionally giving them the opportunity to place their biblical insights through prayer on equal footing with traditional methods of research). Though the students were unaccustomed to citing prayer in their papers (a tragedy in my opinion), many students noted significant breakthroughs in their understanding and nearly one quarter of the class submitted final papers that were of high enough quality to serve as model papers.

---

112. Stamoolis, *Eastern Orthodox Mission Theology*, 15–16, 114–15.
113. Allen, *Spiritual Theology*, 62.

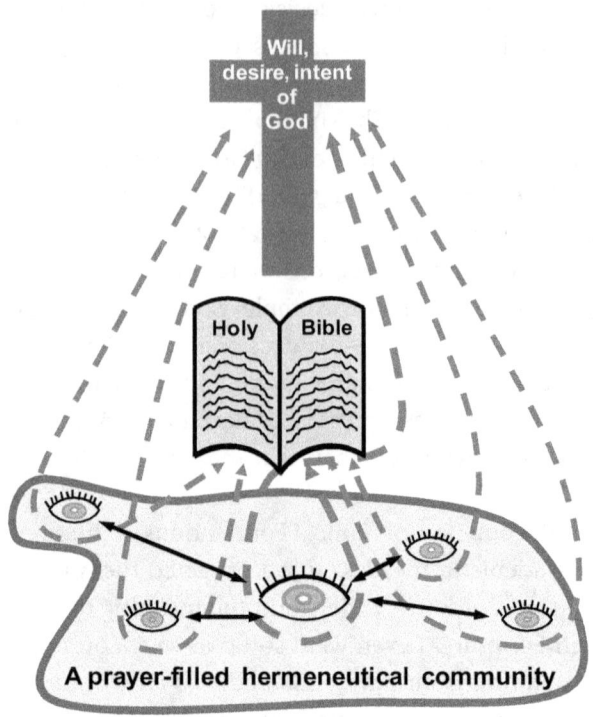

Figure 12: The Role of Prayer

Figure 12 is an attempt to illustrate the dynamic of group prayer. This is a simple diagram focusing on the fact that the prayer-filled hermeneutical community is in conversation with God to understand Scripture and in conversation with one another. There is no separation between the vertical and horizontal. Biblical insights developed through prayer by missiologists should not be independent of others. A community of prayer offers greater protection in addressing individualism and validates the understanding from God through the manifestation of a united effort to seek God. What has already been mentioned about community is critical if prayer is to be given its proper precedence. The process can easily be sabotaged by seeking out others who are in agreement prior to prayer or by remaining within dominating structures. This is one reason why it is beneficial to practice in the classroom because students often come from a variety of backgrounds, which naturally shields against the human tendency toward homogeneity.

A Missional Critique of Current Hermeneutical Theory

Giftedness

Giftedness is an enormous topic that cannot be covered in this brief overview. However, it would be inconceivable to consider the role of spiritual issues related to hermeneutics and not consider the impact of gifting. Giftedness, shown in Figure 11 as a dotted line, is naturally given by God and developed through time in Christian maturation. Gifts are often best developed when natural gifts are stretched through continued effort in mission so that gifting is sharpened. However, gifts can be abused, such as false prophets, who have real God-given prophetic abilities and refuse to use this gifting for God (as already seen in Balaam—Num 22). Gifts can also be given and taken by God at any time.

Since the area of giftedness is so vast, I can only illustrate the role that gifting plays in hermeneutics through an example. Prophetic gifting is the example that I would like to consider. Missiologists would rarely consider their roles prophetic because biblical prophets carry tremendous burden and often tremendous scorn from their audiences. Quite often, the prophets are sent to reform the people of God as were seen in the messages of Isaiah, Jeremiah, Ezekiel, Hosea, Joel, and Malachi.

Missiologists who focus on ecclesiology are likewise prophetic (though I doubt they would be comfortable with this title). They have called the people of God toward their purpose in following their God-given responsibility in mission. Works focused upon reforming the church for mission include William Carey's *An Enquiry into the Obligations of Christians, to use Means for the Conversion of the Heathens*, John R. Mott's *The Evangelization of the World in This Generation*, Lesslie Newbigin's *Is Christ Divided?*, Wilbert Shenk's *Write the Vision* and Charles Van Engen's *God's Missionary People* (certainly more could be listed).[114] These missiologists have written prophetically to the church calling for reform in the Church's understanding and role of their God-given purpose in mission—much in the same way that Old Testament prophets called Israel to faithfulness in their purpose among the nations.

In this example, these missiologists have used their gifting to offer a living hermeneutic that offers greater depth in interpreting the Old Testament. They offer an example that provides a link to the past so that the role of Old Testament prophets is more prominently understood. It is unlikely that this was their intention. However, it is the natural result

---

114. Carey, *Enquiry into the Obligations*; Mott, *Evangelization of the World*; Newbigin, *Is Christ Divided*; Shenk, *Write the Vision*; Van Engen, *God's Missionary People*.

of men and women carrying out God's mission through their gifting that permits the Christian community to re-experience the context and struggle of missionaries in the Bible.

One of the greatest gifts in Scripture is the gift of God's grace. Western society has, however, separated grace from truth in a quest for objective knowledge. In the same way that prophetic gifting offers new interpretation of biblical contexts, the infusing of God's grace is essential for Western Christianity in order to re-interpret the role of truth and theology as it relates to mission.[115] Newbigin, following Augustine's "*credo ut intellegam*" ("[I] believe in order to understand."), addresses the missional interrelationship between grace and truth.[116] "[T]he great objective reality is God but he is also the supreme subject who wills to make himself known to us not by a power that would cancel out our subjectivity, but by a grace that calls forth and empowers our subjective faculties, our power to grow in knowledge through believing. We believe in order to understand, and our struggle to understand is a response to grace."[117]

Scripture in Our Hearts

Scripture memory may not be on the typical list of spiritual disciplines, but this focus is critical for hermeneutics to be sustained in the life of missionaries. In looking at this field, I am not suggesting Scripture memorization, although that may be helpful. I am suggesting that we need to have a living account of Scripture in our hearts that allows us to relate our current missionary context to the biblical contexts, which then re-shapes our understanding of the Bible in the midst of our missionary journey. "The person who allows the biblical story to be the all-surrounding ambience of daily life and who continually seeks to place all experiences in this context finds that daily life is a continuous conversation with the one whose character is revealed in the biblical story taken as a whole. There is a world of difference between this and a concept of God developed out of reflection on life's experience apart from this story."[118]

---

115. Brownson, *Speaking the Truth*, 82.
116. Augustine et al., *Works of Saint Augustine*, 240.
117. Newbigin, *Truth to Tell*, 36.
118. Newbigin, *Proper Confidence*, 88–89.

Scripture memory is shown in Figure 11 as a bowl-shaped object that relates to the Bible through our own cultural lenses and the lenses of Scripture. However, this ultimately resides in the life of the believer, but is consistently related to Scripture (illustrated by the wavy lines). "Through the meditative reading of the Bible we apply the scriptures to our own moral lives, and eventually this reading shapes us in such a way that we can receive greater knowledge of God through the scriptures. As we allow the knowledge of God gained through the scriptures to guide us, nourishing the heart and mind, we are increasingly formed into the likeness of God. Spiritual growth brings illumination of new and deeper meanings hidden in the Bible."[119]

As the witness of Scripture is ingrained in us, meditation upon Scripture follows naturally, leading toward a deeper impact in understanding Scripture. In the midst of this deepening, there is a persistent internalization and integration of God's message since Scripture is at the forefront of missionary thinking. This allows for the reflexive hermeneutic (discussed earlier) that re-interprets mission through Scripture and re-interprets Scripture through mission. "It is [possible] . . . to indwell the story as it is told in the Bible so that we are not looking at it, but looking through it to understand our world. That is what Christians did before they were trained in the critical method. It is how millions of Christians still use the Bible."[120]

Internalization of Scripture occurs in the midst of meditation and re-reading Scripture so that the biblical witness is ingrained in the essence of who we are becoming as missionaries and missiologists. Therefore,

> we have to recognize that we must allow the Bible to provide us with its own account of what it means to speak of the word of God. We have to learn by the actual practice of living with the Bible how and in what ways God speaks. In the words of the Prayer Book collect, we have to hear, read, mark, and learn and inwardly digest the Bible, taking it wholly into ourselves in a way that shapes the very substance of our thinking and feeling and doing. It is less important to ask a Christian what he or she believes about the Bible than it is to inquire what he or she does with it.[121]

119. Allen, *Spiritual Theology*, 125.
120. Newbigin, *Word in Season*, 111.
121. Newbigin, *Proper Confidence*, 86–87.

Only with Scripture memory can we overcome Western fragmentation and achieve the needed integration that occurs as we live out the Christian faith with an ingrained understanding of Scripture that transforms our missionary practice and our interpretation of God's mission in the Bible.

Faithfulness

As a final focus on spirituality in hermeneutics, the importance of faithfulness must be addressed. Faithfulness to God is related to missionary experience. Faithfulness will lead to some type of missionary experience, but the converse is not necessarily true. Experience, in relation to hermeneutics, offers unforeseen perspectives that shed new light upon events in Scripture. As a result, missionary activity infuses our experiences to help those experiences redevelop our hermeneutical method for understanding Scripture. However, faithfulness relates to Scripture through an ultimate focus upon God and God's will in mission. As a result, faithfulness to God's mission provides a hermeneutical lens for those outside the community of Christian faith, which they can use to interpret Scripture.

Faithfulness, as shown in Figure 11, works in the midst of the world and through Scripture to faithfully seek God in the midst of missionary activity. Our action in the midst of the world results in the practice of biblical motifs and indirectly expresses our understanding of the motifs developed in Scripture. For instance, those who never involved themselves in God's mission indirectly imply that the Bible has no interest in mission. Likewise, those who feed the hungry and care for the sick imply that the Bible does have a message about God's mission to the sick and the hungry.

This lived-out action becomes a faithful expression of our interpretation of God's ideas in Scripture. These actions then function as a lived-out understanding and interpretation of the values we find in Scripture. This actually allows the non-Christian community to interpret the message of Scripture through our lives.

If we live out those actions primarily within the church, then non-Christians will view Scripture as having little to do with mission. If we live out those actions primarily involved in God's missionary activity, then non-Christians will understand that mission is integral to the message of Scripture. For the nations observing Christianity, this means that

A Missional Critique of Current Hermeneutical Theory

"the only possible hermeneutic of the gospel is a congregation which believes it."[122]

As the nations interpret the Bible through us, their understanding provides feedback regarding our faithful expression of Biblical themes, belief, and actions. We must prepare to ask, "Do the nations have some accurate understanding of God's nature in Scripture through our missionary activity?"

If the answer is "yes," then those seeking God from the nations have indirectly developed a hermeneutic for the Bible. The nations have then begun the process of interpreting Scripture, which means that biblical interpretation is intrinsically missionary in nature. If nothing else, this implication should give missiologists an overwhelming sense of what is at stake in the field of hermeneutics.

> I am sure that it is vital to insist that the discernment of the Spirit can only come by living in the Spirit; that because there is in truth one Spirit who is Lord and God, He is able to make Himself known as one to those who earnestly seek Him; that all who have ever had any taste of His power to teach, convince and subdue a gathering of Christians coming together with all their clashing wills and affections, know that this is true; and that whenever we try to seek some other sort of security against error and disunity, some criteria of judgment or rules of life which can be operated apart from this discernment of the Spirit in the Spirit, some ecclesiastical order in which we can be secure against error without constantly engaging in the risky adventure of seeking truth, secure against schism without constantly paying the price of unity in costly charity, we are in fact building not according to the Spirit but according to the flesh.[123]

A Priority Lens Based in Humility

A final look at our hermeneutical lens is now in order. Figure 13 illustrates a hermeneutical lens that is prioritized foremost with God (including the Holy Spirit, shown at the top). Other spiritual areas follow along with various human achievements that were initially discussed. It may seem to be an over-reaction to place rational methods at the very

---

122. Newbigin, *Gospel in Pluralist Society*, 232.
123. Newbigin, *Household of God*, 126–27.

bottom, but proper humility before God demands that caution is exercised when human achievements are involved.[124]

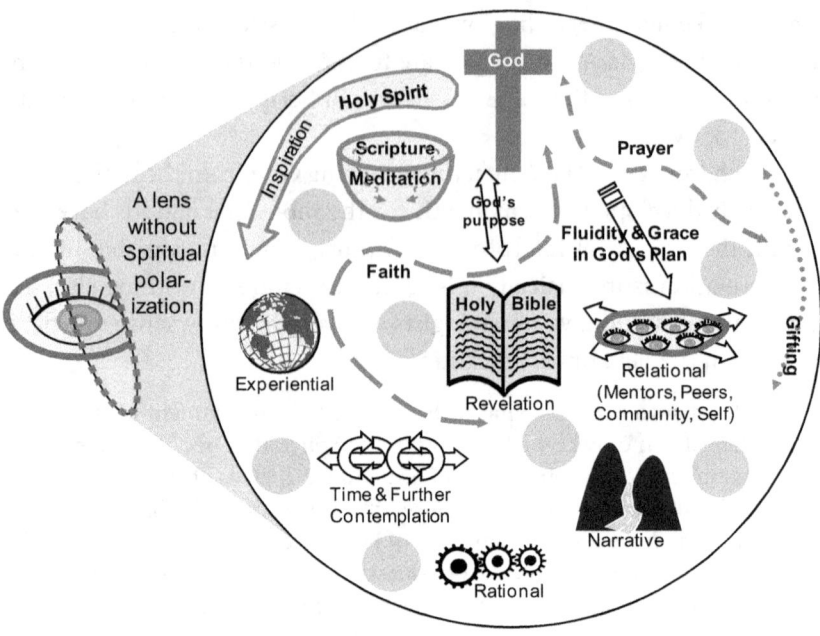

Figure 13: A Priority Lens Based in Humility

The prioritizing of disciplines is important, but the main difference is that spiritual areas are no longer polarized. This does not mean that some sort of objective perspective has been created. Certainly, we will continue to have our blind spots (represented by the darkened circles), but we will at least be addressing issues that we can see. It is still the case that we see imperfectly (1 Cor 13:12), but our vision is more holistic and less filled with prejudice.

The representation given here is not intended to be complete. The list of additional disciplines that could be added would be overwhelming. The main point of this lens is to allow for the integration of the spiritual with the rational, the experiential with the faithful, and so on.

---

124. Allen, *Spiritual Theology*, 78; Beeby, *Canon and Mission*, 113.

A Missional Critique of Current Hermeneutical Theory

Holistic Hermeneutics

The final diagram in this chapter is then the culmination of all the areas we have discussed, which necessarily makes for a complex diagram. Figure 14 illustrates the combination of multiple disciplines integrated synergistically to provide a representative hermeneutical understanding for Biblical Theology of Mission. Faithfulness and experience travel a similar path, but only faith approaches God. Cultural understanding and community influence understanding, but only prayer seeks to enter into dialogue with the author of our faith. History and the holism of the tapestry act as guides but only the Holy Spirit moves pervasively in and through the interpretive process.

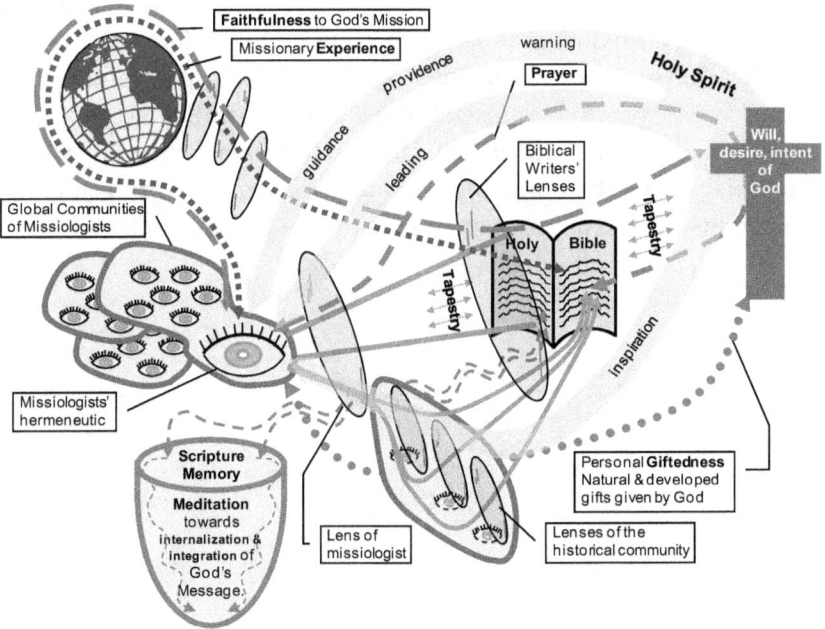

Figure 14: Holistic Hermeneutics

CONCLUSION

The young LDS missionaries who visited me did make a valid request in asking me to pray for God's validity in discerning Scripture. However, the LDS have erred where Western missiology has failed. To the LDS missionaries, I would have to point out that prayer cannot stand as the sole means of discernment. For Western missiology, I would have to point out that prayer (and other spiritual disciplines) must be included if we believe Scripture can be trusted to guide us in hermeneutics.

Various Christian traditions have for some time debated over Christian faith as it relates to prayer for miraculous healings versus the use of modern medical practice. Insightfully, some have solved the dilemma by recognizing that the all-knowing God of the universe could manage to work in the miraculous and in modern medicine at the same time. Therefore, these same Christians faithfully pray for miracles and for God's hand to guide the surgeon's scalpel.

As we now move from hermeneutical theory to case studies in hermeneutics throughout the next two chapters, my hope is that we would never become a polarized discipline in which only one agenda holds priority. Missiologists seeking to interpret Scripture can likewise pray for God's concerns to be made known through spiritual direction while likewise praying for insight in the use of scientific methods such as the historical-critical approach. Ultimately our understanding will be on display before the world. May God transform us as we diligently understand God's missionary nature in Scripture that has so transformed the hearts of faith-filled believers.

FOUR

A Missional Critique of the Hermeneutics Used in a Difficult Missional Issue

A Case Study

Thesis of this chapter: Authors have, for the most part, followed an epistemology based entirely on modernity's assumption of the over-arching supremacy of truth with little or no thought for the role of missiological hermeneutics in guiding their own field response to African polygamy. As such, authors have not attempted to develop a biblical mission practice that informs and critiques their response to polygamy. Instead, they have based their arguments on the false assumption that a given theological stance is the starting point for addressing the practice. Likewise, poorly developed hermeneutics and highly dogmatic interpretations combined with the absence of critique over the failure in biblically informed mission practice are signs that cultural agendas are being thrust upon biblical interpretation.

During the Fall Quarter of 2003, I was teaching on biblical examples of contextual practice with respect to specific messages. In this case, I was illustrating the highly contextual admonishment of Nathan's prophetic rebuke of David (2 Sam 12). Nathan's illustration employs sheep and a herdsman along with other contextual ideas familiar to David, and this allows for David to consider his sin in a far more objective manner.[1] Having had a good response from former classes when teaching this same material, I was unprepared for the question posed by an African student in the front-row—"What do you think his passage is

---

1. Van Engen and Redford, "Syllabus," 106 originally Redford.

saying about polygamy?" Though I was aware of the use of this passage in defending polygamy, I had not read the breadth of authors compiled in this chapter. At the time, I had no idea that some would avoid the passage while others would claim that Nathan's words could not be taken literally and yet others would argue that the passage undoubtedly indicates God's approval of polygamy.

This chapter is a historical investigation of the hermeneutics that have been used to reject, allow or even promote the practice of polygamy. Specifically, this chapter will be limited to writings that address African forms of polygamy.[2] Though this will hopefully provide a helpful critique for a stronger hermeneutic when addressing this topic, the larger framework of the chapter is to critically examine the hermeneutical tendencies. Likewise, the greater purpose is to aid the field of Biblical Theology of Mission by demonstrating biblically founded practices that

---

2. As a case study in looking at hermeneutics in mission, this chapter will look specifically at the integrity of biblical interpretation in relation to the practice of African polygamy. There are at least four main bodies of literature discussing polygamy other than the Bible. (1) The first was most likely polygamy among Muslims, but there is very little literature addressing this group, most likely because of the historically small percentage of missionaries serving among Muslims. (2) The second pre-dates the modern missionary movement and seems to have begun in the 16th century with John Milton. These were primarily unconventional aristocracy who toyed with the idea, although Milton had a genuine interest. (3) The third was most likely African polygamy but this probably received the greatest attention by missionaries due to relatively large missionary efforts in Africa along with the fact that missionaries saw this as a critical issue to address. (4) The fourth were those addressing polygamy among the Mormons or Latter Days Saints.

In order to narrow the field, polygamy among the Church of Jesus Christ of Latter Days Saints (LDS) and the Islamic community are not a focus of this chapter. It should also be noted that polygamy, as seen by the LDS, is more than just a cultural form of marriage. Unlike African polygamy, the LDS historically practiced polygamy because it was considered a good spiritual practice that would benefit the LDS in the afterlife. Furthermore, the present day LDS church continues to practice "celestial marriage" which in essence is a continuation of polygamy in a spiritual form (which the LDS refer to as an "ordinance") even though the practice of physical polygamy was revoked by the LDS church long ago. The "Mormons" who continue to practice physical polygamy today are fundamentalist Mormons who have long ago broken away from the LDS church in discord over this issue. However, addressing polygamy with the LDS church or the fundamentalist Mormon groups takes on a different nature primarily because these forms of polygamy are compounded by the spiritual implications, which are typically not present in African polygamy. Due to the fact that the issues of Mormon polygamy are more complex, I would think that missionary experience among African polygamous families would be an excellent *prerequisite* for Protestant missionaries who plan to work among the LDS or fundamentalist Mormons.

result in stronger and healthier hermeneutics. There are few if any studies that attempt to critique the underlying hermeneutic found in the various arguments over polygamy.[3] In order to provide a valid critique of the underlying hermeneutics, I have provided direction in those cases where there was an obvious interpretational bias.[4] Though some authors exhibited greater hermeneutical problems compared to others, there was no single group that had avoided all hermeneutical pitfalls.

In relationship to the thesis of this chapter, there are a number of lessons for those cases in which the missionaries' culture differs radically from the biblical cultures (or certain cultures today). Notably, poorly developed and highly dogmatic missional hermeneutics are likely signs that cultural agendas have been thrust upon biblical interpretation. The issue of polygamy is also illustrative of a case in which the missionaries' cultural expectations result in human agendas that often manifest questionable hermeneutical tendencies. As such, Scripture must be allowed to inform theology and missionary practice rather than giving a higher priority to a set of worldview values that seem correct.

HISTORY OF BIAS

In order to understand the potential bias, some resources written prior to the modern missions movement, have been uncovered that discuss the issue of polygamy.[5] Two of these works demonstrate significant bias

---

3. Welch's thesis has helpful critiques throughout (Welch, "Biblical Perspective on Polygamy"). Holter makes a very broad critique over the parallels between African polygamy and biblical polygamy, but his underlying thesis is addressed in greater detail in the next chapter. Holter critiques Desmond Tutu's claim that "the Biblical worldview in many ways is far more congenial for the African and for the western man—the African is much more on the wavelength of the Bible than Western man was originally (Tutu, "Some African Insights," 19)." In general, Holter agrees with Tutu's claim, but he is calling for a more fully developed anthropological investigation, rather than a superficial assumption that African and biblical forms of polygamy are identical (Holter, *Yahweh in Africa*, 86–87). Kanyoro's work is an excellent example of a strong anthropological and linguistic comparison showing the differences in African and biblical forms of polygamy, as she specifically demonstrates that Africa has no comparative equivalent for the term "concubine" (Kanyoro, "Interpreting OT Polygamy,").

4. None of the authors declare their own biases or areas where they feel they are unbiased, so I have included a section of that nature in order for future researchers to critique my own work.

5. The modern-day missions movement is typically dated by the publication of William Carey's work in 1792 that acted as a catalyst in moving the church into mission (Carey, *Enquiry into the Obligations*).

with respect to the practice of polygamy. The first is a short work from Charles Leslie who claims that polygamy is based "upon the same loose Principles as the other [fornication and adultery]; to give the Range to our Lusts, and let them endure no Limits."[6]

The second is a much longer work written by Patrick Delany (1685–1768), an Irish clergyman, who discussed both sides of the polygamy debate but was adamantly against the practice.[7] Delany's writing points out the "ignorance" of two loosely associated groups, the Free-Thinkers and Deists who were both addressing the biblical view of polygamy in his day.[8] Delany's work gives the overall impression that anyone who disagrees with his claims must be biased, unlearned, and unwise. While Delany does quote from opposing perspectives, this is done for the sole purpose of correcting them. Likewise, Delany feels that anyone of common sense (in other words, having the same set of cultural values as his) will support his arguments.

However, Delany makes no effort to hide his own biases and for this reason his work is quite helpful since he openly displays his prejudices. Delany's main thesis is that polygamy is an abhorrent sin, forbidden in Scripture, but one that the biblical patriarchs ignored since they did not properly understand God's revelation. Furthermore, he claims that polygamy is a sickness that has only brought harm throughout human history. Finally, Delany claims that polygamy is an evil practice to be driven out of society and likens polygamy to a poison while claiming that his arguments act as the anecdote.[9]

Like many later missionaries, Delany is convinced that polygamy is a tremendous barrier for the nations to convert to Christianity, but he only briefly mentions polygamy in Africa.[10] Nevertheless, Delany's work is helpful in painting a picture of the cultural values and theological ideas that would likely be transferred to later missionaries, who heavily opposed African polygamy themselves. It is uncertain if missionaries were aware of Delany's work, but his cultural values are of great

---

6. Leslie, *Letter of Advice*, 14. Leslie did allow for the possibility that a pre-Christian polygamist could join the church and not become a leader, but this is based entirely on his interpretation of 1 Timothy 3:2, 12.

7. Miller, *John Milton*, 142.

8. Delany, *Reflections Upon Polygamy*, 25–26, 26n, 41; cp. Miller, *John Milton*, 143.

9. Delany, *Reflections Upon Polygamy*, viii, 19.

10. Ibid., 22, 158.

importance since he was a clergyman trained in Scripture and Greek.[11] Furthermore, his position that polygamy was a grievous sin, likewise matches the position of all the missionaries and delegates at the 1888 London Missionary Conference.[12]

Corroborating these biases, current authors have included specific ethnocentric or derogatory terms when referring to African polygamists. It is noteworthy that Westerners advocating permission for polygamy prior to the modern missions' movement were addressed derogatorily. However, the term "savage" was reserved solely for African polygamists. For example, African polygamists have been referred to as "savages" who are "full of lust."[13] Additionally, it was believed that Western cultural values were superior to the cultures of the Old Testament and modern day African cultures.[14] Overall, these trends demonstrate the likely presence of pre-existing agendas and biases when addressing polygamy in the African context.[15]

In terms of my own background and biases, I was born in Salt Lake City, Utah, but spent most of my formative years in Indiana. I was not acquainted with polygamous families. Likewise, growing up in the United

---

11. Ibid., 18n, 87–88n.

12. Johnston and Jackson, *Centenary Conference on Protestant Missions*, 48–81. This was likewise the position of Henry Venn and John William Colenso despite Colenso's claim that polygamists should not be required to divorce in order to join the church (Colenso, *Remarks on Proper Treatment*, 3, 5–8; Knight et al., *Memoir of Henry Venn*, 345–57).

13. Wishard, *Bible against Polygamy*, 61; *The Problem of Polygamy*, 7, 20, 41–42, 66.

14. Parrinder, *Bible and Polygamy*, 65.

15. As my wife and I often discussed this issue throughout my time writing this chapter, we had a very interesting conversation one night. We were watching a documentary on "open adoption" (a form of adoption where the birth-mother and her family are allowed to visit and be involved with the child during the child's upbringing. The show was ABC News 20/20 titled "Be My Baby," airing on Friday April 30, 2004 at 10:00pm PDT). This seemed to be a connection to African polygamy and I said "This is our version of polygamy," thinking that this was an American functional equivalent to polygamy. My wife's immediate response was "Yes, but the birth mother and the adoptive father aren't sexually involved!" She was correct, but her response was typical of most Western assumptions—that polygamy is perceived foremost in terms of sexuality. A common Western suspicion is that polygamy is foremost a sexual issue. While there may be cases where sexual attraction is the primary motivation for polygamy (which also happens in monogamous marriage), there are positive motivations as well, such as infertility, a need for assistance in agrarian contexts, the wife's need for female companionship or even modern-day levirate marriage. In short, Western cultural reflexes are likely to misinterpret the motivations for polygamy.

States, I was only familiar with monogamist families. It was not even part of my thinking to consider that a man could have two or more wives until I was involved in missionary work after college. My first encounter with a polygamous family was among the Maasai of East Africa in 1987. I did not feel troubled by the fact that I had encountered polygamist families, but I did not spend much time with them.

FIVE THEOLOGICAL INTERPRETATIONS

Over the centuries of dealing with African polygamy, there are many who have claimed that the topic did not need to be addressed because it was dying off.[16] Nevertheless, most of these authors addressed the topic. Likewise, others have claimed that polygamy was not dying off.[17] In my own discussions with African students, it has become increasingly clear that the issue of polygamy continues today as a complex issue for African Christians while Western Christians are, for the most part, unaware of the problems.

Since this study is historically focused, I have tried to note those points when an author's self-disclosure of his or her journey regarding polygamy has changed their hermeneutic, but this is rare. However, some authors cite some type of renewed understanding of polygamy from Scripture. This is a good indication that the author was willing to lay down his own agenda and allow the Bible to reshape, transform and critique their understandings, as well as potential ethnocentrism and cultural syncretism.

Additionally, in order to gain a clearer understanding of all the authors involved in this field, Table 6 outlines the major author groupings. This table is an attempt to include all those who have written significantly on a biblical understanding of polygamy. "Significant" for this chart is defined as having written biblical data of at least 10 pages or more. In the case of Hastings and Hillman, their earlier (more than 10 page) articles were not mentioned because of their later, more complete works. Holst was added (though only 8 pages) because of his consistent focus on Scripture and excellent work.

---

16. Adutchum, "Church and Issue of Polygamy," 29–30; Helander, *Must We Introduce Monogamy*, 63 quoting P. Pakendorf, 69 quoting G. Hartmann; Trowell, *Passing of Polygamy*.

17. Horan, "Polygamy Comes Home to Roost," 446, 52; Okullu, *Church and Marriage*, 62; Yego, "Polygamy and African Church," 80.

Beginning with those who condemn polygamy, Group 1 is made up of those who claim that polygamy is a sin once certain passages are retranslated according to their perceptions. Group 2 includes those who claim that polygamy is a sin based on existing translations.[18] Group 3 is made up of those who claim that monogamy is God's ideal. This group has the greatest amount of variation (for example, Helander versus Muthengi), but they all agree that the non-Christian polygamists can be baptized without having to divorce their wives.[19] Group 4 consists of those who claim that polygamy is allowed in the Bible for polygamists coming from a non-Christian background as well as existing Christians. Finally, Group 5 consists of those who claim that polygamy is God's ideal form of marriage.[20]

---

18. Blum's theological arguments fit those of Group 3, but his refusal to allow polygamist baptism places him in Group2 (Blum, *Forms of Marriage*, 264–65, 304–5). Schillebeeckx, might have been included in Group 2, but his work does not focus extensively on polygamy. However, he seems to stand against the practice (Schillebeeckx, *Marriage*, I:90–91, 202). Schillebeeckx might have allowed for a non-Christian polygamist to be baptized, but more than likely he would not have permitted this. Blum likewise compares Schillebeeckx and Hillman and feels that they would diverge on this point (Blum, *Forms of Marriage*, 226). Vollebregt seems to belong to Group 2, but his position is not entirely clear since he foregoes any attempt to discuss whether or not polygamy might be presently permitted. His work is included here because of the significant discussion on polygamy. He describes monogamy as an ideal, but takes a hard stance against polygamy. He never claims that polygamy is a sin, but the overall impression of his work is that polygamy would only be allowed in the Old Testament. Most notably, Vollebregt never shares his view of whether or not polygamy might be allowed in the New Testament church, which is especially surprising since he has a chapter on 1 Corinthians 7, but never discusses 7:17 (compare Vollebregt, *Bible on Marriage*, 105–7).

19. Josphat Yego is one of the few authors who was so entirely objective in his examination of the matter that he never shared his own position, though he quoted heavily from Hastings and Hillman (Yego, "Polygamy and African Church,"). Some authors in this group, such as Trobisch, have some extremely unconventional means of helping polygamists (Trobisch, *My Wife Made Me*).

20. This claim is from a sole author who is the senior pastor of an African Independent Church, but his view may reflect the belief of other similar churches.

Table 6: Five Theological Interpretations on Polygamy

Polygamy Rejected as Sin	Polygamous Converts Accepted	Polygamy Accepted for All
1) Polygamy is a Sin given certain Re-Translations	3) Monogamy is God's Ideal, but a Polygamist Convert is Baptized	4) Polygamy is Allowed for Christians and Converts
du Preez, *Polygamy in the Bible*, 287–89. Kaiser, *Toward Old Testament Ethics*, 183, 89.	Currens, "A Policy of Baptizing Polygynists Evaluated," 79. Gaskiyane, *Polygamy*, 48, 51, 62. Hastings, *Christian Marriage in Africa*, 73, 79. *Helander, *Must We Introduce Monogamy*, 53–54, 69. Hillman, *Polygamy Reconsidered*, 206. * Kiwovele, "Polygyny as a Problem," 13, 24–25. Jasper, "Polygyny in the Old Testament," 41, 56. Mann, "Biblical Understanding of Polygamy," 24–25. Muthengi, "Polygamy and Church in Africa" 76. Nkwoka, "Church and Polygamy in Africa," 145–50, 52–53. Odame, *Christian Approach to Polygamy*, 43, 47, 49, 66–67. Trobisch, *My Wife Made Me*, 30–36. Trowell, *Passing of Polygamy*, 10, 15–16. *Welch, "Biblical Perspective on Polygamy", 126.	*Adutchum, "Church and Issue of Polygamy," 28–29. Buthelezi, "Polygyny in Light of NT," 60, 62, 69. Chime, *Polygamy and Christian Religion*, 7, 17–18. *Holst, "Polygamy and the Bible," 212. Lewis, *Divine Guidance*, 83, 128–33, 207–9. Maillu, *1988 Our Kind of Polygamy*. Omoregbe, "Is Polygamy Incompatible with Christianity," 372. Wambutda, "Monogamy or Polygamy," 84.
2) Polygamy is a Sin based on Existing Translations		
Blum, *Forms of Marriage*, 296, 304–5. Hitchens, *Multiple Marriage*, 144, 48. Parrinder, *Bible and Polygamy*, 64–65. *The Problem of Polygamy*, 3, 63. Urrutia, "Can Polygamy Be Compatible," 276, 78, 81–82, 91 footnote 11. Vollebregt, *Bible on Marriage*, 1–3, 26–27, 46.		
		5) Polygamy is God's Ideal
Citations clarify author's stance * Denotes excellent work		Okotie, *Last Outcast*, 540–43, 46.

A Missional Critique of the Hermeneutics

Finally, the column headings of Table 6 demonstrate a broader level of commonality among authors. The first column includes Groups 1 and 2, who both reject polygamy as a sin. The second column includes those solely in Group 3, who permit polygamy on a limited basis. The third and final column includes Group 4 and 5, who allow polygamists to function equally as monogamists. These authors do not feel that polygamy is a point of division. This does not mean that these authors advocate polygamy, though the sole author in Group 5 leans this direction.

Following the outline of Table 6, I now turn to an in-depth theological and hermeneutical analysis of Groups 1 through 5 followed by a similar analysis of four responses to the difficult missional issue of polygamy.

POLYGAMY IS A SIN GIVEN CERTAIN RE-TRANSLATIONS OF SCRIPTURE

There are four or five passages in the Old Testament that seemingly allow polygamy on some level (Exod 21:7–11; Lev 18:18; Deut 17:17; 21:15–17; 2 Sam 12:7–8).[21] As such, these passages are the most difficult to address if someone wants to condemn the practice. Those who make up this first group of thinkers would like to retranslate some of these passages in order to condemn the practice of polygamy. Most notably, they claim that Leviticus 18:18, when properly translated, condemns polygamy in general rather than preventing a man from marrying two sisters. Once this passage and others are "properly" retranslated, these authors feel that polygamy is clearly condemned.

Walter Kaiser and Ronald du Preez are the two that make up this group. The most troubling aspect of both of these authors is the bias they present at the start of their analysis. Kaiser initially states, "Was polygamy ever lawful for the patriarchs or under the Levitical laws? Clearly, there never existed an express biblical permission for polygamy. The law governing marriage had always looked to Genesis 2:24 as normative."[22]

On the other hand, du Preez, a Seventh-Day Adventist (SDA), has a quite unique bias since his underlying agenda seems to be an attempt to validate SDA prophetess Ellen White's stance on polygamy. Du Preez

---

21. Cp. Kaiser, *Toward Old Testament Ethics*, 184; Odame, *Christian Approach to Polygamy*, 30.

22. Kaiser, *Toward Old Testament Ethics*, 183.

states at the beginning of this work that the accepted SDA writings of Ellen White are an authoritative source and are "given serious consideration" in his work.[23] As he summarizes portions of his work, he states, "Thus, this exclusion of polygamy can be viewed as applying to all members. These conclusions concur with Ellen White's stand that 'the gospel condemns the practice of polygamy.' In both the Old and New Testaments, therefore, there appears to be clear evidence forbidding the practice of polygamy."[24] As such, it is difficult to imagine that du Preez might come to any other conclusions than those of Ellen White.

In terms of the actual arguments, both Kaiser and du Preez lean heavily on Genesis 2:24 in order to build their cases, and both authors claim that the implied monogamy of the Genesis account is an explicitly obvious claim against polygamy (Gen 2:24, NIV—"For this reason a man will leave his father and mother and be united to his wife, and they will become one flesh."). Du Preez even suggests that the passage is a future command that all marriages be monogamous.[25] Interestingly, while both authors argue passionately that this passage is an obvious condemnation of polygamy, neither of them gives strong weight to the New Testament quotations of Genesis 2:24. As such, the latter interpretations of Jesus and Paul do not influence their own interpretations.

When referring to Jesus' quotation of this passage, du Preez states that "the issue considered here is divorce and not polygamy, [but] it would be hermeneutically correct to observe other implications that can legitimately be derived from this statement of Jesus."[26] After du Preez quotes from other authors who agree with his opinion, he skirts the Pauline usage of the passage.[27] As such, du Preez's hermeneutic is problematic in that he draws indirect implications from Jesus' quotation of Genesis 2:24, even though he admits that the focus of the passage is divorce (further analysis of Genesis 2:24 will be developed in the next section on Group 2).

---

23. du Preez, *Polygamy in the Bible*, 28.
24. Ibid., 283.
25. Ibid., 48.
26. Ibid..
27. Ibid., 270 n. 15.

A Missional Critique of the Hermeneutics

Table 7: Comparison of NLT with du Preez and Kaiser

vv.	Typical Translation	du Preez's Translation
Exod 21:10	If he himself marries her and then takes *another wife*, he may not reduce her food or clothing or *fail to sleep with her as his wife* (NLT).	"If he marries a *different* woman, he must not deprive her [the slave woman] of food, clothing, or *shelter*."[28]
Lev 18:18	Do not marry a *woman and her sister* because they will be rivals. But if your wife dies, then it is all right to marry her sister (NLT).	"While your wife is alive, do not marry *another woman*, for she will be a rival to your wife."[29]

vv.	Typical Translation	du Preez and Kaiser Claims
Deut 21:15–17	[15] Suppose a man has two wives, but he loves one and not the other, and both have given him sons. And suppose the firstborn son is the son of the wife he does not love. [16] When the man divides the inheritance, he may not give the larger inheritance to his younger son, the son of the wife he loves. [17] He must give the customary double portion to his oldest son, who represents the strength of his father's manhood and who owns the rights of the firstborn son, even though he is the son of the wife his father does not love (NLT).	du Preez claims, "[I]t is possible to suggest that Deut 21:15–17 may deal with the rights of the firstborn of a woman who is deceased or divorced. If this suggestion is correct, then Deut 21:15–17 would not be addressing a polygamous home but rather a case in which a man has had two wives, a second after the death or divorce of the first."[30] Kaiser makes the above argument and quotes Lev 23:18, claiming "Consequently, as the legislation on harlots in no way authorizes harlotry, so the law on bigamy or polygamy is likewise not a case for its recognition."[31]

Both authors suggest that their interpretation of Genesis 2:24 should guide further biblical investigation, though their thoughts are quite different from Paul's interpretation. As such, they claim that Old Testament passages which seemingly allow polygamy must be retranslat-

---

28. Ibid., 69; cp. Kaiser, *Toward Old Testament Ethics*, 184–85.

29. du Preez, *Polygamy in the Bible*, 77; cp. Kaiser, *Toward Old Testament Ethics*, 185–86.

30. du Preez, *Polygamy in the Bible*, 91.

31. Kaiser, *Toward Old Testament Ethics*, 186–87.

MISSIOLOGICAL HERMENEUTICS

ed or reinterpreted. Leviticus 18:18 is a key passage among those called into question (discussed later). This is the only passage in Scripture that rejects sororal polygamy (the marriage of two sisters, such as Jacob's marriage to Leah and Rachel).

Furthermore, both authors suggest that Exodus 21:10 should be retranslated so that "another wife" is rendered as "a different woman." They also retranslate the verse's ending to eliminate the sexual connotations (discussed later). While the term אַחֵר can mean either "different" or "another," the only other passage using the term in reference to a woman is 1 Chronicles 2:26 and this is a case of polygamy.[32] Du Preez then makes the unfounded assumption, "Since no marital or sexual relations are mentioned in this part of the passage, it appears as though the slave woman is here considered as single and not married to the master."[33] Kaiser makes the doubtful claim that his retranslation of a conditional clause in 21:8 has bearing on the new conditional clause of 21:10.[34] Finally, both claim that Deuteronomy 21:15–17 has a significantly different meaning than it might first appear. In short, the claims of both authors are extremely weak and overly dogmatic. Table 7 outlines the translation changes that both authors suggest.

32. The following is a Libronix search for אַחֵר with the English meaning of "another" or "different" as found in the Lexham Hebrew-English Interlinear Bible (van der Merwe, *Lexham Hebrew-English Interlinear Bible*). The results were then looked up in the 52 verses and each verse is shown with the NLT rendering of the term: Gen 4:25 (another son); 8:10, 12 (2x another seven days); 26:21–22 (2x another well); 29:27, 30 (2x another seven years); 30:24 (another son); 37:9 (another dream); Exod 21:10 (another wife); 22:4 (someone else's field); Lev 27:20 (someone else); Num 14:24 (different attitude); 23:13 (another place); 23:27 (one more place); 36:9 (another [tribe]); Deut 29:27 (another land); Judg 2:10 (another generation); 11:2 (you are the son of a prostitute [a different woman]); Ruth 2:8 (any other field); 2:22 (other fields); 1 Sam 10:6 (a different person); 17:30 (some others); 2 Sam 18:20 (another day); 18:26 (another man); 1 Kgs 13:10 (another way); 20:37 (another man); 2 Kgs 1:11 (another captain); 7:8 (another [tent]); 1 Chr 2:26 (a second wife); 16:20 (another [kingdom]); 2 Chr 32:5 (a second wall); Job 31:8 (someone else); 31:10 (another man); Ps 16:4 (troubles multiply [another suffering]); 105:13 (another [kingdom]); 109:8 (someone else); Prov 25:9 (another person's secret); Isa 28:11 (a strange language); 42:8 (anyone else); 48:11 (share my glory with idols [another]); 65:15 (another name); 65:22 (2x [another] house, [another] vineyard); Jer 3:1 (someone else); 6:12 (turned over to their enemies [someone else]); 18:4 (started over [made another]); 22:26 (a foreign country); 36:28, 32 (2x another scroll); Ezek 12:3 (somewhere else); Joel 1:3 ([another] generation); and Zech 2:7 (a second angel).

33. du Preez, *Polygamy in the Bible*, 68–69.

34. Kaiser, *Toward Old Testament Ethics*, 184–85.

A Missional Critique of the Hermeneutics

Leviticus 18:18 as a Prohibition against Polygamy

Though both authors retranslate Leviticus 18:18 on the same grounds, their claim is not new. Prior to the modern missions' movement, it was said that the Samaritans are so far "from thinking Polygamy [was] permitted by the law of *Moses*, that they think it expressly prohibited by it, in *Lev.* xviii. 18. which they render, (as it is read in the margin of the bible) *Neither shalt thou take one wife to another, to vex her,* &c."[35]

The primary argument is that the phrase "a woman and her sister" is used idiomatically in Hebrew to really mean "a woman and another." Occasionally a similar idiom occurs in English, such as referring to two vessels as "sister ships" or referring to an organization as a "parent company." Clearly in these cases the words "sister" and "parent" are used idiomatically. However, both authors claim that this would prohibit polygamy entirely. Yet, even if one accepts the supposed idiom, "a woman and her sister" would only refer to two Israelite women since "sister" would not apply to foreign women. Therefore, even as an idiom, this would merely limit a man from marrying two Israelite women. Both authors conveniently gloss over this possibility in their rush to force the Bible to condemn polygamy. However, the phrase in Leviticus 18:18 should not be taken idiomatically as will be shown.

In trying to validate the need for a new translation, Kaiser makes a surprising claim. Kaiser states that "[t]he problem phrase is אִשָּׁה אֶל־אֲחֹתָהּ, 'a woman to her sister,' that everywhere else is rendered idiomatically 'one woman to another' or 'one wife to another.'"[36] Kaiser then supports his argument as follows: "[t]he phrase אִשָּׁה אֶל־אֲחֹתָהּ, 'a woman to her sister' is found ten times in Exod. 26:3 (twice), 5, 6, 17; Lev. 18:18; Ezek. 1:9, 11, 23; 3:13. Four more instances of אִשָּׁה אֶל־אֲחֹתָהּ should be mentioned in Isa. 34:15, 16; Jer. 9:20; Zech. 11:9."[37] Kaiser's claim is surprising because none of the supporting verses are rendered "one woman to another" even though all but Ezekiel 1:11 have the exact same construction.[38] Kaiser fails to mention that the meaning of אִשָּׁה can be either "woman" or "each" and this decision is indicated by context. Notably when referring to a female, אִשָּׁה is rendered as "woman" or

---

35. Delany, *Reflections Upon Polygamy*, 72.

36. Kaiser, *Toward Old Testament Ethics*, 185.

37. Ibid., 185 footnote 13.

38. Kaiser's inclusion of Ezekiel 1:11 seems to be a mistake as this verse does not have the same construction.

Missiological Hermeneutics

"wife," and when referring to an object it is rendered as "each." Table 8 outlines each case that Kaiser has cited in his footnote:

Table 8: Leviticus 18:18 translation of "Her Sister"

Passage:	אִשָּׁה (woman/each) refers to a:	אִשָּׁה (woman/each) is rendered as:	אֶל־אֲחֹתָהּ (to her sister) is rendered as:
Exod 26:3	five curtains	each (shall be joined)	to another five curtains
Exod 26:5	the [50] loops	each (shall match)	another set of [50] loops
Exod 26:6	curtains	each (will be joined)	to one another
Exod 26:17	two pegs	each (will be bound)	to one another
Ezek 1:9	their wings	each (touched)	one another
Ezek 1:23	their wings	each (stretched)	toward another
Ezek 3:13	the wings	each (touched)	against another
Lev 18:18	a woman	(do not marry) a woman	in addition to her sister

Only in the case of Leviticus 18:18 is the Hebrew addressing a woman. All of the other cases are non-human objects and these objects are always in the context of other matching objects. Notably, the phrase is used idiomatically only in the case of inanimate objects with matching pairs. Kaiser has simply stretched the idiom beyond its bounds to support his pre-existing agenda of condemning polygamy. Of the following 25 major translations of Scripture, all have translated Leviticus 18:18 as a prohibition against a man literally marrying a woman and her sister (AMP, ASV, CEV, Darby, ESV, GNT, HCSB, KJ21, KJV, Living, MSG, NAB, NASB, NCV, NIRV, NIV, NIVUK, NJB, NKJV, NLT, NLV, NRSV, RSV, Tanakh, TNIV).

Only the Young's Literal Translation (YLT) translates the passage "And a woman unto another thou dost not take, to be an adversary, to uncover her nakedness beside her, in her life."[39] The Hebrew (וְאִשָּׁה אֶל־אֲחֹתָהּ) literally reads "And a woman in addition to her sister . . ." (translation mine).[40] Given that the YLT attempts to be literal, it is quite surprising that this translation includes a questionable idiomatic possibility and then renders the passage in this final form. A literal translation would be the least likely place to find this rendering and as

---

39. The NASB does include a footnote allowing "another" as an option in place of "her sister."

40. Note: "so אֶל in addition to: אֶל־אֲחֹתָהּ Lv 18:18" (Koehler et al., *HALOT*, 50).

such it is hard to perceive that the translation is accurate since it does not even footnote the fact that "another" is an idiomatic rendering of "her sister." By contrast, the *Lexham Hebrew-English Interlinear Bible* follows the same format as Table 8 and gives the literal meaning, "to her sister," as well as the idiomatic meaning, "another." It does this for all the cases shown in Table 8 except for Leviticus 18:18.[41]

Lev 18:18 and the Hapax Legomenon (Rival Wife)

Bias in the translation of Leviticus 18:18 can also be seen when this passage is compared to du Preez and Kaiser's translation of Exodus 21:10. Both passages have a *hapax legomenon* (a word occurring only once in the Bible). In Leviticus 18:18, the *hapax legomenon* (לִצְרֹר) is most often translated as "to be a rival wife." If someone wished to validate polygamy, it would be quite easy for a translator to claim a slightly different meaning for this term. For example, if the translator felt that the *hapax legomenon* was the central focus of the verse, it could be rendered "Do not marry a woman and her sister [in order for her] to become a rival wife." In this case, the verse would be stating that a man should not marry two sisters if they will become obvious rivals, but otherwise it would be acceptable.

The main reason I point out this possibility is because the bias of the translator clearly affects the final rendering. The translation that I have just suggested and Kaiser's idiomatic translation are both weak translations because the translator is trying to force the text to match a pre-existing agenda. However, my facetious example is weak because the wives of polygamists are referred to as rivals throughout much of the Old Testament, whether or not they actually are antagonistic toward one another. Therefore, it is unlikely that Leviticus 18:18 is suggesting that a man try to determine ahead of time whether or not two sisters will be rivals.

Similarly, both Kaiser and du Preez modify the *hapax legomenon* of Exodus 21:10 to their advantage. The term עֹנָה is defined as "sexual intercourse" by the *Hebrew & Aramaic Lexicon*, and this lexicon develops the meaning from extra biblical sources, in contrast to Kaiser's claim that "the translators have been unduly influenced by the Septuagint."[42] However, Kaiser and du Preez claim that the term must mean some-

---

41. van der Merwe, *Lexham Hebrew-English Interlinear Bible*; Lev 18:18.
42. Kaiser, *Toward Old Testament Ethics*, 185; Koehler et al., *HALOT*, 885.

thing else, such as "providing shelter."⁴³ By modifying the term in order to fit their agenda, they are indirectly training others in poor translation methods. As such, I have little doubt that their approach will teach someone in the future to poorly translate Leviticus 18:18 as suggested in my facetious example above.

Additionally, if polygamy were the heinous sin that some have depicted it to be, we could expect to find numerous passages condemning the practice in clear ways without having to decipher a questionable idiom cleverly hidden in a chapter that focuses on improper sexual relationships pertaining to relatives! Furthermore, if the intention was solely to reject sororal polygamy, the given construction would be appropriate. Likewise, since the vast majority of Leviticus 18 is dealing with family relationships and issues of sexuality, this literary context is an appropriate place to reject sororal polygamy.⁴⁴

Internal Evidence of Leviticus 18

Finally, additional concerns related to polygamy are almost certainly envisioned in Leviticus 18. At the start of the chapter, the reader is informed not to have sexual relations with their mother (18:7). In the next verse, however, the passage additionally informs the reader, "Do not have sexual relations with any of your father's wives" and this presents another problem for those who want to claim that verse 18 should be retranslated (18:8 NLT).⁴⁵ If verse 18 were a general prohibition of polygamy, this would mean that verse 8 is a stipulation for those who have failed to follow that prohibition. Such a combination is very unlikely, but the order is even more unlikely. If verse 18 were a general prohibition, then we would expect verse 8 to follow verse 18 and read something like "but if your father has married a woman and her sister (using the same idiom again), do not have sexual relations with any of your father's wives." If the chapter were arranged this way and included the idiom in the suggested linguistic context, this would give much more credibility to the suggested retranslation of Leviticus 18:18.

By contrast, in Tosato's analysis of Leviticus 18, he subjects the Hebrew to Western literary organizational standards and then draws unfounded conclusions. Tosato does this by dividing the passages of

---

43. du Preez, *Polygamy in the Bible*, 69; Kaiser, *Toward Old Testament Ethics*, 185.
44. Contra Tosato, "Law of Leviticus 18."
45. Chime, *Polygamy and Christian Religion*, 5–7.

Leviticus 18 into two categories of "incest" and "general prohibitions."[46] He does this based predominantly on the initial and ending sentence structure, but ignores verb structures that are common between verse 17 and verses 18 through 19.[47] Tosato places 18:18 in the general prohibitions and as such claims that the passage is condemning polygamy as a whole. He likewise assumes that sororal polygamy was thought to be incestuous, but there is certainly no indication of this perception in the Jacob narrative. Leviticus 18:18 simply states that a man should not marry two sisters, and I would speculate that the underlying concern is that this would destroy their relationship as sisters, as was the case with Leah and Rachel. As such, there simply is no indication that the Hebrew writers ever considered ordering their thoughts according to the Western categories that Tosato suggests. Attempting to thrust Western categorical values onto this chapter demonstrates a deeper level of worldview bias by those who are part of this group.

Rejection of the Narrative

Finally, Kaiser rejects the entire Old Testament narrative of polygamy by pointing out that the Jubilee is commanded to take place every 49 years and does not happen for thousands of years. He further claims that God did not discipline this failure and therefore the lack of God's condemnation of polygamy is no evidence that God condoned the practice. I could, like Kaiser, claim that every instance in which Israel did "not heed the voice of God" was in fact referring to their failure to practice the Jubilee. That alone would refute Kaiser, but this would be equally poor hermeneutics.

Foremost, the failure to carry out the Jubilee would be a problem issue twice a century whereas polygamy was happening almost perpetually through the reign of the kings. More importantly, Kaiser is comparing two quite different issues for Israel. Israel's election is for the purpose of becoming a missional nation (as shown in Chapter 2). The Jubilee is internal to Israel even though honoring the Jubilee would have been a powerful centripetal witness in the Old Testament as the poor and

---

46. Tosato, "Law of Leviticus 18," 201, 03.

47. The verb structure of v. 19 is much more closely related to 17 and 18, indicating that v. 19 is most likely a continuation of vv. 17 and 18. However, we must be open to the possibility that the material is simply not organized in keeping with Western standards or Western levels of concern for detail.

enslaved are reinstated. The surrounding nations would no doubt be astounded to witness Israel's demonstration of financial trust in God. Moreover, Kaiser uniquely claims that Israel was required to act centrifugally in mission throughout the Old Testament.[48]

However, Israel rarely responded to their missional calling including the Jubilee. Rather, a great deal of God's effort with Israel in the Old Testament is in dealing with idolatry because Israel's basic allegiance to God was often in question. Intentional missionary activity could only develop from allegiance to God after which mission could flow from that foundation. In this light, God began by addressing those issues that were barriers in developing allegiance to God. Condemning Israel for their consistent failure to carry out God's mission would be similar to chastising non-Christians for their failure to take the Gospel to Africa.

What Kaiser is doing hermeneutically is comparing the so-called sin of polygamy to a pinnacle act of benevolence and missionary practice that could rarely be enforced because God was often addressing basic spiritual problems within Israel. This is simply not a fair comparison. If Kaiser cares to make a fair comparison, he should compare God's response to polygamy with something that he perceives as a similarly heinous act, such as Old Testament idolatry or a commonly listed sexual sin. In such cases, we would expect polygamy to be addressed consistently, whereas the Jubilee would most likely be addressed when God's elected people had their spiritual and missional bearings in place. The narrative record cannot be avoided by contrasting a worse-case scenario with a best-case scenario.

Hermeneutically speaking then, if polygamy is a terrible sin we could expect God to address polygamy in the Old Testament following the nature of other sins in the Old Testament that hinder allegiance to God. However, "[t]he people of Israel reached their unique religious position in the ancient world not by adopting monogamy as against polygamy, but by their faith in God alone and their rejection, at least in their leaders and official teaching, of magic, sorcery and trust in other powers to help them. In the Scriptures this is frequently made an issue upon which men must choose; polygamy is never made an issue in this way."[49]

---

48. Kaiser, *Mission in the OT*, 9.
49. Turner, "Monogamy," 316.

A Missional Critique of the Hermeneutics

Hermeneutical Critique

Throughout their works, du Preez and Kaiser re-translate any passages that stand in their way, and then dogmatically conclude that their translation is authoritative, despite the fact that du Preez claims "it would be inadvisable to dogmatically conclude that Deut 21:15–17 undoubtedly deals with or discusses the issue of polygamy."[50]

Likewise, du Preez claims in his methodology that complex passages should rely on other clearer passages in order to gain a better understanding of the passage. However, when du Preez claims that a condemnation of David's polygamy exists in 1 Samuel 12, he does not consider the clear statements regarding the sinful and righteous acts of the kings (for example, 1 Kings 15:4–5).[51] There are honestly too many areas to critique with these authors and the merit of such a critique would be questionable.

However, in terms of their overall hermeneutic, these authors are ultimately proof-texting, and working from a deep human agenda. That agenda is to prove that polygamy is a sin. From this point, the authors take on a very precarious role of attempting to retranslate the most difficult passages, with foremost focus upon Leviticus 18:18. Once the passages have been modified to their liking, they use these retranslations as a means of reinterpreting other passages. Finally, as we have seen, Kaiser attempts to exclude the narrative of Scripture simply because it does not match his agenda. Figure 15 is an attempt to diagram the overall hermeneutic. The pre-existing agenda influences their interpretation of Genesis. Problematic passages are then retranslated, and utilized to influence the meaning of others. And finally, the narrative is dissected as needed.

---

50. du Preez, *Polygamy in the Bible*, 90.

51. Summers, upon considering this passage, comments that David "did not do wrong in having several wives at the same time; [and] did not commit adultery, except with the wife of Uriah" (Summers, *Bible and Polygamy*, 30).

Missiological Hermeneutics

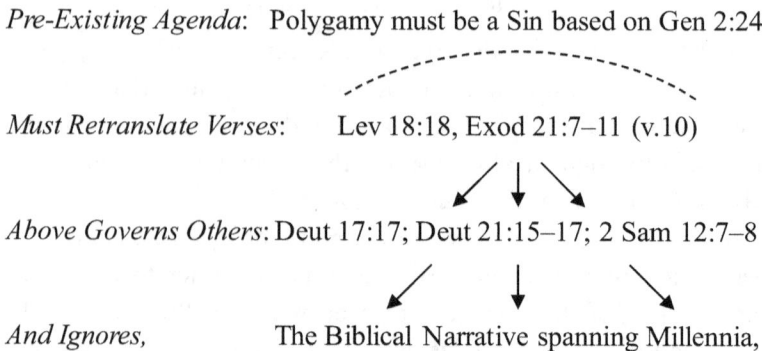

Pre-Existing Agenda: Polygamy must be a Sin based on Gen 2:24

Must Retranslate Verses: Lev 18:18, Exod 21:7–11 (v.10)

Above Governs Others: Deut 17:17; Deut 21:15–17; 2 Sam 12:7–8

And Ignores, Skews or Avoids: The Biblical Narrative spanning Millennia, unless it helps a pre-existing agenda

Figure 15: A Hermeneutic of Proof-Texting

In this way, these authors create a "canon within the canon."[52] That is, they retranslate Scripture by replacing perceived obstacles based on their prerequisites and ultimately invalidating the capacity of Scripture to teach and inform their theology and mission practice.

POLYGAMY IS A SIN BASED ON EXISTING TRANSLATIONS

The primary difference between those we have just studied and those in Group 2 of Table 6 is the way in which they view polygamy in the Old Testament. For the most part, those who accept the existing translations claim that polygamy was being eradicated in the Old Testament and this was a limited act of tolerance that can no longer be allowed.[53] Among these authors, the majority express conservative opinions while Blum is more liberal. Additionally, many of the biblical arguments supported by this group are likewise affirmed by the Group 1 authors that we have just considered.

Nearly all of these authors place great weight on the Genesis 2 creation account. Most feel that "the first marriage presents a strong argument for monogamy since one man and one woman were made 'one flesh.'"[54] Likewise, polygamy and monogamy are compared to Israel's transition from polytheism to monotheism, or more accurately heno-

---

52. Bosch, *Witness to the World*, 46.
53. Urrutia, "Can Polygamy Be Compatible," 282.
54. Hitchens, *Multiple Marriage*, 17; cp. Parrinder, *Bible and Polygamy*, 30; Vollebregt, *Bible on Marriage*, 63.

A Missional Critique of the Hermeneutics

theism to monotheism.[55] "Only with time did the Chosen People come to understand that the deities of other peoples were, in fact, no real gods. Just as God's self revelation occurred in stages, so likewise did God reveal in stages the intimate tie that joined religion and morality."[56]

Additionally, a common claim of this group is that polygamy eventually became a sin through a slow transition on the part of God. "As God's revelation was gradually unfolded in their history, so did they progressively understand its moral teaching, which continually challenged and purified their traditional and borrowed customs, institutions and values, until the coming of the full revelation: in the life and teaching of Christ."[57]

Genesis 2:24 "The Two Will Become One Flesh."

There are many passages that deserve detailed consideration, but two groups of passages in particular require more detailed treatment because of the implications that many authors have drawn from them. The first of these is Genesis 2:24 and its New Testament repetitions (Matt 19:5; Mark 10:7–8; 1 Cor 6:16; Eph 5:31). This passage has a greater need for attention due to the intertextual implications. Beyond the original use of Genesis 2:24, the verse is not directly quoted again in the Old Testament but the New Testament use of this passage offers a window into the passage's interpretation through the eyes of Jesus and Paul.[58]

---

55. Though polytheism, henotheism and monotheism may be used strictly in terms of belief, I am using these terms with respect to belief and allegiance. Therefore, henotheism is allegiance to one god while believing in the existence of other gods, while polytheism is an allegiance and belief in many gods. In contrast, monotheism is the belief in and allegiance to one god.

56. Blum, *Forms of Marriage*, 172; cp. Vollebregt, *Bible on Marriage*, 20. Blum shares the rather popular opinion that Israel is not called to monotheism until late in their history with the prophet Isaiah (Isa 44:6, 8; 45:5–6, 14, 18, 21–22; 46:9; Joel 2:27). However, the much earlier discourse of Deuteronomy contains equally strong monotheistic statements as does 1 Kings (Deut 4:34–39; 32:39; 1 Kgs 8:60). As such, it is quite challenging to support the idea that major theological motifs required millennia to be conveyed. What can be supported is the concept that Israel often did not follow or listen to God. However, this can be said of nearly every era of the People of God.

57. Blum, *Forms of Marriage*, 172; cp. Hitchens, *Multiple Marriage*, 135; Parrinder, *Bible and Polygamy*, 19; Vollebregt, *Bible on Marriage*, 1.

58. "The phrase which is translated into English, as 'becomes attached to his wife', 'joins himself to his wife', or 'cleaves to his wife', is also found in other biblical passages, which arose in the same milieu, as the Yahwist narrative. The phrase was used to describe the sexual love of Shechem for Dinah (Genesis 34:3), and the deep family

The other group of passages to be addressed later are those dealing with leadership in the New Testament (1 Tim 3:2, 12; 5:9; Titus 1:6). Given the controversy that surrounds each of these passages, especially with regard to a biblical understanding of polygamy, we should address these through multiple hermeneutical paths. Likewise, both of these passages should have been given far more attention in terms of original language work and missiological focus.

Within the Old Testament

I would like to begin the investigation of Genesis 2:24 by stating what would seem to be the obvious—namely, that among the thousands of years in which the Old Testament was written, in the midst of a time when the people of God openly practiced polygamy, there is not a single recorded instance in which Genesis 2:24 is quoted in order to address polygamy. This is not a point that should be lightly dismissed. Among a great deal of the modern-day literature on polygamy, Genesis 2:24 is often quoted as the overarching text that validates anti-polygamist concerns. However, throughout the expansive time spans of the biblical record in which polygamy was openly practiced, neither this verse nor the larger narrative of Genesis 2:18–25 was used to deter the practice of polygamy. Furthermore, we do not find God or the prophets of God or even the Levitical law citing this passage to address the practice of polygamy despite thousands of years of Old Testament development. In fact, the only notable Old Testament echo of Genesis 2:24 is Malachi 2:15–16, and the emphasis is toward godly children while condemning divorce, which is very similar to Jesus' use of this passage in the New Testament (Matt 19:5; Mark 10:8). Therefore, the Old Testament backdrop is one that offers no authoritative biblical example in which the passage is interpreted or applied in the same way as that of many modern-day writers.

Some may claim that I am "arguing from the silence of Scripture." My response to that claim is that the thousands of years of silence with respect to the use of this passage is extremely relevant. This is especially the case when modern-day scholars choose to infuse the passage with a meaning that cannot be found in Scripture—even within those portions

---

affection, which led Ruth to remain with her mother-in-law, Naomi, and not to return to her home (Ruth 1:14; 2:23)" (Blum, *Forms of Marriage*, 203).

A Missional Critique of the Hermeneutics

of Scripture at a time when polygamy is openly practiced.[59] However, an enduring silence throughout Scripture cannot be dismissed, especially if one is of the opinion that polygamy is a problem and that Genesis 2:24 addresses the problem.

An argument that could be made in the face of this is that every instance in which this passage was quoted in the Old Testament was simply left out of the record. If that were true, then how many instances might this be? If the New Testament covers roughly a time period of 100 years, with four references to Genesis 2:24, and if the Old Testament were written over 4 millennium with a similar number of citations, then there would be roughly 160 missing citations of Genesis 2:24. Yet we cannot find even one direct quote in the Old Testament. When this or any passage is not utilized within Scripture to address a particular issue that is openly practiced over extended time periods in later portions of Scripture, the pervasive silence substantively communicates to the modern-day reader that the passage in consideration is not relevant to the issue at hand.[60]

Furthermore, the genre assumed for the Genesis account makes it even more difficult to use in a factual manner. Those who would like to use this account to validate their own inferences realize that it has a unique nature that does not always lend itself to a presupposed purpose; "Insofar as it narrates these facts the Eden account is historical, although the description is not one of actual historical events. For this reason the account has been well described as a prophecy of the past."[61] More importantly, an evaluation of the New Testament use of this passage suggests that the Messianic and Pauline interpretations of Genesis 2:24 were not concerned with polygamy.

---

59. I agree that arguments made from silence are precarious especially if the argument focuses on relatively few passages in order to make a claim. For instance, I have had members of the Non-Instrumental Church of Christ tell me that instruments in the church are sinful because two New Testament passages mention the singing of psalms, hymns, and spiritual songs (Eph 5:19, Col 3:16). By avoiding the Old Testament all together and certain portions of the New Testament (for example, Luke 15:25), they force this passage to say something the biblical writers never intended, and they are arguing that the silence of Scripture indicates sin. This is a good example of a very poor hermeneutic.

60. A similar argument is made on p. 33 n. 27 of this work.

61. Vollebregt, *Bible on Marriage*, 56, see also 57.

Missiological Hermeneutics

Within the New Testament

Genesis 2:24 is repeated four times in the New Testament by both Jesus and Paul (Matt 19:5, Mark 10:7–8, 1 Cor 6:16, Eph 5:31). Matthew and Mark are both quoting the same account of Jesus (Matt 19:5, Mark 10:7–8), while Paul interprets the passage in two different letters written to different missional contexts (1 Cor 6:16, Eph 5:31). Among these quotations, only the Ephesians' quotation of Genesis 2:24 is used as part of a metaphor. The other quotations seem to have a more direct relationship with the original passage.

Table 9 compares all three accounts in their original languages, and the Septuagint. In each case, the English and the Greek (NA27) are shown for comparison with other accounts. Notably, the New Testament quotations are identical with the Septuagint (LXX).[62] Consequently, it is a weak argument to claim that the shift from "they" in Genesis 2:24 to "the two" in the New Testament has implications regarding monogamy. The source of the change is almost certainly the Septuagint rather than a theological concern.[63] The consistency in the quotations likewise aids this study, since inconsistent quotations would be expected to have greater variation in their meaning.

All Greek phrases are identically translated "[and] the two will become one flesh" (NIV). Greek italics are original to the NA27 and denotes an Old Testament quotation.

---

62. In 1 Cor 6:16, the post-positive conjunction and verb "γάρ, φησίν," (For, it says,) does not interrupt the flow of the Greek as they would in English. As such, 1 Cor 6:16 is identical except "καὶ" (and) is replaced with "γάρ, φησίν," (For, it says,).

63. The majority of translations of Gen 2:24 render the subject as: "*they*"—"and they (will/shall) be/become one flesh" (Darby, ASV, ESV, KJV, NASB, NIV, NKJV, NRSV, RSV); "and they become one" (GNB); "so that they become one flesh" (Tanakh); "y serán una sola carne" (RVA Spanish). However, some translations of Gen 2:24 are rendered with subject as: "*the two*"—"καὶ ἔσονται οἱ δύο εἰς σάρκα μίαν" (LXX); "suae et erunt duo in carne una" (Latin Vulgate); "and the two of them become one body" (NAB); "and the two will become one body" (NCV); "and the two are united into one" (NLT); "and the two become one person" (TLB).

A Missional Critique of the Hermeneutics

Table 9: The Quotations of Genesis 2:24 in the New Testament

Passage	Original Language	Interpreted by:
Gen 2:24	וְהָיוּ לְבָשָׂר אֶחָד (BHS) and they will become one flesh (NIV)	Original
Gen 2:24	καὶ ἔσονται οἱ δύο εἰς σάρκα μίαν (LXX)	Septuagint
Matt 19:5	καὶ ἔσονται οἱ δύο εἰς σάρκα μίαν (NA27)	Jesus
Mark 10:8	καὶ ἔσονται οἱ δύο εἰς σάρκα μίαν (NA27)	Jesus
1 Cor 6:16	ἔσονται γάρ, φησίν, οἱ δύο εἰς σάρκα μίαν (NA27)	Paul in Corinth
Eph 5:31	καὶ ἔσονται οἱ δύο εἰς σάρκα μίαν (NA27)	Paul in Ephesus

Paul Addressing Sexual Immorality (1 Cor 6:16)

Beginning with the letter to the Corinthians, Paul asks, "Do you not know that he who unites himself with a prostitute is one with her in body?" (1 Cor 6:16 NIV). This is followed by the Pauline equivalent of a bibliographical citation "γάρ, φησίν" (For, it says) as a means of validating his rhetorical question. Paul appears to have a very basic meaning in mind regarding Genesis 2:24. Paul could mean that the phrase "The two will become one flesh" implies sexual intercourse, or this phrase indicates that man and woman are created with the ability to mate through sexual intercourse. Given the context of the Genesis account, both are possible but the latter is favored given that the original narrative focuses on the creation of man and woman.

At a minimum, this means that Paul did not interpret the phrase "the two will become one flesh" to have infused monogamous implications. "That he at all can quote this expression, 'one flesh,' in this connection shows that he thereby simply means physical union, even if repeated with different partners."[64] Furthermore, few of the authors in this group who work with Genesis 2:24 likewise reference this passage.[65] While du Preez and Vollebregt are the only authors to cite this passage, they offer no explanation for Paul's interpretation.[66] This is especially problem-

---

64. Helander, *Must We Introduce Monogamy*, 35–36.

65. not cited in Blum, *Forms of Marriage*; Kaiser, *Toward Old Testament Ethics*; Parrinder, *Bible and Polygamy*; *The Problem of Polygamy*; Urrutia, "Can Polygamy Be Compatible"; Wishard, *Bible against Polygamy*; not cited with respect to polygamy in Hitchens, *Multiple Marriage*, 5.

66. For example, "St. Paul uses the expression 'becomes one flesh,' but applies it to a transitory connection with a prostitute (1 Cor. 6:16). But here the writer has in mind the normal sexual unity between man and woman, and this has its place in marriage.

atic since all of these authors insist that a major concern of Genesis 2:24 is the validation of monogamy and the condemnation of polygamy. This text should not be minimized or excluded because Paul's agenda does not fit the theology of this group. Rather this group must consider modifying their biblical understanding with respect to Paul's interpretation of the text. "For Paul this unity in the 'flesh' is not confined to the conjugal union of one husband and one wife, nor is it limited to the bonds of kinship. Even a man who joins himself to a prostitute becomes 'one flesh' with her: 'for, as it is written, "The two become one"' (1 Cor. 6:16–17). This kind of unity is obviously not exclusive in the way that a monogamous union is supposed to be, for a man can become 'one flesh' with any number of prostitutes."[67] As such, a hermeneutic that consistently excludes or ignores an extremely relevant text is insufficient, especially given the hermeneutical significance that is placed upon Genesis 2:24.

Paul Addressing the Church (Eph 5:31)

By contrast, Paul's quotation in Ephesians 5:31 is the most commonly cited passage to validate a monogamous interpretation of Genesis 2:24.[68] However, this is the only case in which the quotation is clearly used in an analogy of Christ's love for the church. Those who cite this passage superimpose their own analogy on the passage by claiming that monogamy is declared since there is only "one church" that is the bride of Christ.

Moreover, he speaks of the man giving up an enduring connection, since he leaves the family in which he has grown up, he 'leaves his father and mother' in order to enter a new and naturally also enduring bond with the wife of his choice. This enduring quality is implied by the words usually employed, 'to cleave to.' Although this phrase might be used of a temporary connection (cf. 1 Cor. 6:16) and be applied to the many loves of King Solomon (1 Kings 11:2)" (Vollebregt, *Bible on Marriage*, 62). Likewise, "The Pauline usage of this phrase is not addressed here; however, it could be argued that in Eph 5:31, 'Paul is not using monogamous marriage as an analogy at all. He is using the analogy of a relationship—the relationship which exists between Christ and the church;' Welch 96. Also, the phrase 'one flesh' in 1 Cor 6:16 is likewise used in connection with the Christian's relationship to Christ" (du Preez, *Polygamy in the Bible*, 270–71 endnote 15).

67. Hillman, *Polygamy Reconsidered*, 167.

68. Hitchens, *Multiple Marriage*, 134; Parrinder, *Bible and Polygamy*, 56; *The Problem of Polygamy*, 39–40.

A Missional Critique of the Hermeneutics

However, we could respond in kind by asking whether Christ loves only the church.[69] For, it is not difficult to demonstrate God's universal love of all people.[70] For, God so loved the world (and not just the church) that God's only son was given (John 3:16). Likewise, when the Church acts as if it is the sole object of God's love, Christian witness suffers a great deal. However, such a debate drifts from the real focus of the passage.

The main concern of the passage is the nature of Christ and the church. "Paul uses the same parable in another connection (I Cor. 12:12) . . . The thought in itself is not monogamic. The body is one but has many limbs. The family is one but has many members. . . . It is best to let the verse just speak about what it really aims to teach: about love and care, about indissoluble unity."[71]

More than likely, this passage demonstrates that the creation of the church was one that was designed for unity with God and likewise for the purpose of God's mission in the world in order to bring about new spiritual life. God's creation of man and woman makes for a strong analogy if Paul was thinking of man and woman's similar design to be united and to bring about new human life.[72] Paul almost certainly had the unity analogy in mind and the missional analogy would not be surprising given Paul's missionary background. However, to move beyond these themes would most likely stretch Paul's analogy too far. Notably, however, the common interpretation that can be found in both of Paul's quotations of Genesis 2:24 is that of a specially designed unity between man and woman.

Jesus Addressing the Pharisees (Matt 19:5; Mark 10:8)

The primary issue in Jesus' response, quoting both Genesis 1:27 and Genesis 2:24 is to gently rebuke the Pharisees by noting the very antithesis of their concern. Jesus reminds them that their very existence as men and that of their wives is given to them by God (Gen 1:27). In addition, Jesus reminds them that the gift of sexual union that they have

69. Helander, *Must We Introduce Monogamy*, 41–42.
70. Van Engen and Redford, "Syllabus," 42–45 originally Van Engen.
71. Helander, *Must We Introduce Monogamy*, 41.
72. Hillman points out that "[w]hat we have here is the familiar biblical notion of corporate personality: the singular (bride, wife) standing symbolically for the plural (we, the members), the individual representing the collective" (cp. Eph 5:28–33; 1 Cor 5:15; 12:27) (Hillman, *Polygamy Reconsidered*, 168).

is also a gift from God (Gen 2:24). It is as if Jesus is quoting these passages in order to say, "God created you and designed you to unite with your wife, and the attitude and ease with which you entertain divorce demonstrates that you have very little appreciation for God's formative design freely given in your creation." If this is Jesus' meaning, then Jesus' quotation of Genesis 2:24 is consistent with that of Paul. "Jesus used this Old Testament verse to show that the unity of marriage is such that in its very essence it can never be destroyed. Jesus did not intend to indicate what type of marriage, i.e. monogamy or polygamy, was necessary to attain the divine ideal of permanent unity. This divine ideal is as possible (or impossible) in a polygamous as in a monogamous marriage."[73]

More importantly, the emphasis of this passage is to address the issues surrounding divorce and nothing more.[74] Therefore, "[w]e need not expect to find here the answer to a question not being asked."[75]

If there is a common interpretation in the New Testament usage of Genesis 2:24, it would seem to be that of God's blessing in creating man and woman for physical union, as thematically illustrated in Figure 16, Paul's interpretation of the passage in 1 Corinthians 6:16 makes it too difficult to ascribe a far more lofty meaning to the passage. While it is possible that multiple meanings were intended for the original account, those related to monogamy and polygamy do not surface anywhere in Scripture.

---

73. Holst, "Polygamy and the Bible," 208–9.

74. Helander, *Must We Introduce Monogamy*, 23–25; Welch, "Biblical Perspective on Polygamy", 37, 87.

75. Hillman, *Polygamy Reconsidered*, 156. Some authors insightfully have suggested that the implication of adultery intended by Jesus is simply that no legitimate divorce has taken place because the couple is still married in the eyes of God (Colenso, *Remarks on Proper Treatment*, 7; Vollebregt, *Bible on Marriage*, 83). As such, the man is effectively committing adultery if he divorces his wife for an invalid reason and marries again (Matt 19:9). Likewise, since the men had the power to issue the divorce, they were effectively causing their wife to commit adultery if she was divorced for an invalid reason (Matt 5:31–32). Additionally, it would not be hard to imagine a different cultural context were women could issue a divorce, or a case in the Jewish culture where the wife intentionally creates marital turmoil in order to cause her husband to issue an invalid divorce. In either case the woman would be committing adultery herself by trying to force her husband to issue an invalid divorce, hence the wording of Mark 10:12 and Luke 16:18. However, in all of these passages Jesus seems to likewise be warning the community that they will also be committing adultery when they proceed to marry someone who divorced for an invalid reason.

A Missional Critique of the Hermeneutics

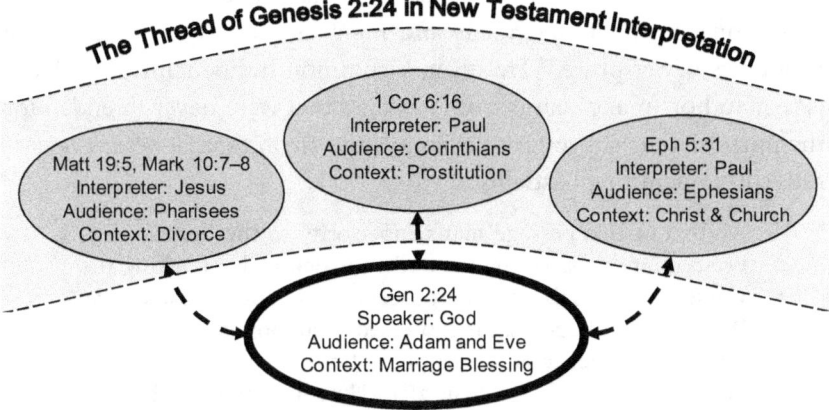

Figure 16: The Thread of Genesis 2:24 in the New Testament

Is Polygamy Comparable to Other Sexual Sins?

Many argue that polygamy is a sin by linking polygamy closely with other sexual sins, such as adultery and lust. This is most common when authors address David's sin with Bathsheba, in which they equate the two or cite polygamy as the root problem that brought about the adultery (2 Sam 12).[76] However, a major difference between polygamy and other true sexual sins is that the latter are explicitly declared in Scripture. Though Schillebeeckx is decidedly in favor of monogamy, he notes a major difference when comparing polygamy to other sexual sins: "Nowhere in the New Testament is there any explicit commandment that marriage should be monogamous or any explicit commandment forbidding polygamy. This presented no concrete problem: monogamous marriage was accepted as a point of departure. Sexual intercourse outside marriage (Jn viii. 41; 1 Cor vi. 12 ff.), sodomy, and homosexual relationships were condemned as sinful (Jude 7; Rom i. 24–7). So were prostitution (1 Cor vi. 12 ff.), which at that time was still practised in the temple, and pederasty (1 Cor vi. 9)."[77]

The main point is that God clearly denounced sexual sins such as lust, adultery, incest, prostitution, homosexuality, and bestiality. In strik-

---

76. du Preez, *Polygamy in the Bible*, 189; Hitchens, *Multiple Marriage*, 53; Vollebregt, *Bible on Marriage*, 26–27; in contrast Blum, *Forms of Marriage*, 191; Welch, "Biblical Perspective on Polygamy," 61–62.

77. Schillebeeckx, *Marriage*, I:202.

ing contrast to polygamy, these sins are condemned through extensive repetitions of direct statements and many negative depictions in the narratives of Scripture.[78] However, a common hermeneutical problem is that authors make claims from passages that were never intended for the purpose they suggest. For example, the claim that Genesis 2 is narratively condemning bestiality;

> And so in this passage man's superiority to the beasts is expressed, and in this way the author is definitely attacking the worship of animals, as it was observed in Egypt and elsewhere. But another antagonism is expressed even more severely: "The man gave names to all the cattle . . . but there was not found a helper fit for him." (20:2) [sic 2:20] Here he condemns bestiality. This practice was widespread in the ancient East. Jewish law imposed the death penalty for it (Exod. 22:18; Lev. 18:23; 20:15–16; Deut. 27:21).[79]

While bestiality is clearly a sin, Vollebregt demonstrates yet another unintended interpretation of Genesis 2. If the passage condemns bestiality, then it can likewise be used to condemn anything else that Adam did not do.

What other practices might be condemned using this hermeneutic? "Some scholars appeal to texts such as Lk. 16:13 'No man can serve two masters' as outlawing polygamy. But someone has rightly observed that it could as well be used to forbid one to have more than one child!"[80]

---

78. The following is not a comprehensive list, but representative passages. Adultery and prostitution are condemned substantially throughout Scripture. Adultery prohibited: Gen 20:3; 26:10; Exod 20:14; Lev 20:10; Num 5:12–13; Deut 5:18; 22:22; 2 Sam 12:7–14; Job 24:15; Pro 6:32; Matt 5:27–28; 15:19; 19:18; Mark 10:19; Luke 18:20; John 8:3–4; Rom 2:22; 1 Cor 6:9; 2 Pet 2:12; Rev 2:22. Prostitution prohibited: Lev 19:29; 21:9; Deut 23:17; 1 Kgs 14:24; 15:12; 22:46; 2 Kgs 23:7; 1 Cor 6:9, 15–16. Homosexuality prohibited: Gen 19:5–7; Lev 18:22; 20:13; Judg 19:22–23; Rom 1:24–27; 1 Cor 6:9; 1 Tim 1:10. Bestiality prohibited: Exod 22:19; Lev 18:23; 20:15–16; Deut 27:21. Improper sexual relations among relatives prohibited: Lev 18:1–17; 20:11–12. Sexual immorality prohibited: Matt 15:19; 1 Cor 6:9, 12ff; 1 Tim 1:10; Jude 7; Rev 22:15

79. Vollebregt, *Bible on Marriage*, 59–60.

80. Odame, *Christian Approach to Polygamy*, 34. The use of inferences hermeneutically is certainly entering into dangerous ground in biblical interpretation. Nearly any issue in Scripture could be labeled as a sin based on an approach of using inferences. It could easily be claimed that anything other than an arranged marriage is a sin, since God arranged the marriage of Adam and Eve (Gen 3). Suppose, for example, that we are exegetes who have lived in a culture in which the government allows only a single child to be born, and we are likewise convinced that this aspect of our culture is a bibli-

Likewise in Genesis 2, Adam did not eat the animals, so we could argue that eating meat is a non-ideal or sinful practice that should be ended. This would give dogmatic vegetarians ample means of condemning those who consume meat. Similarly, Adam did not domesticate the animals or use them for labor, so animal rights activists could theologically argue all attempts to domesticate or control animals are wrong. We could even note that Adam named all the animals, so wildlife biologists could argue that the people of God must be actively involved in searching the globe to ensure that all currently unknown animal species were discovered and named! Adam and Eve likewise were naked and had no children prior to the fall. Therefore, does the ideal marriage imply that couples should be unclothed and childless? Addressing this type of interpretation, Lewis claims; "One is quite as logical as the other. The difference is that none of us wants to go naked, the idea is wholly repugnant. Therefore it never occurs to us to draw such a conclusion from the Adam and Eve account. But in discussing the number of wives a man may have, we are strongly opposed to polygamy and eagerly looking for something to uphold mo-

---

cal ideal. We could easily use inference to show that if Abel had never been born, Cain never would have been jealous enough to kill his brother and that Cain was just never prepared for the irregularity (or "sin") of having siblings. The rivalry prophesied between the descendants of Isaac and Ishmael is quite illustrative. Jacob and Esau "clearly" demonstrate the "sin" of having more than one child. This would have to be due to some sin of Isaac or Rebecca and if nothing suitable is found, then some inference can surely be drawn (for example, Isaac was the son of a polygamist and so having two children was a punishment for his father's sin). Certainly Joseph and his 11 siblings would prove this point. Amnon and Absalom would be another example. Had David only had one child, then Amnon never would have wanted to rape Tamar and likewise Absalom would never have killed Amnon. The pinnacle in this example would be to show Jesus was clearly the only begotten Son of God, and therefore this line of thinking must be true. Of course, we would develop elaborate explanations for passages such as Genesis 1:28; 9:1, 7 ("multiply and fill the earth"). "Clearly" the command to have more than one child existed for special cases such as Adam and Eve in the origin of humanity or Noah in the restoration after great destruction. "Clearly" God did not mean for people to perpetually have more than one child since God promised to Noah that this sort of wholesale destruction would never take place again (Gen 9:8–17). Furthermore, a responsible understanding of that passage shows that we must propagate in a "civilized manner" with ample time to care and train our only child. Debates would surely exist over whether parents of a stillborn child could have another and so on. The main point is that it is quite simple to condemn or commend nearly anything we choose if we begin with the assumption that our cultural values have priority over the concerns of Scripture.

nogamy, so we readily grasp at the fact that God gave Adam only one wife... As a matter of fact, it has *absolutely no bearing* on the case."[81]

The primary reason that the other issues have not surfaced theologically is because Western cultures are not holistically dogmatic regarding childlessness, wildlife biology, animal rights or vegetarianism. All of these are seen as cultural fringes that may be extreme in some cases. However, the West is holistically dogmatic regarding monogamy, and this creates a problem when confronted with Old Testament biblical cultures that do not hold this same cultural values. Consequently, many conclusions can be drawn which have no basis while Genesis 2:24 is co-opted for purposes that were never intended.

Furthermore, Scripture does offer strong examples of passages that tie negative connotations to true sexual sins such as adultery, even though idolatry is the real focus (Jer 3:8–9; 5:7; 7:9; 13:27; 23:14; 29:23; Ezek 23; Hos 4). Idolatry and adultery are paralleled because the inferences are quite obvious. Consider for example, the text of Hosea 4:1–2:

> Hear the word of the Lord, O people of Israel!
> The Lord has brought charges against you, saying:
> "There is no faithfulness, no kindness, no knowledge of God
> in your land.
> You make vows and break them; you kill and steal and commit adultery."

In the last sentence, the association of adultery with killing and stealing gives the reader the impression that adultery is sinful, but the final clause reads "commit adultery," and this independently informs the reader that adultery is probably a bad thing.

However, if this is insufficient, Scripture includes amply redundant passages that directly condemn adultery (and other sexual sins as we have just seen). Where, however, is the clause stating that Israel (or anyone for that matter) "committed polygamy?" God's polygamous marriage of Ezekiel 23 is not such a case any more than monogamy acts a source for the adultery mentioned in Hosea. Likewise, God's chastisement of David is not such a case (2 Sam 12).[82] Polygamy is simply not

---

81. Lewis, *Divine Guidance*, 98.

82. Hillman comprehensively notes that "both Jeremiah and Ezekiel picture Yahweh also as the husband of more than one wife at the same time (cf. Jer 3:6–10; 31:31–32; Ezek 23:2–4)" Hillman, *Polygamy Reconsidered*, 147.

given the same language to denote that it is sin. As such, a hermeneutic that loosely affiliates polygamy with sin will not do.

Throughout the whole of Scripture the language associated with true sexual sins is sufficiently strong. However, authors have instead placed tremendous weight on the implications of Genesis 2:24 and other non-relevant passages while ignoring the clearer portions of Scripture that address polygamy, and through this they demonstrate an incredibly poor approach to biblical interpretation. This is nowhere more clear than in the following extremely weak claim:

> For the sake of showing the absurdity of the polygamist's interpretation [of Exod 21:10] . . . He affirms that because God says, "If he take him another wife, her food, her raiment, and her duty of marriage shall he not diminish," therefore He is regulating plural marriages; that is, if a man do a certain thing, it is right to do it. If a man steal, it is right to steal. For God has said in Exod. 22:1, "If a man shall steal an ox or a sheep, and kill it or sell it, he shall restore five oxen for one ox and four sheep for a sheep." Therefore God is regulating stealing, providing for it by law, and stealing becomes as much a duty as plural marriages![83]

The only absurdity is Wishard's hermeneutic and the fact that du Preez cites the argument for its merit.[84] By reading through the consequences of each passage, it is clear that God is penalizing theft and not penalizing the polygamist husband except in the instance when the husband neglects the basic needs of the slave wife who is more likely to encounter neglect.

Consequently, the penalty of Exodus 21:10 is only enforced when the husband is a bad polygamist! Wishard's argument lacks depth in fully addressing the issue. Furthermore, stealing is known to be a sin because stealing, like the previously mentioned sexual sins, is stipulated as an infraction throughout Scripture (for example, the ten command-

---

83. Wishard, *Bible against Polygamy*, 47.

84. du Preez, *Polygamy in the Bible*, 66. Du Preez cites Wishard in spite of knowing the weakness of the claim: "Wishard's argument has been challenged since the case law in Exod 22:1 has a clearly stated penalty, while the one in Exod 21:7–11 supposedly does not. However, a careful reading of this latter passage reveals that the specific actions to be taken include the loss of material goods (see especially vs. 10)" (ibid., 118 footnote 25). More than likely, du Preez meant to point to verse 11 at the end of this quote, but the loss of a slave wife only occurs if the husband mistreats her, and the regulation of Exodus 21:10 forces the husband to humanize the slave wife by giving her rights for proper treatment, rather than perceiving her as "material goods."

ments, Exod 20:15)! The same cannot be said of polygamy, and there is no indication that polygamy is ever considered a sin (except for the prohibition of Lev 18:18, which prohibits the rare case in which a man might marry two sisters at the same time, and the more extreme case found in Lev 20:14).[85] The extreme bias in these arguments is ultimately overly taxing.

Character Studies

Of all of the hermeneutics used, the character studies of biblical polygamists illustrate the impact of bias. While no one can claim to be without bias, the goal of this section is to illustrate a grace-filled hermeneutic. As such, these alternative readings attempt to address bias straightforwardly and demonstrate strengthened hermeneutics that give biblical figures the benefit of the doubt, while lessening the tendency for critique that is based upon cultural values.

Beginning with Lamech, many authors have surprisingly strong negative comments regarding the first known polygamist. However, very little is written regarding Lamech and his two wives, except that Lamech is a descendent of Cain, and that he killed a younger man while defending himself (Gen 4:19–24). While authors doubt the claim, Lamech was likely acting in self defense because (non-levirate) polygamists often have sufficient wealth to keep additional wives, and Lamech may have been attacked over this. Furthermore, the Bible makes no correlation between polygamy and the man killed by Lamech, so these and other claims are biased assumptions.[86]

Jacob was certainly a scoundrel in stealing his brother's birthright, but his solitary love for Rachel is a quality consistent with monogamy. Jacob has no interest in becoming a polygamist, but he was tricked into it and angry when he discovers Laban's deceit. Nevertheless, numerous authors treat Jacob is if he sought out polygamy. Polygamy could be a source of certain long-term problems with Leah, but Jacob's problems are more likely to have been a lack of attraction (Gen 29:18–19, 30–31), resentment over the marriage itself (Gen 29:25), and the added responsibility that Jacob had thrust upon him (Gen 29:27, 30). Assuming these

---

85. Cp. Lewis, *Divine Guidance*, 88–92.

86. Blum, *Forms of Marriage*, 213; Urrutia, "Can Polygamy Be Compatible," 281. Summers, by contrast has a very positive perception of Lamech (Summers, *Bible and Polygamy*, 13–15).

problems are the result of polygamy demonstrates interpretational bias. Authors writing against polygamy and making this connection should limit themselves to the cases where the Bible makes this type of connection, such as the strife between Leah and Rachel.[87]

Likewise, some authors give great esteem to Joseph over his devout concerns for celibacy and his much later monogamous marriage. Joseph consistently abstained from the daily sexual request sought by Potiphar's wife, who appears to be in a monogamous marriage (Gen 39:7ff). However, it is noteworthy that Joseph demonstrates some of the most impressive sexual control in Scripture even though he was raised in a polygamist home. In contrast, Reuben was raised in the same family and fell to similar temptations with his father's slave wife Bilhah (Gen 35:22). Likewise, the motivation for David's polygamy is consistently perceived as one of lust even though David was raised in a monogamous home.[88] Given Western biases, I have little doubt that Reuben's failure would be ascribed to his rearing in a polygamist family had it not been for Joseph's valor. The biblical narratives demonstrate that the true impact of family values is based upon the family's allegiance to God, regardless of their monogamous or polygamous status.

Finally, it is interesting to note that Jacob's polygamy may have been responsible for some of the stipulations regarding polygamy. Jacob's account gives good reason for the prohibition against marrying two sisters (Lev 18:18). Leah and Rachel's marriage to the same man clearly had a negative impact on their relationship as sisters. Likewise, Reuben's sexual involvement with Bilhah is prohibited in the same chapter (Lev 18:8). However, (and this is pure speculation) Jacob may have been a contributor to the source of the problem if he was not spending adequate time meeting the emotional and physical needs of his slave wives. This may have contributed to the provision stated in Exodus 21:10–11 giving greater rights to a slave wife. I do not mean to imply that this excuses Reuben and Bilhah's sexual involvement, but Jacob's possible neglect of his slave wife may have created a great void. If this conjecture is correct, it would be most important to realize that both of these provisions demonstrate God's attempt to provide boundaries for the polygamist marriage rather than eradicating polygamy entirely, which just as easily could have been done.

87. Blum, *Forms of Marriage*, 183.
88. *The Problem of Polygamy*, 12.

Finally, Samson was born and brought up in a monogamist household and his mother was unable to become pregnant for most of her life (Judg 13:2). This case of infertility would certainly have given Samson's father a commonly accepted reason to take on a second wife. However, they remained monogamous and Samson was born. Certainly we would think that Samson would have had far better morals than Joseph, especially if we are inclined to believe in a progression toward the ideal of monogamy. Yet Samson's lack of interest in Israelite women causes him to marry the Philistine woman in Timnah, but his separation causes his new wife to be given to another (Judg 14:19–20). Moreover, this marriage to a foreign woman is in God's plan (Judg 14:4). However, his infatuation with Delilah eventually leads to his downfall (Judg 16:4ff). How is it that a child of a monogamous family born hundreds of years later is so much worse in terms of sexual control than the son of a polygamist?

More importantly, from a hermeneutical perspective, how unfair is the comparison that I am making? It is extremely unfair because I am comparing one of the best cases in polygamy with one of the worst cases in monogamy. I am comparing extremes, and more than likely I am comparing the two men over the issue of monogamy and polygamy which likely has no impact. It is a faulty hermeneutic to forcibly claim that all the wrong-doings of a polygamist husband, wife or child are due to a polygamist marriage. This approach makes it all the more obvious that the interpreter can have an agenda if not a vendetta when dealing with polygamy.

Other accounts could be easily mentioned, such as the levirate marriage between Ruth and Boaz. The reader is not told if Boaz was married prior to Ruth, but most African interpreters feel this was likely, given his stature. Hosea depicts Israel's covenantal unfaithfulness with God, but this life-metaphor is carried out monogamously. Does this mean monogamy is wrong? No, this is not the point of Hosea.[89]

Likewise, the Parable of the Ten Virgins is the account that seems to be most often ignored (Matt 25:1–13). Simply put, the image of a single bridegroom and ten virgins is one of polygamy.[90] Five of the ten virgins

---

89. Contra Blum, *Forms of Marriage*, 215–17.

90. During the October 14–15, 2001 missiology lectures, guest speaker Eugene A. Nida spoke at the faculty luncheon and stated that the appropriate meaning for the New Testament concept of a "virgin" (παρθένος) was a woman who was single or available to marry, rather than "never had intercourse."

were accepted into the bridegroom's company. It has been said that the New Testament has nothing to say on polygamy, and this is correct, but those who work with inference are presented here with another image of God as a polygamist.

A far better hermeneutic is to stop trying to force a particular interpretation by drawing inferences from Scripture. Over the long term, this hermeneutic will do more damage than good as will be shown later with Group 5.

> There seems to me no compelling reasons for concluding that the marriage analogy used by the Prophets makes the monogamic ideal perceptibly clearer. Their purpose was not to exalt monogamy, but rather faithfulness to the covenant Yahweh had made with the nation. They were not concerned to condemn polygamy, but "spiritual adultery." In so doing they had no hesitation in picturing God as married to two wives at the same time (cf. Jeremiah 3.6–10; and Ezekiel 23.1–43). In the case of Ezekiel, the two "wives" of Yahweh had been prostitutes, and even of doubtful reputation before that. A strange analogy indeed for a prophet who has a clear view of the monogamous marriage ideal God is supposed to be progressively revealing in Israel. In one instance he pictures God as a monogamist; in another as a polygamist. There is an obvious danger in insisting upon a literal interpretation of such analogies.[91]

Hermeneutical Critique

There are some unique hermeneutical pitfalls among this group as well as some common problems. Beginning with the problems, Blum and Vollebregt both lean upon Wellhausen's documentary hypothesis.[92]

91. Welch, "Biblical Perspective on Polygamy", 70.

92. Despite Vollebregt's claim that the Eden account is a unique genre, Vollebregt is dogmatic in both his interpretation and his assumed accuracy in assigning the Yahwist to certain passages, based on Wellhausen theory. Likewise, Vollebregt assigns a great deal more meaning to Lamech's account than can be reasonably drawn from the passage itself. "That the Yahwist tradition in the Garden-of-Eden account regards monogamous marriage as normal is corroborated by the noteworthy remark in the list of Cain's descendants, that Lemech was the first to take two wives (Gen. 4:19). The meaning of this whole Chapter 4 is to show, through tradition that has been handed down, how the descendants of Cain deviated further and further from the original institutions. The writer mentions the first case of bigamy without explicit censure, but it is surely no accident that the so-called Song of the Sword for vengeance is attributed to the first bigamist (4:23–4)" (Vollebregt, *Bible on Marriage*, 63). Likewise, in dealing with

Blum suggests that Scripture may have legitimately or illegitimately been modified to allow for polygamy.[93] Additionally, Blum's overall opinion is that polygamy cannot be allowed in the church, and as such he suggests that the stipulations of Exodus 21:10 and Deuteronomy 21:15–17 are the efforts of a redactor who realized that polygamous families typically degenerated into a loved wife and an unloved wife.[94] However, an overemphasis on redaction does not allow Scripture to speak for itself, and Welch appropriately challenges this claim: "It is exceedingly strange that the so-called Documentists who compiled and edited the Genesis narratives did not meet the polygamy issue head on if they were all that determined to discredit it. Why did they not slay it once and for all with one mighty blow of their literary sword, rather than hide behind verbal rocks and trees and slyly sling innuendo-shaped pebbles at it? Were it so great an evil, why was it not simply and openly condemned?"[95]

Blum likewise avoids the more difficult passages while simultaneously resting his condemnation of polygamy on the creation account in Genesis. "[T]he strongest disagreements revolve around the exegesis of the Creation accounts in the book of *Genesis*. Those accounts are more properly theological, than are some of the other passages, and therefore, we will have to consider them carefully."[96] However, Blum only casually mentions Leviticus 18:18 and never addresses the passage's implications.[97] Furthermore, Blum minimizes the impact that the oral tradition of Scripture might have had on the patriarchs understanding of marriage: "In the time of the patriarchs, Israel possessed no written law, or hard and fast tradition of its own in regard to marriage regulations. As we will see, the patriarchal society seems to have followed the marriage customs of the time."[98]

Genesis 1:26–28, Vollebregt claims to know the mind of the biblical author, "Although the passage makes no definite reference to marriage, marriage is certainly in the author's mind. What he says about man as the image of God he emphatically applies to both man and woman" (ibid., 70, compare 84).

93. Blum, *Forms of Marriage*, 174–75.
94. Ibid., 183.
95. Welch, "Biblical Perspective on Polygamy," 49.
96. Blum, *Forms of Marriage*, 175.
97. Ibid., 217.
98. Ibid., 176–77.

A Missional Critique of the Hermeneutics

On the opposite extreme, the worst hermeneutics are those claiming that passages using the singular form of "wife" are evidence of the biblical preference for monogamy.[99] When Scripture uses the word "child," should we assume that this word implies that families should not have more than one child? Likewise, does the term "brook" imply that there is only one stream on the planet? The fact that such a hermeneutic is used demonstrates the desperation of these authors to make a valid argument given the absence of substantial biblical claims against polygamy.

In terms of the more common hermeneutical problems, two trends can be seen among the majority of those arguing against polygamy. The first is to engage in character assassination in the lives of polygamists, and this demonstrates a bias because the authors do not consider the positive acts that flow from those influenced by polygamy. Likewise, monogamists are not equally scrutinized. Additionally, when comparisons are made, the best-case monogamy scenarios are typically compared with the worst-case polygamy scenarios. As Charles H. Kraft has often stated in his lectures, "a fair comparison can only be made when we compare our best to their best, or our worst to their worst."

A second poor hermeneutic is one that is based upon inferences (which I will refer to as an inference-hermeneutic). The inference-hermeneutic is riddled with problems because the inferences are made in favor of the pre-conceived theological positions and the cultural values of the interpreter. The problem here is that an inference-hermeneutic can be used to validate or invalidate virtually any concern.[100] So, when authors assume that polygamy is the source of the problem or the cause of a sin, they invariably infer that to be the case when approaching Scripture. Furthermore, this approach actually demonstrates the weakness of their claims: "How desperate is the situation of those who feel there must be an explicit scriptural ground for absolute monogamy is shown by the appeal even to such texts as Luke 16.13: 'No one can serve

---

99. Hitchens, *Multiple Marriage*, 128, 34–36; Parrinder, *Bible and Polygamy*, 33; Vollebregt, *Bible on Marriage*, 49–51.

100. "The whole biblical case against the practice of polygamy is developed only by inferences, and it hinges on a number of assumptions which can no longer be taken as self-evident" (Hillman, *Polygamy Reconsidered*, 141).

two masters' as outlawing polygamy. It could about as well be used to forbid one to have more than one child."[101]

The greatest danger of these biases is that Scripture is not permitted to speak to the missional community, because the intended emphases are obscured and unintended emphases are drawn out and highlighted. For example, some later passages in the Old Testament act as commentary upon the lives of well-known polygamist leaders. When this intertextual commentary is taken seriously, polygamy is not cited within Scripture as a problem (Gen 26:5; 1 Kgs 11:1–8; 15:5; 2 Chr 24:2–3; Neh 13:23–30). However, they do point out failures in other areas such as exogamy.[102] The details of these intertextual passages will be discussed in greater detail when looking at Group 4. Additionally, Scripture does not claim that "Lamech killed this man because he was a polygamist" or "David committed adultery because he was a polygamist." Yet these are common conclusions of this group.

> The numerous "conclusive" arguments presented to prove that our Lord had very clear monogamous views about marriage are based primarily on a highly inadequate approach to the exegetical task. In the first place, this approach idealizes one's own culture. Secondly, it projects one's own cultural views onto the Scriptures. And thirdly, it ignores literary, historical, and cultural contexts. It appears that writers such as Parrinder and Vollebregt—and a host of others—have "presupposed the results of exegesis." They have approached the exegetical task with their minds already made up. It is no problem then to find *implicit* condemnation of polygamy in a great many texts. But it is obvious that in many cases it is *projected* meaning rather than *implicit* meaning which they find. This appears to be true in their treatment of the teachings of Jesus as well. He is made to say what they wish him to say.[103]

Finally, Scripture is sufficiently redundant to declare its major concerns over and over, most likely because we have such difficulty listening. We must trust God to make important themes known so that those can be shared with the world, while giving significantly less attention to themes that rarely surface, and no attention to themes that cannot be found.

101. Hastings, *Christian Marriage in Africa*, 74.
102. Summers argues along these lines (Summers, *Bible and Polygamy*, 35–36).
103. Welch, "Biblical Perspective on Polygamy," 93–94.

MONOGAMY IS GOD'S IDEAL

Those in the second column of Table 6 make up the majority opinion of the biblical understanding of polygamy. However, it is difficult to find consistency among authors who claim that monogamy is the biblical ideal. The most common claim is that the New Testament wording of Genesis 2:24 is indicative of an intentional transition toward monogamy.[104] As we have seen, this appears foremost to be a result of quoting from the Septuagint rather than an intentional theological modification. Additionally, many in this group interpret 1 Timothy 3:2, 12 and Titus 1:6 as a requirement for monogamous leadership that also demonstrates the New Testament ideal of monogamy.

For the most part, the notion that monogamy is God's ideal is one that seems correct to many authors which they then confirm throughout Scripture.[105] Biblical compassion is likewise perceived as a part of this perspective; "It would indeed have been difficult for the Jews, springing from Jacob's polygamic marriage, to consider all but Leah's children as being born illegally and in a rejectable type of marriage. The break with polygamy could not be sharp, but only a gradual development."[106]

Some of the authors in this group suggest that polygamy is allowed for the same reasons as divorce, and specifically assign the same saying to polygamy—that it was allowed due to the hardness of men's hearts.[107] For example, "As to divorce, the answer is that, by the precept of Christ, all, both clergy and people, were restrained from unjust divorces. And with respect to polygamy, being an offence against political prudence rather than against morality, it had been permitted to the Jews by Moses, Deut. xxi., 15, on account of the hardness of their hearts."[108] Though Colenso was foremost advocating that polygamists be allowed to remain with their wives as full church members, it was the Africans writing a

---

104. As was shown in the prior section, Gen 2:24 originally reads "they shall become one flesh," but the New Testament quotation reads "the two shall become one flesh" (Matt 19:5; Mark 10:7–8; 1 Cor 6:16; Eph 5:31).

105. E.g., compare Vollebregt, *Bible on Marriage*, 51–52, 63; with Welch, "Biblical Perspective on Polygamy", 35–37, 42, 61–62.

106. Helander, *Must We Introduce Monogamy*, 30.

107. Odame, *Christian Approach to Polygamy*, 31.

108. Colenso, *Remarks on Proper Treatment*, 13. Colenso's primary argument is that Scripture clearly prohibits divorce, aside from adultery, but he does equate polygamy with adultery, and likewise there is no prohibition for polygamy that stands with equal weight as those against divorce (ibid., 5–8).

century later that would argue against projecting the claims for divorce onto polygamy:

> Divorce reflects hardness of heart, Jesus said. "Let no one divide what God has yoked together" (10:9).
>
> Yet, this passage has been taken as authority for condemnation of polygamy. Since Jesus mentions "the *two* becoming one," it is argued that he meant only monogamy is permitted. In reality, the New Testament teaching on marriage—here and in Matthew 5:27–32, Romans 7:2–3, 1 Corinthians 7:2–16, Ephesians 5:22–33—repudiates adultery, divorce, polyandry (many husbands), and consecutive polygamy (marrying and divorcing several wives in succession), but *nowhere* do these texts consider simultaneous polygamy.[109]

Furthermore, the absence of polygamous marriages in the New Testament is one of the more common reasons that has been given to support the idea that monogamy is God's ideal. In general, the claim is that Old Testament acts of polygamy faded away after the kings and what is found in the New Testament is the monogamic ideal. However, the theory that polygamy faded away is a difficult one to justify because the polygamy of the Old Testament spans millennia and the New Testament spans a century of history at the most. Figure 17 is shown primarily to offer a graphical comparison of the vastly different time periods covered by the Old and New Testaments.

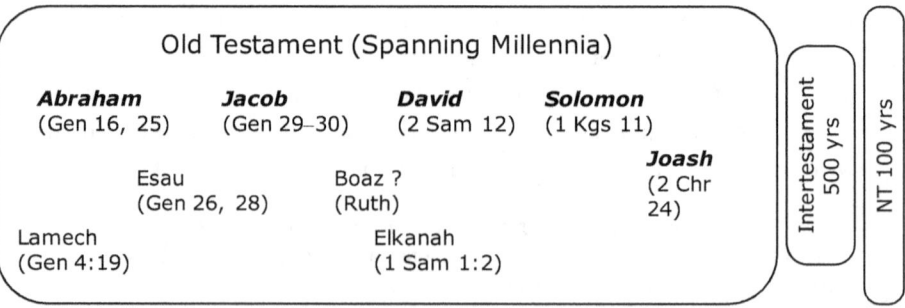

Figure 17: Supposed Fading of Polygamy throughout Scripture

---

109. Gitari, "Rethinking Polygamy," 43.

A Missional Critique of the Hermeneutics

Given the New Testament's much shorter time frame and its highly missional focus, the absence of polygamy in the narratives is not an indication that the practice was ending. Likewise, many who hold this view are under the impression that polygamy did not exist near the first century, but Josephus clearly states that Herod the Great (37–4bc) had many wives and concubines.[110] Furthermore, the Old Testament demonstrates an increase in polygamy as many Israelite kings are polygamists and are likewise highly visible during Israel's strongest political era.

Finally, it may be our cultural coloring that glosses over hints of polygamy within the New Testament. For example, Chime's background as a polygamist causes him to interpret Leviticus 18:7–8 and 1 Corinthians 5:1–2 quite differently than others. He assumes a context of polygamy for both passages, and he perceives that the New Testament passage is an echo of the Old Testament requirement that the children of a polygamist must not be sexually involved with the co-wives of their father (compare Gen 35:20).[111]

1 Timothy 3:2, 12: A Common Hermeneutical Problem

A vast number of authors cite 1 Timothy 3:2, 12 as validation of the existence of polygamy in the New Testament as well as a demonstration of the biblical preference for monogamy. The argument is that the call for monogamous leadership by nature implies the existence of polygamist members in the New Testament church, but the requirement of monogamous leaders demonstrates the greater merit of monogamy (1 Tim 3:2, 12; Titus 1:6).[112] However, this is a common hermeneutical mistake for at least two reasons. The first is that polygamy is among the least likely meanings that Paul might have had in mind. The second is that

---

110. Josephus claims that polygamy was practiced near the first century (Antiquities 17.14; Wars 1.477). Josephus states that Herod the Great had many wives (Antiquities 17.19ff; Wars 1.562). Likewise Herod the Great also had concubines (Wars 1.511).

111. Chime, *Polygamy and Christian Religion*, 5–7.

112. Adutchum, "Church and Issue of Polygamy," 28; Chime, *Polygamy and Christian Religion*, 7–8; Gaskiyane, *Polygamy*, 60–61; Gitari, "Church and Polygamy," 7; Helander, *Must We Introduce Monogamy*, 32–33, 35, 57–59; Hillman, *Polygamy Reconsidered*, 166–67; Hitchens, *Multiple Marriage*, 135; Kaiser, *Toward Old Testament Ethics*, 189; Kiwovele, "Polygyny as a Problem," 14; Maillu, *Our Kind of Polygamy*, 48; Mann, "Biblical Understanding of Polygamy," 21, 25; McGavran, "What Says the Word," 358; Nkwoka, "Church and Polygamy in Africa," 148–49; Odame, *Christian Approach to Polygamy*, 36; Tiénou and Hiebert, "Missional Theology," 234; Wambutda, "Monogamy or Polygamy," 80.

the ambivalence of the passages themselves should cause any interpreter to remain cautious in making authoritative claims without the support of similar passages throughout the remainder of the New Testament or the Bible as a whole.

Yet, it is common to encounter missionaries and missiologists making claims that cannot be substantiated from these passages. For example, Helander claims that Paul's requirement of monogamous leaders "is the simple and obvious meaning of I Tim. 3:2, 12: An episcopos should be the husband of only one wife" and bases this on his conclusion that polygamy prevailed in the New Testament.[113] By one account, this was also the official position in 1951 of the Lutheran Church in Liberia.[114] Quite possibly the worst example of this is McGavran's short article in which his interpretational biases are quite obvious as he claims that 1 Timothy 3:2, 12 is addressing polygamy, and the Paul is offering recommendations for leadership rather than requirements, so on this basis polygamists can become church leaders: "These three passages [1 Tim 3:2, 12; Titus 1:6] then support the position that believing polygamists out of non-Christian society may be baptized. (a) They strongly infer that in the Early Church there were husbands of two or more wives. (b) They may even indicate that in the choice of deacons and elders there was no absolute prohibition of men with two or more wives."[115]

A smaller group of authors claim that the call for monogamous leadership in 1 Timothy 3:2, 12 is based upon Paul's concern to provide contextually appropriate forms of leadership within the missional church.[116] They claim that anything other than monogamous leadership would be seen as indecent given the cultural values of the Greeks and Romans. Hillman is less committed to this idea than Kraft, but summarizes it well stating, "Perhaps this 'one wife' rule came from nothing more than the young Church's need to accommodate itself to the ways of the Greco-Roman world, which saw polygamy as an objectionable

---

113. Helander, *Must We Introduce Monogamy*, 32.

114. Currens, "A Policy of Baptizing Polygynists Evaluated," 76.

115. McGavran, "What Says the Word," 358.

116. Hillman, *Polygamy Reconsidered*, 166–67; Kraft, *Christianity in Culture*, 323–25; Welch, "Biblical Perspective on Polygamy," 9 Welch is following Kraft's lead. Kraft's position on this matter is eventually modified and discussed later in this section.

foreign custom: something forbidden to Roman citizens, hence inappropriate for Church leaders in the Roman world."[117]

Among those writing on these passages in relation to polygamy, the most often overlooked issue is that 1 Timothy 5:9 uses the same Greek construction as 1 Timothy 3:2, 12, but the genders are reversed. Therefore, in the same way that Paul requires that a church leader should be a "one-woman man," Paul also requires that the church should only support a widow who is a "one-man woman."[118] Given that 1 Timothy 3:2, 12 and 1 Timothy 5:9 are written by the same author in the same letter and addressing the virtuous characteristics of their respective subjects, there is no reason why the clauses should not be consistently translated. Nevertheless, the NIV fails in this respect and one author has argued that 1 Timothy 3:2, 12 is addressing monogamy and polygamy, even though he is well aware of the construction of 1 Timothy 5:9.[119]

Table 10 is a comparison of five different intended meanings for 1 Timothy 3:2, 12 and 5:9.[120] The table outlines a consistent translation of each passage and the following paragraphs consider the implication in greater depth, beginning with the most likely and moving to the least likely possibilities. Notably, this analysis is one that demonstrates the merit of grammatical work, but it will later be shown that this is not the only hermeneutic that has potential with respect to these passages.

---

117. Hillman, *Polygamy Reconsidered*, 167.

118. The Greek language uses the same word for man/husband (ἀνήρ) and woman/wife (γυνή). Therefore, μιᾶς γυναικὸς ἄνδρα (1 Tim 3:2, 12) can literally be translated "one-woman man," "man of one woman" or "husband of one wife," while ἑνὸς ἀνδρὸς γυνή (1 Tim 5:9) can literally be translated "one-man woman," "man of one woman" or "wife of one husband." Furthermore, it is insignificant for this comparison that man/husband (ἀνήρ) in 1 Timothy 3:2 is in the plural accusative case because it acts as a direct object, while in man/husband (ἀνήρ) 1 Timothy 3:12 is plural nominative, acting as a predicate nominative. Furthermore, Titus 1:6 is singular nominative, but likewise functions as a predicate nominative. In short, the cases of the clauses are different, but the each clause functions as a direct object or predicate nominative with respect to the subject.

119. Colenso, *Remarks on Proper Treatment*, 8–10.

120. Some have consider a sixth possibility which is that of "married to the church," but this meaning is so unlikely it is not pursued here (compare du Preez, *Polygamy in the Bible*, 261–67).

Table 10: Likelihood of Various Meanings for 1 Timothy 3:2, 12; 5:9

Overall Meaning	μιᾶς γυναικὸς ἄνδρα (one-woman man, 1 Tim 3:2, 12) means:	ἑνὸς ἀνδρὸς γυνή (one-man woman, 1 Tim 5:9) with same meaning would be:	The Likelihood of the Overall Meaning using a Consistent Rendering for Each Passage:
1. Requiring Marital Fidelity	A leader must be faithful to his wife	Only care for widow who was faithful to her husband.	*Most likely* rendering since both passages focus on the virtues of leaders and widows
2. Against Divorce	A leader must not have formerly divorced.	Only care for a widow who had not been divorced.	*Less likely* rendering because women had little choice in the matter of a divorce
3. Against Digamy	A leader, if married at all, must have married only once in life.	Only care for a widow who did not remarry after her first husband died.	*Unlikely* rendering given 1 Timothy 5:11–14 in which Paul encourages widows to remarry (compare 1 Cor 7:39)
4. Requiring Marriage	A leader must have a wife.	Only care for the widow who had a husband.	*Extremely unlikely* rendering given the obvious redundancy of 1 Timothy 5:9.
5. Against Polygamy	A leader must not be a polygynist.	Only care for widow who was not polyandrous.	*Extremely unlikely* rendering since polyandry is never addressed in all of Scripture.

1. With respect to the literary context of 1 Timothy 3:1–13 and 5:3–10, both passages emphasize the virtues of leaders and older widows respectively. Adding "marital fidelity" to the list is consistent with the irreproachable characteristics required in both passages. There is disagreement as to whether or not Ephesus was overrun with sexuality and

A Missional Critique of the Hermeneutics

female deities.[121] Nevertheless, "faithfulness" is much more consistent with the discourse flow in 1 Timothy, which has a consistent emphasis on sexual purity as a means of remaining faithful to God (1 Tim 2:9–10; 3:11; 5:2, 9, 11–14, 21). Likewise, "being faithful" to your wife has much more to do with being blameless.

Some might argue that all Christians are required to be faithful in marriage and as such this would be an absurd addition to this list. However, other qualities ascribed to leaders are likewise required for all Christians (for example not "an active alcoholic, legalistic, greedy or getting into fist-fights" 1 Tim 3:3 translation mine).

For a widow this intended meaning meant that she must have been faithful to her husband in order to receive the church's support. However, faithfulness was not the only criteria. Widows were required to "be at least sixty years old and have been faithful in marriage, and they should have a reputation for doing good things, such as raising children, showing hospitality, humbly doing work that others will not, coming to the aid of those in trouble, and remaining devoted in the midst of all good works" (1 Tim 5:9–10 translation mine).

It may seem harsh that Paul does not call the church to care for the less-than-perfect widow. However, it is important to remember that Paul is restricting the church's support of older widows based on multiple criteria in this case. As such, none of the overall meanings in Table 10 permits the church to support all widows. Nevertheless, marital faithfulness is the most consistent with the virtues mentioned and is likewise the only intended meaning that is consistent for both passages.[122] In support of this possibility, three relatively new translations render these passages with the overall meaning of faithfulness in marriage (NLT, CEV, NIRV).[123]

---

121. Cp. Köstenberger and Schreiner, *Women in the Church: An Analysis and Application of 1 Timothy 2:9-15*; Kroeger and Kroeger, *I Suffer Not*.

122. Notably, ultra-conservatives opt for this intended meaning. John MacArthur, in commenting on 1 Timothy 3:2, states, "A one-woman man . . . maintains sexual purity in both his thought life and his conduct. That qualification was especially important in Ephesus, where sexual evil was rampant" (MacArthur, *1 Timothy*, 104). Dr. Greg Mazak from Bob Jones University claims that 1 Tim 5:9 would be absurd if it was rendered over polygamy (lecturing on "Blameless: A One Woman Man", 29:00, 1 Timothy 3:1–2—Bob Jones University Chapel Hour 7/23/2003). However, MacArthur and Mazak both believe that polygamy is a sin and that Paul could not be referring to polygamy because polygamists would not be allowed in the church in the first place. However, both likewise address 1 Tim 5:9 in making this claim.

123. 1 Timothy 3:2 is rendered: "That's why officials must . . . be faithful in mar-

2. It is possible that 1 Timothy 3:2, 12 is addressing divorce. Paul's wording would not likely differentiate between divorce and digamy unless this phrase was idiomatic.[124] Likewise, it is uncertain if New Testament readers made a distinction between divorce and digamy, or if the Greek clauses in question were in fact idioms that held an obvious meaning for first century readers in Ephesus.[125] Though I am treating the two as separate areas, they could have had a combined meaning in the first century. If Paul's overall meaning is divorce, then Paul would be claiming that the church should not care for widows who are divorced.[126] However, Jewish women had virtually no choice in the matter

---

riage" (CEV). "A leader ... must be faithful to his wife" (NIRV). "For an elder ... must be faithful to his wife" (NLT).

1 Timothy 3:12 is rendered: "Church officers must be faithful in marriage" (CEV). "A deacon must be faithful to his wife" (NIRV). "A deacon must be faithful to his wife" (NLT).

1 Timothy 5:9 is rendered: "a widow must ... have been faithful in marriage" (CEV). A widow "must also have been faithful to her husband" (NIRV). "A widow [must have been] faithful to her husband" (NLT).

Titus 1:6 is rendered: "they must . . . be faithful in marriage" (CEV). "An elder ... must be faithful to his wife." (NIRV). "He must be faithful to his wife" (NLT).

The NIV uses an inconsistent translation that initially reads "the husband of but one wife" (1 Tim 3:2, 12; Titus 1:6) but renders 1 Timothy 5:9 as "widows [must have] been faithful to her husband" with an optional translation that widows must have "had but one husband." However, the NIV has no optional translation for "faithfulness" in the former passages.

The Message (MSG) is inconsistent in the opposite way: "A leader must be ... committed to his wife" (1 Tim 3:2). "Servants in the church are to be committed to their spouses" (1 Tim 3:12). "Is he committed to his wife?" (Titus 1:6). However the rendering for 1 Tim 5:9 is "[W]idows ... must be ... married only once."

124. Digamy is simply "a second marriage after the termination of the first" Online Merriam-Webster: http://www.m-w.com/cgi-bin/netdict?digamy (accessed March 18, 2007).

125. Some idioms make no sense if the gender is reversed as in 1 Tim 3:2, 12 and 1 Tim 5:9. For example, these American English idioms (and their meanings) are usually only used with one gender: "Hell hath no fury like a woman scorned" (a woman will take revenge); "make an honest woman of me" (a man should propose to a woman); "a man's man" (a man respected and popular with other men). However, there are idioms that can function with both genders such as "the man/woman of my dreams" (someone for whom you have great attraction); "a man/woman after my own heart" (someone admired because he or she shares the same beliefs).

126. Albrecht Oepke claims that 1 Timothy 5:9 refers to unfaithfulness and divorce, but it is unlikely given what has already been mentioned (TDNT—ἀνήρ—γυνή) (Kittel et al., *TDNT*, 1:362 footnote 11, 1:778). Likewise, du Preez assigns a double meaning of "faithfully monogamous" (du Preez, *Polygamy in the Bible*, 267).

A Missional Critique of the Hermeneutics

of a divorce, as demonstrated by Jesus chastisement of Jewish men over their fickle grounds for issuing a divorce (Matt 19:3–12; Mark 10:2–12). Additionally, if a blanket decree against divorce is the issue, it would be difficult to deal with other claims by Jesus and Paul (Matt 5:31–32; 19:9; 1 Cor 7:15).[127] Furthermore, God exercised a covenantal break with Israel that was a spiritual divorce (Isa 50:1, Jer 3:7–8).

3. Some believe that Paul is rejecting leaders who married again after the divorce or death of a spouse, which is the practice of digamy.[128] If you married at all, marrying once for life was a culturally esteemed practice in early Christianity. Kraft cites numerous theologians from the early 1900s who think that Paul's statement is a declaration against digamy.[129] However, if 1 Timothy 3:2, 12 is focused upon digamy, then 1 Timothy 5:9 would be stating that the church should only care for non-digamous widows. The initial problem with this is that Paul immediately follows 1 Timothy 5:9 with a claim that the younger widows should remarry (1 Tim 5:11–14). Likewise, Paul encourages widows in the Corinthian church to remarry (1 Cor 7:39). Paul would essentially be saying, "you should remarry, but if you do remarry and become a widow in your old age and are truly in need, you will not be given help from the church."

Kraft adopts a more generalized approach and claims that the real force behind the passage is "the supracultural requirement of irreproachability on the part of Christian leaders" that contextually chooses leaders based on the values esteemed by the culture.[130] Therefore, Kraft is claim-

---

127. I believe it is quite intentional that the exception clause for divorce ("except for marital unfaithfulness") is found *only* within Matthew (5:32; 19:9). It is placed within Matthew for highly contextual reasons—because Matthew is writing to the Jews and there are two threads of divorce running throughout Jewish history (which a specifically Jewish audience needed hear). In Matthew 19, the first is the more obvious thread in the passage regarding the dictatorial and fickle manner in which Jewish men might "validly" claim a divorce. In the background of Israel's long history is the second and critically important thread of God's divorce with Israel due to Israel's marital unfaithfulness. This is the main reason that the clause is added *only* in Matthew. Jesus, aware of the extensive history of God's patience with unfaithful Israel, is indirectly pointing out that God's reason for divorcing Israel was radically different than the whims of these men. Had Jesus used a direct statement, especially in the second case, the Jews would have clearly understood and most likely tried to kill Jesus immediately.

128. Boer, "Polygamy," 25; Parrinder, *Bible and Polygamy*, 50–52; *The Problem of Polygamy*, 28–29.

129. Kraft, *Culture, Communication, and Christianity*, 422–23.

130. Ibid., 425. Since Kraft leans toward digamy as Paul's concern, I am addressing

ing that Paul is, in fact contextualizing to match highly esteemed cultural values such as digamy or monogamy. This would almost certainly not be the case if the passage is referring to marital fidelity.[131] However, Kraft does not consider marital fidelity as a possibility.[132] Therefore, Kraft's underlying assumption is that this passage implies the need for contextually appropriate church leaders. While it is commendable that Kraft is considering the missional dimensions of the passage, he does not adequately consider the implications that this would have for widows.

What are the implications of Kraft's supracultural principle as it relates to the widows (1 Tim 5:9)? If digamy is Paul's intended meaning, it would mean that widows in genuine need of assistance could not be supported by the church solely because they did not match the surrounding culture's concept of irreproachability. While it is conceivable that church leaders might be excluded on this basis, it is unfathomable that Paul would allow widows to suffer solely due to the cultural values of the region where they lived. Likewise, any of the overall meanings in Table 10 would mean that the widows would suffer in one context and be supported in another, with the exception of a biblical concern over marital fidelity. Furthermore, Scripture contains notable accounts when leaders did not conform to highly esteemed cultural values, such as Jesus' validating his disciples picking grain on the Sabbath or Jesus speaking with the woman of Sychar (Matt 12; Mark 2; Luke 6; John 4). As such, there is a valid place for contextual concerns in the leadership

---

his thinking here, but Kraft's analysis is not tied to one of the overall meanings suggested in Table 10.

131. I say "almost certainly" because there are cases in Scripture in which cultural values match biblical requirements, but the motivation for adhering to a given idea appears to rest primarily on cultural concerns. This seems to be the case in Acts 15 when the Gentiles are asked to "abstain from eating food offered to idols, from sexual immorality, from eating the meat of strangled animals, and from consuming blood" (Acts 15:20 NLT). While some of these may not be considered biblical mandates, the New Testament clearly speaks against sexual immorality. However, it is unclear if the Gentiles were asked to meet this requirement due to biblical concerns or the Jewish believers' obsession over ritual purity that flowed from their cultural values. Moreover, the cultural value over ritual purity was a syncretistic "theological" focus that obstructed the Jews from developing a missional hermeneutic.

132. Kraft writes, "Which interpretation is chosen is pretty much irrelevant to the issue at hand, since the statement as it stands, if taken absolutely, prohibits any form of second marriage" (Kraft, *Culture, Communication, and Christianity*, 422).

of the missional church, but above everything else Scripture must be able to critique and inform these concerns.[133]

4. If Paul is requiring marriage in 1 Timothy 3:2, 12, it would mean that an elder or deacon must be married. Paul would essentially be saying in 5:9 "only take care of a widow who had a husband." Certainly the Bible is intentionally redundant at times, but this possibility seems quite unlikely. Furthermore, this would mean that neither Jesus nor Paul could serve as leaders of the church. Finally, given that the focus of 1 Timothy 3:2, 12 is to guide the church in choosing blameless leaders, it is difficult to see how being married causes one to become blameless, especially since Paul advocates celibacy elsewhere (1 Cor 7:7–8).

5. Finally, if Paul is addressing polygyny in 1 Timothy 3:2, 12, it would mean that 1 Timothy 5:9 is addressing widows who were polyandrous. This is extremely unlikely given that polygyny was not a concern in the New Testament and that polyandry was never mentioned. Furthermore, this possibility would include three deepening levels of extreme rarity building one on top of the other as follows: (a) Paul would have to be addressing the rare occasion of polyandrous marriages. (b) Following that rarity, Paul would be addressing the polyandrous widow whose multiple husbands have all passed away, and she has married no additional husbands in their place! Consider for a moment how unlikely it would be for a polygynous man to become a widower. (c) Finally, it is even more unlikely that Paul would likewise choose to write a stipulation upon the rarity of rarities—a requirement that the church should only assist the monogamous versus polyandrous widow.

Of all the authors who address this topic, Holst's short analysis is the strongest, though it is incomplete in two ways. First, he does not consider divorce as one of the possible overall meanings because "Paul permitted a man to divorce his heathen wife (I Cor. 7:15)."[134] Second, he does not consider the ramifications of 1 Timothy 5:9 in all cases. However, he likewise suggests that polygamy is the least likely meaning. "Historical evidence of the times and the culture indicates that it either emphasizes that a man should not re-marry after divorcing his heathen wife or else that a man must be a good husband. If either of these alternatives is accepted there is no Biblical reason to use this passage to prohibit a polygamous man from being baptized and becoming a church

---

133. Cp. Hiebert, "Critical Contextualization."
134. Holst, "Polygamy and the Bible," 211.

leader."[135] Though Kraft's supracultural principle may seem like a similar conclusion, it actually is a far poorer hermeneutic that gives too much weight to cultural values, and negates this specific passage's requirement that leaders be faithful to their wives.[136]

Hermeneutical Critique

The greatest bias demonstrated among this group and those of Group 4 is their zeal to proclaim that 1 Timothy 3:2, 12 validates the inclusion of polygamists in the New Testament church. However in fairness, the analysis of 1 Timothy 3:2, 12 is more complex than other passages. The main point that authors should realize when addressing 1 Timothy 3:2, 12 is that it is highly unlikely that the passage is addressing polygamy, so this passage does not contribute to the discussion. Rather, "[t]he principle stated here would be that a man must not fornicate. This principle would be as valid in choosing church leaders in a polygamous culture as in a monogamous society. In a polygamous society this would mean that a man with many wives must be a good and faithful husband."[137] It is for this reason that Buthelezi takes a more cautious approach when addressing this passage, warning interpreters that "there is no historical evidence of the existence of polygynists in the early Church [and this] only goes to prove that the data are too scanty to enable anyone to hold a dogmatic opinion on the question of polygyny on biblical grounds."[138]

On the whole, missionaries should consider the possibility that the monogamic ideal found in Scripture is really the Western ideal projected onto Scripture. As such, this particular interpretation requires a strong level of cultural humility. It would be appropriate for Westerners to qualify their biblical understanding by claiming that they are unsure of the biblical precedence for the monogamic ideal. The admission that cultural influences could be at work is a level of honesty that is required

---

135. Ibid., 212.

136. In Kraft's final analysis, he writes, "Interpretation of these passages in light of their cultural context and culturally appropriate application of scriptural principles, therefore, supports rather than prohibits the appointment of otherwise qualified polygamists to positions of church leadership in societies that ordinarily expect or demand polygamous marriage of their leadership" (Kraft, *Culture, Communication, and Christianity*, 426).

137. Holst, "Polygamy and the Bible," 211.

138. Buthelezi, "Polygyny in Light of NT," 62.

A Missional Critique of the Hermeneutics

for dialogue with Africans today. Likewise, the West needs to indicate that they are prepared to trust the ability of African Christians to listen to the Holy Spirit and properly interpret Scripture. This not only reflects proper humility in the interpretational process but mission through weakness, and most importantly, mission that trusts in the Holy Spirit's guidance.[139]

POLYGAMY IS ALLOWED FOR THE CHRISTIAN AND NON-CHRISTIAN ALIKE

With the exception of Holst, all of those in Table 6 who believe that polygamy stands on equal footing with monogamy are of African background (see Group 4). For the most part, these authors make strong biblical arguments and do not appeal to inferences when making their arguments. Rather, they most often argue from a thematic or tapestry perspective that perceptively separates true sins, such as adultery and idolatry, from polygamy. In many ways this position represents a truly African reading of Scripture: "Once the Bible was in the hands and in the language of Africans themselves, it became evident that there were differences between what the missionaries said and what the book said. A classic example has to do with polygamy. Although most missionary societies and the churches which they represented condemned the practice, it did not escape the notice of African readers that many of the great "heroes of the faith" had more than one wife."[140]

Many themes emerged from an African interpretation of Scripture that were different than their Western counterparts. For example, some of the major themes related to polygamy were:

1. Throughout the biblical record there is no claim that polygamy is a sin.[141]

2. The biblical narrative shows no indication that God thought polygamous leadership was wrong.[142]

3. Marriages with foreign (non-believing) wives was a sin.[143]

139. Cp. Hastings, *Christian Marriage in Africa*, 62–63.

140. LeMarquand, "NT Exegesis in Africa," 86.

141. Buthelezi, "Polygyny in Light of NT," 62; Chime, *Polygamy and Christian Religion*, ii, 17–18.

142. Holst, "Polygamy and the Bible," 211.

143. Ibid..

4. Scripture does attempt to provide guidelines or regulate the practice of polygamy, and these foremost include the fair treatment of wives and children.[144]

5. Ultimately God is calling for responsible polygamists and monogamists, rather than making a plea for monogamy.[145]

Likewise, the claim of this group that the biblical record does not condemn polygamy is effectively a claim that the pervasive silence of Scripture on this issue cannot be ignored. Otherwise, anything could be claimed. For example, had history been altered so that African missionaries brought Christianity to the West, Africans would likely have considered levirate marriage a normative practice. It would not be surprising if they would have required Western converts to adhere to this custom. Consideration of this possibility would likewise give the West a greater appreciation for the impact of customs drastically foreign to the culture that are imposed in the name of God. More importantly, while biblical guidance on this matter is that levirate marriage in the New Testament was not condemned, there are alternate ways to care for widows from backgrounds in which the levirate practice was foreign (compare Matt 22:23–33; Acts 6:1–6). This demonstrates biblical validation for culturally appropriate practices that meet the biblical concerns of caring for the disenfranchised. The point is that it would be wrong for Africans to force Westerners to adopt levirate practices, just as it was wrong for Westerners to force Africans to become entirely monogamous.

In terms of the tapestry of mission, this position is the most consistent interpretation found through Scripture. It is for this reason that God regulates the practice rather than ending it. God cared about the equal treatment of co-wives, and that slave wives were treated as equals (Exod 21:10). God authorized rights to the wife least likely to be favored (the slave wife) in order to require that the polygamist husband would properly care for his least favored wife (Exod 21:11). As such, God did not decree divorce upon the polygamist, but standards that would internally build up the polygamous marriage. God likewise regulated that the polygamist father could not demonstrate improper favoritism to the children of his most loved wife (Deut 21:15–17). Finally, God's practice of levirate marriage did not prohibit polygamy. Rather, God was uncon-

---

144. Welch, "Biblical Perspective on Polygamy," 52–54.
145. Ibid., 108–9.

A Missional Critique of the Hermeneutics

cerned with the possibility of polygamy in favor of other biblical concerns (Deut 25:5–10). God consistently set standards in place to prevent the mistreatment of wives, widows, and the children of polygamists.

Furthermore, Chime likewise follows the thematic flow of understanding sin in the Old Testament. Following Paul's lead, he claims that one function of the law was to specify that which is sin. Yet, "[t]he Bible contains several passages, about the sins and behaviours which are forbidden by God and which will prevent people from inheriting the Kingdom of God. But polygamy is not one of them" (Rom 7:7).[146]

Intertextual Justification for Polygamy

The authors in this group would benefit from greater consideration of the intertextual commentary that the Old Testament provides on itself (Gen 26:5; 1 Kgs 11:1–8; 15:5; 2 Chr 24:2–3; Neh 13:23–30). These passages in particular provide positive and negative reflection, acting as a biblical summary for the lives of four polygamists, Abraham, David, Solomon, and Joash. Likewise, a comparison of variations in the accounts of King Joash are helpful (2 Kgs 12; 2 Chr 24). The consistent theme that flows through these intertextual passages is that they do not cite polygamy as a problem, in spite of other failures that they do address.

Beginning with Abraham's life, God claims that Abraham listened to God, and obeyed God's "requirements, commands, decrees, and instructions" (Gen 26:5 NLT). Certainly Abraham had problems such as twice claiming that his wife was merely his sister (Gen 12, 20), but on the whole Genesis 26:5 does not suggest that this or any other issue was a significant problem, which likewise means that Abraham's polygamous marriage to Hagar and his son Ishmael were not seen as a point of failure.[147]

Commenting on the whole of David's life, 1 Kings 15:5 claims that "David had done what was pleasing in the Lord's sight and had obeyed the Lord's commands throughout his life, except in the affair concerning Uriah the Hittite" (NLT). Certainly David committed other sins in his life, but this verse likewise acts as an overview, and only the account of 2 Samuel 11 was seen as a great failure. One might argue that the biblical

---

146. Chime, *Polygamy and Christian Religion*, 17.
147. Dean Gilliland made a personal comment stating, "The fact that Sarah brought Hagar to Abraham so the promised son could be conceived by Hagar shows how culturally appropriate polygamous marriage was."

MISSIOLOGICAL HERMENEUTICS

historians were being kind by not smearing the revered names of the former great leaders of Israel. However, 1 Kings 15:5 makes no attempt to conceal David's most significant failure. If polygamy were likewise the great failure that many have claimed, it too should be listed here, but it is not.

In two different instances in the Old Testament, there is a detailed discussion over Solomon's failure, and they both relate to his marriages to foreign women (1 Kgs 11:1–8, Neh 13:23–30). In both cases, the charges leveled against Solomon are that he married foreign women and their influence affected Solomon's faith negatively. Too often Westerners misread these passages and claim that these are a polemic against multiple wives. However, both passages are clear that the problem was specifically Solomon's marriages to foreign women, technically called exogamy (1 Kgs 11:1–11; Neh 13:23–30).[148]

Furthermore, the concerns of this and other biblical accounts are over foreign women who worship false gods, rather than a woman like Ruth who is a foreigner but devoted to God (Narrative Examples: Num 25; 1 Kgs 3:1; 7:8; Ezra 9–10; Mal 2:11; Exogamy Forbidden: Exod 34:16; Deut 7:3–4; Josh 23:12–13). God was well aware of how strong this temptation was for any man, let alone the wisest man on earth, and as such God put a prohibition in place.[149] Certainly if polygamy was a great sin, this would be the prime example in all of the Old Testament.

However, Solomon is not even critiqued over his excessive polygamy or excessive wealth in spite of the limitations imposed in Deuteronomy 17:17, and this all the more illustrates that the major concern was over marriages that negatively impacted a man's faith. Therefore, one would certainly expect polygamy to be mentioned in Solomon's life since it went unmentioned in David's case. However, there is no such claim that polygamy was the problem.

Finally, the account of Jehoiada the priest and the young king Joash is significant. The reader is informed that Jehoiada the priest chose two wives for the young king Joash, and the writer states that Joash "did what was pleasing in the Lord's sight throughout the lifetime of Jehoiada the

---

148. Hillman, *Polygamy Reconsidered*, 145; Odame, *Christian Approach to Polygamy*, 31–32; Schillebeeckx, *Marriage*, I:21 n. 9.

149. Though Schillebeeckx is predominantly against polygamy, he nevertheless claims that Deuteronomy 17:17 is addressing the issue of foreign wives rather than polygamy (Schillebeeckx, *Marriage*, I:21 n. 9).

A Missional Critique of the Hermeneutics

priest" (2 Chr 24:2-3). This claim is in place despite the Chronicler's far more critical commentary on Joash's life, when compared to the parallel account in 2 Kings 12. For example, the Chronicler mentions Joash's idolatry, which is not brought up in 2 Kings (2 Chr 24:17-19; cp. 2 Kgs 12). Likewise, the Chronicler's "positive evaluation of Joash is limited to 'all the days of Jehoiada the priest' (2 Chr 24:2) rather than 'all his (Joash's) days'" (2 Kgs 12:3).[150] Yet, in spite of the Chronicler's more critical review of Joash's life, the Chronicler includes polygamy among the positive acts of Joash (2 Chr 24:2-3).[151]

Finally, the issue of levirate marriage will be discussed in greater detail near the end of this chapter, but it must be pointed out that this is a practice that was required by God with no express reservations that polygamy would be a likely result (Gen 38:8-10; Deut 25:5). Though some authors try to force levirate marriage to be a practice permitted only for monogamists, Gitari is more likely correct when claiming, "It may be assumed that such marriages largely were polygamous. Jesus limited his reply to questions posed in Matthew 22:23 to 'the resurrection.' Jesus made no reference to polygamous implications of the Levirate law."[152]

Without exception, polygamy was not considered a problem in the minds of the Old Testament writers. However, adultery, murder, wife-stealing and marrying foreign women all qualify as problematic. Otherwise, we must assert the alternative which is that God and the Old Testament writers were simply unable to make the proper connections

---

150. The Anchor Bible Dictionary summarizes the main difference between the two passages: "[T]he Chronicler's account supplements and contradicts the material in Kings. Supplementary material includes the account of Jehoiada's death (2 Chr 24:15-16), Joash's subsequent worship of idols (vv 17-19), and the murder of Jehoiada's son, Zechariah (vv 20-22). In 2 Chronicles 24, however, the report in Kings is contradicted at four main points. First, the writer's positive evaluation of Joash is limited to "all the days of Jehoiada the priest" (2 Chr 24:2) rather than "all his (Joash's) days" (2 Kgs 12:4 [—Eng 12:3]). Second, the details of the temple's repairs differ as to who is responsible for the repair (the priests and Levites), for its initial failure (Levites), for the source of its financing (Mosaic tax), and for the making of utensils of silver and gold for service in the temple. Third, the conflict with the Syrians is portrayed as an actual military engagement rather than an adverted threat (2 Chr 24:23-25). . . . Fourth, the servants named in the conspiracy are different. . . . (v 26)" (Freedman et al., *Abd*, 3:857).

151. For further study, refer to Table 16 in Appendix B which is an overview of all polygamists in Scripture.

152. Gitari, "Church and Polygamy," 6; cp. Hillman, *Polygamy Reconsidered*, 164; Welch, "Biblical Perspective on Polygamy," 55; contra Parrinder, *Bible and Polygamy*, 24-27.

to condemn polygamy, and that today we are better interpreters of the biblical text and culture.

Hermeneutical Critique

African writers make it very clear that the Bible is their authority. Chime says, "I was inspired by the Holy Spirit to write this small book in order to correct the wrong notions and impressions being spread by the Church with regard to polygamy. In doing so, I decided to base my research on discovering what the Bible tells us about the subject."[153] Likewise, it is encouraging to consider that this group represents the majority African position, at least with respect to the works used in the study. Furthermore, this group contains the only work by an African polygamist.[154]

Like Group 3, this group must avoid the pitfalls of 1 Timothy 3:2, 12. Furthermore, this group should stipulate the biblical limitations of polygamy. For example, in spite of Chime's claim that he and his wives have read through the entire Bible three times, they never mention Leviticus 18:18 which was surprising.[155] Additionally, there should be greater use of the internal evidence of Scripture, as already shown.

A thematic or tapestry approach should be more obvious among this group. Too often the writers here are responding to specific Western arguments which detract from developing the larger themes. Those in opposition will undoubtedly fragment the claims of this group, but a thematic approach has the greatest validity and cohesion, and this is especially true because the claims of this group have the greatest thematic continuity in Scripture, such as the themes mentioned at the start of this chapter.

The real challenge for this group is that they are almost immediately put on the defense. However, it will be important to shed a defensive stance in the interpretational process. Certainly, great harm has been done to polygamist families in the name of Christianity, but the continued frustrations over Western biases must not enter into the interpretational process. Otherwise, a corresponding African bias will most likely

---

153. Chime, *Polygamy and Christian Religion*, iii.
154. Ibid., 15.
155. Ibid., ii.

A Missional Critique of the Hermeneutics

limit biblical understanding. Defending polygamy is fine, but doing it defensively makes for an unreliable hermeneutic.

Finally, Africa is rich in spirituality and family. These are at least two areas where Africa can lead the way and offer a carefully defined spiritual hermeneutic that avoids the pitfalls of the lone and overly assertive interpreter, while also validating the impact that prayer and other spiritual disciplines have in the hermeneutical process. The West can learn a great deal from Africa in this area. Likewise, Africa has kinship bonds that far exceed those of typical Western families. Africans must call all families and all marriages into greater relationship using their unique hermeneutical insights that flow from this experience.

POLYGAMY IS GOD'S IDEAL

Many African Independent Churches have responded to the issue of polygamy by ignoring the thoughts of the Western missional community entirely. This is not a new phenomenon, but as African Independent Churches have gained stronger footing, they are speaking out specifically on the topic of polygamy.[156]

As such, the African Independent Churches are openly addressing the issue of polygamy apart from the influence of Western missionaries, whereas Africans in mission founded churches have been trained to follow the missionary. "[M]any church members either secretly engage in the custom [of polygamy] while maintaining their church membership or they fall away. Or, they become members of the thousands of independent churches that have separated from the missionary churches (especially in Africa)."[157]

Due to the variety of responses among African churches, these churches have not developed a consistent stance with respect to polygamy. However, we can understand the perception of at least one African Independent Church through the writing of Pastor Chris Okotie. Okotie is one of the few to suggest that polygamy is the ideal form of marriage when compared to monogamy. However, Okotie proclaims this unique twist in biblical interpretation through a fictional narrative. In Okotie's

---

156. Cp. Helander, *Must We Introduce Monogamy*, 9, 57–59; Okullu, *Church and Marriage*, 69; Nkwoka, "Church and Polygamy in Africa," 140, 51; *The Problem of Polygamy*, v; Turner, "Monogamy,"; Yego, "Polygamy and African Church," 72, 78.

157. Kraft, "Polygamy and Church Membership," in *Evangelical Dictionary of World Missions*, ed. Moreau, et al. (Grand Rapids, MI: Baker, 2000), 766.

Missiological Hermeneutics

book, *The Last Outcast*, the entire biblical interpretation is done through fictional characters and as such, Okotie could claim at any time that the ideas are merely fiction. However, Okotie and his followers have stated that the book is a prophetic interpretation of Scripture. The book covers numerous areas, and in the 77th chapter, the issue of polygamy is expanded upon as follows:

> "It is important to understand that God did not stop his people from having more than one wife under the old covenant. The only thing he spoke against was divorce and that is a different matter altogether.
>
> I have heard some of my colleagues say that God tolerated polygamy in the Old Testament but will not do so in the New Testament. They say so out of a good and sincere motivation but there is no sin that is tolerated in the Old Testament and forbidden in the New Testament. The only things that have been put aside are the ceremonies and rituals that pointed to Jesus Christ because now that he has appeared physically, they are no longer requirements that need to be observed....
>
> ... [H]owever, the greatest and earliest display of rebellion against God took place in a monogamous home. Cain was raised in a monogamous home where the living presence of the Spirit of God on his parents could still be felt. Solomon who became the wisest man on earth was raised in a polygamous home....
>
> To understand what God's position is on the matter [of marriage], we must look again at the third chapter of the Book of Genesis. In that chapter, God made a declaration concerning the woman. He said, 'Thy desire shall be unto thy husband and he shall rule over thee.' What was he talking about? He was not referring to the fact that Adam would have authority over her. That was already in existence since God made Adam lord over the woman from the very beginning....
>
> ... For you to rule spiritually, you must be less in number than what you rule over. When God said that Adam was going to rule over the woman, he was saying that Adam will one day acquire more than one wife. In other words, he would have several wives under him as a demonstration of his rulership. God was not speaking about the harshness of Adam's lordship, he was prophesying that polygamy would soon emerge as a physical demonstration of Adam's rulership. That prophecy was fulfilled in Lamech. Since then, men have had wives according to their desire. That is why God told the woman that she will have a long-

A Missional Critique of the Hermeneutics

ing or a desire for her husband. A desire to return to the old arrangement [of monogamy]."

"I am not recommending polygamy, I am simply stating the mind of God on the issue."[158]

Okotie's claims are quite interesting, but even more interesting is the hermeneutic that he has adopted. Okotie is drawing an inference from the narrative of Genesis 3 and the hermeneutic that Okotie uses in order to validate his interpretation is identical to those who condemn polygamy based on the inferences that they draw from Genesis 2.

Hermeneutical Critique

Okotie's underlying hermeneutic and those of Groups 1 and 2 is an attempt to validate a particular interpretation by drawing an inference that is not central to the passage. Furthermore, neither interpretation can be validated throughout Scripture, except through making more inferences of the same type from passages that are not intended to validate or invalidate polygamy. Therefore, we see the culmination of what should have been expected through the exceedingly poor interpretational approach associated with Genesis 2—an identical method but reversed interpretation based on Genesis 3, and one that seems to be based on a pre-existing agenda.

It is precisely for this reason that Genesis 2 never should have been interpreted in the way it was. The interpretational model of Genesis 2 served as an example of biblical hermeneutics that was unwittingly transferred to African Christians. Moreover, the fact that missionaries were dogmatic with respect to their particular interpretation communicated the fact that loosely based inferences combined with heavy-handed ethnocentrism were a more than adequate hermeneutic even when the implications would result in forced divorces, motherless children and broken families. Pastor Okotie has "correctly" learned how to interpret the Bible from the missionaries, so that the real failure surrounding this particular interpretation rests primarily on the shoulders of missionaries who transferred this hermeneutic as the result of a failure to address their own cultural biases.

---

158. Okotie, *Last Outcast*, 540–43, 46.

INTERPRETATIONAL GOALS

Most of the above authors have attempted to discuss polygamy in terms of whether it is a sin or not. Why have authors focused on this aspect of polygamy? For the most part, the deliberation over the "sinful" state of polygamy is the first step for many authors who then intend to use these findings in order to stipulate the grounds for proper missionary practice when addressing polygamous families. This is understandable because it is the most common hermeneutic that missionaries employ when encountering foreign practices that do not have biblical precedence.

For example, when missionaries encountered marriage ceremonies in Africa that took years before the consummation of the marriage and likewise included intimacy between the bride and groom in the midst of this time, there was no biblical equivalent, so the missionaries approached the problem by considering the biblical principles involved and then applied those to this situation.[159] Likewise, when a modern-day tribal society makes use of blood sacrifices as a praise offering rather than a means of atonement, missionaries are challenged to understand if any type of blood sacrifice can be a valid expression subsequent to Christ's atonement.[160] Standing at an even greater "cultural distance" from biblical cultures, some Western missionaries will have to make biblically informed decisions regarding computer gaming or online virtual churches.[161] The point is that missionaries who seek biblical direction for modern-day missional dilemmas are familiar with the journey of translating traditional exegetical insights into principles or meanings that can guide them in answering contemporary questions.[162]

However, if our sole goal is to determine the proper missional approach in dealing with polygamy, there is no need to debate over whether or not polygamy is a sin. This is because we have an ongoing record of God's missionary involvement in the midst of polygamy for thousands of years through the Old Testament.[163] Of course, it could be argued that

---

159. Kraft, *Anthropology for Christian Witness*, 301.
160. Priest, *Doing Theology with Maasai*, 190–91.
161. Redford, "Missiology and Internet," 215–24.
162. Cp. Shaw and Van Engen, *Communicating God's Word*, 83–92.
163. In opposition to the following: "The Old Testament makes no issue of it [polygamy], and the instructions in the New Testament are for leaders in the church. . . . We need also to look at how polygamy has been viewed throughout history. In the Old Testament little is said about it. In the New Testament Paul makes reference to it

the New Testament brings significant discontinuity in this area in the same way that the requirement for animal sacrifice as a sin offering is nullified in Christ's sacrifice. However, an unbiased reading of the New Testament shows that there is no significant discussion that relates directly to a change of direction with respect to polygamy or levirate marriage in the New Testament.[164] In this light, the Old Testament stands as the example of God's missionary response to the issue of polygamy.

Therefore, while the entire preceding theological discussion on the nature of polygamy is interesting, it holds very little weight in determining what our actions should be as missionaries today when encountering polygamy in the church or on the mission field. It is extremely important that missionaries remain equally vigilant in looking to Scripture when addressing the issue of polygamy.[165] As such, to discern the proper missional approach for addressing polygamy, we must look at God's example of mission in the Old Testament.

Helander, in typical fashion, asks these questions in the same order that they were sought out historically:

> It seems therefore imperative that we earnestly (*if somewhat belatedly*) try to find a valid answer to these two questions:
> Is monogamy the only permissible form of marriage for a Christian?
> If the answer to that question is yes, *are then the methods used by the missions to introduce monogamy the right ones?*[166]

However, unlike Helander, I do not think that the former question is a prerequisite for the latter. The prerequisite for the latter is God's missionary response among polygamists in the Old Testament.

FOUR MISSIOLOGICAL INTERPRETATIONS

The most notable difference in the debate over polygamy in the 19th century versus the twentieth century is the respective emphasis upon missional concerns versus theological concerns. Though Colenso was seen as a renegade in his time, he did not believe that polygamy was

---

with regard to elders" (Tiénou and Hiebert, "Missional Theology," 234).

164. Hillman, *Polygamy Reconsidered*, 139; Maillu, *Our Kind of Polygamy*, 48; Odame, *Christian Approach to Polygamy*, 34; Schillebeeckx, *Marriage*, I:202.

165. Cp. Bosch, *Transforming Mission*, 3–6.

166. Helander, *Must We Introduce Monogamy*, 8 italics mine.

in any way equal to monogamy.[167] Rather, the main thrust of Colenso's argument was that the Bible clearly condemns divorce and this alone was reason enough to call the existing mission policies into question.[168] Likewise, in the 1888 London Missionary Conference, there was a commonly held perspective that polygamy was a sin, and as such the debate is entirely over the issue of the proper mission policy to address polygamy.[169] However, even in this era it was rare for the mission policy to be heavily guided by Scripture.

During the twentieth century, Hillman's work became a central focus that broke new ground in the theological debate over polygamy. Hillman was calling into question whether or not polygamy should be perceived as anything other than a cultural phenomenon that was foreign to the West. As a result, the energy in addressing polygamy shifted from concern over the best mission policy to the theological arguments that have already been investigated. In essence, Hillman's claims refocused the efforts of scholars and missionaries to bolster the theological foundation against polygamy that had gone relatively unchallenged up to that point. The impact of this change in venue, however, meant that little energy was being directed toward biblically informed mission practices in addressing polygamy. Likewise, the discussion of the nineteenth century is helpful, but the literature of this type pales in comparison to that already addressed.

The end result was that the most needed work was to focus biblical efforts upon missional examples within Scripture, and this had come to the foreground only occasionally in the nineteenth century. Yet, this was eclipsed by the theological momentum of the twentieth century, which brought a larger mix of writers to the topic. On the one hand, many of those writing major works during the twentieth century were not field missionaries.[170] On the other hand, African nationals only began publishing significant works on polygamy in the latter half of the 20th century.[171] By contrast, throughout the twentieth century the discussion took place almost entirely among Western field missionaries.

167. Colenso, *Remarks on Proper Treatment*, 3.

168. Ibid., 5–8.

169. Johnston and Jackson, *Centenary Conference on Protestant Missions*, 48–81.

170. Hitchens, *Multiple Marriage*; Kaiser, *Toward Old Testament Ethics*; *The Problem of Polygamy*; Schillebeeckx, *Marriage*.

171. Adutchum, "Church and Issue of Polygamy"; Buthelezi, "Polygyny in Light of

A Missional Critique of the Hermeneutics

Our interest, therefore, in the remainder of this chapter is to consider the far more fruitful focus of examining the biblically, missional, and hermeneutical merit of four main mission policies and practices. Though there was a great deal of variation in the mission policies and practices, I have grouped the practices according to their impact as it relates to African polygamists coming to Christ. For the most part I am likewise focused on the way that these practices impacted polygamist converts, rather than polygamists who were already involved in the church. The four categories are: (1) divorce, (2) ecclesiastical restrictions, such as the inability to take communion or be baptized, (3) allowance for baptism but a restriction on becoming a leader in the church, and (4) no restrictions for the polygamist.

POLYGAMISTS MUST DIVORCE THEIR WIVES

With very few exceptions, the policy that polygamists must divorce their wives is held by those who claim that polygamy is a sin.[172] Though these authors spend enormous exegetical energy using the Bible to validate the sinful nature of polygamy, they often proclaim divorce as the best resolution in less than a page with virtually no biblical support. For example, in an appendix to his work with no biblical validation, du Preez advocates his best "solution [which] is for the dismissed wives to find new husbands."[173] In contrast, Parrinder lacks a basic missional hermeneutic as he briefly discusses the proper response to polygamy and claims, "These are questions into which we cannot go here. Our sole aim

---

NT"; Chime, *Polygamy and Christian Religion*; Kanyadago, *Evangelizing Polygamous Families: Canonical and African Approaches*; Kanyoro, "Interpreting OT Polygamy"; Kiwovele, "Polygyny as a Problem"; Maillu, *Our Kind of Polygamy*; Muthengi, "Polygamy and Church in Africa"; Nkwoka, "Church and Polygamy in Africa"; Odame, *Christian Approach to Polygamy*; Okotie, *Last Outcast*; Okullu, *Church and Marriage*; Omoregbe, "Is Polygamy Incompatible with Christianity"; Urrutia, "Can Polygamy Be Compatible"; Wambutda, "Monogamy or Polygamy."

172. Trobisch is the only author who feels that polygamy is a practice that should be ended through marital counseling, rather than ecclesiastical control. To such an end, he attempts to find new suitors for the additional wives, followed by subsequent divorce from their existing husband and remarriage to the suitor. However, in cases where Trobisch feels that a suitor could not be found or that the husbands motives for marriage are more genuine (non-sexually motivated), such as the case of a blind woman who was married under African levirate customs, Trobisch does not care to take action (Trobisch, *My Wife Made Me*, 35–36).

173. du Preez, *Polygamy in the Bible*, 337; cp. Trobisch, *My Wife Made Me*.

in this little work has been to examine the Biblical basis for Christian teaching."[174] Others claim that the Bible condemns polygamy, but give no thought to a biblically informed missional response.[175]

The converse is not true however. Many of those who believed that polygamy was a sin, likewise rejected divorce as a proper response to the issue and argued this from a biblical perspective. For the most part, those who took this latter position were long-serving field missionaries who felt deep internal conflict over the practice and some likewise felt that Christ's sufficient condemnation of divorce was reason enough to look for other alternatives. Among these were notable names such as J. Hudson Taylor and the Anglican Bishop of Natal, South Africa, John William Colenso.

Colenso was one of the earliest African missionaries to claim that divorce was an improper response to polygamy. This claim caused Colenso to be seen as a liberal in his day despite the fact that he maintained solidarity in the belief that missionaries should actively try to eradicate the practice of polygamy.

> I believe, of course, that the practice [of polygamy] is at variance with the whole spirit of Christianity, and must eventually be rooted out by it, wherever it comes. And I believe that it is our duty, as Christian men and Ministers, to aim at its extirpation among the natives of this land, as speedily as possible.
>
> But I certainly expressed a doubt, in my published Journal, whether the method, at present adopted by the Missionaries, of requiring a man, who had more than one wife, to put away all but one, before he could be received to Christian Baptism, was the right way of accomplishing this end. I have since given much closer consideration to the question, and I have now no hesitation in saying, that I believe the above-mentioned rule to be *unwarranted by Scripture, opposed to the practice of the Apostles*, condemned by common reason, and altogether unjustifiable.[176]

Colenso is likewise one of the first to base his rejection on biblical grounds. However, Colenso died prior to the 1888 London Missionary Conference.

---

174. Parrinder, *Bible and Polygamy*, 65.
175. Vollebregt, *Bible on Marriage*, 3.
176. Colenso, *Remarks on Proper Treatment*, 3 italics mine.

A Missional Critique of the Hermeneutics

Despite his death, his concerns were addressed at the conference, and the voice of another surprising veteran came to the foreground. J. Hudson Taylor quoted from an unknown source that expressed his view,

> This pamphlet is a brief examination of the Old and New Testament Scriptures on marriage, polygamy, and concubinage. There is one sentence in it which gives you briefly the conclusion that we were led to in considering this matter:— "Thousands of persons were speedily converted when the Holy Ghost came down, and were received as members; but there is no proof that before they were received any inquiry was made as to their previous family arrangements, or that any who were found to be the husbands of more than one wife, were constrained to retain only one and to put the others away. Nevertheless," says the author, "without violence or harshness to those who had previously been entangled with the sins of polygamy, its speedy extirpation was made."[177]

Though it could be claimed that this argument is based on a hermeneutic of the silence of Scripture, the full extent of the author's argument is unknown (since only a portion is quoted). However, this argument does draw from a pervasive silence in Scripture on the matter of polygamy and allegiance to God, and therefore has a great deal of validity.

Likewise, some who argued against the policy of divorce claimed that Paul's marital advice in 1 Corinthians 7 was reason enough for the admittance of polygamous converts into the church ("Each of you should continue to live in whatever situation the Lord has placed you, and remain as you were when God first called you. This is my rule for all the churches." 1 Cor 7:17 NLT). This is likely one of the strongest claims in the New Testament to support the idea that polygamist marriages should remain intact as they join the church. Commenting on 1 Corinthians 7:17–20, Hillman claims; "It is certainly possible that there may also have been called to the faith at that time some Jewish families that were polygamous before being called: new Christians "already circumcised" and living by the law of Moses. Would Paul's rule have applied to them and to their marital status? Would a Jewish polygamist have been required, before answering the call to Christian faith, to divorce all but one of the mothers of his own children? The

---

177. Johnston and Jackson, *Centenary Conference on Protestant Missions*, 74.

answer to this question would have to be no."[178] If 1 Corinthians 5:1 refers to a polygamous situation, 1 Corinthians 7 would have direct implications for this matter. Additionally, there are numerous Old Testament narratives that offer significant guidance in determining a biblically informed missional response to polygamy. We now turn to one of the most controversial of these.

2 Samuel 12:1–12: The Strength of a Missional Hermeneutic

David's failure in 2 Samuel 12 and the subsequent events are a good example of a passage that has strong implications for Biblical Theology of Mission. However, the persistent momentum devoted to theological arguments has obscured the larger and more relevant missiological implications. A quick survey of the arguments will illustrate the way that theological agendas have obscured a missional hermeneutic.

Many of those who argue in favor of polygamy cite 2 Samuel 12:8—"I [God] gave you [David] your master's house and his wives"—as a clear indication that God sanctioned polygamy. "[T]he charge against David is threefold: adultery, murder, and misuse of power. Polygamy is not implicated at any point. God indicated to David that he would have given him other wives; there was no need to take by force from a poor man who had only one. To find in this episode, as Vollebregt does, condemnation of polygamy and approval of monogamy is remarkable interpretation indeed. It indicates the lengths to which some theologians are willing to go to prove that God never at any time sanctioned polygamy."[179]

Of course, comments such as these spark a highly charged but decidedly non-missiological debate. Those refuting such claims argue three common points.

1. They claim that Saul's wives were known in there entirety.[180]

---

178. Hillman, *Polygamy Reconsidered*, 166.

179. Welch, "Biblical Perspective on Polygamy," 62. Vollebregt claims that, "the whole story of David's adultery is a clear illustration of the decadence of the feeling for moral rules as a consequence of polygamy: only through the words of the prophets does the King come to realize his guilt. Thus it can be interpreted as a protest against polygamy itself. In his parable of the rich man with the flocks and herds and the poor man with one ewe lamb Nathan clearly indicated his approval of monogamous marriage and at the same time implicitly criticized David's harem" (Vollebregt, *Bible on Marriage*, 26–27). Du Preez quotes Vollebregt's above statement in agreement with him (du Preez, *Polygamy in the Bible*, 189).

180. du Preez, *Polygamy in the Bible*, 190; Kaiser, *Toward Old Testament Ethics*, 188; *The Problem of Polygamy*, 13.

2. Based on the first assumption, they then claim that "There is no proof, however, that David took even one of his master's [Saul's] wives to be his own wife. Had he done so it would almost certainly have been mentioned."[181]

Both of these points are excellent examples of arguments based on the silence of Scripture since the authors make claims from missing details.[182] By comparison, not all of David's wives were listed by name (1 Sam 18:27; 25:39-44; 2 Sam 3:2-5; 11:27; 1 Chr 3:1-9 are named; 2 Sam 5:13; 1 Chr 14:3 are unnamed). Likewise, we should not even imagine that Solomon's wives would be listed in their entirety (1 Kgs 11:1-3). Yet there would be far more reason to completely list the wives of these two highly esteemed kings in comparison to Saul. As such, Scripture demonstrates silence in regard to the names of the kings' wives. Greater balance is found in noting that:

> The Scriptures actually tell us very little of the family life of Saul. In 1 Samuel 14.50 we are told that his wife's name was Ahinoam, suggesting that he had only one wife. But in 2 Samuel 12.8 Nathan the prophet, speaking of Saul, said to David: "I gave you his kingdom and his wives . . ." (TEV), referring of course to David's elevation to power. Nothing else is said of Saul's marital life, or whether he had children other than those mentioned in 1 Samuel 14.49. The Scriptures have far more to say about his successor, David.[183]

3. Finally, through a variety of unconvincing arguments, authors claim that 2 Samuel 12:8 does not indicate God's sanctioning of polygamy in giving David multiple wives.[184] For example, one author as-

---

181. *The Problem of Polygamy*, 12-13; cp. Kaiser, *Toward Old Testament Ethics*, 188. Specifically, the issue of Michal's mother Ahinoam is at the fore by those challenging the passage. The only mentioned wife of Saul is Ahinoam, the mother of Michal (1 Sam 14:49-50). Saul also had a concubine named Rizpah (2 Sam 3:7; 21:8). However, since David married Michal (1 Sam 18:20-27), most argue that it would have been incestuous or at least inappropriate for David to later marry Ahinoam, even though Saul gave Michal to another in marriage long before the account in 2 Samuel 12 (1 Sam 25:44) (du Preez, *Polygamy in the Bible*, 190-91; Kaiser, *Toward Old Testament Ethics*, 188; *The Problem of Polygamy*, 13).

182. As such, these claims are examples of poor hermeneutical arguments based on the silence of the Bible, in contrast to the pervasive silence I have already discussed in this chapter.

183. Welch, "Biblical Perspective on Polygamy," 60.

184. du Preez, *Polygamy in the Bible*, 195.

serts that 1 Samuel 12:7–8 "is certainly nothing more than a figure of speech to emphasise the fact that God had given to David, as king of Israel, everything that had belonged to his predecessor."[185] In contrast, Welch notes the inconsistency that these perceived actions of God have with other responses in the Old Testament, "God seems to be saying, 'If you were not satisfied with the number of wives I gave you, I would have given you others—even twice as many.' If God wished to idealize monogamous marriage what better place to begin that with the ruler of the nation? Are we to believe that God simply catered to David's lustful whims because he saw no way of changing him?"[186]

Furthermore, in addition to adultery and murder, David's wife-stealing was the central focus of Nathan's highly contextual and prophetic admonishment.[187] Those arguing against polygamy have claimed that wife-stealing is the same thing as polygamy.[188] However, the Israelites did not engage in wife-stealing with one another as a legitimate means of monogamous or polygamous marriage. Nevertheless, du Preez and Vollebregt's emphatic need to make the passage address polygamy demonstrates a hermeneutic that builds upon questionable passages. Furthermore, though many object to the possibility that God implemented polygamy in David's life, Lewis is not as influenced by his western instincts:

> [I]f it did refer to Saul's wives, the Lord still makes the statement that He gave *wives* into David's bosom. Regardless of who they were or where they came from, the Lord lists these plural wives among the good things He had given to David and calmly adds the statement that if that had not satisfied David, He would have given him more.
>
> Rebel against the idea as we may, we simply cannot escape from the clear attitude here expressed by the Lord toward plural wives. God was quite willing to give them to His servant, as many as he wanted. Instead of rebelling against the idea, would it not be better to humbly try to adjust our thinking to God's attitude and face the meaning as applied to our dealing with polygamous converts?[189]

185. *The Problem of Polygamy*, 13.
186. Welch, "Biblical Perspective on Polygamy," 61.
187. Van Engen and Redford, "Syllabus," 106 originally Redford.
188. E.g., du Preez, *Polygamy in the Bible*, 194–95.
189. Lewis, *Divine Guidance*, 83.

A Missional Critique of the Hermeneutics

Appropriately, Lewis redirects the focus of the passage toward mission practice.

The clear trend that we can see in the discussion to this point is that the theological energy has obscured the missiological analysis. Those trying to discern proper ways to deal with polygamy have, for the most part, missed the strongest emphases in the passage, which is that God's response to David's sin in the midst of his polygamous lifestyle is biblically authoritative for guiding mission practice today!

Given that David's crimes include adultery, murder, wife-stealing, abuse of power and a public cover-up, this extreme case can inform mission practice if we are willing to address the matter through a missional hermeneutic. Such a hermeneutic begins by asking, "What was God's response in addressing David the polygamist who married Bathsheba after numerous crimes?" Lewis perceives this text to have field-practice implications and claims, "The Lord was greatly displeased and pronounced heavy punishment but no suggestion was ever made that he should put her away."[190]

In terms of God's authoritative missionary example; (1) David was allowed to remain married to Bathsheba after all this took place.[191] Likewise, David was permitted to remain in leadership most likely because he thoroughly repented of his sins (Ps 51). (2) God did not invalidate the marriage by claiming it was "no marriage at all." God did not dissolve the marriage even though it was based on ungodly origins. (3) God did not excommunicate David from the people of God in spite of his taking an additional wife after having committed himself to God. (4) Finally, the adultery of this passage cannot be equated with polygamy, because David who is already a polygamist is permitted to marry Bathsheba and she remains his wife. Had polygamy been the issue, David would have been in store for one punishment after the next. Likewise, the intertextual evidence already discussed with respect to

---

190. Ibid., 41.

191. Gaskiyane argues that the example of David and Bathsheba's pregnancy is similar to those cases where an existing Christian takes on a second wife and then she quickly becomes pregnant. He claims that these are mitigating circumstances that require a more complex disciplinary response (Gaskiyane, *Polygamy*, 58–59). However, he argues that the second wife must be immediately divorced otherwise, in spite of the fact that he is willing to allow non-Christian polygamists to join the church (ibid., 50–57). However, there are many Old Testament cases of followers of God taking a second wife, and God issues no such response.

1 Kings 15:5 adds another level of biblical validation. That is, this account is not addressing polygamy since polygamy was an ongoing aspect of David's life. All of this should inform our understanding of the validity of any sanction imposed with respect to polygamy.

Certainly God does not validate David's adultery or the murder of Uriah, but God does allow for David to take Bathsheba in marriage. God did punish David through a sovereign act over David and Bathsheba's son. Though the death of David's son seems to misplace the punishment, any concerned father could easily relate to the level of anguish and pain this would present. God's sovereign act caused the king to beg for his son's life. This would unquestionably be a life scarring punishment, as David would live with the pain of knowing that his son died as a result of his sin (2 Sam 12:16).

Some might claim that David's wives were "divorced" from him as punishment for stealing Bathsheba based on Absalom's overthrow (2 Sam 12:11).[192] However, no matter what ethical lens is used to color this account, Absalom's ensuing actions did not constitute divorce, but a similar act of wife-stealing focused solely on David's concubines (2 Sam 16:21–22).[193] As such, if God did not require David to divorce his wives, nor even require David to divorce Bathsheba, there are few more extreme examples for the church to follow today. Any church that would call for divorce among polygamists could only do so through ignoring this and numerous other Old Testament accounts.[194]

Yet, what church today would then recommend that the adultering-murdering polygamist should validly be married to Bathsheba?[195] This is

---

192. Furthermore, the only other account in which men loose their wives has nothing to do with polygamy, but rather everything to do with those who misinterpret Scripture for their own gain as mentioned in Chapter 2 (Jer 8:10).

193. Amnon and Absalom's later revolt are more likewise an indication that David's parenting was weakened by his own sins which prevented him from appropriately addressing Amnon's rape of Tamar, and ultimately contributed to Absalom's anger and revolt.

194. Once again, the argument that David was not required to divorce Bathsheba could be perceived as one that is made from the silence of Scripture until it is realized that there is no account of any Old Testament polygamist being required to divorce his wives. As such, this is a pervasive silence and a hermeneutically strong argument.

195. If this account were to have taken place among modern-day Western-led churches, David would not have been allowed to marry Bathsheba. He almost certainly would have been removed from his position of leadership. He would then most likely be excommunicated from the church if he did not divorce Bathsheba. It is quite prob-

not a case of a pre-convert who has no relationship with God! This is not a case in which a second wife was needed to help work the fields in an agrarian society. This would even break the norms for levirate marriage if Uriah's closest male relative chose to redeem Bathsheba. In fact, this is a case where the motivation to marry this wife began with lust while also avoiding the public embarrassment of her pregnancy. Yet, the marriage is still permitted!

Aside from the complexity of this account, there were many notable leaders in the Old Testament who were polygamists, but *God never responded to the polygamists by a call for divorce.* "Solomon took [foreign] heathen women for his wives though God had strictly commanded that His people should not intermarry with the heathen. God was angry, not because Solomon took many wives but because he took them from the heathen nations. . . . Yet no suggestion was ever made that he should put away one of those wives."[196]

We could likewise traverse the Old Testament narratives and continue to trace this theme of God's response to the issue of polygamy even among Israel's highly visible leaders. These leaders are not only well-known to the people, but many regularly interact with God. David and Solomon are two of the strongest examples, and yet David's commitment to God is portrayed as exemplary apart from this account (1 Kgs 15:5). There is no call for divorce in the extreme cases, let alone the more mundane cases in which God deals with polygamists.

What then should guide a missionary in considering their response to the issue of polygamy? This passage and others should cause missionaries, regardless of their position on polygamy, to take notice and realize that there is no biblical validation for requiring a polygamist, whether Christian or non-Christian, to divorce their wives. If one chooses "inference" as a primary hermeneutic, then infer from the many Old Testament examples. However, David's case, like many others, is not a case that requires inference. It is a substantially obvious case in which God addresses numerous sins, none of which is polygamy. The main

---

able that his marriage to Bathsheba would not have been validated as a true marriage in order to claim that this was not a true divorce. Finally, a number of churches would have required David to divorce all his remaining wives except for one before being reinstated into the church.

196. Lewis, *Divine Guidance*, 41.

Missiological Hermeneutics

point is that certain mission policies regarding polygamy have entirely ignored God's response to the practice for those of faith and non-faith.

Ultimately then, this account and many other narratives involving polygamy offer missional guidance for those who follow God's example in addressing this matter. Likewise, we have seen that God's response to polygamy does not include divorce in spite of the consistent practice of polygamy among many of Israel's most notable leaders. As such, a missiological hermeneutic must engage these passages in terms of their authority to guide mission field practice with equal validity and standing as that of any theological claim that can be drawn from them.

Ezra 9–10: Validation for Divorce?

The great missionary statesman Henry Venn, however, made the unique claim that Ezra 10 validated mission policy that polygamists must divorce. His claim was that this passage;

> should have great weight with those who argue the question upon considerations derived from the hardships to the women and children who may be put away. During the captivity the people of Israel, priests and Levites, had married heathen wives. Much might have been pleaded in respect of such wives and their children; but under Ezra's remonstrances the people determined, "Now, therefore, let us make a covenant with our God to put away all the wives, and such as are born of them, according to the counsel of my lord, and of those that tremble at the commandment of our God; and let it be done according to the law." (Ezra x. 3.) The last clauses of this text intimate that a proper reverence for the Word of God will overcome a variety of perplexing questions which may otherwise entangle a scrupulous mind.[197]

The group-divorce of Ezra 9–10 takes place over the issue of foreign wives. Though there is the possibility that this account is actually a form of ethnocentrism hiding beneath the marriage prohibitions to foreigners, there is also the possibility that Israel's leaders perceived this as a threat to their missional identity.[198] Far too often in the Old Testament,

---

197. Knight et al., *Memoir of Henry Venn*, 355.

198. In dealing with the request to put away foreign wives, Lewis believes that Shechaniah was in error and was not acting on God's behalf, "No more striking example can be found of a religious leader using human reasoning and by means of forceful personality carrying out a conclusion at variance with God's commands" (Ezra 9–10) (Lewis, *Divine Guidance*, 42).

A Missional Critique of the Hermeneutics

there were prevalent signs that the people of God were surprisingly weak in their ability to remain spiritually devoted to God in the midst of other religious systems (compare Deut 27–32).

> The Mosaic law, which by now was the constitutional foundation, as it were, for this emerging community, gave no direct guidance on the central issue that Ezra had to face. In consequence, as our exegesis of 9:1–2 has tried to show, he taught, and the community accepted, an interpretation of the law according to its "spirit," as he understood it. We may not agree with certain aspects of Ezra's interpretation, but his motivation and method here remain ones we would still acknowledge as valid today.
>
> We have noted in connection with the list in the second half of chap. 10 that only the leadership of the community was directly involved in these proceedings. The survival of the whole stood no chance at all if the center became "soft." Israel's election was not merely for her own comfort, but so she might shine as a witness to the nations for God and his standards (see Gen 26:4). This could not be achieved without the maintenance of her distinctive self-identity, and this was thought to be threatened by mixed marriages.[199]

As has been shown, the New Testament expresses concern over spiritually mixed marriages (1 Cor 7).[200] The primary difference in the New Testament, however, is that there is an affirmation regarding the potential for a believing spouse to witness to his or her unbelieving spouse. Despite the Old Testament prohibition to avoid marriages to women devoted to foreign gods, Paul does not advise believers to end their marriage with a non-believing spouse for the same reasons. In essence, Paul's advice is opposite of the actions found in Ezra 9–10. This in itself is eye-opening because Paul's missional hermeneutic allows him to foresee the possibility for marital witness even when facing a spiritual threat that is outlined quite clearly in the Old Testament.

Lewis goes so far as to draw from New Testament correctives regarding divorce, and claims that Shechaniah's request to put away foreign wives was a serious error and was not acting on God's behalf, "No more striking example can be found of a religious leader using human

---

199. Williamson, *WBC Ezra-Nehemiah*, 160; cp. Odame, *Christian Approach to Polygamy*, 33.

200. Cp. Vollebregt, *Bible on Marriage*, 93.

reasoning and by means of forceful personality carrying out a conclusion at variance with God's commands" (Ezra 9–10).[201]

While the account of Ezra 9–10 is a difficult one to solve, it is commendable that Venn attempts to draw upon an Old Testament narrative in order to develop some biblical basis for field practice. However, Venn's missional hermeneutic is problematic in a number of ways. First of all, Ezra is the sole passage cited despite the fact that the passage's validity is controversial. The main problem in drawing from a single account is that it is too easy to make the obscure occurrence normative (compare Num 25:6–13). Venn could have drawn from numerous other accounts such as Paul's statements in 1 Corinthians 7. Furthermore, Boaz marries Ruth who is a foreign wife, as does Joseph who marries the daughter of an Egyptian priest (Gen 41:45).[202] Yet these men seem to hold steadfastly to their faith and in Ruth's case she demonstrates clear allegiance to God despite her limited exposure (Ruth 1:16).

More importantly, the account in Ezra 9–10 involves monogamous marriages and the concern is solely over the spiritual impact of the foreign wives rather than the number of wives. As we have already seen, God's response to Solomon's foreign wives does not include a request to divorce those wives despite expressed biblical sanctions against this. However, instead of considering the relatively few cases that involve foreign wives, Venn could simply have drawn from the more numerous accounts of polygamists throughout the Old Testament in which foreign (non-believing) wives were not involved. In this way, God's response (or policy) to the sole issue of polygamy could be understood and followed. And what is that response? Simply put, there is no point at which God requires polygamists to divorce their wives. At the most, we could only claim that Scripture is pervasively silent in addressing the matter.

Hermeneutical Critique

Of all the missional responses, the call for polygamists to divorce their wives demonstrates (1) an absent missional hermeneutic, and (2)

---

201. Lewis, *Divine Guidance*, 42.

202. Though it might be thought that Hosea married a foreign woman to further accentuate the living imagery of Israel's unfaithfulness, there is nothing to indicate this. However, the name Gomer does have heritage outside of Israel as Genesis 10:2 notes a Gomer who is a descendant of Japheth, while Abram is a descendant of Shem (Gen 11:10–26).

overwhelming bias in the interpretational process. For example, when considering a passage on divorce, Hillman notes the hermeneutical hypocrisy over the passage's direct focus, despite the confidence asserted over the polygamous implications that are not addressed:

> It is remarkable, therefore, that some of the scholars, for whom the meaning of indissolubility [of marriage] is an open question, are, nevertheless, able to affirm without any hesitation that the question of simultaneous polygamy is settled by the words of Matthew 19:3–9 and its parallels. Indeed, it could be only by some exegetical sleight of hand that a question, which is neither mentioned explicitly in this passage nor even implied in the historical context, is somehow answered definitively, while the question of divorce and remarriage, which is dealt with explicitly here, remains open for further discussion.[203]

For the most part, there has been a lack of commitment to the hermeneutical effort extended toward the missional response to polygamy, despite the fact that the policy on polygamy has deeply affected the lives of polygamists. This has caused honest missionaries and Africans to ask questions such as, "What have we done to the Africans in the name of Christianity? Polygamy which Christ does not forbid, we have fought against as the greatest of all evils, but divorce and remarriage which He does forbid, we have introduced."[204]

It is not surprising, therefore, that the claim of the sole Christian polygamist writing among these authors is that, "Any objective reader of the Synoptic Gospels will agree that Jesus Christ did not make any specific pronouncement on polygamy. Rather he roundly condemned divorce" noting Mark 10:9.[205]

In terms of the issue of divorce, the field experience of missionaries has likewise been a harsh taskmaster. The superintendent of the Moravian Mission in South Africa was adamantly opposed to the official position of the Moravians. He describes their position of forced divorce as biblically unfounded and heartless: "I feel that by our narrow approach of the problem influenced by European theories, a tremendous harm is done to the African people. I myself shall never ask a man to dismiss his wives. It is cruel, immoral and has nothing to do with Christ

---

203. Hillman, *Polygamy Reconsidered*, 157.
204. Helander, *Must We Introduce Monogamy*, 40.
205. Chime, *Polygamy and Christian Religion*, 7.

at all. Nothing but stubborn theories, doctrines as hard as a stone without understanding of the problem and without love. I have done it once in my life and never again."[206]

Likewise, Helander outlines a case in which the wives of a polygamous family actively tried to prevent their husband from becoming a Christian, due to the mission practice at the time:

> As stated, the mission policy is to allow the *wives* in polygamic families to become full members of the Church, since each of them only has one husband? There are plenty of such families in Zululand where the husband, owing to mission policy, remains a heathen though he might go to church, but where the wives are Christian. Generally speaking, they seem to live quite a happy family life together, and one never hears about a wife wanting to be parted from her husband just because he is a polygamist. Should their husband decide to become a Christian, it would mean a great disaster and unhappiness to those Christian women, since mission policy demands that all but one be divorced. If they are bound to him with deep affection, they must view with anxiety any pious tendencies on his part.
>
> Such a woman, having become "one flesh" with her husband, might feel consoled by Christ's words: "What God has so joined together let no man put asunder." But she will have to accept the missionary's word that Christ means precisely the opposite, namely that they *should* be divorced.[207]

Notably, it requires a serious bending of Scripture to claim that polygamy is a sin, but a hermeneutical train wreck is required to claim that polygamists must divorce their wives.

POLYGAMOUS CONVERTS MAY REMAIN POLYGAMOUS UNDER SEVERE RESTRICTIONS

Many of those holding the view that polygamous converts can join the church do so only under severe restrictions that make polygamists second-class Christians. Often this appropriation is based on the idea that the church should offer some level of grace to a potential polygamous convert.

---

206. Helander, *Must We Introduce Monogamy*, 69 quoting from a questionnaire submitted by Superintendent G. Hartmann of the Moravian Mission.

207. Ibid., 20.

A Missional Critique of the Hermeneutics

In terms of the actual restrictions, the two most common were that polygamous converts could not take communion or be baptized. However, the matter strangely grew out of hand from there. Some could be baptized but not until they were on their deathbed. Other restrictions are astounding. For example, "Some Kenyan bishops felt that to refuse them baptism or to make them monogamist or *to cause them to wait until they were incapable of sexual intercourse* imposed a burden contrary to the gospel."[208] Who would have thought that impotency would lead to "salvation!" There was even an attempt to eradicate polygamy through a supplementary tax levied against every wife after the first.[209] "Such [negative] generalized allegations provide a good example of ethnocentric moralizing, and they reveal a vast ignorance of the socio-cultural reality of African polygamy."[210]

The Impact of the Restrictions

However, Africans responsibly asked, "On what basis do the church authorities exclude polygamists from the Holy Sacrament, otherwise called the Holy Communion?"[211] One unforeseen problem with the inconsistent discipline levied upon polygamists was that it weakened the church's capacity when real discipline was needed. One such example flows from African church members interpreting Scripture in ways that many Western missionaries would not:

> [An] objection raised is that even if the Church must continue to discipline its [polygamous] members it should not use the sacraments as the form of punishment. Some people have come to doubt whether the Church has any rights at all to punish or to excommunicate. They support this by Scripture that Jesus commanded his disciples to go teach and baptise, and the only criterion was faith. Or that Jesus, knowing fully well that Judas was His betrayer still ate the last supper with him, and did not excommunicate him. All these are very strong arguments against any kind of discipline by the Church.[212]

---

208. Newing, "Baptism of Polygamous Families," 130 italics mine.
209. Hunt, "Noise over Camouflaged Polygamy," 474.
210. Hillman, *Polygamy Reconsidered*, 182.
211. Chime, *Polygamy and Christian Religion*, 19.
212. Okullu, *Church and Marriage*, 70.

Okullu continues by stating that he is not ready to place a moratorium on all forms of church discipline, but he clearly understands the rift that is caused by improper forms of punishment that are all-together undeserved.

Likewise, the restrictions sometimes produced inappropriate motivations for new converts. For example, a husband who has marital trouble with one of his two wives may intentionally become a Christian solely for the motivation of abstaining from the unwanted wife. Aside from the divorce policies, there were policies that called for the family to remain together, but for the husband to be sexually involved with only one wife. Such a policy, however, would allow a man to keep his children nearby and benefit from the labor of his unwanted wife while justifiably excluding her needs for emotional and sexual intimacy. A woman in this case could easily feel trapped in a functional divorce.

No policy has fully remedied this problem, including those that essentially require a continued but non-sexual marriage with the "extra" wives. However, the primary reason for the failure is a continued resistance to consider the implications of God's attempts to regulate polygamy in the Old Testament, rather than prohibit polygamy (compare Exod 21:10–11).

Like the issue of divorce, few attempts have been made to consider whether or not God has a similar policy among the many Old Testament cases of polygamy. Did God forbid an Israelite to be involved in a given Old Testament practice due to his status as a polygamist? A man is never forbidden to be circumcised or undergo ceremonial washing because he is a polygamist. Likewise, a man is never forbidden to engage in a practice that infuses life, purpose, and meaning into the people of God because he is a polygamist.

Similarly within the New Testament,

> Jesus Christ did not say that the Apostles, or the Bishops, who came after them, should use the solemn ceremony as an instrument of victimization, discrimination and punishment. But the Church has turned this solemn ceremony, ordained by God for every body, into a punitive instrument. It is significant to note that some of the people who partake in the Holy Communion are murderers, armed robbers, or criminals of various types. But people who married more than one wife, and who, other-

wise, have not done any thing against the law of God or the law of man, are denied the sacrament.[213]

Hermeneutical Critique

Nearly all of those who have developed the vast array of policies enforced by the churches, likewise believe that God implemented gradual changes in Scripture that ended the practice of polygamy. However, these missionaries must consider that they are bound by the same methods that they claim God used in Scripture![214] If, by their own claims, God's missionary practice consisted of inferences, images, and subtle connections to make this known, then by what basis do they adopt another practice? If in fact polygamy is wrong, it is quite likely that God's use of inference was in place because it was the only way the problem could be addressed.

Gaskiyane is one of the more helpful examples in this discussion, because he clearly holds the position that monogamy is God's ideal form of marriage, and that it would be wrong for an existing Christian to become a polygamist.[215] However, he is likewise adamant that "[r]efusing to baptize polygamous converts is a refusal to obey the will of God."[216] And while he only briefly touches on the subject of a biblically informed missional response, he does draw upon the Old Testament to do so: "[I]t is clear that it is God's will to change a polygamous culture to a monogamous one as He did with His people in the Bible. In the Old Testament He did this by speaking to His people within the moral framework in which they lived, but this took time. It did not happen in one generation. God does His work by gradually changing the inner moral character of His people within the culture where they live."[217]

In spite of his demonstration of a missional hermeneutic, Gaskiyane goes on to add his own list that the church should teach on the matter which includes "clear Bible teaching" so that new Christians can "understand the reasons for God's plan of monogamy."[218] If he were to continue to follow God's example in dealing with polygamy, he could only work

---

213. Chime, *Polygamy and Christian Religion*, 19.
214. Contra Urrutia, "Can Polygamy Be Compatible," 282.
215. Gaskiyane, *Polygamy*, 28–30, 51.
216. Ibid., 48.
217. Ibid., 37.
218. Ibid., 40.

through inferences to suggest monogamy, because that is the strongest form of teaching that flows from the Old Testament. Nevertheless, Gaskiyane has at least demonstrated that a proper missional response to the issue of polygamy must be developed from continued biblical investigation.

However, most of those establishing policies against polygamy have failed to ask crucial questions related to mission such as: "Since I believe polygamy is a sin, what is the missionary nature of God in addressing this issue in biblical contexts?"; or "Since I believe that non-Christian polygamists may become baptized (but that all following generations of Christians should be only monogamists), how does God convey this message to the people of God in biblical contexts?" Questions such as these are the starting point for a biblically informed mission practice, but they are either rare or entirely absent.[219]

If God did in fact condemn polygamy through an indirect, patient, and graceful approach to the issue, this becomes the biblical example for addressing the problem.[220] However, those writing against polygamy are so engrossed in showing that polygamy is a sin that they rarely give thought to considering what the Bible has to say in informing Christian workers on how to address this so-called sin. These writers have made the grave mistake of assuming that the Bible exists solely to inform theology while ignoring the role of the Bible in terms of mission practice. They appear to be so influenced by the theological ideals of modernity that they are unaware of the blatant syncretism they propagate by integrating modernity and theology in place of a missional hermeneutic.

As a result, a biblically unfounded response to polygamy demonstrates at least three major failures. (1) God's missional example is not seen as a directive, which (2) results in poor or culturally biased hermeneutics that offer no helpful example of missional hermeneutics, and (3) the African reaction to undeserved punishment results in a weakened capacity for the church to address genuine matters of discipline.

---

219. When I say they are "rare," I am being generous because many writers briefly suggest ideas for the missional implementation of their particular theological stance, but the use of Scripture in this matter occurs only in the most general sense (for example, concern for non-Christian; compassion) (Hitchens, *Multiple Marriage*, 139–44).

220. The only direct or propositional statements addressing polygamy are those of Leviticus 18:18 (ending the practice of sororal polygamy) and those who improperly claim that Titus and 1 Timothy are statements against polygamous church leaders.

Furthermore, Africans have responded to the problem by removing the Western interpretational bias:

> Why is the baptism of polygynists a problem? Africa has not found it to be a problem to have polygyny as a valid and accepted form of marriage. Monogamy, however, is not rejected, but it is part and parcel of another valid and accepted structure of marriage. This is because man in the African concept is a family.... A person in Africa does not act according to his individual conscience, but according to that of the family. How far is this African social structure wrong, even sinful? The Western missions and Churches say they know it.... Africa goes together with the missions and Churches to say that adultery, fornication, prostitution etc. are evil, but it does not understand what is wrong with polygyny. In polygynous families, there are problems, but those are internal family problems and no more. They cannot be classified as evil as the above-mentioned evils, which even Africa would not tolerate.[221]

Even though Colenso claimed that polygamy was wrong and needed to end, he properly adopted the only proper missional hermeneutic to match his view, namely that "It was, therefore, to be corrected mildly and gradually, by example, rather than by express precept."[222] Given that so many of the biblical arguments used inference upon inference to claim that polygamy was a sin, the only valid missional response to this perspective would be to use inferences rather than policy to end polygamy as a whole.

"[W]e might say that the Bible slowly creates *the ideal* of monogamy, but without being categoric or fanatic about it, and that it tolerated existing polygamic marriages."[223] Likewise, for those who have claimed that polygamy has always been a sin, they would have all the more reason to consider God's grace in the Old Testament that was consistently extended in the midst of this sin.[224] For those who concluded that monogamy was God's ideal form of marriage expressed over thousands of years, it is inescapable to likewise conclude that God's grace extended to polygamists over thousands of years through the witness of one inference after another.

---

221. Kiwovele, "Polygyny as a Problem," 10–11.
222. Colenso, *Remarks on Proper Treatment*, 13.
223. Helander, *Must We Introduce Monogamy*, 30.
224. du Preez, *Polygamy in the Bible*; Kaiser, *Toward Old Testament Ethics*, 182–92.

POLYGAMOUS CONVERTS ARE ALLOWED BAPTISM BUT DENIED LEADERSHIP

The missional position that polygamous converts can be baptized but that they cannot lead was most often based on an improper interpretation of 1 Timothy, which assumes that Paul's overall meaning of 1 Timothy 3:2, 12 is one that is "against polygamy" (referring back to Table 10). Though it has been shown that polygamy is among the most unlikely meanings that Paul had in mind, this passage was often cited to validate the inclusion of polygamists in the church while likewise excluding them from leadership.[225]

However, the irony of this response is that polygamists were often included in the church as a result of misinterpreting 1 Timothy 3 and then proof-texting from that misinterpretation. Some who had a stronger missional focus, however, argued that non-Christian polygamists could not have understood their error apart from knowing Christ. Therefore, it was felt that the church must offer grace for those new converts already involved in polygamy. Notably, the emphasis upon Christ's grace given for sinners and Paul's advice was actually a much stronger missional hermeneutic than those who misinterpreted 1 Timothy 3 (compare 1 Cor 7:17–20).

Most of those who implemented this mission policy felt that monogamy was God's ideal form of marriage and some felt that polygamy was a sin. Interestingly, many of those from the second and third aforementioned theological positions were divided in terms of their theology but had greater cohesion in terms of field practice. At the same time, numerous mission agencies who once called for great condemnation of the practice now began to believe that their earlier stances were wrong. "[S]ince the 1950s a greater appreciation has arisen as to how God works with culture, even with customs that are less than ideal. This has brought a greater openness among missionary theorists and some mission lead-

---

225. Chime, *Polygamy and Christian Religion*, 7–8; Gaskiyane, *Polygamy*, 60–61; Gitari, "Church and Polygamy," 7; Helander, *Must We Introduce Monogamy*, 32–33, 35, 57–59; Hitchens, *Multiple Marriage*, 135; Kaiser, *Toward Old Testament Ethics*, 189; Maillu, *Our Kind of Polygamy*, 48; Mann, "Biblical Understanding of Polygamy," 21, 25; Nkwoka, "Church and Polygamy in Africa," 148–49; Odame, *Christian Approach to Polygamy*, 36; Tiénou and Hiebert, "Missional Theology," 234; Wambutda, "Monogamy or Polygamy," 80. Nevertheless, it is possible polygamists may have been part of the New Testament church given some African perceptions (1 Cor 5:1–2) (Chime, *Polygamy and Christian Religion*, 5–7).

ers to rethink the church's position [on polygamy]. Large numbers of indigenous leaders who are now in charge of the churches have, however, refused to change."[226]

Polygamy, Leadership and the Tapestry of Scripture

Not only is "faithfulness" the strongest overall meaning of 1 Timothy, it likewise provides the strongest match for the tapestry of Scripture. Since it is the least likely possibility that the passage is prohibiting polygamist leadership in the church, this means that Abraham, David, Solomon, and other polygamist leaders could just as validly lead the church today.[227] Furthermore, David was praised for his faithfulness to God and referred to as a man after God's own heart. However, the biblical record demonstrates consistency with the leadership requirements of 1 Timothy when God chastised David over his unfaithfulness and murder of Uriah (2 Sam 12)!

Though not a case of marital unfaithfulness, Solomon's condemnation took place over spiritual unfaithfulness as he worshipped the gods of his foreign wives (1 Kgs 11). When combined with other accounts regarding faithfulness, such as Hosea and Jonah, a clear theme emerges indicating that God places a high value on faithfulness to God, the Church, and God's mission to the world.

Hermeneutical Critique

The former grammatical study of 1 Timothy 3:2, 12 was a helpful example of the benefit of traditional hermeneutical tools. However, that analysis could benefit from a variety of additional work, such as traditional historical studies in first century culture and a firm anthropological understanding of the nature of culture. Nevertheless, these skills are primarily the hermeneutical tools of seminary trained "experts" who have learned the language and methods to enable them to perform such work.

Africans, who were not trained in seminary, demonstrated an alternative hermeneutic that did not require this level of background.

226. Kraft, "Polygamy and Church Membership," 766.

227. Of all the work I have done in looking at the issue of polygamy and the Bible, I find this the most freeing. There is no justifiable way to biblically validate the claim that Abraham, David, and Solomon could lead God's missionary people while today's polygamous believers cannot. Such a claim simply stands on shaky ground.

Essentially, they looked thematically at the narrative of the Old Testament and found the practice of polygamy to be a consistent theme flowing through the pages of Scripture.

The same hermeneutic can and should be investigated with respect to Christian leadership and it is not difficult to fathom that such a study would demonstrate God's acceptance of polygamists in the Old Testament as leaders. Barring an expressed claim that God had condemned the practice (such as is found over the flippant reasons for divorce), there is no reason to think that 1 Timothy 3 should abruptly alter this theme. Therefore, a thematic analysis of polygamous leadership should likewise lead to the conclusion that 1 Timothy 3 is discussing another matter.

Certainly the collective effect of multiple hermeneutics provides greater interpretational confidence, especially if each analysis arrives at similar conclusions. However, most Western missionaries failed to carry out either analysis, despite the fact that many missionaries were seminary trained. Moreover, Africans were naturally illustrating the tapestry of Scripture as it relates to polygamy in general. The major missional failure was one of listening to the Holy Spirit through the eyes of new believers and a minor failure to undergo the more complex grammatical work.

Hermeneutically speaking, Paul's concern in 1 Timothy 3:2, 12 can join the greater chorus of passages that consistently require "faithfulness" or the meaning can be subjugated to match the Western agenda obsessed with polygamy. In this latter case, the passage becomes an isolated text that only finds corroboration through similar distortions of other portions of Scripture. For those who take the latter approach, the increasing ambiguity of these passages as they relate to polygamy is reason enough to avoid a theology and mission practice that stands or falls based on these passages alone.

POLYGAMOUS CONVERTS FUNCTIONING EQUALLY WITH MONOGAMISTS

"My plea with the Church and missions, therefore, is that the pre-baptism polygynists should be baptized together with their wives and children without being forced to divorce their wives. They should also be accepted into full church membership. The post-baptism polygynists also should not be excommunicated from church membership because of their wives they married besides the first wife. In other words, monogamy should not be a condition for church membership."[228]

Those claiming that polygamists can function equally as monogamists are those found in the third column of Table 6. With the exception of Okotie, these authors present a balanced theological and missiological response to the majority Western voice that has argued against polygamy.[229] Likewise, these authors offer the least biased reading of the Old Testament. As such, their theological and missiological claims hold the greatest consistency with God's treatment of polygamists in the Old Testament.

As has so often been the case in the history of mission, unrealized syncretism among the missionaries led to non-biblical requirements that produced separatist reactions, sometimes resulting in new-found biblical values. However, such a moratorium would likely have never come about had the missionaries acted as biblical partners rather than overbearing parents. "As the missionaries cease to control the indigenous churches, there exists a definite possibility that some of such churches reintroduce polygamy if they have not been convinced of the necessity of monogamy. There have been plenty of tendencies in that direction. In numerous smaller independent churches and sects in South Africa, polygamy is today a fact."[230]

Polygamy among Existing Christians

The possibility that an existing Christian might become a polygamist is probably the most controversial of all issues surrounding polygamy. Since polygamy was tolerated as an act of grace or as something less than the ideal, it was not tolerated among existing Church members who wanted to take additional wives. This was true for the Christian monogamist who wanted to become a polygamist, or the existing Christian polygamist who wanted to marry an additional wife. In both cases, it was recommended that those engaged in this practice be excommunicated.[231]

---

228. Kiwovele, "Polygyny as a Problem," 24–25.

229. Okotie, *Last Outcast*.

230. Helander, *Must We Introduce Monogamy*, 9.

231. Gaskiyane, *Polygamy*, 50–59; Odame, *Christian Approach to Polygamy*, 51, 54, 67.

Odame, for example, presents convincing evidence to allow a non-Christian polygamist to join the church.[232] However, his views are irreconcilable at points. Odame claims that, "Upon reflection therefore one may say that God permitted it [polygamy] because of the hardness of human heart" and that "The New Testament position then is a clear affirmation of monogamy but we have no biblical basis for condemning polygamy."[233] He further affirms, "I have thoroughly read all the relevant texts on this subject and no single text from Genesis to Revelation legislates against the practice of polygamy. We should not misrepresent scripture."[234] On what biblical basis, then, does Odame make the following claim: "While we have to have mercy on the pagan polygamist who wants to become a Christian, I earnestly urge the Church not to tolerate the Christian polygamist. Strictly speaking, if a Christian flouted the advice or authority of the Church and succeeded in taking a second wife, I should have no qualms if he were excommunicated from the Church. I make this statement without any mental reservations."[235]

If there is no biblical basis for condemning polygamy, why is it then that the non-Christian polygamist is in need of mercy? Furthermore, why is it that a Christian polygamist is likely to be excommunicated? The only answer can be that there is some form of non-biblical bias in addressing the issue. More importantly, Odame does not look to Scripture to determine if his Church's policy is biblically valid. He re-affirms his perspective that monogamy is God's ideal by drawing upon Genesis 2 and other passages, but he never considers God's response to men of faith in the Old Testament as an example that should be followed.

However, Okullu offers greater options for the Christian polygamist. On the one hand, he accepts a non-Christian polygamist primarily on the basis that they cannot be expected to know biblical standards apart from Christ.[236] On the other hand, when addressing those who have become polygamists, Okullu suggests that a grace-filled attitude must be adopted: "[T]ension must be held between our acceptance of monogamy as the ideal Christian form of marriage on one hand and the grace and willingness to live with those who have failed to reach it on the

---

232. Cp. Odame, *Christian Approach to Polygamy*, 34–36, 38–41, 49.

233. Ibid., 31, 34.

234. Ibid., 47.

235. Ibid., 49.

236. Okullu, *Church and Marriage*, 63.

A Missional Critique of the Hermeneutics

other hand. Personally, I believe that where monogamy is clearly taught as the form of marriage which is more in line with Christian teaching, those who attain it should take pride in it and continue to teach it rather than be defensive and unforgiving in their attitudes."[237] However, Okullu likewise points out that many polygamists "are still strongly believing Christians but have had to excommunicate themselves to escape the judgemental eyes they encounter in church from some of those whose only qualification to be called Christian is that they have one wife."[238]

Finally, Kiwovele considers God's response to polygamists and appropriately questions the consistency of the practice of missionaries in comparison to the Old Testament:

> Monogamy is one of the conditions for baptism as well as church membership for Christians. In other words, there is no salvation for a polygynist. This has led to the excommunication of all post-baptism polygynists. The latter aspect of polygyny is regarded by the Church and missions to be worse than the former one. However, most churches and missions in Africa accept wives and children of polygynous husbands for baptism and church membership.
>
> The problem seems to be made more serious partly by the fact that the church-accepted holy book, the Bible, contradicts itself with regard to this problem. This is especially true in the Old Testament. This shocks some of our readers very much unless they are eye and brainwashed when they read those passages. The people of God in the Old Testament who were polygynists were not excluded from the membership of the community of the people of God.[239]

Kiwovele is one of the few who looks to the biblical accounts of those involved in polygamy and finds no similar stipulations to those of Western missionaries. Furthermore, Kiwovele appropriately asserts that the "Church and missions are requested to reconsider methods" due to the vast inconsistency of responses in dealing with the issue.[240] Unfortunately, Kiwovele does not address the matter at length.

---

237. Ibid., 67.
238. Ibid., 68–69.
239. Kiwovele, "Polygyny as a Problem," 7.
240. Ibid., 8; cp. Helander, *Must We Introduce Monogamy*, 67; Yego, "Polygamy and African Church," 79.

However, of all the cases we have studied, levirate marriage is the one issue that stands out prominently in terms of theology and mission for existing Christians. Many Africans societies have levirate customs similar to those in Scripture, and as such the levirate expectations create a dilemma for believers wanting to take an additional wife. This is especially confounding for the Christian who is trapped between ecclesial policies and a need to provide a culturally appropriate response to their family.

In the case of levirate marriage, there is a combined theological and missional mandate. The theological aspect is that it is commanded in the Old Testament. Shame is thrust upon those who did not follow this command (Deut 25:5–10). Furthermore, Onan was struck down by God over the issue of failing to comply with levirate marriage requirements (Gen 38:9–10). Given that many African cultures have similar customs for very similar reasons, I cannot fathom condemning the same practice today.

Missionally, this mandate foremost focuses upon keeping the family name, but this likewise had a great deal to do with giving rights and land to widows (Ruth 4:10). Women and children are some of the poorest in Israel and this command places them in care while preserving their inheritance if something tragic happens to the husband. Israel is given an edict that causes them to care for the disenfranchised, and Israel was similar to many societies that had unfair levels of male dominance.

Likewise, Israel was learning a lesson that God cares for the poor and disenfranchised. This is a lesson that could have been taken to neighboring nations (such as Ruth) and a lesson that ultimately acts as imagery for Israel in terms of seeing other nations as orphaned from God (such as Jonah). There is no getting around the fact theologically or missionally that levirate marriage held a firm place in God's vision of proper practice for Israel.

Likewise, in the New Testament the practice of levirate marriage is discussed but it is not condemned (Matt 22:23–33). However, alternate ways of caring for the Greek-speaking widows are found in Acts 6:1–6. This does not replace levirate marriage, but it demonstrates the possibility of caring for widows through a combination of biblically and culturally appropriate systems which may or may not include levirate practices. Finally, levirate marriage is rarely motivated by lust. Rather, the motivations have often been quite pure and caring motivations

A Missional Critique of the Hermeneutics

(Ruth 3:10–13; 4:9–15).[241] In this light, there is no biblical justification for preventing this practice among Christians who have similar desires to fulfill their cultural expectations today.

God's Response to Polygamous Marriage

In all that has been discussed up to this point, we have looked at the fact that God did not carry out action against polygamists, even though the church, almost as a matter of form, has presupposed an authority to do so apart from Scripture's guidance. However, we need to ask, "What actions did God actually take throughout the narratives in which polygamy is found?" Just as certain Old Testament passages regulate the practice of polygamy, God's involvement in the narratives likewise demonstrates a desire to strengthen the polygamous marriage.

In the more extensive narratives in Scripture that allow the reader an insider's view into a polygamous family, God takes actions to build up the polygamous marriage rather than tear it down. In the instances of Jacob with Rachel and Leah as well as Elkanah with Hannah and Peninnah, both men seem to favor one wife (Gen 29:31; 1 Sam 1:5). However, in response to the husband's favoritism, God sovereign actions appear to bring greater balance to the polygamous family.

In the case of Jacob with Leah and Rachel, God sovereignly responds by opening Leah's womb early in the marriage. Might God have brought about this act of grace in order to bring greater balance in Jacob's love toward Leah? Such an act would most likely decrease the strife and increase the stability in a polygamous marriage (Gen 29:31). By contrast, it is far later in the relationship that Rachel and Leah's continued prayers are together answered allowing them to both become pregnant (though another pregnancy for Leah at this point) (Gen 30:17–22).[242] This again would bring greater stability to the relationship at this later time period because Jacob was caught in the middle of both his wives frightfully competitive need to bear children (Gen 30:1–16).

---

241. Trobisch, *My Wife Made Me*, 35–36. Trobisch points out that Scripture illustrates many different motivations for polygamy: "For Abraham and Elkanah (1 Sam. 1) it was barrenness; for Lamech (Gen. 4:23) it was pride; for Gideon (Judg. 8:30) it was prestige; for Boaz, who married Ruth, the widow of one of his cousins (Ruth 4), it was the levirate marriage; for David and Solomon it was power and sexual lust" (ibid., 26).

242. God likewise sovereignly closed the wombs of Abimelech's household, but the act here is used to warn Abimelech (Gen 20:17–18).

Similarly, in the case of Elkanah with Hannah and Peninnah, Hannah's womb was closed by God in order to bring greater appreciation toward Peninnah and thereby balance Elkanah's love for both of his wives (1 Sam 1:5). However, Hannah's womb was later opened to relieve her personal torment as well as the intentional torment of her co-wife (1 Sam 1:10–20). Once again, God's actions appear to have the intent of bringing greater balance to the polygamous marriage. It is likewise notable in this case that we see God affirmatively answering the prayer of the polygamous wife and blessing her with a child, rather than finding a new husband for one of the wives. It is worthwhile to consider that modern-day mission agencies with a policy against baptizing the children of polygamists would ironically have to restrict the prophet Samuel from baptism.

In each of these accounts, God's sovereign actions appear to be designed to increase the husband's loyalties and affections for the less-loved wife.[243] These examples, therefore, should be included among writers who only cite Sarah's eviction of Hagar as a validation for enforcing divorce (Gen 21:8–21). Likewise, it should be noted that it is Sarah's disdain which causes the separation. Though God permits the separation to take place, God sovereignly cares for Hagar and Ishmael and likewise sovereignly provides an inheritance for Ishmael even in the aftermath of a broken polygamous family.

> What is God's ideal for marriage? Most theologians will undoubtedly reply that the ideal form is clearly an indissoluble union between *one* man and *one* woman. But surely this is to miss the point. The divine ideal is not to be found in a *form*, but in a *relationship*. Marriage is to be a mutually responsible, supportive, loving and reciprocal relationship. It is to be the source of the basic social unit—the family. It is to provide the context into which children are born, and in which they are physically and spiritually nurtured. The question then becomes: Which social form of marriage is best able to express this kind of relationship and meaning?[244]

---

243. I owe the synthesis of this summary sentence to my wife, Kristin Redford, who is a California licensed Marriage and Family Therapist and likewise has a background as a missionary and a Master of Arts degree in missiology from Fuller Theological Seminary.

244. Welch, "Biblical Perspective on Polygamy," 108–9.

A Missional Critique of the Hermeneutics

Therefore, God wanted husbands to love their wife or wives responsibly. Much like the issues surrounding baptism, missionaries have been so occupied with the form (sprinkling, pouring or immersion), that they have failed to focus on the meaning of identification with God's mission and Christ's atonement (Acts 2; Rom 6). One of Africa's natural strengths is an extremely strong understanding and appreciation for family. In my experience with the Maasai, the one thing that poignantly stood out was their level of family cohesion. This background will give them a much stronger lens for biblical interpretation of the family. As such, Africans should ignore the sterile debate of monogamy versus polygamy and inform the West on the deeper meaning of family!

Hermeneutical Critique

In effect, the majority of Africans and a minority of Western missionaries have provided their own hermeneutical critique. Their claim is essentially that the failure to engage Scripture with a missional hermeneutic has resulted in potential converts being unjustly turned away from the Christian message over a non-essential issue. Consequently, the manifestation of a failed missional hermeneutic had dreadful consequences for Africa. As missionaries operated from their own agenda, they preached monogamy as a requirement rather than following Christ, and in doing so they drove willing followers away from the Christian message with no biblical basis whatsoever:

> Even before they have been approached by missionaries, the polygamists themselves are apt already to have received the message that admission into the Church depends on the law of monogamy no less than it depends of faith in Jesus Christ. Precisely because this legal condition is both intolerable and incomprehensible to them, polygamists find it hard to listen to the whole Christian message, so they are unable to respond fully to the call of Christ. Since the law of monogamy is often the first thing that people hear about Christianity, many do not care to hear any more. The message of Christian freedom does not liberate them, because it is presented equivocally under the burden of a law (cf. Acts 15:10–11).[245]

There was likewise a failure in trusting the Holy Spirit to make the matter clear since Western biases were seen as a source of the problem.

---

245. Hillman, *Polygamy Reconsidered*, 205.

If the issue was so vital to the church and so relevant for mission, the Holy Spirit could certainly have manifested this same concern in the hearts of African believers. However, the failure to trust the Holy Spirit to hermeneutically reveal this same interpretation meant that a great deal of mission flowed from human authority. Western paternalism became the primary driving force behind the non-biblical concern to instill monogamy as a biblical ideal. As a result, mission was perceived as the enforcement of Western values rather than a spiritual act of gracefully sharing the message of Jesus Christ:

> If the truth of Christianity, as revealed in the Bible, was not diluted with Western European customs and traditions, before it was brought to us in Africa, there would have been no heathens remaining in Africa today.
>
> But the impracticable doctrine about polygamy which cannot be rationalized, brought so much hindrance to the evangelization of [the] African population. The Europeans, who brought Christianity to us, preached against polygamy which is part and parcel of the customs and traditions of Africa. They told us that polygamy is a practice of adultery. If polygamy is adulterous, as taught by the Church, a logical question follows, thus: "If people like Abraham, Jacob, Moses and David who are patriarchs of our faith, married more than one wife, why were they not rebuked by God who talked directly to them in those days?"[246]

Though Ofora may overstate his case in terms of Africa's complete acceptance of the Christian message, the deterring impact that polygamy has had is a common complaint. Far too many missionaries have responded in claiming that this is an offence of the true Christian message. However, they will not be able to find a biblical figure who was unwilling to follow God over the practice of polygamy, and this is because polygamy is not presented as a prerequisite for faith within Scripture.

Likewise, Africans were thrust into a defensive position when addressing polygamy. As Ofora points out, missionaries did not give the Bible to Africans and casually ask them to report back if they felt there was anything wrong with polygamy. Rather, missionaries assumed that Africans could not carry out an unbiased reading of Scripture because of the existence of polygamy, and preemptively asserted heavy dogmatism and paternalism by dictating the response that they felt African's should

---

246. Foreword written by L Ofora in Chime, *Polygamy and Christian Religion*, iv.

A Missional Critique of the Hermeneutics

adopt. "Missionaries assumed it was their task, indeed their right to interpret the Bible and in the early days Africans could not even read the Bible which only added to missionary paternalism."[247]

However, from a hermeneutical standpoint, it is extremely difficult to respond to an issue that goes unmentioned in God's mission as found throughout Scripture. When Western trained missionaries claimed that polygamy is an evil in God's sight, those coming to Scripture for the first time would certainly love to find a passage declaring that polygamy was accepted by God and was not evil. However, this cannot be found just as the passages referring to polygamy as an evil cannot be found.

As it stands, the strongest claims concerning the practice are that the Bible does not condemn polygamy or the slightly stronger claim that the Bible regulates the practice of polygamy (Exod 21:7–11, Lev 18:18, Deut 17:17; 21:15–17). This, however, was hardly enough to reverse the watershed of claims that drew upon any mention of monogamy and poor hermeneutics as a means of condemning polygamy. The incredibly poor inference-hermeneutic could be used to validate or critique nearly anything. As we have seen, one African has used this identical hermeneutic to note that polygamy is God's preference, and the most likely basis for adopting this hermeneutic were the missionaries' own arguments.

The real irony, however, is that the Africans had manifested the strongest interpretation even though they had the least training and background with Scripture. This was true both in terms of their theological understanding and their missional response. Though the process was extremely painful, Africa had begun to develop a missional hermeneutic in spite of its absence among missionaries with respect to polygamy. This was and is, in many ways, a testimony to the Holy Spirit's power to work through obstacles raised by the missionary and is all the more reason to keep a text such as Jonah at the forefront of mission studies. There is no stronger example of this than that of African evangelist William Wadé Harris:

> The prophet had, in fact, preached submission to authorities under God's law, denounced alcohol abuse, and had clearly affected the moral climate of the populations by his denunciation of adultery. . . . Eight times Harris attempted to return to the Ivory Coast but was always stopped by the colonial authori-

247. A personal comment written by Dean S. Gilliland.

ties. But he went up and down the Liberian coast with his mission, often penetrating into the interior where missionaries had never gone. He went to Sierra Leone three times on foot: in 1917, 1919, and 1921. His ministry in Liberia, even if it gave problems to the Methodist missionary Walter B. Williams because of their differences over polygamous marriage, nevertheless provoked a mass "revival movement" in 1915 and the years following. Harris did not denounce polygamy but accepted it as a fact of African life, and this led to continuing problems with the Methodist groups and others. . . . Dr. Frederick A. Price described it as a "real tidal wave of religious enthusiasm which swept hundreds of people into the Christian church . . . It was nothing else but Pentecost in Africa." But he also pointed out that because of their refusal to abandon polygamy, countless numbers were also refused by the [Western] churches, obviously in contradiction to Harris's understanding and preaching. . . . The new dimension in Harris's strategy was the administration of baptism immediately following the shift growing out of the power-confrontation; this was to keep people from returning to the old powers—a preventive measure.[248]

MISSIONAL RESPONSES DRAWING FROM SCRIPTURE

From these final four categories, we should realize that the way in which we address polygamy must likewise flow from Scripture. We are bound by Scripture in both understanding the nature of sin and in determining the proper missional action for addressing a sin.

The issue of polygamy is probably the most critical example of the cultural differences between Scripture and the West. It demonstrates the difference in perception between deeply ingrained Western values and the quite different values that we find in Scripture. Specifically, within Scripture, we do not find the same level of repugnancy toward polygamy. Among the most prominent sins throughout the Old Testament, we do find a great deal of hatred toward idolatry. When the people of God are idolatrous, God addresses this harshly and swiftly.

However, when the people of God involve themselves in polygamy, many of whom were leaders, God did not address this in the same way that he addressed idolatry. Polygamy, if it ever was addressed by God, was given great patience since the practice existed for thousands of years

---

248. Shank, "William Wadé Harris," 159–60, 62–63.

within Scripture. Likewise, there is not a single punishment that can be derived from Scripture in order to address polygamy (excepting the very specific case of Lev 20:14). The only mandates regarding polygamists are essentially that they treat their wives as equals, with equal love for both, and that they treat their children with the same sort of fairness. In essence then, God's heart for the polygamist families was that the husband act responsibly and with equal care toward his family.[249]

CONCLUSION

There has been at least a four-part failure in the hermeneutics related to the theological and missional issues addressing African polygamy and early hermeneutical failures have had cascading implications that obscured the way to better practices.

1. Foremost, intense Western biases were never sufficiently addressed and these remained evident within many hermeneutical tendencies. While these biases did influence the theology on the topic of polygamy, a far more tragic effect was an unrealized scientific modernist epistemology that pushed theology to the foreground and likewise dictated the underlying hermeneutical approach. As a result, interpreters began addressing polygamy through a theology that supposedly flowed from Scripture. However, the theological outcome was of such concern for the interpreters that it rarely seemed as if they had allowed Scripture to inform their theology. As a result, Scripture was rarely permitted to speak for itself and when interpreters did allow it to break through their pre-existing agendas, Scripture remained imprisoned in theological debates. The consequence is that the missional response to polygamy was developed almost entirely through human reasoning. This, likewise,

---

249. The only thought that convinces me that polygamist relationships are difficult has nothing to do with Scripture. Polygamist marriages, by their very nature have a greater number of relationships making the family dynamics naturally more complex. In a monogamous marriage, there is one relationship and yet a good monogamous marriage requires a great deal of relational effort. In the case of a polygamist with two wives, there are three relationships; with three wives, there are six relationships; with four wives, there are ten relationships (to illustrate this just draw a single mark representing the husband followed by four marks to represent the wives. You will find that there are ten individual relationships among the five marks). The greater number of relationships would seem to imply that even greater effort is needed to sustain the marriage.

resulted in diversity and conflict with respect to the policies themselves and their implementation.

2. The Western preoccupation with theology that flowed from absolute truth led to the second hermeneutical failure, which was a near eclipse of missional hermeneutics. Missional hermeneutics were needed to define and guide mission practices that were biblically informed. Likewise, they were needed to biblically critique the wide variety of ecclesial policies. From a biblical standpoint, missionaries had not given equal weight to God's Old Testament response toward biblical figures practicing polygamy. Had there been clear narrative examples in which God ended the practice of polygamy, I have little doubt that Western authors would have swarmed to such passages. However, the biblical narrative did not support their agenda and this likewise meant that Western authors minimized the impact of a missional hermeneutic.

3. Much of this could have been remedied by trusting African Christians to theologize over an area that is decidedly a non-issue within Scripture. However, Western dogmatism forced the issue of polygamy to have an almost equal standing as the lordship of Jesus Christ, leading to a third hermeneutical failure. Western paternalism obscured the more important need of an indigenous African hermeneutic that could develop a biblically informed theological and missiological understanding of polygamy. Given the African response shown in this chapter, such a hermeneutic would most likely have been thematically consistent with Scripture and integrated in terms of its theological and missiological understandings. This would also have tested the capacity of missionaries to separate their cultural values from central biblical themes, and would have additionally served as an excellent case study for the training of new missionaries.

4. However, the failure in all of these previous three areas led to the greatest hermeneutical failure, which was a lack of trust in the Holy Spirit's capacity to biblically inform the lives of new believers in the African church in order to effect change where change was needed. Deep down, I suspect that many from the West felt that the gracious Holy Spirit would not match the same levels of dogmatism brought by Western missionaries. Likewise, Western hermeneutics were so infused with scientific agendas that there was little room for a spiritual hermeneutic that relied upon the Holy Spirit as biblical figures did.

A Missional Critique of the Hermeneutics

These four hermeneutical failures culminated in a final failure that had tragic consequences. Families were destroyed. Children were left without their father or mother. Some banished wives entered into prostitution, remarried into traditional religion and hated the church. Divorces were enforced in the name of Christianity and partiality was shown in baptism. Many polygamists interested in following Christ were turned away for absolutely no biblical reasons.

Finally, this particular issue was one wedge among many that fragmented African churches from their Western counterparts. It is my humblest prayer and apology that such acts were ever condoned through Scripture. There is simply no biblical validation for the condemnation of polygamy or the insidious policies that the church adopted to address this so-called sin.

> There is no subject before us which requires to be approached in a more prayerful spirit than this [polygamy], and I am exceedingly thankful that our Chairman has called for prayer. I went out to China some thirty-four years ago, holding very strongly the view that I suppose most hold, namely, that every man having more than one wife, if converted, must be prepared to put them aside.... [However,] I [now] hold that there is no lawful cause to put away a wife except that of adultery.
>
> So strongly do I feel on this question that if a man were to come and say, "I am married to two wives; I am prepared to put one away; I will turn her out; I want you to receive me and baptise me," I should tell him I could not do it under the circumstances.[250]

J. Hudson Taylor spoke these words at the 1888 London Missionary Conference. Taylor's words were the first that turned the tide of the discussion and allowed a handful of other seasoned missionaries to express their similar convictions. However, Taylor's heart-felt concerns arose through his missionary experience in China causing him to return to Scripture with a convicted heart and the guidance of a missional hermeneutic. We now turn from a painful black-eye in the history of missions to a final case study where, like Taylor, we encounter the positive impact of missionary experience that further develops missional hermeneutics in ways that other disciplines cannot.

---

250. Johnston and Jackson, *Centenary Conference on Protestant Missions*, 73–74.

FIVE

The Role of Mission Praxis upon Missiological Hermeneutics

A Case Study

Thesis of this chapter: While living in a cross-cultural setting provides a more robust framework for understanding other cultural perspectives (including biblical cultures), it is actually cross-cultural missionary practice that provides an integrative compliment that correlates closely with the activity and context of Scripture (and unintentionally challenges present-day worldview and theological assumptions). Therefore, missionary experience in the mist of other cultures provides one of the strongest hermeneutical lenses for biblical interpretation because this type of missionary activity so closely matches the practice and setting of many biblical accounts.[1]

I FIRST BEGAN TO think about the role of missionary experience in relationship to biblical interpretation while in the midst of teaching graduate-level studies and trying to understand certain statements found in 1 Timothy 2:1–15. As I was trying to understand this passage,

---

1. When reading the following quote, it seems that Nissen is suggesting a similar hermeneutic to what I am advocating in this section. However, Nissen is trying to bridge traditional biblical disciplines with missiology rather than suggesting that missional experience can function as a hermeneutical lens in itself. "A new model of interpretation has emerged. It is based on the belief that deepest insight and relevance lie neither in the original meaning of the Bible alone nor in the contemporary context but in the to-and-fro of question and answer between them. This model of interpretation is that of a conversation.... What we need is an interaction between text and contemporary experience.... From the works I have consulted it can be seen that I have learned much from third world theologians as well as missiologists" (Nissen, *NT and Mission*, 13–14).

I began to think back to an account that only seemed like a winsome missionary tale until this point.

When working with missionaries among the Maasai in 1987, I encountered a very interesting account of mission practice that was developed to counter some deeply ingrained cultural values within the Maasai society. Some of the missionaries felt that they had unintentionally made a critical blunder in the process of developing new churches. After years of missionary practice they realized that the churches were often lacking male leadership. These same missionaries believed that their error originated in their all-inclusive practice (with respect to age and gender) when sharing the Christian message.

CMF missionaries taught the men, women and children together when sharing Christ with the villages.[2] Even though CMF missionaries lived in the African bush and spoke the mother tongue of the Maasai (Maa), they had to travel vast distances to reach some of their teaching points due to the dispersed living of the semi-nomadic Maasai pastoralists. To prepare separate lessons for the men, women and children would have been an overwhelming task, given the difficulties that the missionaries faced on a daily basis.[3] The main problem, however, was that teaching the men, women and children together countered the indigenous teaching style of the Maasai.

Among the Maasai, the most important meetings regarding the most important matters are attended by men only. Consequently, it was natural for Maasai men to assume that any matter open to women and children is relatively unimportant. Therefore, the missionaries unknowingly were communicating that the Christian message was unimportant, given their inclusive teaching style. There might have been a number of ways to correct this problem, but what the missionaries did was quite unique.

---

2. The Christian Missionary Fellowship (CMF) is based in Indianapolis, IN and was the first mission agency from the tradition of the Independent Christian Churches/Churches of Christ, which was also part of Donald McGavran's background.

3. It was common for the missionaries to be sought out by the Maasai for medical and financial needs. All of the missionaries faced requests or trade-offers for material goods such as food or financial loans. Furthermore, the missionaries were likewise the best hope for retrieving a seriously ill relative that might need to be driven to a major hospital or could simply be suffering from a bad cold. Given that the missionaries were scattered at vast distances from one another, they became a central resource for a relatively large population of Maasai some of whom would walk for days to make their requests.

Upon entering a new village, the missionaries informed the Maasai that, "What we have to teach you is so important that we will only teach the men!" The result had surprising impact. Due to the importance of the discussion, the men were immediately queried by their wives regarding the missionary message. As a result, the men had to repeat the ideas just shared with them, reinforcing the Gospel message in their own minds and words. Likewise, the children would ask their mothers about the discussion and once again the Gospel message was reinforced in the mothers' minds.

This transfer of thought had the additional advantage of providing a means of feedback for the missionaries to understand how well their teaching was received by the men. Likewise, the men saw themselves in a more esteemed role and the modification made by the missionaries allowed for slow change within the culture given the deeply ingrained pride of the typical Maasai man.

In the midst of grappling over the implications of 1 Timothy 2:1–15, this missionary encounter caused me to see the passage in a new light. These problematic verses have wreaked havoc on the role of women in the church, predominantly because of the assumption that Paul is trying to espouse a particular theological point regarding women.

I thought about the phrase that the missionaries had used when approaching the Maasai villages, "What we have to teach you is so important that we will only teach the men!" I began to wonder how I would interpret this phrase if I was unsure of the original context. What if this statement was made over two-thousand years ago, and I could not interview any of the missionaries? How would I know that the phrase was developed by missionaries? Might this phrase have devastating implications if I were to assume that the missionaries were making a theological statement? Certainly, a conservative face-value interpretation of this phrase would mean that women could not take part in learning about God.

Though I will come back to the issues surrounding 1 Timothy 2:1–15, the failure to read Scripture with a missional perspective slights the hermeneutical process to a point where it must be questioned. This is not to say that every passage in Scripture has direct missional implications, but neither does it mean that by default every passage has direct theological implications. In order to balance the overwhelming inertia of theological energy, I would like to present some of the hermeneutical

The Role of Mission Praxis upon Missiological Hermeneutics

trends found in the lives and work of Dr. Kenneth E. Bailey and Dr. J. Dudley Woodberry.

I have chosen to look at Bailey and Woodberry's hermeneutical tendencies for two reasons. First of all, Bailey and Woodberry have lived for years among societies that have very similar cultural values to that of first century Palestine. Second, the missionary experience of Woodberry in Islamic countries is very similar to the missional activity found in the Gospels (for example, the missional dynamics today in many Islamic contexts is very similar in nature to the missional dynamics of first century Judaism). Throughout this chapter, we will be asking, "How does their cultural and missional experience impact biblical interpretation?" However, before looking at the hermeneutical trends of these two men, let us first look at biblical examples dealing with missionary experience and the interpretation of God's revelation, through the accounts of Balaam and Peter.

BALAAM'S "MISSIONARY" EXPERIENCE (NUM 22–24)

Having already discussed Balaam's relationship to Genesis 12:1–3 in depth in Chapter 2, this section will be intentionally brief. Balaam is by all accounts a corrupt prophet. Nevertheless, he does seem to have the ability to hear God's voice (for example, Num 23–24). However, Balaam does not appear to have insight into Israel's missional election through his own prophetic gifts, and as such does not realize the potential backlash for taking part in Balak's curse upon Israel.[4] Considering that prophets are the means for a considerable volume of the biblical revelation in the Old Testament, it is interesting to see the way in which God reinterprets earlier portions of Genesis for Balaam. The book of Genesis, even as an orally transmitted body of literature, was most likely unknown to Balaam. However, as already mentioned, the entire nation of Israel was at God's disposal to witness to Balaam and Balak regarding their history and revelation of God.

Yet, it is precisely through Balaam's role in Balak's attempts to curse Israel that Balaam eventually understands a great deal regarding God's protection and plans for this nation! They are told of the chosen and blessed nature of Israel through Balaam's three repetitive acts of "witness" to Balak (Num 23–24). In a missional climax, Balaam repeats por-

---

4. It is also likely that Balaam has no interest in understanding what God is doing through Israel, since he was so often motivated by personal gain.

235

tions of the promise found in Genesis (compare Gen 12:1–3 and Num 24:9), and through this Balak should have understood how graceful God had been. The hermeneutical shock of this account is that the biblical reinterpretation came in the midst of Balaam's ingenuine attitude toward mission and proper interpretation took repeated efforts on God's behalf. Therefore, in this case even unwanted missionary experience was a stronger interpretational lens than Balaam's squandered prophetic gifting.

Throughout mission history, less-than-reputable missionaries have been involved in sharing God. This passage illustrates that training can take place through experience and that God will begin even with corrupt hearts that would prefer to intentionally misuse God-given gifts for their own gain. It is most impressive that God makes use of Balaam to interpret the Genesis account, in spite of Balaam's sole interest in his own financial gain, the protection of his image (since he does not like being embarrassed by his donkey's wisdom), and the fact that he seemingly would prefer to serve a god that he can manipulate for his own means.

Hermeneutically speaking, we see signs of God's grace and patience in order for both Balaam and Balak to arrive at a proper understanding of Israel. Eventually Balaam realizes that God is calling him to be a witness to Balak. Moreover, God does manage to transform Balaam into someone who can witness for this kingdom. Foremost, this should provide all of us with missional and hermeneutical hope since God can and does work through men like Balaam.

Likewise, if there comes a point when we think that our hermeneutics are indubitable, we should consider how God took hold of this corrupt prophet and eventually caused him to understand something of Israel's missional election not to mention his "sharing" that message with a neighboring ruler who was intent on destroying Israel. Consequently, in missionary service we should never rule out the possibility of God working through anyone, even when it comes to a correct interpretation of Scripture.

Similarly, the hermeneutical struggle with Balaam is repeated on some level with Jonah and even Peter in Acts 10–11, but never to the same degree as found in Numbers 22–24. Yet, God's patience in teaching Balaam was a minor effort when compared to the investment made in Peter, to which we now focus our attention.

The Role of Mission Praxis upon Missiological Hermeneutics

PETER'S MISSIONAL HERMENEUTIC (ACTS 10–11)

The account of Peter and Cornelius in Acts 10 is a powerful example of the way in which mission experience impacts biblical interpretation as well as the barriers that prevent proper biblical understanding. In order to understand the full impact of this chapter, Peter's worldview assumptions must be taken into account.

The Barriers—Peter's First Century Jewish Worldview

Peter's perception of God's mission was heavily governed by his Jewish worldview (just as modern-day worldview influences missionaries today). Peter has the history of Israel's walk with God flowing through his community, but this community itself is a double-edged sword in understanding God's mission. At any point in the millennia of Israel's journey with God, this elect community could have taken hold of their missional purpose and begun to act as a witness to the nations. To be fair, there were strong punctiliar expressions of mission throughout the Old Testament in which mission flourished, such as Joseph's witness to the world in Egypt and Daniel's witness to Nebuchadnezzar in Babylon (among others). However, the norm of the Old Testament is very similar to the norm of the church today in that an all-encompassing determination to carry out God's mission is the exception even though the people of God have been and are called to be the reigning manifestation of God's presence on earth.

As such, Peter's Jewish upbringing infused him from birth with a misconception of how to express one's zeal for God. A prevalent distortion in first century Jewish culture was the idea that dedication to God required strict personal purity. This naturally imposed a separation from those lacking the same religious fervor.[5] The Pharisees typified this as they separated themselves into a puritanical group who saw themselves as "keepers of the law (*haberim*)," while the average Jew who was not pharisaically trained was treated as a "lawbreaker (*'am ha-'arets*)." This separation between the *haberim* (friends/companions [of God]) and the *'am ha-'arets* (people of the land, law-breakers) is well documented.[6]

---

5. Though later monastic movements espoused different theological motivations, the impact of living out these ideals meant that a separation from the world took place and mission was likewise obscured as a result.

6. Bailey, *Finding the Lost*, 25–26, 59–60, 81–82; Bailey, *Poet & Peasant*, 2:148;

In light of this cultural division, Peter's perception of zealous religious devotion is characterized by pharisaical misunderstandings that are syncretistically devoted to "remaining pure." Consequently, Peter's Judaizing tendencies and those of his Jewish-Christian colleagues found throughout Acts and Galatians, are not merely an authoritative display of ethnocentric values. Rather, prior to significant religious devotion, they were guided by the deeply ingrained religious-worldview tendencies that would have existed even in the minds of those who had little concern for the law (*'am ha-'arets*).

The Baffling—How Might God Have "Properly" Explained It?

Therefore, how might Peter have arrived at a proper missiological understanding of God's concern for the salvation and missionary partnership of the Gentiles, and what would be needed in order to break through the barriers of Peter's worldview tendencies? If we were to follow modern-day methods for discerning God's will, we would have to go back to the Bible and do a proper study using the "correct" historical-critical hermeneutic.

When it came to understanding God's will for his involvement in mission, Peter had a wealth of privileges available. It is likely that the Torah and much of the Old Testament would have been available at a synagogue. Furthermore, the Scripture available to Peter did contain an understandable message that God's mission was to be carried out by the Jews to the nations. While there are many passages in the Old Testament that support this (Gen 12:3; 18:18; 26:4; Josh 4:24; 2 Kgs 5, etc.), the book of Jonah is the missiological meta-narrative for the Old Testament that typifies God's missionary heart and Israel's response to it. It displays God's will, desire, and command for Israel to seek out the nations, even among hated nations like Assyria that were the fiercest of enemies. However, it likewise typifies Israel's response to this call through Jonah's anger over God's grace given to the Ninevites.

The main point here is that the Old Testament offers a discernable missionary message that could have been re-interpreted by Peter and other Jews. However, a comparison of Acts 10 and Jonah further illustrates God's struggle to involve the Jews in mission. Although the Book of Acts is a post-resurrection narrative in which mission is gener-

---

Bailey, *Jacob & the Prodigal*, 24–25, 191–92; Evans and Sanders, *Luke and Scripture*, 35–36.

ally thought to be flourishing, it is a tell-tale sign that Peter's account in Acts 10 has more continuity with Jonah than anything else. With Peter, each situation is not as brazenly against God's mission as Jonah, but the similarities strikingly demonstrate the longevity and continuity of the obstacles that God faced to involve Israel in mission to the nations.

Table 11 illustrates the similarities with the main difference shown in point 5b. Given these similarities and initial barriers in mission, could Peter have understood God's missionary message through biblical study? It is unlikely. Peter probably did not have personal access to the Torah, and he probably had only limited access to this as the synagogue met each week and read from the Torah. More importantly, it is unlikely that the synagogue and the readings of the Torah would have helped overcome these barriers to God's mission, since the self-confidence of the scribes and Pharisees in their own interpretational process had so much religious momentum. In other words, a missiological interpretation based purely on biblical study would require overwhelming courage and skill against the tidal wave of the Jewish preoccupation in following the law.

Table 11: Comparing Peter in Acts 10 with Jonah

The Account	Jonah as an Old Testament image of Israel's mission to the nations	Peter as a New Testament image of certain Jewish-Christian Missionaries
Both originate in Jewish territory	1) Jonah's initial origin is unknown but he travels to Joppa to actively disobey God	1) Peter is in Joppa praying
Initial Response to God's call is a failure	2) Israel, represented by Jonah, avoided and did the exact opposite of what God had requested.	2) Jewish-Christians from the center of Jewish control, Jerusalem and Judea, (represented by Peter), had to be summoned to move toward the Gentiles because the Jews assume that God has no concern for them.

Missiological Hermeneutics

The Account	Jonah as an Old Testament image of Israel's mission to the nations	Peter as a New Testament image of certain Jewish-Christian Missionaries
The extraordinary efforts of God that cause mission to take place	3) They were involved in mission only when God forced them to be involved through extraordinary means, such as the storm, spiritually discerning sailors, and a great fish that did not eat its helpless prey.	3) This required supernatural efforts by God in sending an angel to the Gentile "convert" to retrieve the "missionary" and if this was not enough three visions from God are given to Peter along with specific permission from the Holy Spirit.
Both are called to territory of political enemies and ironically the Nations are obedient to God	4) The notoriously cruel Ninevites (Assyrians) are immediately repentant to the degree that their animals are even repentant and all of this is done in the spirit of the fact that no hope is offered for a reversal of God's destructive statute.	4) A Gentile Roman centurion representing notoriously cruel Rome, living in Caesarea, is someone of great spiritual stature, already involved in daily prayer to God, giving liberally to the poor and is respected by Jews.[7] Cornelius is seemingly more involved in carrying out God's mission than Peter.
Response to God's blessing	5a) Even once they were involved in mission, their heart was one of hatred for the nations and even hatred for God when God's mercy was offered to the nations.	5a) Peter's initial understanding of the vision does not grasp that mission to the Gentiles is for the purpose of salvation to the Gentiles.
Response to God's blessing (*primary difference*)	5b) Jonah is angry that God cares for the nations and has mercy upon them. However, the nations are blessed *despite* the hard-hearted "missionary." The narrative echoes the Genesis 12:3 promise, but Jonah is the sole opposition to blessing the nations.	5b) *Unlike Jonah,* once the experience of God's hand upon the Jews or Gentiles is shared, all the Jewish-Christians respond with joy. Furthermore, the Genesis 12:3 promise echoes loudly in the narrative as the nations are blessed *and* the missionary is transformed.
The Result of Mission	6) The Ninevite King, subjects, and animals are eager to follow God and God has mercy upon them.	6) The Holy Spirit falls upon the Gentiles even before Peter can finish a very basic message regarding Christ.

It is noteworthy that God did not give Peter today's standard guidelines for historical-critical hermeneutical practice and then set before him selections of the Old Testament which Peter would need to correctly exegete. Rather, God chose to instruct Peter through the experience of a carefully devised real-life narrative that Peter and his fellow Jews could not refute. Therefore, despite the availability of Old Testament resources, God does not utilize an Old Testament study in order to help Peter correctly interpret God's missionary concern for the Gentiles. God elects to transform Peter's perspective through another means, most likely because the barriers were so high due to the domination of the existing perceptions of the Bible and the reigning interpretations of the day.

Peter's Actual Interpretation of What Happened

What then was God's specific hermeneutical approach to re-training Peter in developing a missionary mindset that included the non-Jew? First of all this took a great deal of time and continuity in teaching. Acts 10 did not take place in a vacuum. Peter was trained by the greatest missionary to ever walk the planet. Peter did not spend three years in seminary with Jesus. Rather, Peter spent three years in an apprenticeship-life-learning-experience with the God-made-flesh. Apprenticeship models like that of Jesus and his disciples are virtually unknown in the West today, but I am convinced that this method of teaching builds a much more holistic connection between real life and the ideas learned, not to mention the student-teacher connection. As such, Peter was a first-hand witness to the actions of the living God on a daily basis and learned from this holistic lifestyle.

Through this Peter was privileged in many ways as a disciple, such as being part of the inner circle that was allowed to hear the private explanations of the parables. Peter was commissioned by the risen Lord to continue the ministry that he had been taught. Even the personalized scolding of Jesus had great benefit because it taught his disciples specifically when they had stepped out of line (Matt 16:23; 26:33–35; Mark 10:35–40). It is impossible to list the full impact of Peter's training through Jesus, but it is hard to imagine that there could ever be a

---

7. "[T]he pièce de résistance of Herod's building projects in honor of the emperor was the construction of two cities he named Sebaste and Caesarea" (Freedman et al., *Abd*, 3:166).

more encompassing missiological training than that which Jesus gave to the disciples. Nevertheless, Peter's tendency to revert to his religio-cultural values, focusing upon purity and cleanliness, demonstrates how intensely powerful one's worldview can be, even when it is wrong and contradicts intense training carried out directly from Jesus.

Therefore, in addition to Peter's earlier training, God takes more drastic measures, and the starting point for this missionary endeavor is unique. Instead of beginning with the missionary, God begins by sending an angel to the would-be convert, an unclean Roman centurion, asking the convert to summon the missionary. Though Peter eventually makes his way to the Gentiles through even more of God's miraculous acts, it is difficult to perceive this account as centrifugal (outward-focused) mission because so much effort is expended in getting the missionary to arrive at the converts' door-step. What is even more unique about the account of Acts 10 is that Peter immediately repeats the account in Acts 11.

In order to understand Peter's interpretation of what took place, a comparison of Peter's account of the incident (Acts 11) with the original account of Peter's encounter with Cornelius (Acts 10) makes a helpful evaluation (see Appendix C for a line by line comparison of Acts 10 and 11). One of the most obvious differences is that Acts 11 repeats nothing of the fourfold accolades describing Cornelius. In four separate instances impressive spiritual qualities are attributed to Cornelius, two of which were direct responses to Peter's questions. From these we learn that Cornelius is a God-fearer, that his household are God-fearers, that he is respected by Jews, that he prays regularly and that Cornelius gives generously to the poor (Acts 10:2, 4, 22, 31—v.31 is a restatement of v.4). Moreover, these spiritual qualities have so moved God that an angel and the Holy Spirit are at work to overcome some deeply ingrained barriers among the missionaries.[8] Peter's failure to mention any of this in Acts 11 gives the impression that Peter never considered the possibility that Cornelius had placed his faith in God before Peter's arrival.

Furthermore, Peter (or possibly Luke), when retelling the story to the Judaizers in Acts 11, fails to include the initial perplexity regard-

---

8. "Peter had to allow the Holy Spirit to expose and root out some pernicious prejudices, both religious and racial, before he, as a Jew, could share the good news with a Godfearing man of a different nationality" (Chapman, "Thinking Biblically About Islam," 69).

The Role of Mission Praxis upon Missiological Hermeneutics

ing the vision, and Peter's initial attempts to provide an answer for the vision. Immediately after the three visions we are twice told that Peter was puzzled or perplexed as to the meaning (Acts 10:17, 19), but this is not included in Acts 11. Though the Holy Spirit has choreographed this missiological training with near perfect timing, Peter still manages to formulate an initial interpretation. Peter seems to converge on the idea that God has no bias when it comes to people (Acts 10:28). Though this is true, this initial interpretation does not capture the full breadth of God's missionary transformation for Peter.

More than likely, Peter is now thinking that he can become involved with the Gentiles and he will not become ritually impure due to this contact. Though his challengers in Acts 11:1 demonstrate the same ingrained worldview misconceptions, they are never informed of Peter's partially correct and incorrect interpretation of the vision (as Acts 10:28 is not mentioned in Acts 11). While Peter's discard of specific details might have been an attempt to avoid feelings of foolishness or embarrassment, it is more significant to note that Peter felt free to disregard that information because he realized it was no longer relevant. This gives the impression that Peter realized his initial attempts to correctly interpret the vision were insufficient.

This point is more obvious when comparing the words initially given by the Holy Spirit and Peter's recounting of this (Acts 10:20; 11:12). In Acts 10:20 we are told that the Holy Spirit requested that Peter "Get up, go downstairs, and go with them. *Do not hesitate because I have sent them* (μηδὲν διακρινόμενος ὅτι ἐγὼ ἀπέσταλκα αὐτούς)." However, in Acts 11:12 the *hoti* clause is missing, "The Spirit told me to go with them *without hesitating* (μηδὲν διακρίναντα)" (translation mine).

When Peter is told "I have sent them," this leaves open the possibility that a mission is unfolding for both Cornelius and Peter. The obvious mission to Cornelius and those with them is to share the message of Jesus Christ, which Peter eventually delivers. The equally important but far less obvious mission is the one directed to Peter, his six colleagues and those that hear his repeated account in Acts 11. The central transformation of chapters 10 and 11 is really to bring new understanding to Peter and his fellow Jewish-Christians since they still do not realize that God's mission extends beyond those who are ethnically Jewish.[9] By comparison, it is entirely unclear if Cornelius and other Gentiles in Acts 10 are

9. Van Engen, "Peter's Conversion," 136–37.

even in need of Peter's testimony since the Holy Spirit comes upon them even before Peter is finished. As such, the additional account of Jewish evangelism among Gentiles taking place in Antioch is not a separate account but one that bolsters the missiological re-interpretation that now understands God's salvation to the Gentiles and equal inclusion of the Gentiles as missionary partners with God (Acts 11:19–30).

It is also relevant that Jewish-Christians from Cyprus and Cyrene were the first to preach to "Greek speakers" (Gentiles, Greeks, Hellenists) for the following reasons. (1) Though Jewish in their background, they did not live in a region in which Jews were the majority and had to interface more consistently with Gentiles. (2) Living outside of Judea also meant that these Jews were not as infused with Jewish puritanical practices. (3) As such, Jewish-Christians that did not live in Judea were not as heavily influenced by the misguided Jewish syncretism of the Judean religious leaders (for example, Acts 15:5). By this, I mean that the Jewish leaders' failure to perceive or follow God's missional calling was concealed by their preoccupation with the syncretistic practice of remaining pure. This actually contributed to a lack of missionary involvement, since the world was essentially unclean and therefore untouchable. (4) The geographic buffer between Judea and distant Jewish populations, such as Cyrene (in modern-day Libya) or an island like Cyprus, acted as a positive filter. These Jewish-Christians were removed from the religious pressure of those steeped in pharisaical traditions, which allowed them to consider mission to the Gentiles as a viable option.

It is quite possible, therefore, that the Jewish-Christians coming from Cyprus and Cyrene had already been sharing the good news of Jesus Christ with Gentiles prior to their arrival at Antioch. Regardless of whether or not Antioch was the first location of Gentile evangelism (outside of Caesarea), the Acts 10–11 account indicates that the barriers of the Judean Christians was substantial. This is because of the effort that God exerted to break down these barriers, and because of the self-imposed jurisdiction that the Jerusalem Christians assumed in evaluating the practice of those already involved in mission to the nations (for example, Acts 11:2–3, 22; 15:1–5). The positive response from Barnabas regarding the evangelism of the Gentiles may seem to contradict the Jerusalem mentality described here until one recalls that Barnabas originally came from Cyprus (Acts 4:36).

The Building Blocks

How is it then that Peter and others willingly accept a radically different interpretation of God's missionary concern for the world? As we have seen, God addresses Peter's biblical misunderstandings apart from biblical study and makes adjustments through the hermeneutical lens of missionary experiences that Peter and his colleagues cannot deny.[10] The miraculous agents (angel, Holy Spirit) and events (visions, Holy Spirit's instruction) have penultimate roles in the interpretational process since they are merely catalysts to bring the Jews and Gentiles into contact with one another.

The ultimate event in Peter's correct interpretation is his observation of the Holy Spirit being received by the Gentiles in the midst of his missionary experience. Once Peter observes this phenomenon, his only hesitation is to ensure that he has the support of his fellow Judaizers before proceeding toward baptism. Interestingly, the one "biblical passage" that does enter Peter's mind at this point is one yet to be written—Acts 1:5 (quoted in Acts 11:16). Despite the fact that Peter is not flooded with Old Testament understandings of God's mission, *he does correctly interpret God's missionary concern for the Gentiles based ultimately on his missionary experience.* As such, Peter uses his missionary experience as a hermeneutical lens to unknowingly develop an appropriate biblical and missiological interpretation of the existing body of Scripture.

This account demonstrates two very important principles in overcoming barriers to biblical interpretation. *When the reigning interpretations and hermeneutics are so imposing that a missional understanding cannot be developed, one's own experience in mission may have the greatest impact on a correct biblical interpretation* even if that is not realized at the time.[11] This is yet another act of God's grace in understanding Scripture because Peter is not subsequently bombarded with the long standing Jewish failure to perceive God's missionary intentions. Rather, God gracefully gives Peter and others the space and time needed to re-

---

10. The closest thing to biblical study in Acts 10 is Peter's testimony of Jesus' death and resurrection.

11. This is not to say that any experience has equal merit. Experiences that take place in life apart from missionary engagement are unlikely to have the same benefit. Furthermore, the experiences themselves should lead to a more holistic interpretation of Scripture even though this may be a radically different understanding from former ideas that were developed apart from a missional perspective.

interpret Scripture in light of their missionary experience that becomes a natural hermeneutical lens. *As a result of this, the Old Testament took on new meaning for Peter in that it was now infused with a missional hermeneutic at its core.* For example, in 1 Peter 2, Peter makes use of the concept of "living stones" and a "royal priesthood," both of which draw heavily from Old Testament concepts that were most likely misinterpreted until Peter's missional understanding of Scripture was further transformed through experiences similar to this account.

A second principle to be gleaned from this account is that *accepted hermeneutical trends and the accompanying interpretation may be widely accepted and yet far from ideal.* The parallels between the dynamics of Acts 10–11 and the modern day are striking. Just as first-century Jews were swayed by the obsession over purity, the syncretistic tendency found today is that most modern-day Christians believe that true dedication and understanding of God is properly expressed through in-depth theological study. I cannot remember the number of times that I have heard would-be missionaries state that they went into traditional theological studies because they wanted to understand the Bible better. In my opinion, modern-day theological study generally tends to demonstrate our own syncretism that allows theological zeal to eclipse a biblical understanding of mission and mission practice, and some proponents of the former seem to think that Biblical Theology of Mission is a farce in the first place.

I have always felt a sense of sadness for students who mistakenly assumed that traditional theology would equip them to be better missionaries. For the most discerning students, this possibility exists, but many are sucked into the vortex of endless theological discussions (the vast majority of which do not even have a remote connection to mission), and as such their missionary fervor is left unsupported or becomes extinguished altogether.[12] It is for this reason that missionary work must not only be practiced, but we must enter into such work with the painful expectation that God will transform our misconceived hermeneutics and reshape us to become aware of those deeply ingrained worldview assumptions that have obscured a proper biblical understanding of God's mission.

---

12. Though this point may seem harsh, it is not my desire to be intentionally harsh. These are real factors that affect the progress of mission as it relates to biblical and missiological training.

CULTURAL DYNAMICS AS AN INTERPRETATIONAL LENS—BAILEY

Peter's account in Acts 11 demonstrates the value of mission experience as a hermeneutical lens for the first century missionary, but for the most part we assume that Peter is acquainted with the cultural nuances of his day. What means can the modern-day biblical interpreter utilize in order to know the culture in which Peter lived, or any of the biblical cultures for that matter? For those of us who are distant from first century culture, the answer has typically been a combination of library research including linguistic, historical and archaeological data.

Many missionaries have had experiences in a particular cross-cultural context that exposed them or stretched their own cultural understanding. Most cross-cultural missionaries later recognize that their biases were unrealized until they were exposed through service in a cross-cultural setting. Furthermore, a common report from missionaries is that indigenous Christians will often develop unique interpretations of Scripture, and the missionaries are challenged by these interpretations because they (1) often make a great deal of sense to cultural insiders, and (2) some interpretations hold as much validity as the traditional theology that the missionary learned in seminary.[13] Taber cites a common missionary occurrence when those with fairly different worldviews come to Scripture: "Westerners who have interacted seriously with non-Westerners about biblical passages and themes have inevitably experienced astonishment, not to say dismay, at what their interlocutors purported to see there. But they also inevitably experienced personal enlightenment as previously obscure or irrelevant passages took on new life and meaning when examined from a fresh point of view."[14]

As missionaries traverse the continuum between "dismay" and "new life" they will inevitably accept some interpretations while leaving others in silence. Historically, the reactions to these unique interpretations have varied. Some culturally insensitive missionaries have simply discarded the interpretations as fanciful ideas from untrained minds. However, missionaries with anthropological training have been taught to be sensitive to any cultural interpretation and as such they

---

13. Cp. Sugirtharajah, *Voices from the Margin*.
14. Taber, "Missiology and the Bible," 239.

may avoid making critical assessments.[15] Finally, in cases such as the following account, missionaries can become enchanted with a romantic concern for cultural "purity" and as such they fail to interact with issues that will fester into future problems. "African Christians who have not been Westernized . . . often approach the Bible . . . [seeking] a God who accepts and confirms the African's experience of life and the world. This produces, in the first place, a strong sense of kinship to the Old Testament. For many African independent churches the Old Testament is the only Bible."[16]

I would suggest that missional hermeneutics can equip missionaries to help in accessing the benefit of interpretations that flow from a particular cultural hermeneutic. But how do missional and multicultural hermeneutics differ? Biblical interpretation based on cultural hermeneutics (also called ethnohermeneutics, contextual hermeneutics or indigenous hermeneutics) is not the same as biblical interpretation based on missiological hermeneutics.

The primary difference is that cultural hermeneutics are built upon the worldview assumptions and cultural tendencies of the interpreter, while missiological hermeneutics are built upon the missionary nature of God that is disclosed throughout Scripture. They are related in the sense that missionaries and mission are always bound by their cultural context, but missiological hermeneutics draw upon a perception that moves beyond linguistic and anthropological understandings. As such, the former is culturally infused while the latter is foremost infused with a combination of reflection, activity, and partnership in God's mission.[17]

For example, within the Bible, midrashic hermeneutics seem to be foremost a cultural hermeneutic, while much of the New Testament hermeneutics of Jesus and Paul are missional hermeneutics. The exception would be in cases similar to Galatians 4 in which Paul appears to be intentionally using an accepted cultural hermeneutic and therefore applies midrashic hermeneutics for the sake of introducing Christ to Judaizers. Likewise, a hermeneutic based entirely on scientific theory

---

15. Cp. Hiebert, "Critical Contextualization."

16. de Groot, "One Bible and Many Interpretive Contexts," 147–48.

17. Of course, every missionary will be influenced by his or her cultural background and in that sense, missional hermeneutics will always be influenced from a contextual origin, but missional hermeneutics attempt to stretch beyond a purely cultural framework and toward a framework that matches the nature of God's missionary character.

The Role of Mission Praxis upon Missiological Hermeneutics

with an unspoken avoidance of spiritually-infused interpretation is a cultural hermeneutic.

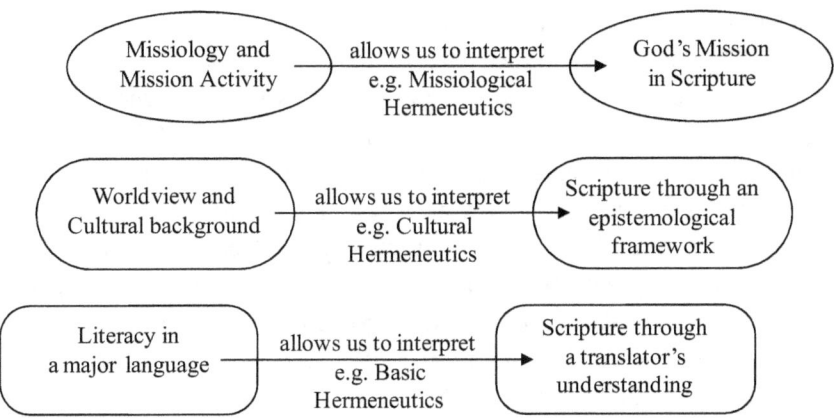

Figure 18: Hermeneutical Building Blocks

As one way to compare the differences, consider Figure 18 which illustrates the ideas that missiological hermeneutics build on top of cultural hermeneutics, but do so because they naturally match Scripture's intrinsic missionary emphasis.

A Case for the Value of Modern Day Cultures

How then can missionaries identify the more beneficial cultural interpretations while simultaneously avoiding those interpretations that are simply the societal equivalent of reader-response hermeneutics?[18] Part

---

18. An example of the societal equivalent of reader-response hermeneutics is the Maasai response to Jesus' parable of the two sons (Matt 21:28–31). When Jesus asks, "Which of the two did what his father wanted?" (NIV), the Maasai will typically say "the second" because in Maasai culture it is always better to save face by saying the right thing to your father, even if you have decided not to do it. This is seen as saving face for the father and son. Textual variants on this passage indicate that a similar struggle may have taken place as the New Testament Scripture was copied. The NA27 textual critical apparatus notes "εσχατος loco πρoτος"—meaning "'The final [son]' in place of 'The first [son]'" (Aland, *Greek-English New Testament*, 60). Likewise, the NLT summarizes the variants, "Other manuscripts read 'The second.' In still other manuscripts the first son says 'Yes' but does nothing, the second son says 'No' but then repents and goes, and the answer to Jesus' question is that the second son obeyed his father" (Tyndale House Publishers, *Holy Bible: New Living Translation*, Matt 21:31). Surprisingly, Metzger offers no such cultural possibility for this change, affirming the position that it was "due to

of the answer must lie in the similarity of the culture in which the missionary serves with a given biblical culture. In other words, a society today that has numerous cultural parallels to that of Peter's first century society would be a better indicator of Peter's cultural values than a society that has undergone radical changes since Peter's day.

One New Testament theologian who has given credence to this approach is Kenneth Bailey. Bailey has served among Middle Eastern cultures for over 40 years and he feels that his experience in the Middle East offers great validity as a means of developing cultural understanding. "To be properly interpreted, any story must be seen from within the culture of the storyteller and his/her audience.... Having struggled for more than a generation with this problem in both the East and the West, it is my perception that for us as Westerners the cultural distance 'over' to the Middle East is greater than the distance 'back' to the first century. The cultural gulf between the West and the East is deeper and wider than the gulf between the first century (in the Middle East) and the contemporary conservative Middle Eastern village."[19]

Bailey offers a comparison that not only perceives cultural "distance" in terms of anthropological variations (such as worldview universals), but also one that perceives the effect of cultural changes over time.[20] However, is it reasonable for Bailey to make this comparison between modern-day cultures and first-century Jewish culture? What basis can Bailey use to analyze a first-century culture that he cannot personally encounter?

The most tangible way that Bailey validates his claim is through his reading of ancient Arabic manuscripts. When doing so, Bailey has discovered that practices taking place centuries before Christ continued centuries after Christ, and he even witnesses them in the societies among which he lives today.

---

copyists who either committed a transcriptional blunder or who were motivated by anti-Pharisaic bias" (Metzger and United Bible Societies, *Textual Commentary on Greek NT*, 45). As such, understanding Maasai culture may be helpful in determining the motives for this variant. More importantly, this variant might be better understood using the ideas presented in this chapter.

19. Bailey, *Finding the Lost*, 28–29. For longer discussions, see Bailey's argument, relying heavily on Newbigin, in which he argues that we all have intrinsic cultural assumptions (Bailey, *Jacob & the Prodigal*, 36–44).

20. Kearney, *World View*, 65–107.

> The custom of wrapping babies at birth appears in the birth story of Jesus (Luke 2:7). The only other time this custom is recorded in Scripture is in Ezek. 16:4. The same custom prevails today among Palestinian peasants. The Ezekiel reference is appropriately seen as important background for the Lucan account, even though the book of Ezekiel is more than 500 years older than the gospel of Luke. One could argue, 500 years is a long time. Culture changes. Surely such a long passage of time makes the Ezekiel text worthless as background to Luke 2:7. However, Middle Eastern cultural patterns have millennia behind them and are extremely slow to evolve. If this is the case for 500 years *before* the NT period, what about 500 years *after* that same period? Surely the answer is the same. Thus, for example, Ps. 23:5 (dated ca. 1000 B.C.) talks of the anointing of the head with oil. Luke 7:46 discusses the same cultural practice. What then of a text from the Mishnah (A.D. 200) or the Babylonian Talmud (ca. A.D. 400)? The latter two texts are 800 and 600 years closer to the NT than the psalm! If we are discussing the history of the development of *ideas,* much of the Jewish oral law is too late to help us. But if we are looking for a *culture* other than our own as a place to stand as we view the metaphors and stories of the NT, they can prove invaluable.[21]

Here and elsewhere Bailey asserts the correlation between New Testament biblical culture, historic Middle Eastern cultures as found in literature, and Middle Eastern cultures today. In this sense, Bailey's experience today affords him the closest thing to a personal encounter with first-century Jewish culture found in the New Testament. Furthermore, continuity is a primary value of many traditional societies and as such, these societies intentionally discourage change.[22]

Bailey's experience working in the Middle East has also given him the perception that long standing cultural practices are slow to change. He notes,

---

21. Bailey, *Finding the Lost*, 29–30.

22. This stands in stark contrast to Western culture in which changes highly valued. For example Western consumers seek the most recent version of something because Westerners assume that a changed product is changed for the better (for example, higher resolution cameras, more ergonomic appliances, faster computers, more productive software, safer and more reliant cars, better insulated homes, etc.). In the computer field, some Westerners will contact manufacturers to learn their plans solely to ensure that they obtain the newest machine. In short, Western worldview assumes "change" is a good quality.

as a life-long observer of change in the Middle East, some of it dramatic and rapid, a number of observations can be made. . . . *Cultural mores are the slowest to change.* This is our concern. To interpret the parables of Jesus, the interpreter (consciously or unconsciously) will inevitably make decisions about attitudes toward women, men, the family, the family structure, family loyalties and their requirements, children, architectural styles, agricultural methods, leaders, scholars, religious authorities, trades, craftsmen, servants, eating habits, money, loyalty to community, styles of humor, story-telling, methods of communication, use of metaphor, forms of argumentation, forms of reconciliation, attitudes towards time, towards governmental authority, what shocks and at what level, reactions to social situations, reasons for anger, attitudes toward animals, emotional and cultural reactions to various colors, dress, sexual codes, the nature of personal and community honor and its importance, and many, many other things.[23]

In making this critique, Bailey helps us to understand that living in a particular culture has the added benefit of making us sensitive to the entire gamut of cultural values rather than the atomized learning style of library research that supposedly allows us to learn one particular value apart from the rest.[24] As such, living in the midst of a culture close

---

23. Bailey, *Finding the Lost*, 32.

24. In pointing out that Bailey builds upon Middle Eastern cultural practices today, I am not trying to imply that Bailey avoids other forms of study. Bailey does not use modern-day Middle Eastern societies as a crutch to avoid doing good historical research. Rather, he builds upon the historical information available as well as noting the similarity in modern-day Middle Eastern societies. "What is to be done if the reader of a story does not participate in the culture of the storyteller and his audience?. . . [One option] is to pretend the problem simply does not exist. . . . A second option is to assert that the parables of Jesus are universal in nature and apply to all cultures. . . . A third option is to plead Hellenism. . . . But the question remains: Is Greek culture an adequate lens through which to examine and understand the culture of the parables of Jesus the Jew? If we desire to break out of our own cultural imprisonment to hear the Gospel as its first listeners heard it, it is obvious that we must turn to the Hebrew Scriptures, the Dead Sea Scrolls, and many other Jewish documents from before the time of Jesus to understand the culture of his world. But Middle Eastern sources, written in the early centuries after the time of Jesus, are also important. . . . The Gospels originated in that Eastern world from which we have been isolated since A.D. 451. Surely Western Christianity is the poorer if it fails to do its best to recover the ways in which the Eastern Semitic Christian tradition has understood the text of the New Testament. Finally, there is the possibility of obtaining insights from surviving conservative traditional Middle Eastern culture. . . . It will not do to blithely say, 'Middle Eastern traditional culture has changed over the years and thus is of little value as a grid for understanding the culture

The Role of Mission Praxis upon Missiological Hermeneutics

to that of a given biblical culture offers the biblical interpreter a more comprehensive perspective on the cultural values found in the text.

The impact of Bailey's cross-cultural experience in the Middle East and his detailed historical research in ancient Arabic yields very impressive cultural insights. Missionaries often feel that their cross-cultural experiences allow them deeper insights into Scripture, but Bailey rightly points out the critical insight that certain cultures overlap to a greater extent with cultures found in the Bible. If we were to diagram this perspective, it might look something like Figure 19. The key point to keep in mind is that cultural values do not change at the same rate, causing some cultures to stand at a much greater distance than others.

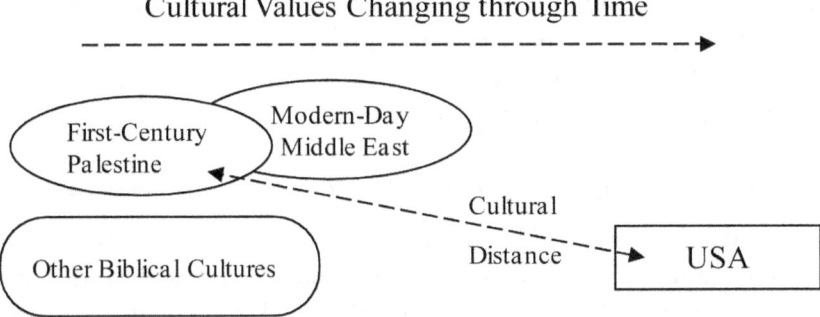

Figure 19: Cultures Change at Different Rates

In terms of hermeneutics, Bailey notes how important it is "for us to take seriously . . . the biblical perceptions of early (and modern) Middle Eastern Christians who live in societies closer to the cultural world of Jesus."[25] This claim will come as no surprise to most cross-cultural missionaries because one of the great stresses of cross-cultural missionary work is adapting to a new context. This process of cultural adaptation, takes years and a great deal of personal transformation through unforeseen levels of humility, sensitivity and personal introspection. Furthermore, it is this transformation that gives many missionaries a unique brokenness (and rebuilding) that is very difficult to describe or quantify.

---

of Jesus.' Superficially, this is true. But, should we fall back on our own culture?" (Bailey, *Jacob & the Prodigal*, 38–44).

25. Ibid., 40.

However, the value of this for biblical interpretation is that the missionary's journey can then be drawn upon so that he or she approaches Scripture with appropriate levels of cultural sensitivity and grace. I would suggest that this transformation is the main reason that missionaries develop an intuitive sense for deeper insights into passages that were once seen as problematic, as well as the fact that missionaries often serve among societies that are in close cultural proximity to those found in Scripture.

The benefit of this transformation has rarely been affirmed in hermeneutics. This is most likely because missionaries have served in such a variety of cultural contexts, and for the most part their insights have been met by skepticism from the "experts" in biblical interpretation. To the best of my knowledge there has not been any intentional effort by missionaries to document the closest biblical parallels to their own ministry contexts or the ways in which their cultural adaptation has influenced their understanding of Scripture.

Historical-Critical Insights That Flow from Cultural Experience

It is important to keep in mind that Bailey does not use modern-day Middle Eastern societies as a crutch to avoid doing good historical research. Rather, he looks for consistency among historical literature and historical translations, and modern-day Middle Eastern practices.

> Briefly, the method we have evolved is to make use of four tools. The first is to discuss the cultural aspects of the parable with a wide circle of Middle Eastern friends whose roots are in isolated conservative village communities and try to find how the changeless Middle Eastern peasant sees things. The second is to examine carefully twenty-four translations of the New Testament in Syriac and Arabic to see how Christians in this part of the world have understood the text from the second to the twentieth centuries. The point here is that translation is *always* interpretation.... Through a careful reading of a series of such translations one is able to learn a great deal about how Middle Easterners themselves have understood a given text. The third is to look for parallels in literature as close to the New Testament as possible. Finally, the literary structure of the parable or parable passage must be examined with care.
>
> But the principle of "discussions with contemporary peasants" always raises the question, "How do you know that the

peasants of the Middle East have not changed their culture over the centuries?" Obviously, if we can confirm in ancient literature a cultural pattern that we find surviving in the contemporary conservative Middle Eastern village, there is no problem. For example, we observe that the Middle Eastern gentleman in the village always walks down the street at a slow, pompous pace in order to preserve his honor. The father of the prodigal in Luke 15:20 *runs* down the street. For the village patriarch today to run down a village street would be humiliating and degrading. Was it the same for the village father in the time of Jesus, or has the pattern of life changed? In this case we are fortunate. Ben Sirach, a gentleman scholar in Jerusalem early in the second century B.C., tells us plainly that a "gentleman is known by his walk" (Sir. 18:20). Thus pre-New Testament literature confirms what we discover in isolated villages today in northern Syria and Iraq, in the highlands of Galilee, and in the south of Egypt.

[But] if we had not found the Sirach text confirming the significance of the slow walk for a gentleman in the village, what then? We could then say, "Thus we cannot assume the father's run down the road to be significant!" But to do so is to *make* a cultural judgment. In this case the judgment is to decide that his run is not significant. We then fall back on our own subconsciously assumed Western culture as a base for interpretation. For the American, the people in a parable start acting like Americans, and for the French, they look like French, and for the German, they become Germans. When there is no alternative it seems better to start with the Middle Eastern cultural pattern with the full awareness that *if* we find more evidence our present assumptions may be confirmed, revised, or rejected. In the meantime, let us do our best. The question is not, Shall we make cultural judgments as we interpret or not? Rather, there is no escape from asking, Whose culture is to inform our interpretations? Ours or someone else's.[26]

It is clear that Bailey has often been challenged over the single issue of drawing upon modern-day cultures as a hermeneutical tool. However, the question itself illustrates the hermeneutical bias of Bailey's critics, as well as the approaches that they do not challenge. It is most interesting that Bailey is not often plagued with questions such as "How do you know that the historical literature and translations reflect the culture of the New Testament?"

---

26. Bailey, *Poet & Peasant*, 2:xiv-xv; cp. Bailey, *Jacob & the Prodigal*, 38–44.

I would suggest that the reason this question is not often asked (if at all) is because other exegetes assume that historical research is a valid hermeneutical tool, since Western exegetes also emphasize historical research as a guide. Furthermore, it would not be too surprising to find that many of Bailey's critics have blinders that prevent them from understanding these modern-day cultural parallels. This is because they lack the cross-cultural experiences that help one to see the same sort of parallels that Bailey has found.

Bailey's works offer some of the strongest examples of (1) cultural insights developed from his experiences living among Middle Eastern societies combined with (2) outstanding historical research. Furthermore, Bailey's willingness to (3) live immersed in Arabic thought and the ancient commentaries of Arabic Christians provides a greatly improved cultural understanding of the passages that he addresses. Bailey's historical studies are still governed by a principle that he learned through life in a cross-cultural setting—and this is the idea that today's Middle Eastern societies have the best instincts for understanding certain biblical cultures. As such, Bailey's historical research is validly based on the assumption that Middle Eastern societies from long ago have even better instincts for understanding certain biblical cultures.

Bailey's Missiological Insights

Given the widely accepted tendency of the historical-critical method, most theologians seem to believe that a proper exegesis of a particular biblical culture and language will result in a generally consistent and correct interpretation of the theological ideas intended by the original authors of Scripture.[27] However, Bailey raises the bar for hermeneutical commitment by integrating exegetical research with a life lived among societies similar to those in the Bible. Though this is standard practice for missionaries, few biblical scholars in the modern-day have so completely committed all aspects of their lives to biblical research in the manner that Bailey has. Bailey demonstrates that even theological study benefits extensively from cross-cultural commitment.

---

27. In dealing with hermeneutical paths taken by various scholars working on issues of divine election, Berkouwer notes a similar problem on a more basic level: "We face the fact that even a formal agreement with respect to the authority of Scripture has not always led to an agreement regarding the doctrine of election" (Berkouwer, *Divine Election*, 23).

However, even with his great commitment, Bailey does show signs of one domineering Western hermeneutical assumption. A grave problem with Western hermeneutics is the assumption that Scripture is primarily intended to espouse theology. The West, in particular, seems to have fallen prey to the idea that a complete understanding of Scripture will result in a fully integrated systematic theology. As a result, Western concerns for integration and systemization are unconsciously placed upon Scripture forcing it to become predominantly a theological document. In spite of Bailey's extensive cultural and theological research, his Western theological background prevents him from recognizing the breadth and depth of mission within Scripture.

Jesus the Metaphorical Theologian

From the perspective of missiology, the most obvious barrier in Bailey's work arises from his claim that Jesus and the biblical writers are "metaphorical theologians." In his most recent volume, Bailey states that Jesus "was clearly a 'metaphorical theologian' whose primary style of creating meaning was the skillful use of metaphor, parable and dramatic action."[28] Furthermore, Bailey even ascribes this characteristic to the biblical writers. "If Western theologians had written the Bible it might have read like George Orwell. They didn't. Rather Middle Eastern metaphorical theologians wrote the Bible."[29]

Jesus may be a theologian on some level, but the downside of Bailey's extensive historical-critical research that flows from ingrained Western training is that this causes him to think of Jesus primarily as a theologian. In short, Bailey's cultural influences cause him to overemphasize the theological nature of Jesus. While the same could certainly be said of a missiologist calling Jesus a missionary, the biblical text supports the latter claim far more extensively.[30]

Furthermore, if the authorial intent of Scripture was meant to lead people to Christ with comparatively less concern for theology, then we should expect to find that the biblical arguments for following God are theologically weaker (according to Western standards) and missiologi-

---

28. Bailey, *Jacob & the Prodigal*, 22; cp. Bailey, *Finding the Lost*, 15–28.

29. Bailey, *Finding the Lost*, 19.

30. I have no doubt that I have my own set of biases and that I do not understand the full implications of Jesus' missional nature, but this does not make Jesus a theologian by default or circumvent the fact that Jesus was foremost involved in God's mission.

cally stronger than currently realized. The case for a Bible that is focused upon mission holds even greater validity if it is God's intention to bring salvation to the lost and this God-focused missionary concern (*missio Dei*) is woven into the fabric of Scripture. While it is beyond the scope of this work to validate the missional intent of the biblical authors and God, it is a perspective held by many.[31]

In terms of a missional mindset, Bailey shows some hope. He does address the issue of Jesus' mission when looking at The Great Banquet.[32] Furthermore, Bailey does demonstrate familiarity with a few missiologists such as Johannes Blauw, Lesslie Newbigin and Andrew Walls.[33] However, even in Andrew Walls' case he is referred to as a "church historian and specialist in non-Western Christianity."[34]

And certainly, Bailey offers numerous themes related to mission throughout his exhaustive research on Luke 15. Bailey discusses themes such as the searching father who willfully endures public embarrassment while running to the boy in the hopes of shielding the son from public humiliation.[35] Likewise, there are themes such as the kinship concern of the father for his children, tenderness toward the older son, atonement, reconciliation, restoration and redemption.[36] He even touches upon evangelism, but only in the context of explaining Andrew Wall's mission theory.[37]

---

31. It must be pointed out that everyone comes to Scripture with assumptions that bias their interpretation, including theologians. Although it may be argued that one set of assumptions has more or less credibility than another set, the main difference seems to be the degree to which the interpreter(s) are open to recognizing and modifying their assumptions. Ultimately those spending a great deal of time in biblical interpretation should be able to stipulate their assumptions and biases while giving reasonable justification for them. There are many authors who claim that the authorial intent of Scripture must foremost be understood through the Bible's over-arching missional nature. This is just a sampling (Beeby, *Canon and Mission*, 113; Beeby, "Missional Approach to Renewed Interpretation," 282–83; Hesselgrave, "Missionary Hermeneutic," 17; Horton, *Bible: A Missionary Book*, 16; McLean, *Where the Book Speaks*, 9; Montgomery, *Bible and Missions*, 8; Taber, "Missiology and the Bible," 231–32; Van Engen, *God's Missionary People*; Van Engen, "Relation of Bible," 33–34; Van Engen, *Mission on the Way*, 40–43).

32. Bailey, *Poet & Peasant*, 2:101–11.

33. Bailey, *Finding the Lost*, 12; Bailey, *Poet & Peasant*, 2:60, 2:102–3; Bailey, *Jacob & the Prodigal*, 36–41, 133–34; Bailey, *Cross & the Prodigal*, 9.

34. Bailey, *Jacob & the Prodigal*, 133.

35. Bailey, *Finding the Lost*, 143–44.

36. Ibid., 140, 149, 150, 169, 185, 192, 211.

37. Bailey, *Jacob & the Prodigal*, 133.

The Role of Mission Praxis upon Missiological Hermeneutics

However, in trying to demonstrate that Jesus was a "metaphorical theologian," Bailey's quest prevents him from arriving at the full missional depth of the parables in Luke 15. In essence, the intensely missional aspects of the Luke 15 parables are overrun by lesser theological motifs. As such, Bailey's interpretations have astounding cultural insights that ultimately lead the reader into theological directions that are foreign to the real missional emphases answered in the Luke 15 parables.

Bailey is well aware that such biases are largely unseen as he notes: "It is impossible to communicate in writing the utter frustration I have endured as I have, across the years, read the works of very able Western scholars who time and time again have read into the text of the NT their own Western attitudes toward the above topics, with little or no apparent awareness that their own feelings and attitudes on these topics are not universals."[38]

However, Bailey does not seem to realize the degree to which his goals reflect deeply ingrained Western attitudes about the very nature of Scripture. For example, as Bailey reflects on his love of the Parable of the Prodigal Son, he says, "For over 30 years . . . it has been my privilege to study and teach this great text. The goal has always been to rediscover its authentic Middle Eastern cultural assumptions and to understand its theological content in the light of those assumptions."[39]

The real source of blame, however, does not lie with Bailey, because the problem found in Bailey's work is a systemic Western hermeneutical issue and the massive amounts of theological momentum in existence today indicate that this problem will continue for centuries. Furthermore, Bailey, who is foremost a New Testament theologian, demonstrates how powerfully ingrained Western hermeneutical tendencies are, in that (1) the theological bias unintentionally eclipses missional insights even when these are more true to the text, and (2) even the extensive cross-cultural service of Bailey is insufficient to break the grip of Western dominance.[40] Missionaries should take note of this because serving as a

---

38. Bailey, *Finding the Lost*, 32–33.
39. Ibid., 109.
40. In an e-mail received from Paul E. Pierson on June 2, 2006, he wrote, "Ken Bailey is a good friend and a great scholar. He is primarily a New Testament scholar but has lots of gifts."

missionary is no guarantee that this deeply embedded assumption will be seen or broken—for Bailey also considers himself a missionary![41]

Luke 15 from a Missional Perspective

Continued critique of Bailey will not solve the hermeneutical crisis that missiologists encounter. This crisis is one of being subjugated to hermeneutics predominantly void of missional concern, and lack of direction in our own hermeneutical journey. Therefore, let's look at a positive example that draws upon Bailey's many impressive insights and allows the parable of the Prodigal Son to express its natural missional insights. So how might Luke 15 be interpreted if we were to use a missional hermeneutic?

Bailey suggests a wonderful hermeneutical tool when he tells us that he consults a wide circle of Middle Eastern peasants whose "roots are in isolated conservative village communities" in order to discuss the cultural aspects of the parable.[42] However, the overall thrust of the Luke 15 parables is one of Jesus giving a powerful answer for his involvement in God's redemptive mission amidst the missional incredulity of his accusers. Here, Jesus the missionary is under attack for maintaining steadfast allegiance to God's mission. Therefore, the missional dynamics of the parable carry just as much weight as the cultural values found in the parables.

Similar to Bailey, we need to consult a wide circle of missionaries who have had to defend their missional allegiance among those who have none (and this certainly happens)! Their experience will likely have impact as they interpret this parable. Therefore, we must begin by asking the relevant missional questions and avoid spending all efforts in intensive literary and cultural research. The older hermeneutic is simply inadequate to interpret a parable bursting with missiological implications.

In a separate situation, D. A. Carson summarizes the biblical analysis of Sawyerr by illustrating the sort of tendency to which we are all prone:

---

41. In a telephone conversation with Kenneth E. Bailey on June 1, 2006 (6pm PDT), he indicated that he intentionally went to the Middle East to witness and did not see this as a stepping stone for another teaching position. Likewise, he described himself as a "preacher in witness" and intentionally learned Arabic for his teaching. Most importantly, he is involved in more than teaching theology.

42. Bailey, *Poet & Peasant*, 2:xiv.

The Role of Mission Praxis upon Missiological Hermeneutics

Sawyerr has exposed some of the unwitting "pre-understandings" of the West, and is creatively trying to think through what implications might follow. But *Tiénou* rightly points out that before long Sawyerr is introducing some "pre-understandings" of his own, making the New Testament text seem to justify things which are nowhere near its focal concerns, and which are in some cases antithetical to them. What started off as a valid critique of western preunderstandings has degenerated into the adoption, witting or unwitting, of African pre-understandings, both sets rather distortive of Scripture, and neither side sufficiently self-critical to introduce the necessary changes to bring church life into greater conformity with the Scriptures.[43]

Likewise, we must not superimpose mission blindly upon the text.[44] We must have eyes to see mission taking place even in something as difficult to interpret as a parable, but we must allow the broader context and activity found in Scripture to guide us in knowing when God's mission is at the forefront.

We must also consider what the larger community of missiologists have to say on these parables. Do Anderson, Bosch, Glasser, Kirk, Newbigin, Shenk, Sugirtharajah or Van Engen have anything to add to this conversation? In this case, many other missiologists and even some theologians, such as Ladd, have indicated that this passage is without question missional even though they have not uncovered the details that Bailey has found. Since Bailey has spent most of his energy dealing with the parable of the prodigal son, his insights are an important corrective for this community as well.

For example, Glasser states that the parables of Luke 15 "so relentlessly reiterate God's delight in the repentance with which sinners turn to him that we regard them as mission parables."[45] Newbigin even goes so far as to link the Pharisees with some modern-day theologians:

43. Carson, *Biblical Interpretation*, 14

44. "Missiologists tend far too easily to read back into the Bible aspects of the missionary enterprise in which they are involved today" (Nissen, *NT and Mission*, 13). "One of the problems, however, might be that a mission perspective in the study of the New Testament might mean just looking for evidence of things we can call 'missionary'. We would just read into our texts what we want to find" (Church of England Mission Theological Advisory Group and Churches Together in Britain and Ireland, *Presence and Prophecy*, 119).

45. Glasser, *Announcing the Kingdom*, 197. Horton claims that in parables like that of "the prodigal son, which are particularly directed to the Jewish people, the object is only to cancel that exclusiveness and to show that the message is not for them but for

> I find it astonishing that a theologian should think he has the authority to inform us in advance who is going to be "saved" on the last day.... This is the exact opposite of the teaching of the New Testament. Here emphasis is always on surprise. It is the sinners who will be welcomed and those who are confident that their place was secure who will find themselves outside. ... The honest, hard-working lad will be out in the dark while the young scoundrel is having a party in his father's house (Luke 15).[46]

Newbigin's emphasis is helpful in the sense that theologians and missiologists are in danger of becoming the equivalent of New Testament Pharisees if we simply devote ourselves to theory (as a replacement for the Pharisees concern over purity) and hold no allegiance to the practice of God's mission.

Let us now look further into the details of the parable. One of Bailey's concerns is that the proper interpretation of this parable must include the initial framework for telling these parables. The context begins with a complaint issued by the Pharisees and other religious teachers of the law that touches on Jesus' association with "sinful" people (Luke 15:1–2). Bailey explains that the religious Jews of the first-century and the average or unclean Jew represented two distinct Jewish audiences.

As briefly mentioned in the discussion of Acts 10, the Pharisees, scribes, and other religious teachers perceived themselves as law-keepers with a critical emphasis on remaining pure. Reference should be made once more with respect to the terms *haberim* and *'am ha-'arets*. The Pharisees were part of the *haberim*, which literally meant "friends" or "companions" of God. In contrast, average Jews who had no formal religious training were part of the *'am ha-'arets*, which literally meant

---

the world" (Horton, *Bible: A Missionary Book*, 51). Contrary to Bailey, Bashford and Peters assert that the older son represented the Jews, while the younger son represented the nations (Bashford, *God's Missionary Plan*, 55, 65, 70; Peters, *Biblical Theology of Missions*, 50; cp. Bailey, *Finding the Lost*, 192). Bosch indicates that the parables of Luke 15 represent the "lost" (Bosch, *Witness to the World*, 70). Newbigin feels that God's concern over the one lost sheep is a proper counter balance to mission theory focused upon numerical growth (Newbigin, *Open Secret*, 125). Ladd's theological background even allows him to claim that "the central truth of all three parables is that of the yearning God. God is like one who seeks lost sheep, who searches for a lost coin, who longs for the return of a prodigal. This is a parable about the Father, not about the son" (Ladd, *Theology of the NT*, 85).

46. Newbigin, *Open Secret*, 173.

"people of the land."⁴⁷ Though we often naively perceive the Jews as having solidarity, given the political threat of Rome, the level of conflict between the two groups is shocking: "The *haberim* lived in an apparent perpetual state of hostility with the *'am ha-'arets* (the people of the land). These latter where those who (in the eyes of the former) did not keep the law in a precise fashion. Intense hostility between these two groups is reflected all through the tradition. The *'am ha-'arets* were consistently seen by the *haberim* as impious slackers in religious matters. Any contact with them was defiling for the *haber* (associate)."⁴⁸

Given the perception of the *haberim*, it is no surprise that the *'am ha-'arets* held an equal level of hatred for the *haberim*. It is against this backdrop that the Pharisees ask "why does Jesus eat with sinners?", making all three of the parables in Luke 15 a response to the Pharisees.

Bailey's research on the *haberim* and *'am ha-'arets* is extremely important for proper interpretation. Through further research, Bailey believes that the older son is representative of the *haberim* while the younger son is representative of the *'am ha-'arets*. As such, it is most likely that Jesus' parable is directed to two different Jewish audiences rather than the approach that some missiologist have taken—interpreting the younger son as representative of the nations.⁴⁹

Likewise, Bailey did extensive research and found that "in Middle Eastern culture, to ask for the inheritance while the father is still alive is to wish him *dead*."⁵⁰ As such, the younger son's request reflects that of someone who has no concern for his father, and his actions demonstrate no allegiance with family matters. The younger son is interested in distancing himself from the father. At this point we are building upon cultural values and moving into the realm of action which is where missional dynamics will be found.

The distancing in the parable is likely to be representative in part of the (*'am ha-'arets*) false-absorption of their own religious leaders message—"you are unclean." Self-righteous leaders often have more impact than often realized because their pervasively wrong message can still be

---

47. Bailey, *Finding the Lost*, 25–26, 59–60, 81–82; Bailey, *Poet & Peasant*, 2:148; Bailey, *Jacob & the Prodigal*, 24–25, 191–92.

48. Bailey, *Finding the Lost*, 25.

49. Contra Bashford, *God's Missionary Plan*, 55, 65, 70; Peters, *Biblical Theology of Missions*, 50.

50. Bailey, *Finding the Lost*, 112, 14.

wedged in the minds of those who perceive their self-esteem through things like education, money or power. It may well be the case that this misguided self-perception was adopted by the average Jew (*'am ha-'arets*) causing them to think they are not worthy to stand in God's presence and therefore distancing themselves from God (much the same way that some non-Christians feel when surrounded by those fervorently spouting "christianese").

In contrast, Jesus was indirectly informing the scribes and Pharisees (*haberim*) that they are like the older son. When the younger son comes home and is restored to the father, the older son's response is the exact opposite of a good missionary. Jesus is illustrating their failure in allegiance to God's mission and lack of concern for the lost. In so doing, Jesus was answering the initial question of the Pharisees through the character of the older son.

Jesus is pointing out that he is surrounded by two Jewish audiences neither of which has allegiance to God's mission. Both need the father's care and protection, as the father loves them into his care. Moreover, they need to follow in the ways of the father, as Jesus subtly illustrates the failure of both groups through the character of each son. Here we find an image of a lone father whose children either reject him or misunderstand him entirely.

This is the image of Jesus who stands before "righteous" Jewish persecutors who are accusing him of doing wrong while he carries out his mission to the Jewish "sinners" who need to find their way home. All the while, neither group understands Jesus' mission. In the parables, the younger son returns, indicating that the *'am ha-'arets* are moving closer in allegiance, while the only one without allegiance (missional or otherwise) is the older son, the *haberim*.

If either group had embraced an allegiance to God's mission during Jesus' ministry, we would not have had to wait until Acts to see one attempt after the next designed to cause the Jews to move forward in carrying out God's mission to the Gentiles. Mission would have happened through the Jews during Jesus ministry. Ironically, and in spite of these failures, mission does flow to the Gentiles through the Jews in the New Testament even when surrounded by great Jewish reluctance.

In explaining to both the law-keepers and the law-breakers that they do not understand the depth of God's missional nature or concern for the lost, the ultimate insights to be drawn from this parable are missional ones.

Stepping out of the interpretation itself for a moment, what else could be done hermeneutically? Given what I have just presented, some might call this conjecture because I have few, if any, sources to demonstrate the validity of my interpretation beyond what I have drawn from Bailey. On one level their claim is valid because the next step in this interpretation would be to do further work to see if I could verify some of my claims above.

For example, is there anything to indicate that the 'am ha-'arets did have some sort of inferiority complex due to the false-sense of superiority exhibited by the *haberim*? If so, would the 'am ha-'arets or a historian be aware of this and willing to record it? This is possible but unlikely. However, resolving this quest as an individual would mean learning Arabic and then searching through the volumes in the same way that Bailey has done. If a missiological interpretation of Luke 15 were to be my life's work then this may well be warranted. Resolving this problem corporately would mean that I could politely ask Bailey for assistance and learn from his expertise.

However, in going back to the initial concern of this being conjecture, there is a sense in which this accusation holds little validity. How so? When I draw upon my own missionary experience to move into an understanding of the action in the text, I am not operating from mere speculation. I am allowing that experience to act as an interpretational lens in order to credibly develop support for areas that I could not otherwise interpret. I am carrying out the same process with respect to mission that Bailey was carrying out when using modern-day culture.

It would certainly hold more credibility if I were a missionary in the Middle-East. I would then have even better reflexes for understanding the missional implications of the text. And, of course, it would be conjecture if I had no experience as a missionary and had no involvement in understanding the human religious response to self-righteousness, or experience with those who claim to follow God and have no allegiance to God's mission. However, since I have not served as a missionary in the Middle East, drawing upon those who have served in this context is our next task!

MISSION DYNAMICS AS AN INTERPRETATIONAL LENS— WOODBERRY[51]

J. Dudley Woodberry, a long-term missionary in the Middle East and missiologist at Fuller Theological Seminary, has caught my attention because he often redefines the understanding of a passage in Scripture through the lens of his own missionary activity. While understanding the type of insights that Bailey develops are one goal of this chapter, our concern is to understand the ways in which modern-day missionary activity acts as a lens for understanding biblical mission practice. Woodberry does this seemingly without realizing it. As such, this section most directly develops the thesis for this chapter, demonstrating the ways that missionary experience plays a vital role in forming and shaping our understandings of portions of the Biblical text.

Woodberry often uses a comparative hermeneutical method that begins by looking at the parallels between the missionary dynamics of Scripture and the dynamics of modern-day missionaries.[52] In doing this, Woodberry seems to be trying to demonstrate the ways in which Scripture can guide the practice of missionaries interacting with Muslim believers.[53]

---

51. The term missionary dynamics is used in favor of the terms "circumstances" or "context," because dynamics describes both the problems that the missionaries face and the missionary response to those problems, while context is typically thought to be the cultural problems.

52. Other authors, such as Bailey, appear to do something similar, but Woodberry's method sets him apart from the norm because he moves beyond cultural parallels and considers the parallels between the *missionary activity* of the Bible and the *missionary activity* of his own experience or others he has known as a missiologist.

53. Woodberry bases his ideas in part upon Chapman who states, "If Jesus knew how to meet people as people, his example has much to teach us about all our relationships. But when we consider the extensive debt which Islam owes to Judaism, a study of Jesus' relations with his fellow Jews may have special relevance to the way we should seek to relate to Muslims" (Chapman, "Thinking Biblically About Islam," 66). Woodberry is also intentional in his theology of mission, for example:

The theological questions impact practice. First, is Islam a friend or a foe or both? Second, how do we understand the finality of the two faiths? Third, do we worship the same God though understand different things about him? Fourth, how do we answer Jesus' question, "Who do you say that I am?" Fifth, is there salvation through Christ but outside Christianity? Sixth, does or can Islam have a patriarchal or mosaic place in God's plan of salvation? Seventh, was Muhammad a prophet-in a BC context though he was AD? Eighth, does God speak through the Qur'an or do we hear his echoes there?

What guidelines do we get from Jesus and Paul in dealing with Muslims to overcome current issues? These include ethnic prejudice (with the woman of Samaria in John 4),

The Role of Mission Praxis upon Missiological Hermeneutics

Yet, it does not appear that Woodberry was intentionally trying to develop a new hermeneutical tool when making these comparative analogies. Nevertheless, that is what has happened. In this section, we will develop three cases that illustrate this hermeneutic. These will be (1) the use of parables, (2) the use of questions and (3) the role of visions.[54]

Woodberry's primary question that he brings to Scripture is "What would Jesus say to Muslims?" Woodberry refines this question through further delineation;

>"What would Jesus say to Muslims...
>...concerning social obstacles (John 4)?
>...concerning orthodox legalism (John 3)?
>...concerning theological problems (Matt 16)?
>...concerning popular practices (Luke 10, Acts 19)?
>...concerning militant activism (Acts 9)?
>...concerning [folk] religious forms (1 Cor. 9:19–22; Acts 15)?"[55]

In order to answer these questions, Woodberry begins by comparing the parallels between the Bible and modern-day Islam. Some parallels have greater depth than others, but the important thing to consider for this study is the method.[56] Woodberry's approach may be summarized as follows:

Are there parallels between the missionary dynamics of the Bible and Islam? These parallels may be found in areas such as cultural norms, folk religion, orthodox religion, militant activism, politics, etc. that a missionary would face or address.

If there are parallels, what are they and how closely do they match?

---

orthodox legalism (with the Pharisee Nicodemus in John 3), theological issues (with the disciples in Matthew 16), popular practices (with the magic of Ephesus in Acts 19), and cultural issues (with the Judaizers in 1 Corinthians 9 and Acts 15) (Woodberry, "Syllabus," 232).

54. Each of these cases draws from devotions in Woodberry's lectures given throughout his Introduction to Islam (MR550) course that ran from October 10–21, 2005, and the accompanying syllabus.

55. Woodberry, "Syllabus," 237.

56. Although Woodberry does not do as detailed of an analysis as some scholars might like, Woodberry's instincts for understanding the biblical culture may serve him well. Certainly those untrained in anthropology and unaccustomed to interacting with other cultures are likely to exhibit ethnocentric traits and instincts that cannot be trusted. However, those who have served as missionaries for decades in foreign societies similar to specific biblical societies will most likely have instincts that can be trusted when interpreting Scripture to solve difficult missional questions.

267

Missiological Hermeneutics

Based on those parallels, how closely should modern-day missionaries follow the biblical accounts, such as adopting the content and communication styles of biblical missionaries?

For example, one of Woodberry's more developed accounts considers the parallels between Orthodox Legalistic Judaism and Orthodox Legalistic Islam, as follows:

1. Both have very similar law (Woodberry offers an extensive list of similarities between Exodus 20 and Islamic law). Woodberry points out that Islamic law is borrowed even in its most minute details from Rabbinic law, such as the allowance of having a maximum of four wives, or knowing when to break a fast by using light and dark colored threads to discern the time of day.[57]

2. Both have similar creedal affirmations
"The lord our God is One lord." // "There is no god but God." (compare Shema Deut 6:4 and Q. 112:1–23)

3. Both have shared prophets

4. Both see religion as a total way of life including "church" and "state."

5. Both reject a suffering Messiah.[58]

In most cases, Woodberry believes that when parallels are found, Scripture then becomes a useful guide from which his questions ("What would Jesus say to Muslims . . .?") can be answered and principles can be developed to further improve missionary efforts. Moreover, because Western missionaries are easily tempted to operate from a position of power, the majority of Woodberry's parallel accounts illustrate ways in which mission can flow from weakness.[59]

---

57. Woodberry, *Audio of Woodberry Lectures*, 29 MP3 files. When referencing Woodberry's lectures, the format will be to cite the lecture date (Oct 10 in this case), the lecture on this date (typically there were three lectures with breaks in-between). Therefore, L1 stands for lecture 1 (of 3). Finally, the 28:00 reflects the minutes:seconds (roughly accurate within 15 to 30 seconds) at which Woodberry's ideas are referenced.

58. Woodberry, "Syllabus," 241–42; cp. Chapman, "Thinking Biblically About Islam," 75–76.

59. It should be noted that this is a corrective needed for many Western missionaries and Woodberry issues this correction quite gracefully (through seemingly simple biblical study). As such Woodberry demonstrates a grace-filled approach in his teaching that models his expectations for the style of witness that he would like to see his students demonstrating before Muslims.

The Role of Mission Praxis upon Missiological Hermeneutics

Furthermore, Woodberry does not try to force the parallels into place. In those cases in which the parallels do not fit, Woodberry is clear to point them out. For example, when discussing the way in which militant Islam parallels militant Judaism of the first century, Woodberry points out the similarity between Rome as a superpower and the USA today. As such, he adds "this one clear distinction: Today America represents Rome, whereas in the first-century it was the persecuted church that was the evangelizing agency."[60] Woodberry makes it clear that Christian missionaries of the first century were perceived by the Jews as having no associated political power, while present-day USA missionaries going to Muslim countries may be seen as oppressors.

The Missiological Role of Telling Parables

Woodberry's understanding of parables is quite possibly one of the best examples of the ways in which missionary experience impacts biblical interpretation and therein offers a glimpse of an unfolding missiological hermeneutic. Woodberry has always worked among people living in

---

60. Woodberry, *Audio of Woodberry Lectures*, 29 MP3 files. Chapman advocates the merit of building upon these parallels throughout his article, but likewise mentions three major differences that need to be kept in mind.

[Muhammad's] background [with the Jews of his day] should help us to understand not only the most obvious similarities between the doctrines of Judaism and Islam (for example, their understanding of the oneness of God), but also some of the deeper similarities between the spirit of the two religions (for example, their understanding of the role of the law). It should therefore make it easier for us to put ourselves into the shoes of the Muslim and to see Jesus as the Muslim sees him.

This parallel between Judaism and Islam needs to be qualified at three points. In the first place, we need to recognize that Muhammad was too much of a creative genius to be described as one who simply "borrowed" from Jewish sources. Everything that he absorbed was stamped with the imprint of his own creative mind, as we see in the distinctive thrust that is given to the story of Joseph (Sura 12).

Secondly, some of Muhammad's teaching was influenced, if not actually determined, by the negative response he received from the Jews in Medina. . . . Any attempt, therefore, to draw a parallel between Judaism and Islam must take into account this tortuous love-hate relationship between Muhammad and the Jews, which has coloured relations between Muslims (particularly the Arabs) and Jews ever since, not least in the twentieth century.

Thirdly, in spite of all the similarities between the two religions, the Jewish people had special privileges because of their special place in God's plan of salvation . . .

If, however, these qualifications are not serious enough to make us abandon the attempt to see Islam in the light of New Testament Judaism, this approach may help us to come to terms with the bewildering variety of Christian responses to Islam (Chapman, "Thinking Biblically About Islam," 71).

"closed lands." Early in his work in Afghanistan, this provided opportunity for him to consider ways in which the propagation of the gospel could take place in regions where direct presentations of the Christian message were illegal or extremely limited. Therefore, he learned to "speak in such a way that the receptive [would] understand and the others [would] not."[61]

In most cases, Woodberry developed ways of indirectly communicating the message of Jesus Christ by drawing upon contextually appropriate forms of communication.[62] Through this struggle to find tangible ways to share the Christian message, Woodberry developed a new appreciation for the missional use of parables that he had not fully realized prior to his missionary involvement.[63] This new insight afforded him a fresh perspective when interpreting Scripture, adding also further depth for Jesus' own use of parables.

In terms of Woodberry's actual insights, he foremost believes that Jesus' use of parables are an intentional form of indirect communication designed to sift out persecutors while simultaneously allowing interested followers to learn the Christian message. Persecutors, in order to charge Jesus with a crime would need a direct statement. However, as Woodberry points out, Jesus' early parables are the most difficult to discern while latter parables have a much more obvious meaning. Finally, as Jesus approaches the final days of his life, he issues direct statements that ultimately lead to his crucifixion. Woodberry believes that Jesus was intentionally delaying the crucifixion to lengthen his time of ministry

---

61. Woodberry, *Audio of Woodberry Lectures*, 29 MP3 files. Woodberry points out that when telling the parable of the sower in the field, Jesus uses the parable so that only the receptive would understand Jesus claim that he was the sower, while the nonreceptive would not understand.

62. Woodberry drew from indirect communication forms found in his ministry context. Many of these match New Testament forms of indirect communication, most likely due to the similarities in first-century biblical culture and modern-day Middle Eastern culture. However, there are forms of indirect communication that are quite different such as Trinidadian calypso songs that carry embedded meaning and could yield helpful insight into songs in the Old Testament (Mulrain, "Is There a Calypso Exegesis?," 39–42).

63. Interestingly, Woodberry asks his class, "Why did Jesus use parables?" To which a student humorously responds, "To confuse us!" (Woodberry, *Audio of Woodberry Lectures*, 29 MP3 files). Though this answer is made in jest, it does reflect the perplexity that most Americans feel when trying to understand Jesus' use of parables.

upon the earth, noting that, "it is as though Jesus was trying not to get himself crucified too soon."[64]

Woodberry was most likely able to gain this insight because (1) Woodberry, like Bailey, was immersed in a culture similar to that of the New Testament, (2) Woodberry was involved in the activity of mission and (3) Woodberry faced the same type of barriers in sharing the Christian message as that of Jesus (for example, persecution and barriers regarding direct communication).[65] As such, Woodberry was able to see what others have not seen—the missiological nature of Jesus' communication through parables. This is a much deeper insight than simply a cultural or linguistic understanding because Woodberry's combined cultural experience and mission practice allowed him to gain insight into the activity flowing through Scripture.

Without the similarity of Woodberry's missional dynamics to that of Jesus, Woodberry's missionary practice would not have the same level of insightful guidance into Jesus' first century missional dynamics. If, by chance, Islam were to have no opposition to Christian evangelism, then he would not have faced the struggle of trying to understand how to share the Christian message in the midst of persecution. As it was, Woodberry's missionary difficulties in facing persecution became the unlikely but helpful lens that allowed him to gain greater understanding into Jesus' mission practice. Furthermore, Woodberry was able to discern the reason for those parables that were more difficult to understand versus those that were fairly obvious. As such, Woodberry's praxiological movement between missionary experience and biblical reflection is exemplary of a unique and powerful missional hermeneutic that can be generated from one's missionary experience.

---

64. Ibid., Oct 14 L1 23:30.

65. Though Christianity emerges in the midst of Judaism while Islam emerges in the midst of Christianity, this temporal inconsistency has little bearing upon the issues that Christian missionaries must face in their day. For example, there is little question that persecution was severe for Christians in the New Testament. Jesus faces severe persecution from the Jews to the point of death. Stephen is stoned to death (Acts 7:57—8:1) Saul holds official documents from the High Priest that allows him to persecute Christians (Acts 9:1–2). James is killed and Peter is imprisoned simply because Agrippa I wanted to appeal to the Jews (Acts 12:1–2). Paul is stoned, left for dead and persecuted throughout Acts (Acts 14:19).

The Missiological Role of Asking Questions

Similar to his missiological understanding of parables, Woodberry discovered that there is great merit in "asking questions." Because he was an outsider, he could ask questions about Islam that allowed him to prod the mind of the average Muslim believer. These are questions that the average Muslim would not normally ask, let alone questions for which they would publicly seek answers. However, when he began asking questions he found further missiological significance that caused him to reinterpret Scripture in light of this practice. These are as follows:

- Reinstating levels of dignity and honor (John 4)
- Reciprocal relationships (Matt 16:13–28)
- Developing a Group Understanding (Matt 16:13–28)
- Prodding the minds of potential converts (Matt 16:13–28)
- Asking questions rather than making a direct attack (Acts 9).

Reinstating Levels of Dignity and Honor (John 4)

The Islamic societies within which Woodberry worked had strong values of honor and shame, leading Woodberry to discover that one of the ways to achieve honor is based upon the level of generosity that one might offer. When dealing with those who had been shamed by the society, Woodberry looked for ways to restore honor. Likewise, it is essential in the societies to share a meal before discussing any business concerns. However, when coming in contact with those of extreme poverty, offering a meal was often beyond their capacity. As such, Woodberry focused on other ways in which he could restore honor to the poor.

For example, he discovered that being willing to receive any gift from the poor, such as a cup of coffee or tea, gave them a sense of honor. Woodberry likewise realized that the Western tendency in these situations was to focus on doing things for the poor. As such, the untrained or inexperienced Western missionary might try to politely refuse a gift of coffee or tea, while simultaneously giving food or other supplements to the poor. However, in doing so the missionary would have stifled the very small act of the poor, and likewise stifled an opportunity for them to gain honor.

In an attempt to find other ways of honoring the poor, Woodberry began to realize that he could ask questions that would allow the poor to share their knowledge and experience with him. In doing this, he discovered the importance of "being willing to ask questions and learn from [those in extreme poverty] which also gives [the poor] a sense of honor."[66]

As such, the missional experience of asking questions of the disenfranchised became a new interpretational lens for understanding Christ's missionary practice in Scripture. Woodberry's interpretation of John 4 reflects these hermeneutical trends as he points out that "[Jesus] didn't give her anything initially. He said, 'give me a drink'... and Jesus being willing to receive from her, gave her an honor that ultimately would allow him to give her something much more."[67] Once again, we find a hermeneutical model in which the very act of serving in God's mission provides the insight and framework for understanding Scripture in missiologically relevant ways.

Though Charles Taber represents a somewhat different approach to this issue, he offers us another perspective on the role of the poor related to biblical interpretation.

> I have been increasingly wondering whether it might not be the case that the biblical emphasis on the priority of the poor in God's salvific concern is not only an important soteriological and eschatological theme, but also an important hermeneutical principle.... [M]ight it not be the case that the poor need fewer illusions to justify their status in the world and have no vested interest in the enjoyment of unjust privileges, and are thus in a better position not only to receive the gospel but even to understand it?... There seems to be a real sense in which complacent enjoyment of any great unfair advantage over others—economic, social, political, or intellectual—may in itself constitute an impediment to the understanding of the good news. Might this not be the reason for the extraordinarily convoluted hermeneutics of apartheid used by South African white churches?
>
> What are the implications of all this for biblical scholarship? Should we forthwith abandon the tools and findings of the trade? Of course not! But I suggest that we need to be attentive, expectant, and respectful when our sisters and brothers in other cultures and social situations tell us what they see in the Bible. We have grown so accustomed to being the world's experts, the world's teachers, that it may be a salutary exercise for us to sit at

---

66. Woodberry, *Audio of Woodberry Lectures*, 29 MP3 files.
67. Ibid., Oct 11 L1 29:30, 34:00.

the feet of the world's destitute, the world's oppressed, the world's babes, and so learn of Christ.[68]

If Taber is correct, then learning from the poor is not simply an act of charity. Rather, it is an act of genuine recognition that the poor may interpret Scripture in ways that others cannot. Taber does not tell us if this hypothesis sprang from his missionary service, but it is not hard at all to see this possibility arising. Certainly, Taber sees the life experience of the poor as a hermeneutical advantage. Furthermore, it can easily be seen how the poor would likely provide some of the most honest interpretations of the Jubilee (Lev 25, 27) or the Sermon on the Mount (Matt 5; Luke 6) to name a few passages.

Reciprocal Relationships That Develop Understanding (Matt 16:13–28)

Woodberry likewise found that questions are one of the best ways to discover the perceptions of an individual or group. The attitude of the missionary is an essential trait that can be sensed to a greater depth than we often realize. In asking questions about a Muslim's understanding of God, we must prepare for answers that go far beyond an orthodox understanding of Islam, and this was likewise the experience of Woodberry. In his own words, the "value of questions and listening" is that it shows "[g]enuine interest, [that] they are important, [encouraging a] reciprocal relationship, [and seeing] where they are for relevance."[69]

If done properly and genuinely, this can encourage a reciprocal relationship as our own learning attitude will most often foster a learning attitude in those same relationships that we develop. Chapman and Woodberry have similar experiences in this particular area, especially in the sense that both are very serious about evangelism even in a context that calls for these indirect ways of expressing their faith.[70] Like Woodberry, Chapman's interpretation of Jesus as a boy (Luke 2:46) flows from years of insight as a missionary: "This kind of sharing was possible only because Jesus was *sitting among them* and *listening* in order to

---

68. Taber, "Missiology and the Bible," 241–42.

69. Woodberry, "Syllabus," 236, 245.

70. Chapman adds, "perhaps we need to make a double plea: on the one hand that those who believe they are practising 'dialogue' with people of other faiths stop to ask themselves whether it is leading them in anything like the same direction as we see in this dialogue between Jesus and the Jews: and on the other hand, that those who think simply in terms of 'evangelism' ask themselves if their proclamation of the gospel allows for this kind of meeting of minds" (Chapman, "Thinking Biblically About Islam," 67).

know how they thought and felt. He had begun to learn the art of *asking questions,* not to trip up and embarrass, but to draw others out into a real meeting of minds. He had the *understanding* which enabled him to grasp the real issues and discern the things that really matter. When he offered *answers,* it was in response to questions that were understood and expressed."[71]

In relating the difference between group and individual understanding, Woodberry was well aware that the orthodox Islamic understanding of Jesus was that he was "only a prophet." This was the group understanding. However when discussing the nature of God with a Bengali Muslim (in current-day Bangladesh), this man asserted that he believed "God is like a father."[72] This man's individual understanding went far beyond the orthodox system of Islam, which teaches that "God does not beget and is not begotten."[73] As a result of this and other missionary experiences, Woodberry came to believe that missionaries should witness both to individual Muslims and to Islam as a system. More importantly, he realized that some individuals, like the Bengali man, are much further along in understanding God and Jesus Christ.[74]

Once again, turning to Scripture, Woodberry considered the parallels between this experience and certain reactions to Jesus in the New Testament. For example, when interpreting Matthew 16:13–28, Woodberry points out that the Jews, like modern-day Muslims, thought Jesus was a prophet (Matt 16:14). Similarly, even though Peter saw Jesus as a messiah, he misunderstood the role of the Messiah because the thought of a suffering Messiah was unthinkable to Peter (Matt 16:16, 21–22). A suffering Messiah is likewise a stumbling block for modern-day Muslims and is another parallel with first century Jewish thought.

As a result of his mission experience, Woodberry perceived that Jesus is addressing the Jews, the disciples, and Peter on increasingly deeper levels throughout Matthew 16:13–28. Jesus begins by asking the disciples "Who do *people* say that I am?" (16:13, paraphrase mine), but

---

71. Ibid., 66.

72. Woodberry, *Audio of Woodberry Lectures,* 29 MP3 files; Woodberry, "Syllabus," 245.

73. Woodberry, "Syllabus," 246; Woodberry, *Audio of Woodberry Lectures,* 29 MP3 files.

74. Woodberry, *Audio of Woodberry Lectures,* 29 MP3 files.

shortly after that query, Jesus becomes more personal and asks "Who do *you all* [ὑμεῖς—2nd per. pl.] say that I am?" (16:15, translation mine).

Eventually the discussion centers entirely around Peter's response. Uniquely, Woodberry feels that Jesus seemingly harsh words toward Peter ("Get away from me, Satan!" Matt 16:23, NLT) are really expressing anguish toward the reigning Jewish perceptions that "kept Peter from [understanding] God's revelation."[75] As such, Woodberry perceives that Jesus' reaction is primarily against the Jewish group understanding that had so colored Peter's understanding about the true nature of God.

Interestingly, Chapman comes to very similar conclusions when dealing with separate passages in which Jesus expresses similarly harsh words toward the group understanding:

> [W]e need to go back to the words of Jesus himself and ask how it was that he could say to one Jew, "You are not far from the Kingdom of God" (Mk. 12:34), but on another occasion to a group of Jews, "You are of your father the devil" (Jn. 8:44 RSV). Part of the answer needs to be that there is a difference between "Judaism" and "Jews"—between the body of beliefs and traditions, and the people who hold them with varying degrees of conviction. We also need to be suspicious of sweeping generalizations and simple categories, whether they spring from an attitude that is excessively generous or excessively negative.
>
> If we base our understanding of Judaism only on the scribes and the Pharisees described in the New Testament, we may be incapable of recognizing a Nicodemus who has grown up in the same tradition but is reaching out for something more (Jn. 3:1–13).[76]

Strikingly, Chapman's description of Nicodemus is the identical biblical equivalent to Woodberry's missionary encounter with the Bengali man. Although some feel shock or surprise that Nicodemus lacks the vision to see Jesus as the Messiah, the missionary experience of Woodberry and Chapman gives them a common missiological view of Scripture to see Nicodemus as someone likely to place his faith in Christ.

---

75. Woodberry, "Syllabus," 245.

76. Chapman, "Thinking Biblically About Islam," 72; cp. Chapman, *Cross and Crescent*, 226–31.

The Role of Mission Praxis upon Missiological Hermeneutics

Prodding the Minds of Potential Converts (Matt 16:13–28)

In the same way that Jesus spent a great deal of time understanding the perception of his disciples, Woodberry found that his asking questions modeled a genuine attitude of learning by the missionary and this openness was generally appreciated (not to mention something that many American missionaries needed to appreciate). As relationships moved to deeper levels of trust, Woodberry found one of the most positive consequences of asking questions. This was that certain questions had the power to awaken Muslims spiritually.[77]

Depending on the depth of friendship and trust building, some relationships allowed Woodberry to ask questions such as, "If people are basically good, how do we account for the qur'anic quotations of most people rejecting right guidance?"[78] However, in the deepest relationships, he could even ask the most disturbing questions, such as, "How can I reconcile the fact that the Qur'an claims that Jesus is sinless even though the Qur'an likewise states that Muhammad had to ask forgiveness for his sins?"[79]

In the midst of reciprocal relationships, the learning process moves both directions and Woodberry notes that ultimately "[w]e are offering answers to questions that are not being asked (i.e., we are offering salvation when they are only looking for right guidance)."[80] Once again, in interpreting Matthew 16:13–28, Woodberry observes that the questions and answers move from less significant implications—"Who do *people* say that I am?" (v.13) to more personal and vital decisions—"Who do *you* say that I am?" (v.15).[81]

The Missional Role of Dreams and Visions

A much more difficult matter for any missionary is dealing with militant forms of a particular religion. Christian missionaries have faced the threat of martyrdom from its birth during first century Judaism to certain extreme forms of Islam today. Though these extremists (or zealots

---

77. Woodberry cautions that when asking a question to a Muslim, the question should be asked politely as one that the missionary was trying to solve for his or her own understanding.

78. Woodberry, "Syllabus," 86.

79. Woodberry, *Audio of Woodberry Lectures*, 29 MP3 files.

80. Woodberry, "Syllabus," 79.

81. Woodberry, *Audio of Woodberry Lectures*, 29 MP3 files.

Missiological Hermeneutics

in the Bible) were a minority in their respective faiths, they have been willing to fight or die for their causes, which were all tied closely in their minds to faith. In this brief look at the role of visions and dreams, we will consider the way in which Woodberry's missiological and mission experience integrate to give him another understanding of the role of visions and dreams, as well as yet another understanding of the use of questions.

For many Christians, the concept of visions and dreams conjures up thoughts of charismatic Christian movements that exuberantly proclaim God's continued use of prophetic dreams and visions as a sign of God's modern-day direction. By contrast, Woodberry's missiological understanding of dreams and visions is drawn from extensive surveys showing that dreams and visions have been a common instrument in Muslim conversions.

The role of visions in Woodberry's experience is decidedly missiological in at least three ways.

1. Woodberry notes that "for militants it is almost like there needs to be something dramatic to shake them out of the direction they are going."[82] "If they come to realize that their very militancy is persecuting . . . Jesus . . . that is again something that God uses."[83] The dreams and visions, that were the driving factors for Muslim conversions to Christ in so many cases, were not all that different from Paul's vision on the Damascus road.[84] Paul, as a biblical example, needed this "about face" to recognize the Messiah and end his militant persecution.

2. Missionaries, such as Peter (discussed in the first section of the chapter) had a vision that caused him to reassess the missionary scope of God's redemption for humanity (for example, Jews and Gentiles). Therefore, the role of visions had missional impact not only to halt the fierce persecution of the non-believer, but to likewise correct the misconceptions of Christian missionaries.

---

82. Ibid., Oct 20 L1 27:30.

83. Ibid., Oct 20 L1 28:30.

84. One very interesting aspect of Woodberry's missiological discoveries is that many Muslims who came to place their faith in Jesus Christ developed a great love for the Savior even though they retained levels of disdain for Christianity as a religion. Woodberry refers to this trend as "The veneration of Jesus in Islam" (Woodberry, "Syllabus," 254; Woodberry, *Audio of Woodberry Lectures*, 29 MP3 files). In the same way that American slavery of Africans in the nineteenth-century should have left them no witness for Christ, Jesus managed to act as a witness and venerate his nature even in the face of very poor Christian witness.

3. Woodberry reminds us that "God seems to honor [those who value dreams and visions] and used it in the Bible and [God] uses it today. At the least, we need to be open to [the role that dreams may have in helping others to come to faith in Jesus Christ]."[85] Therefore, even missionaries who feel that dreams and visions are inconsequential should respect the historical pragmatism of the missionary God who has demonstrated their effective use time and again.

Relating to the former section, a final insight regarding "asking questions" is that questions have a much softer impact when one might be prone to issuing a direct attack. Once again, Woodberry's missiological study of these encounters gave him new eyes to see Acts 9. Woodberry emphasizes the fact that Jesus begins with a question rather than declaring "You are persecuting me!"[86] Furthermore, he notes that "[Jesus] helps the militant, [through] questions [to] see the implications of his/her actions."[87]

Rather than seeing Jesus as attacking Paul during what must have been an overwhelming encounter (Acts 9), Woodberry feels that Jesus "help[ed] the militant, by [asking] questions [to] see the implications of his/her actions—persecuting the prophet Jesus in the name of religion."[88] Furthermore, Woodberry feels that Jesus' response to Paul's question is likewise a gracious sign of concern for peace as Paul understands that the Savior "identifies himself as the Jesus of history—the humble and despised—whose followers Paul persecuted."[89]

Uniquely, Woodberry has attempted to discover ways to discern the questions that Muslims are asking. Given strong social pressure to conform, people are normally not going to raise questions themselves. However, Woodberry has found that reading novels is a helpful way, because a good author will often put the questions into the mouths of their fictional characters. In this way, the characters can ask ques-

---

85. Woodberry, *Audio of Woodberry Lectures*, 29 MP3 files. Woodberry recalls an event when the late M. Scott Peck brought together ten Christians, ten Jews, and ten Muslims in New Orleans to get to know one another. During this event, they told their dreams to each other in the morning, but there was no interpretation. Later in the day, the Jews and Muslims were to interpret their own dreams and interpret the dreams of the Christians (ibid., Oct 20 L1 20:30–24:30).

86. Ibid., Oct 20 L1 30:00.

87. Woodberry, "Syllabus," 254.

88. Ibid..

89. Ibid..

tions that the people cannot. Naguib Mahfouz is a Nobel Peace Prize winning novelist who raises these sorts of questions through his characters and was nearly killed for doing so.[90] Though not mentioned by Woodberry, Bailey does point out that Jesus used the parables in this same manner, and this is nowhere more obvious than in the parable of the prodigal son.

Beyond the role of these three areas (Parables, Asking Questions, Visions, and Dreams), there are other examples in which Woodberry's missionary experience has hermeneutical significance.[91] These include the missional role of public praying and fasting. Woodberry notes that Muslims had trouble deciding if Christians in their area were "spiritual" because they never saw Christians openly praying and fasting.[92] Woodberry is clear to point out potential biblical parallels, once again

---

90. Woodberry, *Audio of Woodberry Lectures*, 29 MP3 files.

91. An excellent example of a current issue in mission with significant hermeneutical implications is the topic of "insider movements" in Islam (technically C5 in the C1-C6 continuum). Woodberry and Larry Owens (pseudonym) both attempt to consider the issue from a biblical standpoint and both call for hermeneutical and missional grace especially because they realize the potential for Western values to become dominant while also wanting to follow biblical guidelines (Owens, "Syncretism and the Scriptures,"; Woodberry, "To the Muslim,"). Interestingly, Woodberry once again interprets Scripture through his own mission experience noting, "We do know that the early Jewish Christians, like many Messianic Jews today, continued to attend the synagogue (Acts 9:1–2; 23:2). And the Judaic establishment at the time was hostile to Christians (Acts 9:1–2; 23:2) even as many Muslims are today. . . . In studying Muslim followers of Christ over a number of years, I have found them less interested in the Qur'an as they read the Bible and less interested in the mosque as they worship with other believers" (ibid., 154). Woodberry works from Scripture to demonstrate the early church's approach to dealing with Jewish syncretism, but in his last sentence he is making a connection from his present day missions experience which essentially links the mission to the Jews in Acts and his mission experience to Muslims today pointing out that each can address syncretism without too much fear because the Christian faith will continue to attract new believers.

I would add that one of the very best ways to curtail syncretism would be for missionaries to present consistent missional interpretations of Scripture in hopes that such a hermeneutic will be inductively passed onto the insider movements. This would have the hopeful effect of avoiding Western syncretism as well as some future syncretism of their own. Furthermore, this will eventually lead them to become a missionary movement. This is essentially what Paul is doing in Galatians 3–4 since he adopts a quite possibly syncretistic midrashic hermeneutic in order to demonstrate a missiological hermeneutic as he addresses familiar Old Testament passages amidst a syncretistic Jewish audience.

92. Woodberry, *Audio of Woodberry Lectures*, 29 MP3 files.

demonstrating the impact of hermeneutical insight drawn from his missionary practice: "Christians are given warnings against the misuse of fasting (Mt. 6:16–18; Lk. 18:10, 12), but Jesus expected his disciples to fast (Mk. 2:18–20). It is interesting that Paul includes his going hungry as one of the deprivations he endured so that he would "put no obstacle in any one's way" (2 Cor 6:3). Lack of fasting is seen by Muslims as being irreligious. God asked the Israelites, "Was it really for me that you fasted?" (Zech 7:5). We need to ask ourselves the same question."[93] Though not mentioned by Woodberry, genuine observance of praying and fasting may have more correlation with God's intention for Israel's mission as they tabernacled in the Old Testament. In the same way that the nations were permitted to be spectators as Israel surrounded the tabernacle, praying and fasting may have been intentionally centripetal aspects of Israel's witness.

Finally, the nature of the Christian church in Islam offers insights into the appropriate levels of permeability of the church. Much like the reaction to Paul's conversion after Acts 9, the Christian church in many Islamic countries is bonded tightly but not always for the sake of mission. When a Muslim comes to Christ, there is appropriate concern over whether the conversion is genuine, or a case in which the convert will later revert to Islam, or even cases of the ingenuine informer.[94] In such cases, the bonding of the church may be too rigid, while at the same time they must have discerning skills for the inclusion of the convert and the growth of the church. As Woodberry put it, "the church wanted to have enquirers but not converts."[95]

Implications

In each of the above cases, we observe some very impressive hermeneutical trends. Strikingly, Woodberry's suggestions for missionary practice are equally impressive to his biblical insights due to the way he illustrates missionary practice working from weakness; that is, mission that flows from questions resulting in dialogue or parables resulting in further thought are main forms of communication. Likewise, there is human weakness found in a missionary community that is dependent on God's

---

93. Woodberry, "Syllabus," 161.
94. Woodberry, *Audio of Woodberry Lectures*, 29 MP3 files.
95. Ibid., Oct 20 L1 45:30.

intervention through spiritual visions and dreams, as well as quiet public acts of prayer and fasting. These missionary practices are both subtle and substantive, and are profoundly dependent upon God.

Given the strong-arm tactics typical of Western evangelism, a striking difference can be seen between those who operate from a perception of power compared to those who do not.[96] Mission from weakness therefore has great application for evangelism in the West as it naturally reduces levels of dogmatism, impatience and confrontational encounters. Furthermore, in the same way that Taber argues that the poor have the least reason for bias, mission from weakness is likewise instrumental in developing a proper hermeneutic that will parallel many of the missional dynamics found in the Bible. As such, we should likely expect that missionary practices based foremost upon human strengths (such as Constantinian or colonial mission—for example, absent of sustained persecution due to political dominance) will likely result in a lack of parallels to missional dynamics found in the Bible, such as Jesus' missionary activity in the New Testament. Therefore, mission that flows from power is more likely to result in misguided biblical interpretations.

The implications of this are enormous for hermeneutical development. This means that even a flawless understanding of the biblical culture and language are inadequate in themselves. Instead, a well-developed understanding of Scripture must be found through God's missionary efforts and the missionary efforts of biblical authors. It follows that the most relevant hermeneutical path taken is one immersed in understanding mission theory and practice. Once in place, missionary experience can provide a basic framework for understanding the missionary activity of Scripture. This does not mean that a proper understanding of the biblical cultures and languages is unimportant for understanding the missionary practice of Scripture. However, it does mean that the biblical cultures and languages play a supporting role to that of the missionary practice found in Scripture.

MISSIONARY PRACTICE INFLUENCING

---

96. Interestingly, I once heard a first-hand account of prayer-evangelism in the USA. Christians simply went from one home to the next asking if the residents would like them to pray for a matter on their heart. They also encouraged the residents to pray with them. They found a very high response from those they approached. This practice of prayer-evangelism is fundamentally based on human weakness and reliant on God's faithfulness to answer prayer.

The Role of Mission Praxis upon Missiological Hermeneutics

HERMENEUTICAL THEORY

What then are the relevant hermeneutical understandings that can be drawn from the role of cross-cultural exposure and missionary experience? Furthermore, can these integrate with traditional historical-critical hermeneutics? The vast majority of seminary students develop their hermeneutical understanding through courses thought to give them those skills, such as Greek, Hebrew, and their corresponding courses in exegetical methods. As such, they follow the progression shown in points 1 and 2 at the bottom of Figure 20.

Unfortunately, Greek and Hebrew are not required by most schools of missiology, but students of missiology are trained anthropologically which often gives them much stronger skills in understanding culture and worldview. As already discussed, traditional biblical theology courses assume that the principal purpose of Scripture is to present the theological ideas depicted in the text, and as a result they truncate the hermeneutical process through this assumption.

Given Biblical Theology of Mission's claim that Scripture is foremost missional in purpose, there is a great deal of hermeneutical potential to be found in the typical practice of most missionaries. Most missionaries engage in years of linguistic and cultural study in the midst of their ministry, and the cultural context of the missionary may have biblical parallels in the Old Testament or New Testament. Bailey is the obvious example that I have chosen to illustrate this tendency.

Although I have critiqued Bailey's theological assumptions, he does consider himself to be a missionary (though most likely not a missiologist). This means of understanding cultural values and worldview (shown as point 3 in Figure 20) is far more holistic than library study. Even though most missionaries only learn a few of the world's cultures at this depth, it does give many of them great expertise in understanding these cultures, and as such it gives them far more hermeneutical expertise than they realize. Theologians would be wise to draw upon missionaries as a primary resource for understanding biblically similar cultures.

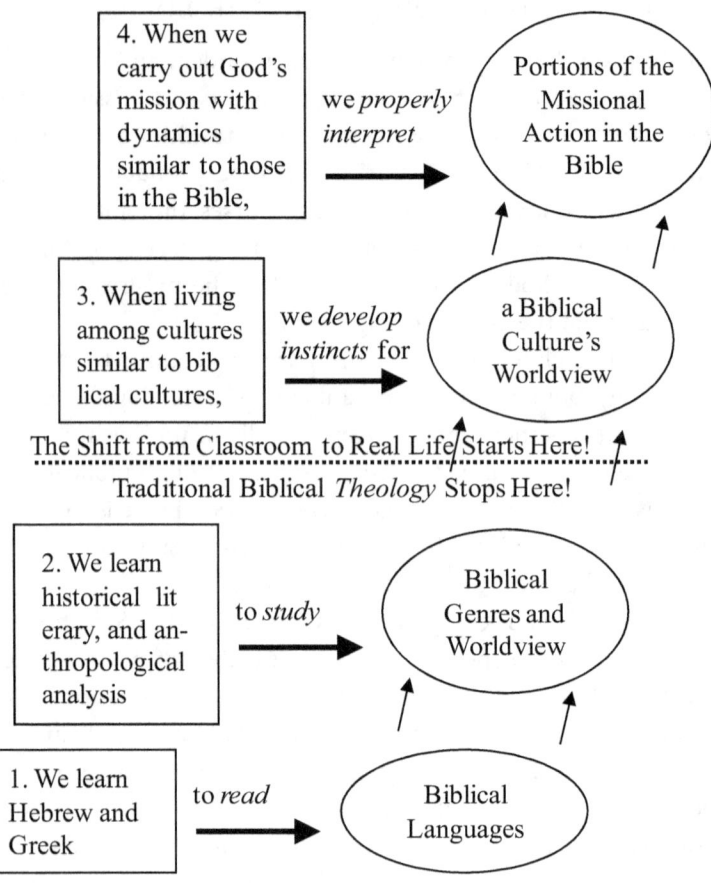

Figure 20: Hermeneutical Commitment

Therefore, we can say that our given experience in a culture may act as a hermeneutical guide in understanding Scripture. The important point to remember, however, is that a relevant biblical parallel is needed for the biblical culture in view and of course this must not be forced upon Scripture. As such, *if our cultural experience is similar to a specific biblical culture, then our cultural instincts may act as a useful guide in understanding the cultural aspects of that portion of Scripture.*[97] As an

---

97. Some may present the question, "How can you know a given biblical culture's values without having done the proper historical research?" I am not advocating that missionaries should avoid proper historical research, but *no one* has the ability to step back into time and make definitive claims regarding specific cultural values, includ-

example, those who serve among people in a modern-day monarchy may have valuable insights in understanding the books of Samuel, Kings and Chronicles. Those who serve in the tribal setting may develop good instincts for understanding the Pentateuch.

Furthermore, we have seen that those serving in the Middle East have developed good instincts for understanding Jesus' mission in the New Testament (shown as point 4 in Figure 20). Therefore, *the activity of carrying out God's mission provides a desperately needed framework of missional understanding that may bring to light missional dynamics found throughout Scripture.* Though it goes unrealized by most missionaries, their allegiance to God's mission represents hermeneutical commitment as well as the more obvious missional commitment.

In terms of understanding the missionary practice in Scripture, modern-day missionaries are the greatest hermeneutical resource for the appropriate interpretation of the missionary activity found in Scripture. Woodberry is likewise the obvious example chosen to illustrate this critical hermeneutic. Missionaries need to follow Woodberry's example in documenting insights relating to their own missional dynamics and those found in Scripture. Missionaries also need to feel a great deal more confidence when contending with scholarly interpretations.

Even though missionary experience may act as a lens upon Scripture, we should not expect that every activity in mission will have an obvious parallel in the Bible, due in part to a lack of equiva-

---

ing those who do historical research. Certainly missiologists and theologians can all contribute together toward this understanding, but modern-day traditional societies that demonstrate strong parallels with a given biblical society should be given a very high priority for cultural understandings because they are the best *societal* representation of a once living society. Historical records explaining cultural values of the day would be another obvious resource, but even these are generally only the views of a single author who may or may not reflect an accurate depiction of his own society. Kraft points out that individuals do not necessarily reflect societal norms when writing, "It is very important for us to recognize that there is great individual variability within each society. It is very easy for an outsider to come to a people and . . . to assume that they are all the same. . . . Such a view is simplistic. Rather, there are people in all societies who have learned their culture or language imperfectly or do things idiosyncratically" (Kraft, *Anthropology for Christian Witness*, 157). Many missionaries have experienced this lesson firsthand when, after months of language study, they discover that they have unknowingly adopted the lisp or archaic words of their language helper. Theologians need to likewise consider that individual sources for cultural data may have their own idiosyncrasies. As such, Bailey's approach of drawing upon both modern-day societies and historical records provides the greatest overall confidence.

lent modern-day cultures. However, we must be vigilant in searching for parallels between the Bible and mission for at least three reasons; (1) it provides the entire missional community with needed insights, (2) it prevents missional passages from being co-opted by mission-less theological interpretations, and (3) if there are no parallels it may be a sign that something needs to be re-thought in modern-day mission practice.

As an example of the above, it is important to keep in mind that a missionary could be in a context of persecution that does not have a good cultural match, such as the former USSR, which persecuted Christian missionaries. Communism may not offer close cultural parallels to that of first century Palestine. However, in this case the missional dynamics may have somewhat close parallels in the Bible, allowing the missionary to develop understandings of biblical missionary activity, while the cultural nuances may be amiss.[98]

CONCLUSION

Returning then to the attempt by CMF missionaries to develop male leadership in their churches, you will recall that they told the Maasai, "What we have to teach you is so important that we will only teach the men!" However, did they believe that statement was true? Of course not! In fact, they believed the exact opposite.

More to the point, if God's mission to the Maasai were by some chance included in the biblical canon, I would first have to face the problem that there would be over two millennia of time spanning my reading of this "verse" and its origin. I have already mentioned that a conservative face-value theological interpretation of this would be devastating

---

98. Tiénou and Hiebert offer a model to help validate biblical hermeneutics related to a particular field practice by using a case-law comparison, but the main problem as I see it, is that traditional biblical and systematic theology still play a large part in determining the "law" while mission theology offers a multiplicity of cases to stretch and test the former (Tiénou and Hiebert, "Missional Theology," 224–35). For the most part, biblical and systematic theology in the West have such a lack of vision for mission in Scripture that these disciplines are suspect in their ability to contribute to the overall scheme. Only a few theologians (that do not have a background in missions or missiology) have contributed in significant ways (Hahn, *Mission in the NT*; Kaiser, *Mission in the OT*; Martin-Achard, *Light to the Nations*; Nissen, *NT and Mission*; Schnabel, *Early Christian Mission*; Wright, *Mission of God*).

for women. Furthermore, it would be devastating to the missionaries if they realized how the phrase was interpreted.

Does the phrase have cultural implications? Yes, but the cultural implications are not nearly as relevant as the missional reasons for its origin even though the two are intertwined. Knowing the culture would offer some clues to the proper interpretation of the phrase, but cultural study in a total absence of missiological understanding would not offer a correct interpretation. Therefore, if I lived a life focused entirely on theology and void of missionary practice, how likely is it that I would interpret the original authors' missional intent?

The potential for interpretational disaster when considering the mission to the Maasai most certainly influenced the way that I perceived 1 Timothy? Most of the arguments that I had read surrounding this passage were foremost theological in nature while a few focused on culture. Furthermore, 1 Timothy is thought of as a "pastoral epistle" in which the genre is thought to be one of Paul giving Timothy theological training.

If the passage is predominantly theological in nature, then we should adopt consistency in our hermeneutic. By this I mean that if we are going to assume that women cannot teach in the Church (1 Tim 2:10), then we should just as fervently proclaim that women are saved through child-bearing (1 Tim 2:15). We should not be allowed the luxury of switching from a very literal hermeneutic in verse 10 to one that ignores or spiritualizes the claims within a matter of a mere five verses. We are dealing with the same genre.

Or, is 1 Timothy knee-deep in missional issues and is Paul's genre missiological in style? My point is not that this must be a passage of missional dynamics, though I find that position far more tenable than any other. The point is that such a possibility radically transforms the way we teach, the way we treat women, the way we minister in the church, and the freedom with which the Christian message is accepted in certain societies.

Furthermore, the claims of 1 Timothy must be balanced with the entire canon of Scripture. It is irresponsible hermeneutically and missionally to focus on a single passage that does not have other consistent theological counterparts throughout the tapestry of Scripture. It will not do to atomize the text and force it into a theological mold. Nor will it due to atomize Paul's nature in 1 Timothy and ignore the fact that Paul's allegiance to missionary action is undaunting.

Finally, some will make the complaint, "what might provide coherence as Scripture is interpreted using missiological hermeneutics?" Foremost, we should recognize that theology as a discipline will not provide coherence, because the discipline is too often divorced from God's mission, God's action and most importantly the central concerns of God's word. As such, seeking theological coherence is inherently flawed.

Missionaries devoted to understanding Scripture rarely debate over topics theologically irrelevant to mission, because their first concern in learning theology is to understand how it benefits God's missionary activity.[99] Furthermore, missionaries devoted to understanding the Bible often have healthy instincts (far better than they realize) when it comes to recognizing mission practice in Scripture (especially when they intentionally practice missional hermeneutics). Finally, missionaries often have an Ockham's-razor level of practicality that appropriately rejects highly convoluted forms of theology (extreme forms of redaction theory for example).[100] They reject these not because they are too complex for the missionary to understand. Rather, they reject them because traditional theology most often fails to present any missiological interpretation even when the text begs for missiological interpretation.[101] Therefore, the overriding means of developing reasonable levels

---

99. The appropriate response to insider movements in Islam (C1-C6) is an example of a debate that directly affects field practice. Similarly, the debates over church growth were ones that affected missionary field practice.

100. Ockham's-razor is a principle noting that given two or more explanations, the simplest answer (often thought of as the one with the least number of assumptions) is most often the correct explanation.

101. In my own experience, one of the most startling examples of this took place in 1998 when C. K. Barrett, the highly esteemed New Testament scholar, came to Fuller Seminary to lecture and discuss Acts 15. The audience was made up nearly equally of students from the School of Theology and the School of World Mission. Throughout C. K. Barrett's lecture he never brought up even the possibility that the Acts 15 council was foremost resolving a clash between Jewish and Gentile cultures. Most of the students of missiology were shocked and waited until the end as the final panelist, G. Walter Hansen, asked C. K. Barrett "about the feasibility of the rather common interpretation that the decree [of Acts 15] had more to do with mission than salvation" (Hengel and Barrett, *Conflicts and Challenges*, 89). It seemed surprising to me that Hansen was the only panelist to point out the missiological possibility of this account. However, it was even more shocking to hear C. K. Barrett's reply, "I have not heard that interpretation." The students of missiology in the audience were stunned, especially since this highly touted scholar came to speak solely on Acts 15 and was entirely unaware of this interpretation. This portion of his response was not published, but in the midst of his response to Hansen, Barrett is quoted as saying "That is a first impression" (ibid., 90).

of coherence is allegiance and involvement in God's mission mixed with the proper amount of grace in recognizing our human ability to misinterpret Scripture. Together these provide the strongest hand in forging continuity in biblical interpretation.

SIX

Conclusion

MISSIOLOGISTS AND MISSIONARIES MUST move forward towards a biblically informed, spiritually grounded, and missionally sensitive hermeneutic. What can be done to move towards this hermeneutic in the future? Traditional hermeneutical methods have emphasized the biblical languages and an understanding of biblical cultures.[1] However, traditional hermeneutics have been insufficient in missional and spiritual dimensions. Foremost, any hermeneutic must allow for Scripture to be seen as more than a compilation of theological concepts.

Figure 21 is an overview diagram that represents a commonly held perception of Scripture. When a given curve approaches the top of this diagram, this represents the perception that a given concern occurs consistently within Scripture. Conversely, curves at the bottom of the diagram represent the perception that certain concerns are not generally found in Scripture. Figure 21 portrays theology as "heavily embedded" within Scripture while mission is "rarely found." Therefore, when interpreting Scripture, line T (the dashed line) in this diagram is representative of the expectation that Scripture contains consistently strong theological content. For the most part, it has been assumed that every portion of Scripture is meant for theological purposes. Line C (the dotted line) illustrates the idea that some aspects of Scripture are surrounded by heavy cultural embedding, while other portions of Scripture have less cultural overlay. For example, women wearing head-coverings during prayer is often seen as a cultural form that contains deeper meaning, while the statement "God is love" requires less cultural background

---

1. Having said this, theologians are not generally trained in linguistics or cultural anthropology. However, missiologists are typically trained in these fields, which often means that they have a stronger understanding of the nature of culture.

even though it will carry some cultural nuances.² Finally, Line M (the solid line) represents the fairly common view that Scripture has little missional content.

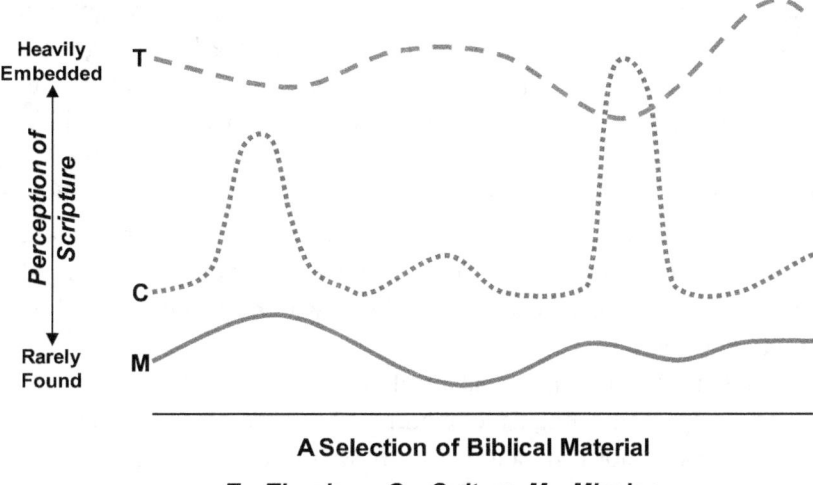

Figure 21: A Commonly-Held Perception of Scripture

Sadly, this perception is nearly the opposite of what Scripture presents. With respect to the perception of mission in Scripture, theologians have had a devastating impact as they remain steeped in unspoken assumptions of a theologically-overflowing and mission-less Scripture. Missionaries have also allowed theologians to set their underlying biblical perspective, and this has had at least a three-fold impact.

1. As a result of following the lead of theologians, many field missionaries continue to teach a theologically-filled and mission-less Bible (Figure 21). This perception of Scripture is so common that indigenous Christians outside of the West often hold this view without realizing it. This particular perception is one of the most errant "Christian" values of our time and it deeply affects the role of the church today—from leadership to laity, from those with long experience in the Christian life to the newly converted.³

2. Cp. Kraft, *Christianity in Culture*, 140–46.
3. Stephen Travis writes, "This is why when we look, for example, at Mk. 2:1–3:6 we find a collection of short paragraphs (known as pericopae), each complete in itself and with no essential connection with what precedes or follows" (Travis, "Form Criticism,"

2. The genuine mission activity in Scripture is drowned out by a hurricane of contemporary "theological" force (line T), leaving Christians and non-Christians with the perception that Scripture has little to say in terms of mission (line M).[4] This massive amount of theological energy further consumes the thoughts of missionaries as they are caught in the flow. This results in missionary churches that have been taught (and themselves teach) the same mission-less conception of Scripture, causing a continued propagation of a fundamentally flawed hermeneutic.

3. Furthermore, many missionaries do not realize that the Bible can (and should) guide their mission practice because they lack the ability to see anything other than theology in the Bible. As a result, they attempt to utilize a hermeneutic that is missionally and spiritually weak in order to answer questions that are often infused with deep spiritual and missional implications.

What might be a more balanced perception of Scripture? The Bible contains significant linguistic, cultural, theological, and missional insights. What is not generally found in Scripture is theology that exists independently of mission or theology that is divorced from missional intentions.[5] Rather, theology supports the practice of mission and is infused with missional purpose.[6]

---

154). This is a good example of how traditional interpretation fails to consider mission, because these passages that parallel Matthew 8–12 have a great deal of continuity. The continuity is over Jesus' attempts to carry out mission and the attempts of leading religious teachers to stop Jesus' mission. The failure to see these passages from a missional perspective causes a cascading failure in terms of the overall interpretation. For the form critics, this is effectively a failure to consider that "mission" is the *Sitz im Leben* ("life-situation") from which the passage arose and the purpose for which the passage was intended.

4. Cp. Wright, *Mission of God*, 30.

5. The exception to this would be those who understand God but are intentionally anti-missional. For example, Jonah is someone who theologically understands God's grace, but has no interest in the missional flow of that grace. Likewise, the religious leaders in the New Testament do at times understand something of God, but their overall concerns demonstrate anti-missional tendencies.

6. Cp. Wright, *Mission of God*, 48–51.

Conclusion

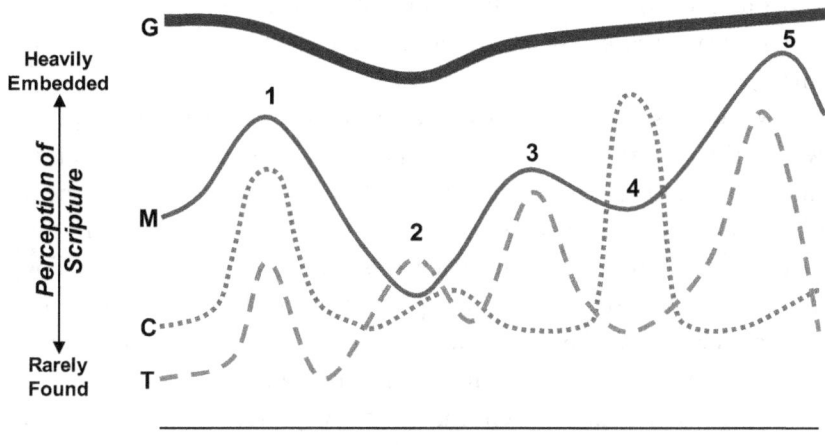

A Selection of Biblical Material
*G—God's Missional Intentions,
M—Human Missional Response, C—Culture, T—Theology*

Figure 22: A Balanced Perception of Scripture

As such, Figure 22 is a more appropriate perception of the nature of Scripture. Given a large selection of Scripture, God's missional intentions are consistently embedded within the larger flow of Scripture (line G). However, the human response to God's missional intentions rises and falls throughout Scripture (line M). Most of the cases in which mission diminishes are due to a lack of human allegiance to the mission of God. Likewise, there are cases in which a basic allegiance to God is missing all-together—a state which itself significantly hampers mission. In these cases, we often find God addressing basic issues hence the "apparent" dip in line G. Additionally shown in Figure 22 are culturally embedded values (line C) that rise and fall according to the many cultural contexts and factors that are found within Scripture. Finally, the theological ideas found in Scripture (line T) also rise and fall and rarely exceed the missionary activity of Scripture because they act in a supporting role to the mission that is taking place.

There are exceptions (such as point 2) when theological understanding is evident, but the human response to mission is low. This is most often due to a failure on the part of the people of God to take on genuine missional concerns that exist in the broader scope of Scripture. There can be cases in which valid understandings of God are expressed and mission takes place in the midst of opposition, such as Jonah 4.[7] Syncretism is a case in which mission and theology are both significantly misunderstood.

Other cases also are illustrated in the diagram, such as point 1 in which there is extensive mission taking place and extensive cultural information. Often the complexity of these two will mean that the associated theological statements are simplistic. Points 3 and 5 are cases of good mission practice in which mission is supported by theology, and the theology serves its proper purpose in furthering mission rather than acting as an end in itself. Likewise, it is more common for theological peaks to take place in the midst of significant missiological activity. Finally, there are times when mission activity takes place in the midst of complex and commonly accepted cultural values, such as point 4. Regardless of the interplay between mission, theology, and culture, the main point is that Figure 22 is a more appropriate model for perceiving the nature of Scripture.

Having considered both diagrams, it is important to keep in mind that these models are tools and as such they include limitations, one of which is simply the fragmented categories of mission, theology, and culture presented in each diagram. Scripture and modern-day mission practice both move much more fluidly among these and other categories since they stem from real life. Consequently, David Bosch called for "missionary theology," nothing more and nothing less, since studying Scripture and doing theology are from beginning to end, intended to serve the mission of God.[8]

In order to move towards missionary theology we must transition from the one-sided concepts of Figure 21 to the more balanced perspective of Figure 22. This is not an easy process, especially given our starting point. However, it is best thought of as a process that takes place through a transformational mindset that builds with continual time and effort.

In moving towards that end, I would like to offer some practical guidelines that will hopefully help facilitate the process. These suggestions are those that I would offer to seminary students with little background in missions, field missionaries reflecting on their experience in times of study, and field missionaries currently active in ministry. As I

---

7. A similar trend occurs in the modern day, but it is often the result of being enamored with theology and apathetic towards mission.

8. Bosch, *Transforming Mission*, 492–96.

address each group, my hope is that I can set forward some suggestions as to how to develop the kind of missiological hermeneutic that has been advocated throughout this work.

1. In many cases, this transformation begins either at an academic or a devotional level with those who do not have a great deal of field experience. Those coming from this background should initially try to suspend their judgment while reading Scripture and allow their mind to wander into the possibilities that may be happening in terms of mission. It is important to dissociate from the traditional theological perspectives that one may already have learned, because these interpretations, in many cases, obscure the actual mission that is found in Scripture. Every effort should be made to shed the theological dogma that has submerged the missional components of the passage, while continuing to test whether or not there are missional elements in the passage. A proper balance must be struck between allowing genuine missional dimensions to surface and avoiding any tendency to impose mission onto Scripture that does not exist.

Reading the full narrative flow of Scripture is extremely important. Often it is helpful to read at least five chapters, but reading ten or more chapters can be very helpful in perceiving the mission that is happening. This is especially true when reading narrative accounts. It is important to allow this to be a process of re-reading Scripture with openness towards the possibility that God's mission is at work. One should be prepared for accounts when the people of God reject God's missionary call. At the same time, there are instances when God's mission takes place in unconventional ways that only God could direct.

The passage should be read more than once. Reading the passage at least three to five times allows the broader strokes of the narrative to become familiar, allowing the interpreter to feel as if he or she is part of the account. While reading, it is important to pray for guidance and expect God to be involved. Praying with a community of fellow Christians focused on the same passage, if possible, can draw upon the strength of combined insights and discussion when gathering with others who are also trying to discern the missional intentions of Scripture. Finally, once the biblical work is underway, field situations should be envisioned (or recounted if the interpreter has mission experience). During this entire exercise, it is helpful to ask basic questions such as, "What is happening in terms of God's mission?"

Those needing assistance should not run immediately to theological commentaries. These typically will not help. If examples are needed, it is most helpful to consider those who have written in Biblical Theology of Mission. Their insights will often act as examples of a missional hermeneutic. Classic works such as those by Roland Allen, Johannes Blauw, David Bosch, Helen Barrett Montgomery and Lesslie Newbigin are very helpful, as well as those from more recent authors such as Richard De Ridder, Dean Gilliland, Arthur Glasser, Roger Hedlund, Paul Hertig, Walter Kaiser, Robert Gallagher, Johannes Nissen, James Okoye, Donald Senior, Carroll Stuhlmueller, Charles Van Engen and Christopher Wright.[9] All of these authors have written works that have been used at the seminary level to help students think through the process of understanding God's missionary activity in Scripture.

2. There is also work to be done for those reflecting from extensive amounts of field experience. From the onset, it is important to assume that Scripture can speak to any field situation. A student in class once claimed that the Bible could not help her with the management of her medical clinic, but it was later observed that the Bible had a great deal to say about healing and practical advice on preventative medical care.[10] The ideas in Scripture that occur consistently can speak to everything from missional dilemmas to future direction. In other words, it is best to use an approach that looks for themes coursing through Scripture, from the Old to the New Testament. As themes are discovered, it is helpful to ask, "How would these themes impact today's missionary situations?" Reliance on a single hermeneutic should also be avoided when interpreting Scripture. Multiple hermeneutics leading to similar conclusions offer greater confidence and narrow the range of interpretations. Furthermore, spiritual disciplines, such as prayer and biblical meditation, should be included among the hermeneutical paths chosen.

---

9. Allen, *Missionary Methods*; Allen, *Spontaneous Expansion*; Blauw, *Missionary Nature of Church*; Bosch, *Witness to the World*; Bosch, *Transforming Mission*; De Ridder, *Discipling the Nations*; Gallagher and Hertig, *Mission in Acts*; Gilliland, *Pauline Theology & Mission Practice*; Glasser, *Announcing the Kingdom*; Hedlund, *God and the Nations*; Kaiser, *Mission in the OT*; Montgomery, *Bible and Missions*; Newbigin, *Open Secret*; Nissen, *NT and Mission*; Okoye, *Israel and the Nations*; Peters, *Biblical Theology of Missions*; Senior and Stuhlmueller, *Biblical Foundations for Mission*; Van Engen, *God's Missionary People*; Van Engen, *Mission on the Way*; Wright, *Mission of God*.

10. Cp. Fountain, *Health, Bible and Church*.

Conclusion

Finally, it is essential to avoid the temptation of assuming that we already know the biblical direction on a given matter. Human agendas can often get in the way of the interpretational process. Therefore, any prior agenda that is brought to Scripture should be released. Like those with strong pre-existing opinions on polygamy, we must assess any agenda that we bring to Scripture. If one has passionately debated colleagues over a passage that is now being addressed, it should be forgotten. Releasing this baggage and coming to Scripture with a learning attitude will allow Scripture to speak in a fuller capacity. If one senses a need to prove an idea, then an agenda is in the background. The interpreter should reflect and try to discern why his or her agenda is so strong. God will speak through Scripture, but only if we are ready to lay down our agendas and listen to God's concerns. For those who find themselves anxious in the process, be at peace—God's central concerns arise again and again within Scripture to help those of us who are hearing impaired.

3. Missionaries actively involved in mission practice hold both great strength and great weakness in further defining a missional hermeneutic. In terms of weakness, there are numerous challenges that draw a missionaries' attention. Given the everyday demands of the mission field, missionaries often feel that it is a luxury for them to engage in Scripture as a means of guiding them in their missional action. The problem is further exacerbated by the fact that some missionaries simply do not explore Scripture in order to guide their missional actions.

However, those engaged in field practice should re-read Scripture in order to address matters that will otherwise consume the time of many Christians who lack significant missional experience. It is important to begin by looking for parallels in the mission activity of Scripture and present-day mission activity. What are the missional parallels? What factors define your mission activity? What are the limitations or barriers in sharing the gospel? How enthusiastic or apathetic is the church towards mission? Looking through Scripture for signs of similar mission practice will offer guidance. What biblical figures faced similar challenges in their own mission? What similar problems did the church face in Scripture with respect to mission?

When numerous parallels are found, accounts having similar cultural elements to a ministry's modern-day culture will help further narrow the relevant passages. An assessment of the cultural parallels in Scripture and the ministry context(s) will be needed. Do the Maasai, for example, have good interpretational instincts for understanding the Pentateuch? They understand the impact of living in drought, the fear of loosing livestock in the midst of drought and the fear of famine. They live in a region that offers very little national military protection, so they understand the need for personal military protection and as such they carry spears and swords.

When considering similar biblical passages, it is helpful to ask what the biblical accounts have to say in terms of guiding mission practice. Do the biblical accounts confirm, refine or correct missionary field practice? Listening to the biblical insights of new Christians is important, not simply because of their unique ethnohermeneutical tendencies, but because they may have well developed "biblical reflexes," especially as they become involved in mission practice and relate their experience to parallel portions of Scripture.[11]

Those involved in mission have a great deal to offer in defining a hermeneutic that will correctly draw out important missional motifs. The parallels of modern-day mission activity are essential for perceiving mission in Scripture and allowing Scripture to speak into today's field practice. Without this, Scripture will most likely be misinterpreted by those lacking mission experience. As such, it is important to actively relate one's field experience to Scripture in order to properly perceive what is taking shape within a given passage. This reverse approach is a critically important step in a missional hermeneutic.

Has your missionary practice given you new eyes to see what you formerly could not see in Scripture? Likewise, are there signs that God is using spiritual activity to reshape your missional perspective? If so, it can be useful to reengage with Scripture to see if your modern-day mission practice and spiritual understandings have reshaped your view of passages that you may not have formerly perceived as missionally significant. These passages are examples of biblical parallels with similar missional and spiritual dynamics. Missionaries should consider documenting and sharing these understandings in order for the church,

---

11. New Christians should be encouraged to follow a missionally strong discipleship model that integrates mission practice, apprenticeship and theological understanding. Those who follow this model without being subject to cultural or religious dogmatism will likely have the capacity to recognize mission in Scripture when it matches similar mission dynamics in their context. Similarly, commonality between the modern-day culture and certain biblical cultures may also allow for good interpretational instincts among those portions of Scripture where a match occurs.

potential converts and other missionaries to gain strong hermeneutical footing. Ultimately, the mission of Scripture cannot be understood apart from mission practice.

4. Finally, the interpretational insights that flow from this process should become a significant part of the teaching content on the mission field. As missionaries develop a new outlook on Scripture, their perceptions in Biblical Theology of Mission offer a proper balance with traditional theological emphases. Missionaries can look back on passages that were once viewed as primarily theological in nature and share the process and the interpretational insights that have been found. If there is significant missional understanding that was once obscured, these matters should be taught to new converts and the church so that a missional hermeneutic can be incorporated into the discipleship process. When missionaries share the transformative power of Scripture upon their mission practice, this integration of mission and theology allows the church to begin with a more balanced view of Scripture. Furthermore, the church is given the freedom of engaging Scripture with a missional hermeneutic. Therefore, missionaries can implicitly demonstrate a missional hermeneutic while leading others to live out active mission practice in the church.

Missionaries and missiologists should confront the secularization and de-missionizing of Scripture, to address what is a long lasting and unforeseen spiritual battle: the disempowerment of mission in Scripture which leads to the disempowerment of mission practice in general. However, there is no reason to propagate the pitfalls of traditional hermeneutics. This hermeneutical struggle must move from a defensive critique to a progressive position that appropriately develops missional hermeneutics to consistently interpret God's missionary mindset for the privilege of continued participation in God's mission. The field of Biblical Theology of Mission has made great strides in trying to correct the above issues, but the field is still comparatively young and the discipline is not perceived as a requirement by many mission agencies or seminaries, even though they often require traditional theological training. The situation is even more critical in terms of the field of hermeneutics, and this has an even deeper effect because the failure to perceive mission at the hermeneutical level is the root problem that spawned the discipline of Biblical Theology of Mission.

Missionaries must be open to perceiving new ways in which the hermeneutical process can take shape. This is necessary, both in order to see God's direction and movement in defining mission, as well as avoiding the tendency of making any hermeneutic overly rigid. Missionaries can begin this process by remaining open to the insights and the underlying hermeneutics that are displayed by new converts. It will be important to properly decipher good and bad hermeneutical directions, and we should expect some insights and ideas to feel unfamiliar.

Finally, we must actively end the trend of being closet Christians when it comes to hermeneutics, at the very least to provide continuity between academic missiological training and field practice. God and the missional community must be included as active agents in the hermeneutical process. Biblical interpretation cannot remain the role of the individual separated from the trusted community who perceive and understand God's mission. The true nature of any missionary is that of a spiritual ambassador crossing barriers to bring the good news of Jesus Christ to those who would like to know the risen Savior. The missional community, as a spiritual people, must embrace the active agency of God in the problems, joys, and everyday lives of the new convert as well as the mature missional church. We are a spiritual people, called by faith to faithfully take Christ's message to the nations. Our hermeneutics must not only reflect our missional and spiritual nature, but our hermeneutics must be a visible witness that reflects our faith in the living God who is invited to inform and speak into our understanding even as we seek to interpret God's revelation.

Appendix A

The Promise to Bless all Nations

Table 12: Outline of Themes in Genesis

Themes	Abraham	Isaac	Jacob	Joseph
Promise given *miraculously* in the midst of weakness	12:1–3—fear of being foreign, of famine, of death over wife 18:13–19—fear for Lot and loss of military ally; mistreatment of righteous 22:2–18—fear for loss of Son, promise as a nation, care as you grow older	22:18—fear of death! 26:2–24—fear of being foreign, of famine, of death over wife (*identical* to Abraham)	28:13–15—fear of death from Esau's anger; fear of becoming a foreigner 31:3, 21—A veiled promise of the land is given as Jacob leaves under God's command in fear of Laban and his sons.	37—Dream given sends Joseph on his way. 41—Dream interpreted allows for major influence
Blessing related to Obedience	12:4–6—leaves 18:19—expected 22:16–18—obeys	26:5–6—Isaac stays in the land as did Abraham	31:3–18—Jacob obeys and leaves 35:2—no gods	Gen 39 Gen 40 Gen 41
Nations bless the people of God (land is offered 4 times by the nations)	12:17–20—Pharaoh interprets the signs of God and relates them to Abraham. 20:1–18–Abimelech speaks to God and learns that Abraham is a prophet. (20:15)—Land of Abimelech given (21:22–23, 32–34) results in witness to Philistines 23:5–11—Burial cave offered by Ephron (Hittite)	26:11—Isaac's family protected by Abimelech despite the same lie by father and son. 26:15, 19–22—Isaac among Abraham's wells so land theme is here also.	34:1–31—A mixed blessing given Dinah, but all are killed even though Shechem (and other Hivites) are open to the sign of covenant.	47:5–6—King of Egypt offer the very best land.

Themes	Abraham	Isaac	Jacob	Joseph
Blessing to all the nations of the earth interpreted	24:6–7—Does not mention the blessing to all the nations. 25:5—no details given.	27:29; 28:3–4—Does not mention this blessing and claims there is nothing more. Wants the nations to bow (similar verb in Hebrew)	32:12; 48:3–4 – Does not mention the blessing to all the nations. 49:8–10, 22–26—Jacob's military focus is reduced compared to Isaac. Judah has a conquest focus but is prophetic (10, 22) is an image of nations being blessed.	50:24—Joseph focuses on the land in his death, but he likely never heard the promise to the nations. 45:5–8; 50:20–21—Joseph sees his missional purpose in all that he has gone through.
Mission ceases with Power and Security	12:20—Pharaoh removes Abraham from Egypt 14—Military campaign (Is this protection of Lot or revenge?) Abraham is *not* involved until Lot is taken, so the life of others is not a priority.	26:16—Isaac *accumulates* beyond his needs. His power becomes a threat!	34:1–31—Levi and Simeon use military power through spiritual abuse! (compare Gen 48:22 [NCV], 49:5–7) Jacob likely kills solely because his sons lives are at risk (or he is lying)	47:13–26—Joseph builds economic power through hunger

303

Themes	Abraham	Isaac	Jacob	Joseph
Mission takes place in the midst of weakness (as the nations see God's blessing	18:18–33—Prays for Sodom and Gomorrah (19:29) Lot is saved because God remember Abraham! 21:22–23—Philistines *see* God's *blessing* and make a treaty 24:12–60—chief servant (12–15, 26–27) prays, understands God and witnesses (30–48) to Laban and Rebekah; Laban follows (50–51); servant praises God (52) and Rebekah is blessed (60) 21:13; 25:1–6—Abraham marries again and some of the children become nations (Fulfillment of Abraham's name and witness to family may have been further mission).	26:12–33—Isaac is willing to make peace despite being forced out (not a strong witness, but Isaac does not resort to force)	30:25–31:55—Jacob is blessed, in the midst of Laban's shifting agreements (30:25–35), and God's hand on Jacob is obvious. (31:24, 52–53) Laban knows God! 35:2—calls for no foreign gods 47:7–10 Joseph introduces Jacob to the king of Egypt and he twice blesses him. 50:7–11 The Canaanites realize that someone of great stature is being buried—Jacob's greatest witness may have been in his death.	39:3—Potiphar 39:21–23—trust by warden 40:8—wine-server and baker witness God's power in dreams 41:6—King of Egypt witness God's power to interpret dreams 41:37–40—King of Egypt witness Joseph's wisdom and God leading 41:45–50—Wife of Joseph is from Egypt; her father is a Priest of On 41:56–57—Food for the world!

Themes	Abraham	Isaac	Jacob	Joseph
Tragedy related to beauty causes mission to cease	12:10–20; 20:1–18—both times Abraham lies and claims that his wife is his sister (*3 times Abr. & Isaac lie to nations, 3 times later the nations afflict the people of God*)	26:7–10—Isaac likewise lies and claims that his wife is his sister	Gen 34:2–3—Dinah is violated by Shechem but he asks to marry her. All in his town are killed.	38:18 Tamar prostitutes herself to Judah 39:6–18 Joseph's handsomeness

Table 13: Occurrences of the Promise with respect to Land, Growth, and Blessing the Nations

Passage	Land	Growth	Nations	Speaker	Notes
Gen 12:1–3		X	X	YHWH	
Gen 12:7	X			YHWH	
Gen 13:14–17	X	X		YHWH	First account in which YHWH promises land and growth solely—Gen 13:13 prepares for Gen 18
Gen 15:4–20	X			YHWH	
Gen 17:3–21	X	X	x	YHWH	The blessing of Ishmael blesses other nations.
Gen 18:13–19		X	X	YHWH	Promise to Sarah relates to growth (v.18) and God hears Abraham's prayer in v.29!!!
Gen 20:15	x		x	Abimelech (Philistine)	The nations (via Abimelech) offer land to Abraham! See also 21:22–23, 32–34
Gen 22:2–18		X	X	Elohim & Angel of YHWH	The promise of growth is seen as "the Lord provides" a ram saving Isaac. Also explicitly promised in 22:17.
Gen 23:5–11	x			Ephron (Hittite)	Ephron the Hittite offers Abraham the best tomb available in order to bury Sarah
Gen 24:7	x			Abraham	Abraham repeats/interprets God's promise
Gen 26:2–24	X	X	X	YHWH	26:22, 23–24 echo the focus on land and growth

306

Promise of:	Land	Growth	Nations	Speaker	Notes
Passage					
Gen 27:29			X	Isaac	Isaac repeats/interprets God's promise
Gen 28:3–4	X	X		Isaac	Isaac again repeats/interprets God's promise
Gen 28:13–15	X	X	X	YHWH	
Gen 31:3–18	x			YHWH	An inference of the "giving of the land" (compare 37:1)
Gen 32:12		X		Jacob	Jacob repeats/interprets God's promise
Gen 34:1–31	x	x	x	Shechem (Hivite)	Land, growth, and blessing are all offered, and acceptance of circumcision, but revenge takes place
Gen 35:11–12	X	X		God	The promise follows Simeon and Levi's revenge which caused Jacob to have a fear of being destroyed
Gen 41–50		x	x	(God)	The promise to bless all of the nations of the earth is narratively displayed in Joseph's life for all to see, and growth flows from that
Gen 47:5–6	X			Pharaoh	Offers the best land to Joseph's family
Gen 48:3–4	X	X		Jacob	Jacob repeats/interprets God's promise to Joseph
Num 24:9		X	X	Balaam	
Ps 72:17			X	David	
Isa 61:9			X	Isaiah	
Acts 3:25			X	Peter	
Gal 3:8			X	Paul	

There are vast references to the land that followed Genesis, but in most cases the phrase, "the land . . . promised to your forefathers" becomes the equivalent of a proper name. As such, it is primarily the references in Exodus and the ending references of Joshua that are focus specifically on reminding the people of God of the promise (Exod 3:8, 17; 13:5, 11; 33:1–3; Num 11:12; Deut 1:35; 6:18, 23; 7:13; 8:1; 11:9, 21; 19:18; 26:2–3, 9,15; 28:11; 31:7, 20; Josh 1:6; 21:43; Judg 2:1).

Table 14: Detailed Summary of the God-Given Promises in the Old Testament

	Gen 12:1–4 (NSRV)	18:18–19 (NSRV)	22:16b-18 (NSRV)	26:3–5 (NSRV)	28:14 (NSRV)	Num 24:9 (NLT)
Declared by:	God to Abraham	God to Abraham	God to Abraham (& Isaac)	God to Isaac	God to Jacob	God & Balaam to Balak
Promise of Land	Go from your country and your kindred and your father's house to the land that I will show you.			for to you and to your descendants I will give all these lands, and I will fulfill the oath that I swore to your father Abraham.	the land on which you lie I will give to you and to your offspring;	
Promise of Growth	2 I will make of you a great nation, and I will bless you, and make your name great, so that you will be a blessing.	seeing that Abraham shall become a great and mighty nation,	17 I will indeed bless you, and I will make your offspring as numerous as the stars of heaven and as the sand that is on the seashore.	4 I will make your offspring as numerous as the stars of heaven, and will give to your offspring all these lands;	14 and your offspring shall be like the dust of the earth, and you shall spread abroad to the west and to the east and to the north and to the south;	23:10a Who can count Jacob's descendants, as numerous as dust? Who can count even a fourth of Israel's people?

	Gen 12:1–4 (NSRV)	18:18–19 (NSRV)	22:16b–18 (NSRV)	26:3–5 (NSRV)	28:14 (NSRV)	Num 24:9 (NLT)
Protection	3 I will bless those who bless you, and the one who curses you I will curse;		And your offspring shall possess the gate of their enemies,	3 Reside in this land as an alien, and I will be with you, and will bless you;	15 Know that I am with you and will keep you wherever you go, and will bring you back to this land; for I will not leave you until I have done what I have promised you."	23:8, 21–23; 24:8–9 24:8b He devours all the nations that oppose him, 24:9 Blessed is everyone who blesses you, O Israel, and cursed is everyone who curses you."
Agent	and in you	in him	18 and by your offspring	and through your offspring,	in you and in your offspring.	
Recipient	all the families of the earth	and all the nations of the earth	all the nations of the earth	all the nations of the earth	and all the families of the earth	24:9 everyone
Verb	shall be blessed."	shall be blessed	shall gain blessing for themselves,	shall gain blessing for themselves	shall be blessed	

	Gen 12:1–4 (NSRV)	18:18–19 (NSRV)	22:16b-18 (NSRV)	26:3–5 (NSRV)	28:14 (NSRV)	Num 24:9 (NLT)
Because	4 So Abram went, as the Lord had told him; and Lot went with him.	19 . . . for I have chosen him, that he may charge his children and his household after him to keep the way of the Lord by doing righteousness and justice; so that the Lord may bring about for Abraham what he has promised him."	Because you have done this, and have not withheld your son, your only son. . . . . . . because you have obeyed my voice."	5 because Abraham obeyed my voice and kept my charge, my commandments, my statutes, and my laws."	compare Gen 35:1–15 (Gen 32:22–32)	23:9 I see them from the cliff tops; I watch them from the hills. I see a people who live by themselves, set apart from other nations. 23:10b Let me die like the righteous; let my life end like theirs."

Table 15: Detailed Summary of the
Re-Statement or Interpretation of the Promises

Declared by:	Abraham calls his servant	Isaac blesses Jacob	Isaac sends off Jacob	Jacob recounts God's message	Jacob blesses Judah, Joseph	Joseph to his brothers
	24:7 (NSRV)	27:29 (NSRV)	28:4 (NSRV)	32:12; cf. 48:4	49:8–10, 22–26	45:5–8; 50:20
Reinterpretation	The Lord, the God of heaven, who took me from my father's house and from the land of my birth, and who spoke to me and swore to me, "To your offspring I will give this land,"	28 May God give you of the dew of heaven, and of the fatness of the earth, and plenty of grain and wine. 29a Let peoples serve you, and nations bow down to you. Be lord over your brothers, and may your mother's sons bow down to you.	May God Almighty bless you and make you fruitful and numerous, that you may become a company of peoples. 4 May he give to you the blessing of Abraham, to you and to your offspring with you, so that you may take possession of the land where you now live as an alien—land that God gave to Abraham.	31:12 I will surely do you good, and make your offspring as the sand of the sea, which cannot be counted because of their number. 48:4 I am going to make you fruitful and increase your numbers; I will make of you a company of peoples, and will give this land to your offspring after you for a perpetual holding.	49:10 The scepter shall not depart from Judah, nor the ruler's staff from between his feet, until tribute comes to him; and the obedience of the peoples is his (NRSV). 49:22 Joseph is a fruitful tree, a fruitful tree beside a fountain. His branches reach over the wall (NLT). 49:25–26 [Many blessings will rest] on the brow of him who was set apart from his brothers.	45:7 God has sent me here to keep you and your families alive so that you will become a great nation. 50:20b He brought me to the high position I have today so I could save the lives of many people (NLT).

312

Declared by:	Abraham calls his servant	Isaac blesses Jacob	Isaac sends off Jacob	Jacob recounts God's message	Jacob blesses Joseph	Jacob blesses Judah, Joseph	Joseph to his brothers
Protection	he will send his angel before you, and you shall take a wife for my son from there.	29b Cursed be everyone who curses you, and blessed be everyone who blesses you!"	Go at once to Paddan-aram to the house of Bethuel, your mother's father (to escape from Esau)	48:5 Therefore your two sons, who were born to you in the land of Egypt before I came to you in Egypt, are now mine; Ephraim and Manasseh shall be mine, just as Reuben and Simeon are.		49:23 He has been attacked by archers, who shot at him and harassed him. 29:24 But his bow remained strong, and his arms were strengthened by the Mighty One of Jacob, the Shepherd, the Rock of Israel.	50:20a God turned into good what you meant for evil (NLT).

Appendix B

Chart of All Known Polygamists in Scripture

Table 16 is an attempt to list all known polygamists in the Bible, and expands upon Pamela Mann's work. However, this table differs from her work by considering the positive and negative traits of the polygamists whenever possible. In Mann's work, she considers the positive or negative effect of polygamy upon the family.[1]

---

1. Mann, "Biblical Understanding of Polygamy," 16.

Table 16: All Known Polygamists in the Bible

+ Good
- Bad
? Unsure

		Number of wives	References	Names of Wives	Comments
?	Lamech	2	Gen 4:19	Adah, Zillah	He killed a young man who attacked and wounded him (Gen 4:23).
+ -	Abraham	More than 3	Gen 16:2; 25:1, 6	Sarah, Hagar, Keturah, unnamed slave wives	(+) Faithful to God in leaving Ur. (-)Lied twice about Sarah being his wife. May have allowed Sarah to vengefully act upon Hagar. Keturah and other wives are after Sarah's death. (+) Faithful to God with Isaac.
- +	Esau	2	Gen 26:34; 28:9	Judith, Basemath, and later Mahalath	(-)Both wives were foreign women (Hittites). (+)Esau hated Jacob but later reconciled without bloodshed.
- +	Jacob	4	Gen 29:28; 30:3, 9	Leah, Rachel, Bilhah (Rachel's maid), Zilpah (Leah's maid)	(-)Stole Esau's birthright. Devoted to Rachel. Jacob did not want to marry Leah, but was tricked by Laban. (+)Progeny from four wives and Joseph's half-Egyptian children become the 12 tribes of Israel.
+	Moses	2	Exod 2:21; Num 12:1	Zipporah and the Cushite Woman	There is no indication that Zipporah and the Cushite woman are the same person. Moses is criticized for his later marriage, but God defends him in general (Num 12).

+	Good				
−	Bad				
?	Unsure	Number of wives	References	Names of Wives	Comments
?	Jair	?	Judg 10:4	Unknown	There is no assurance he was a polygamist, but he had 30 sons and was a Judge, so polygamy is more likely than divorces.
?	Ibzan	?	Judg 12:8–9	Unknown	Like Jair above, there is no assurance he was a polygamist, but he had 30 sons and daughters and was a Judge.
?	Ashur	2	1 Chr 4:5	Helah, Naarah	
+ −	Gideon	Many	Judg 8:30–31	Unnamed wives and a slave wife in Shechem	(+) Was faithful in following God as one of the Judges, (−)but is involved in idolatry at the end of his life.
+	Elkanah	2	1 Sam 1:2	Hannah and Peninnah	(+)Loved Hannah. (+)Hannah is the mother of Samuel, and a deeply spiritual woman.
+ −	David	More than 8	1 Sam 18:27; 25:39–44; 2 Sam 3:2–5; 5:13; 11:27; 1 Chr 14:3	Michal, Abigail, Ahinoam, Maacah, Haggith, Abital, Eglah, Bathsheba, and more unnamed wives and slave wives married in Jerusalem	Michal is Saul's younger daughter who is taken away. Abigail is the widow of Nabal from Carmel. Ahinoam is from Jezreel. Maacah is the daughter of Talmai, king of Geshur! David is permitted to *remain married* to Bathsheba in spite of the fact that (1) (−) he committed adultery with her, (2) (−) arranged for the death of her faithful husband, Uriah the Hittite and 3) he is already a polygamist and leader of Israel. (+) In spite of this, David is called a "man after God's own heart!"

+ Good
− Bad
? Unsure

	Name	Number of wives	References	Names of Wives	Comments
+ −	Solomon	1000	1 Kgs 11:1–8	700 wives and 300 slave wives	(+) Supposedly, he was the wisest man of all time. (-)In spite of this, he married foreign women who influenced him enough that he setup idolatrous gods in Israel. He taxed the Israelites heavily.
?	Rehoboam	More than 2	2 Chr 11:18–23	Mahalath and Maacah (David's granddaughters), other wives and slave wives	Solomon's son was a young and inexperienced King of Judah who listened to young counsel and ignored older and wiser counselors.
+	Abijah	14	2 Chr 13:21	14 unnamed wives	Good King of Judah. Rejected the false gods of Israel.
−	Jehoram	More than 1	2 Chr 21:6, 14–17	Married one of King Ahab's daughters and other un-named wives	Bad King of Judah
+ −	Joash	2	2 Chr 24:3	Two unnamed wives	"Joash did what was pleasing in the Lord's sight throughout the lifetime of Jehoiada the priest. Jehoiada chose two wives for Joash" (2 Chr 24:2–3). Later allows idolatry and kills Zechariah (son of Jehoiada the priest 2 Chr 24:17–21)
−	Ahab	Uncertain	1 Kgs 16:31; 20:3–7	Jezebel (the daughter of King Ethbaal of the Sidonian), and other un-named wives	Extremely Bad King of Israel (1 Kgs 16:30–33). Ahab is the only recorded King of Israel who had multiple wives.

+ Good
− Bad
? Unsure

	Name	Number of wives	References	Names of Wives	Comments
−	Jehoiachin		2 Kgs 24:15	Queen mother and other wives	Bad King of Judah who was defeated by Nebuchadnezzar (2 Kgs 24:9–12)
−	Zedekiah		Jer 38:23	Only "wives" are mentioned	The last King of Judah who would not listen to Jeremiah. Zedekiah watched as his sons were killed by Babylonian forces after which he was tortured and bound (2 Kings 25:6–7)
−	Belshazzar		Dan 5:2, 23		Foreign King, Nebuchadnezzar successor. God destroys him over issues of idolatry but polygamy is never mentioned.
	Jerahmeel	2	1 Chr 2:26	Unnamed first wife and Atarah	The son of Kish, and a Levite (1 Chr 24:29). He gave his name (meaning "may God have compassion") to a group of non-Israelites in southern Judah. Is this mission?

Appendix C

Comparison of Acts 10 and Acts 11

The following shows the parallels and discrepancies in Acts 10 and 11. The differences in highlighting correspond to: *Cornelius*, **Missional Reversals**, Parallel Accounts, and Peter and Missional Transformation.

Acts 10:1–48, NLT	Acts 11:1–26, NLT
In Caesarea there lived a Roman army officer named Cornelius, who was a captain of the Italian Regiment. *He was a devout, God-fearing man, as was everyone in his household. He gave generously to the poor and prayed regularly to God.* One afternoon about three o'clock, he had a vision in which he saw an angel of God coming toward him. "Cornelius!" the angel said. Cornelius stared at him in terror. "What is it, sir?" he asked the angel. *And the angel replied, "Your prayers and gifts to the poor have been received by God as an offering!* Now send some men to Joppa, and summon a man named Simon Peter. He is staying with Simon, a tanner who lives near the seashore." As soon as the angel was gone, Cornelius called two of his household servants and a devout soldier, one of his personal attendants.	Soon the news reached the apostles and other believers in Judea that the Gentiles had received the word of God. But when Peter arrived back in Jerusalem, the Jewish believers criticized him. "You entered the home of Gentiles and even ate with them!" they said. Then Peter told them exactly what had happened.
He told them what had happened and sent them off to Joppa. The next day as Cornelius's messengers were nearing the town, Peter went up on the flat roof to pray.	"I was in the town of Joppa," he said, "and while I was praying,
It was about noon, and he was hungry. But while a meal was being prepared, he fell into a trance.	I went into a trance and saw a vision.

319

Acts 10:1-48, NLT	Acts 11:1-26, NLT
He saw the sky open, and something like a large sheet was let down by its four corners.	Something like a large sheet was let down by its four corners from the sky. And it came right down to me.
In the sheet were all sorts of animals, reptiles, and birds.	When I looked inside the sheet, I saw all sorts of small animals, wild animals, reptiles, and birds.
Then a voice said to him, "Get up, Peter; kill and eat them."	And I heard a voice say, 'Get up, Peter; kill and eat them.'
"No, Lord," Peter declared. "I have never eaten anything that our Jewish laws have declared impure and unclean."	"'No, Lord,' I replied. 'I have never eaten anything that our Jewish laws have declared impure or unclean.'
But the voice spoke again: "Do not call something unclean if God has made it clean."	"But the voice from heaven spoke again: 'Do not call something unclean if God has made it clean.'
The same vision was repeated three times. Then the sheet was suddenly pulled up to heaven.	This happened three times before the sheet and all it contained was pulled back up to heaven.
Peter was very perplexed. What could the vision mean?	?
Just then the men sent by Cornelius found Simon's house. Standing outside the gate, they asked if a man named Simon Peter was staying there.	"Just then three men who had been sent from Caesarea arrived at the house where we were staying.
Meanwhile, as Peter was puzzling over the vision,	?
the Holy Spirit said to him, "Three men have come looking for you. Get up, go downstairs, and go with them without hesitation. Don't worry, for I have sent them."	The Holy Spirit told me to go with them and not to worry that they were Gentiles.

| Acts 10:1-48, NLT | Acts 11:1-26, NLT |

So Peter went down and said, "I'm the man you are looking for. <u>Why have you come?</u>" They said, *"We were sent by Cornelius, a Roman officer. He is a devout and God-fearing man, well respected by all the Jews.* <u>A holy angel instructed him to summon you to his house</u> **so that he can hear your message.**" So Peter invited the men to stay for the night.

The next day he went with them, accompanied by some of the brothers from Joppa. They arrived in Caesarea the following day. Cornelius was waiting for them and had called together his relatives and close friends. As Peter entered his home, Cornelius fell at his feet and worshiped him. But Peter pulled him up and said, "Stand up! I'm a human being just like you!" So they talked together and went inside, where many others were assembled. <u>Peter told them, "You know it is against our laws for a Jewish man to enter a Gentile home like this or to associate with you. But God has shown me that I should no longer think of anyone as impure or unclean. So I came without objection as soon as I was sent for.</u> *Now tell me why you sent for me."*

These six brothers here accompanied me, and we soon entered the home of the man who had sent for us.

Cornelius replied, *"Four days ago I was praying in my house about this same time, three o'clock in the afternoon. Suddenly, a man in dazzling clothes was standing in front of me. He told me, 'Cornelius, your prayer has been heard, and your gifts to the poor have been noticed by God!* <u>Now send messengers to Joppa, and summon a man named Simon Peter.</u>

He told us how an angel had appeared to him in his home and had told him, 'Send messengers to Joppa, and summon a man named Simon Peter.

321

Acts 10:1–48, NLT

He is staying in the home of Simon, a tanner who lives near the seashore.' So I sent for you at once, and it was good of you to come. Now we are all here, waiting before God to hear the message the Lord has given you."

Then Peter replied, *"I see very clearly that God shows no favoritism. In every nation he accepts those who fear him and do what is right.*

This is the message of <u>Good News for the people of Israel</u>—that there is peace with God through Jesus Christ, who is Lord of all. You know what happened throughout Judea, beginning in Galilee, after John began preaching his message of baptism. And you know that God anointed Jesus of Nazareth with the Holy Spirit and with power. Then Jesus went around doing good and healing all who were oppressed by the devil, for God was with him. "And we apostles are witnesses of all he did throughout Judea and in Jerusalem. They put him to death by hanging him on a cross, but God raised him to life on the third day. Then God allowed him to appear, not to the general public, but to us whom God had chosen in advance to be his witnesses. We were those who ate and drank with him after he rose from the dead. And he ordered us to preach everywhere and to testify that Jesus is the one appointed by God to be the judge of all—the living and the dead. He is the one all the prophets testified about, saying that everyone who believes in him will have their sins forgiven through his name."

Even as Peter was saying these things, the Holy Spirit fell upon all who were listening to the message.

Acts 11:1–26, NLT

He will tell you how you and everyone in your household can be saved!'

"As I began to speak," Peter continued, "the Holy Spirit fell on them, just as he fell on us at the beginning.

Acts 10:1-48, NLT | Acts 11:1-26, NLT

Then I thought of the Lord's words when he said, 'John baptized with water, but you will be baptized with the Holy Spirit.'

The Jewish believers who came with Peter were amazed that the gift of the Holy Spirit had been poured out on the Gentiles, too. For they heard them speaking in tongues and praising God. Then Peter asked, "Can anyone object to their being baptized, now that they have received the Holy Spirit just as we did?" So he gave orders for them to be baptized in the name of Jesus Christ.

Afterward Cornelius asked him to stay with them for several days."

And since God gave these Gentiles the same gift he gave us when we believed in the Lord Jesus Christ, who was I to stand in God's way?" When the others heard this, they stopped objecting and began praising God. They said, "We can see that God has also given the Gentiles the privilege of repenting of their sins and receiving eternal life."

Meanwhile, the believers who had been scattered during the persecution after Stephen's death traveled as far as Phoenicia, Cyprus, and Antioch of Syria. They preached the word of God, but only to Jews. However, some of the believers who went to Antioch from Cyprus and Cyrene began preaching to the Gentiles about the Lord Jesus. The power of the Lord was with them, and a large number of these Gentiles believed and turned to the Lord. When the church at Jerusalem heard what had happened, they sent Barnabas to Antioch. When he arrived and saw this evidence of God's blessing, he was filled with joy, and he encouraged the believers to stay true to the Lord. Barnabas was a good man, full of the Holy Spirit and strong in faith. And many people were brought to the Lord. Then Barnabas went on to Tarsus to look for Saul. When he found him, he brought him back to Antioch. Both of them stayed there with the church for a full year, teaching large crowds of people. (It was at Antioch that the believers were first called Christians.)

Glossary

Evangelism — A focus within the field of mission activity that attempts to communicate the message of reconciliation to God through Jesus with those who have little or no allegiance to God, primarily through some verbal means, such as discussion, dialogue, proclamation, or story telling.

Exegete — An exegete is someone who is generally trained to use a particular hermeneutic. When applying his or her hermeneutic in the process of interpreting Scripture, this is referred to as "exegesis."

Hermeneutic — Hermeneutics traditionally deals with the methods, guidelines or principles used in the process of interpreting Scripture.

Intertextual — This is the mention or quotation of biblical passages within later portions of Scripture. Unlike synoptic accounts in the Gospels, intertextual quotations apply Scripture in a new context and in doing so; the author demonstrates some type of underlying hermeneutic.

Mission — For the most part, I prefer Charles Van Engen's definition of mission, which is based upon a statement made by Stephen Neill.[2] Mission is defined as follows: "God's mission works primarily through the People of God intentionally crossing barriers from Church to non-church, faith to non-faith, to proclaim by word and deed the coming of the Kingdom of God in Jesus Christ through the Church's participation in God's mission of reconciling people to God, to themselves, to each other, and to the world and gathering them into the Church through repentance and faith in Jesus Christ by the work of the Holy Spirit with a view to the

---

2. Neill, *How My Mind Changed*.

Glossary

transformation of the world as a sign of the coming of the Kingdom in Jesus Christ."[3] I do not define mission in terms of cross-cultural engagement. Mission may be cross-cultural but it is certainly no requirement. Bosch is correct that "mission was understood in the typical, activistic Western categories of the crossing of (remote) geographical boundaries. . . . The Church does not become missionary only when she crosses geographical boundaries. As a matter of fact, she may cross such boundaries without becoming missionary in the true sense of the word. She may be crossing geographical frontiers without crossing the many other frontiers that count so much more."[4] More importantly, I claim that mission can and does take place within one's own cultural context by indigenous workers—see also "Evangelism."

Nations Throughout this research the term "nations" refers to those who are outside of the people of God and in need of God's direction and salvation. The boundary between the people of God and the nations is not always clear but the boundary is primarily defined in terms of a person or groups allegiance to God. In the Old Testament, it was those from Israel who most often held high allegiance to God and witnessed to the nations, but there are non-Israelites who also held allegiance to God. Similarly, in the New Testament, the church often held high allegiance to God and witnessed to those who did not know God. The nations, however, are those who held little allegiance to God and were often in need of missionary help to know God.

---

3. Van Engen and Redford, "Syllabus," 25.
4. Bosch, "Hermeneutical Principles," 440, 51.

Bibliography

Achtemeier, Paul J., Harper and Row Publishers, and Society of Biblical Literature, eds. *Harper's Bible Dictionary.* 1st ed. San Francisco, CA: Harper and Row, 1985. Logos CD-ROM.

Ad Gentes; Decreto Conciliare Sull'attivita Missionaria Della Chiesa. Vol. 153, Il Pastore, Serie 1,. Roma: Edizione Paoline, 1966.

Ådna, Jostein, and Hans Kvalbein. *The Mission of the Early Church to Jews and Gentiles,* Wissenschaftliche Untersuchungen Zum Neuen Testament 127. Tübingen, Germany: Mohr Siebeck, 2000.

Adutchum, Ofusu A. "The Church and the Issue of Polygamy." *Africa Theological Journal* 22 (1993) 21–33.

Aland, Kurt. *Greek-English New Testament: Greek Text Novum Testamentum Graece, in the Tradition of Eberhard Nestle and Erwin Nestle.* 8th rev. ed. Stuttgart, Germany: Deutsche Bibelgesellschaft, 1994.

Allen, Diogenes. *Spiritual Theology: The Theology of Yesterday for Spiritual Help Today.* Cambridge, MA: Cowley, 1997.

Allen, Roland. *Missionary Methods; St. Paul's or Ours?* Grand Rapids: Eerdmans, 1962.

———. *The Spontaneous Expansion of the Church: And the Causes Which Hinder It.* Grand Rapids: Eerdmans, 1962.

Amstutz, John L. "Humanitarianism with a Point." In *Missionary Care: Counting the Cost for World Evangelization,* edited by Kelly S. O'Donnell, 37–40. Pasadena, CA: William Carey, 1992.

Anderson, Gerald H. *The Theology of the Christian Mission.* 1st ed. New York: McGraw-Hill, 1961.

Archer, Kenneth J. "Pentecostal Hermeneutics and a Critique of the Evangelical Historical-Critical Method." Paper presented at the 2002 Annual Meeting of the Society for Pentecostal Studies (SPS), Southeastern College, Lakeland, FL, March 14–16, 2002 2002.

Augustine, Edmund Hill, John E. Rotelle, and Augustinian Heritage Institute. *The Works of Saint Augustine: A Translation for the 21st Century.* Translated by Edmund Hill. Edited by John E. Rotelle. Brooklyn: New City, 1990.

Bailey, Kenneth E. *The Cross & the Prodigal: Luke 15 through the Eyes of Middle Eastern Peasants.* 2d ed. Downers Grove, IL: InterVarsity, 2005.

———. *Finding the Lost: Cultural Keys to Luke 15.* St. Louis: Concordia, 1992.

———. *Jacob & the Prodigal: How Jesus Retold Israel's Story.* Downers Grove, IL: InterVarsity, 2003.

———. *Poet & Peasant; and, through Peasant Eyes: A Literary-Cultural Approach to the Parables in Luke.* Combined ed. 2 vols. Grand Rapids: Eerdmans, 1999.

Barth, Karl. *Credo.* New York: Charles Scribner's, 1962.

Bibliography

Bashford, J. W. *God's Missionary Plan for the World*. New York; Cincinnati, OH: Eaton & Mains; Jennings & Graham, 1907.

Bauckham, Richard. *Bible and Mission: Christian Witness in a Postmodern World*. Grand Rapids: Baker Academic, 2003.

Beale, Gregory K. "Eden, the Temple, and the Church's Mission in the New Creation." *Journal of the Evangelical Theological Society* 48 (2005) 5-31.

———. *The Right Doctrine from the Wrong Texts? Essays on the Use of the Old Testament in the New*. Grand Rapids: Baker, 1994.

Beeby, H. Daniel. *Canon and Mission*, Christian Mission and Modern Culture. Harrisburg, PA: Trinity, 1999.

———. "A Missional Approach to Renewed Interpretation." In *Renewing Biblical Interpretation*, edited by Craig G. Bartholomew, Colin J. D. Greene, and Karl Möller, 268-83. Grand Rapids: Zondervan, 2000.

Berkouwer, G. C. *Divine Election*. Grand Rapids: Eerdmans, 1960. Logos CD-ROM.

Bevans, Stephen B. "God inside Out: Toward a Missionary Theology of the Holy Spirit." *International Bulletin of Missionary Research* 22 (1998) 102-5.

Blackman, E. C. *The Biblical Basis of the Church's Missionary Enterprise*, Essays on Mission 3. [London]: London Missionary Society, 1961.

Blauw, Johannes. *The Missionary Nature of the Church; a Survey of the Biblical Theology of Mission*. 1st ed. New York: McGraw-Hill, 1962.

Blomberg, Craig L. "The Globalization of Hermeneutics." *Journal of the Evangelical Theological Society* 38 (1995) 581-93.

———. "New Testament Miracles and Higher Criticism: Climbing up the Slippery Slope." *Journal of the Evangelical Theological Society* 27 (1984) 425-38.

Blum, William G. *Forms of Marriage: Monogamy Reconsidered*, Spearhead 101-7. Eldoret, Kenya: AMECEA Gaba, 1989.

Boer, Harry R. "Polygamy." *Frontier* 11 (1968) 24-27.

Bosch, David J. "Reflections on Biblical Models of Mission." In *Toward the Twenty-First Century in Christian Mission*, edited by James M. Phillips and Robert T. Coote, 175-92. Grand Rapids: Eerdmans, 1993.

Bosch, David Jacobus. *Believing in the Future: Toward a Missiology of Western Culture*. 1st US ed, Christian Mission and Modern Culture. Valley Forge, PA: Trinity, 1995.

———. "Hermeneutical Principles in the Biblical Foundation for Mission." *Evangelical Review of Theology* 17 (1993) 437-51.

———. *Transforming Mission: Paradigm Shifts in Theology of Mission*, American Society of Missiology Series 16. Maryknoll, NY: Orbis, 1991.

———. "The Why and How of a True Biblical Foundation for Mission." In *Zending Op Weg Naar de Toekomst*, 33-45. Kampen, Netherlands: Uitgeversmaatschappij J H Kok, 1978.

———. *Witness to the World: The Christian Mission in Theological Perspective*. Atlanta: John Knox, 1980.

Briscoe, Jill. *Jonah and the Worm*. Nashville: Thomas Nelson, 1983.

Brownson, James V. *Speaking the Truth in Love: New Testament Resources for a Missional Hermeneutic*, Christian Mission and Modern Culture. Harrisburg, PA: Trinity, 1998.

Brunner, Emil. *The Word and the World*. New York: Charles Scribner's, 1931.

Burnett, David. *The Healing of the Nations: The Biblical Basis of the Mission of God*. Rev. ed. Carlisle (Cumbria), UK: Paternoster, 1996.

Burrows, William R. "A Seventh Paradigm? Catholics and Radical Inculturation." In *Mission in Bold Humility: David Bosch's Work Considered*, edited by Willem A. Saayman, and J. N. J. (Klippies) Kritzinger, 121–38. Maryknoll, NY: Orbis, 1996.

Buthelezi, Manas. "Polygyny in the Light of the New Testament." *Africa Theological Journal* 2 (1969) 58–70.

Caldwell, Larry W. "Ethnohermenutics: The Author Responds Further." *Journal of Asian Mission* 2 (2000) 135–45.

———. "Syllabus." *Interpreting the Bible in Cross-Cultural Contexts, MT524*. Pasadena, CA: Fuller Theological Seminary, School of Intercultural Studies, 1998.

———. "Towards the New Discipline of Ethnohermeneutics: Questioning the Relevancy of Western Hermeneutical Methods in the Asian Context." *Journal of Asian Mission* 1 (1999) 21–43.

Carey, William. *An Enquiry into the Obligations of Christians to Use Means for the Conversion of the Heathens*. Reprinted from an 1891 facsimile edition of the MDCCXCII original ed. London: Hodder and Stoughton, [1792] 1891.

Carriker, Charles Timothy. *Missão Integral: Uma Teologia Biblica*. São Paulo: Editora Sepal, 1992.

———. *O Caminho Missionário de Deus. Uma Teologia Bíblica de Missões*. São Paulo: Sepal, 2000.

———. *A Visão Missionária da Bíblia. Uma História de Amor*. Viçosa: Editora Ultimato, 2005.

Carson, D. A., ed. *Biblical Interpretation and the Church: Text and Context*. Exeter, UK: Paternoster, 1984. Logos CD-ROM.

Carver, William Owen. *The Bible a Missionary Message; a Study of Activities and Methods*. New York; Chicago: Revell, 1921.

———. *Missions in the Plan of the Ages: Bible Studies in Missions*. 4th ed. Nashville: Broadman, 1951.

Chapman, Colin Gilbert. *Cross and Crescent: Responding to the Challenge of Islam*. Downers Grove, IL: InterVarsity, 2003.

———. "Thinking Biblically About Islam." *Themelios* 3 (1978) 66–78.

Chime, Igwe Kingsley. *Polygamy and Christian Religion*. 2d ed. Enugu, Nigeria: Johnny Harmony, 2002.

Church of England Mission Theological Advisory Group, and Churches Together in Britain and Ireland, eds. *Presence and Prophecy: A Heart for Mission in Theological Education*. London: Church House, 2002.

Colenso, John William. *Remarks on the Proper Treatment of Cases of Polygamy: As Found Already Existing in Converts from Heathenism*. Pietermaritzburg, South Africa: Printed by May & Davis Church Street, 1855.

Cook, Edmund F. *The Missionary Message of the Bible*. Nashville, TN; Richmond, VA: Cokesbury, 1926.

Culver, Robert Duncan. *A Greater Commission: A Theology for World Missions*. Chicago: Moody, 1984.

Currens, Gerald E. "A Policy of Baptizing Polygynists Evaluated." *Africa Theological Journal* 2 (1969) 71–83.

de Groot, A. "One Bible and Many Interpretive Contexts: Hermeneutics in Missiology." In *Missiology: An Ecumenical Introduction; Texts and Contexts of Global Christianity*, edited by Frans J. Verstraelen, Arnulf Camps, Libertus A. Hoedemaker and Marc R. Spindler. Grand Rapids: Eerdmans, 1995.

Bibliography

de Groot, A. T. *The Bible on the Salvation of the Nations.* De Pere, WI: St. Norbert Abbey Press, 1966.
De Ridder, Richard. *Discipling the Nations.* Grand Rapids: Baker, 1975.
———. "The Old Testament Roots of Mission." In *Exploring Church Growth*, edited by Wilbert R. Shenk, 171–80. Grand Rapids: Eerdmans, 1983.
Delany, Patrick. *Reflections Upon Polygamy, and the Encouragement Given to That Practice in the Scriptures of the Old Testament.* 2d ed. London: Printed for C. Rivington, J. Walthoe, and T. Woodward., 1739.
DeYoung, James B., and Sarah Hurty. *Beyond the Obvious: Discover the Deeper Meaning of Scripture.* Critical Issues Series. Gresham, OR: Vision House, 1995.
Dietrich, Walter, and Ulrich Luz. *The Bible in a World Context: An Experiment in Contextual Hermeneutics.* Grand Rapids: Eerdmans, 2002.
Dodd, C. H. *The Old Testament in the New*, Facet Books Biblical Series 3. Philadelphia: Fortress, 1963.
Driver, John. *Understanding the Atonement for the Mission of the Church.* Scottdale, PA: Herald, 1986.
du Preez, Ronald A. G. *Polygamy in the Bible with Implications for Seventh-Day Adventist Missiology.* Berrien Springs, MI: Adventist Theological Society Publications, 1993.
DuBose, Francis M. *God Who Sends: A Fresh Quest for Biblical Mission.* Nashville, TN: Broadman, 1983.
Evans, Craig A. *The Interpretation of Scripture in Early Judaism and Christianity: Studies in Language and Tradition.* London: T. & T. Clark, 2004. Logos CD-ROM.
Evans, Craig A., and James A. Sanders. *Early Christian Interpretation of the Scriptures of Israel: Investigations and Proposals*, Journal for the Study of the New Testament. Supplement Series 148. Sheffield, UK: Sheffield Academic, 1997.
———. *Luke and Scripture: The Function of Sacred Tradition in Luke-Acts.* Minneapolis, MN: Fortress, 1993.
———. *Paul and the Scriptures of Israel*, Journal for the Study of the New Testament. Supplement Series 83. Sheffield, UK: JSOT, 1993.
Fee, Gordon D. *Listening to the Spirit in the Text.* Grand Rapids: Eerdmans, 2000.
Filbeck, David. *Yes, God of the Gentiles, Too: The Missionary Message of the Old Testament.* Wheaton, IL: Billy Graham Center Wheaton College, 1994.
Flannery, Austin. *Documents of Vatican II.* Grand Rapids Mich: Eerdmans, 1975.
Fountain, Daniel E. *Health, the Bible and the Church.* Wheaton, IL: Billy Graham Center Wheaton College, 1989.
Freedman, David Noel, Gary A. Herion, David F. Graf, John David Pleins, and Astrid B. Beck, eds. *Anchor Bible Dictionary.* 1st ed. New York: Doubleday, 1992. Logos CD-ROM.
Frei, Hans W. *The Eclipse of Biblical Narrative; a Study in Eighteenth and Nineteenth Century Hermeneutics.* New Haven, CT: Yale University Press, 1974.
Fuller, Daniel P. "The Holy Spirit's Role in Biblical Interpretation." In *Scripture, Tradition, and Interpretation*, edited by W. Ward Gasque and William Sanford LaSor, 189–98. Grand Rapids: Eerdmans, 1978.
Gallagher, Robert L., and Paul Hertig, eds. *Mission in Acts: Ancient Narratives in Contemporary Context*, American Society of Missiology Series 34. Maryknoll, NY: Orbis, 2004.
Gaskiyane, I. *Polygamy: A Cultural and Biblical Perspective.* Carlisle (Cumbria), UK: Piquant, 2000.

Bibliography

Gasque, W. Ward. "Nineteenth-Century Roots of Contemporary New Testament Criticism." In *Scripture, Tradition, and Interpretation: Essays Presented to Everett F. Harrison by His Students and Colleagues in Honor of His Seventy-Fifth Birthday*, edited by Everett Falconer Harrison, W. Ward Gasque, and William Sanford LaSor, 146–56. Grand Rapids: Eerdmans, 1978.

Gilliland, Dean S. *Pauline Theology & Mission Practice*. Grand Rapids: Baker, 1983.

———, ed. *The Word among Us*. Dallas, TX: Word, 1989.

Gitari, David M. Bp. "The Church and Polygamy." *Transformation* 1 (1984) 3–10.

———. "Rethinking Polygamy: Jesus Spoke against Divorce, Not Polygamy." *Other Side* 24 (1988) 42–43.

Glasser, Arthur F. *Announcing the Kingdom: The Story of God's Mission in the Bible*. Edited by Charles E. Van Engen, Dean S. Gilliland, and Shawn B. Redford. Grand Rapids: Baker Academic, 2003.

———. *Kingdom and Mission: A Biblical Study of the Kingdom of God and the World Mission of His People*. Pasadena, CA: Fuller Theological Seminary, 1989.

Glover, Robert Hall. *The Bible Basis of Missions*. Los Angeles: Bible House of Los Angeles, 1946.

Gnanakan, Kenneth Romesh, ed. *Biblical Theology in Asia*. Bangalore, India: Theological Book Trust for Asia Theological Association, 1995.

———. *Kingdom Concerns: A Biblical Exploration Towards a Theology of Mission*. Bangalore, India: Theological Book Trust, 1989.

Goerner, Henry Cornell. *All Nations in God's Purpose: What the Bible Teaches About Missions*. Nashville, TN: Broadman, 1979.

Gordon, A. J. *The Holy Spirit in Missions*. 4th ed. London: Hodder and Stoughton, 1905.

Guder, Darrell L. *The Incarnation and the Church's Witness*, Christian Mission and Modern Culture. Harrisburg, PA: Trinity, 1999.

Guder, Darrell L., and Lois Barrett. *Missional Church: A Vision for the Sending of the Church in North America*. Grand Rapids: Eerdmans, 1998.

Hahn, Ferdinand. *Mission in the New Testament*, Studies in Biblical Theology 47. Naperville, IL: Alec R. Allenson, 1965.

Harris, R. Laird, Gleason Leonard Archer, and Bruce K. Waltke, eds. *Theological Wordbook of the Old Testament*. Chicago: Moody, 1980. Logos CD-ROM.

Harrison, Everett Falconer, W. Ward Gasque, and William Sanford LaSor, eds. *Scripture, Tradition, and Interpretation: Essays Presented to Everett F. Harrison by His Students and Colleagues in Honor of His Seventy-Fifth Birthday*. Grand Rapids: Eerdmans, 1978.

Hastings, Adrian. *Christian Marriage in Africa; Being a Report Commissioned by the Archbishops of Cape Town, Central Africa, Kenya, Tanzania and Uganda*. London: SPCK, 1973.

Hays, Richard B. *Echoes of Scripture in the Letters of Paul*. New Haven, CT: Yale University Press, 1989.

Hedlund, Roger E. *God and the Nations: A Biblical Theology of Mission in the Asian Context*. Delhi, India: ISPCK, 1997.

———. *The Mission of the Church in the World: A Biblical Theology*. Grand Rapids: Baker, 1991.

Helander, Gunnar. *Must We Introduce Monogamy? A Study of Polygamy as a Mission Problem in South Africa*. Pietermaritzburg, South Africa: Shuter & Shooter, 1958.

Bibliography

Hengel, Martin, and C. K. Barrett. *Conflicts and Challenges in Early Christianity*. Edited by Donald A. Hagner. Harrisburg, PA: Trinity, 1999.

Hesselgrave, David J. "A Missionary Hermeneutic: Understanding Scripture in the Light of World Mission." *International Journal of Frontier Missions* 10 (1993) 17–20.

Hiebert, Paul G. "Critical Contextualization." *International Bulletin of Missionary Research* 11 (1987) 104–12.

———. "Critical Contextualization." *Missiology* 12 (1984) 287–96.

———. *The Missiological Implications of Epistemological Shifts: Affirming Truth in a Modern/Postmodern World*, Christian Mission and Modern Culture. Harrisburg, PA: Trinity, 1999.

Hillman, Eugene. *Polygamy Reconsidered: African Plural Marriage and the Christian Churches*. Maryknoll, NY: Orbis, 1975.

Hitchens, Robert J. *Multiple Marriage: A Study of Polygamy in Light of the Bible*. Elkton, MD: Doulos, 1987.

Holst, Robert. "Polygamy and the Bible." *International Review of Mission* 56 (1967) 205–13.

Holter, Knut. *Yahweh in Africa: Essays on Africa and the Old Testament*, Bible and Theology in Africa 1. New York: Peter Lang, 2000.

Horan, Hubert. "Polygamy Comes Home to Roost." *Missiology* 4 (1976) 443–53.

Horton, Robert F. *The Bible: A Missionary Book*. New ed. Edinburgh, UK: Oliphant, 1908.

Howard, David M. *Student Power in World Missions*. 2d ed. Downers Grove, IL: InterVarsity, 1979.

Hunt, Nancy Rose. "Noise over Camouflaged Polygamy, Colonial Morality Taxation, and a Woman-Naming Crisis in Belgian Africa." *Journal of African History* 32 (1991) 471–94.

Hutchison, William R. *The Modernist Impulse in American Protestantism*. Durham, NC: Duke University Press, 1992.

Jasper, Gerhard. "Polygyny in the Old Testament." *Africa Theological Journal* 2 (1969) 27–57.

Johnston, James, and Samuel Macauley Jackson. *Report of the Centenary Conference on the Protestant Missions of the World: Held in Exeter Hall (June 9th–19th), London, 1888*. 2 vols. New York: Revell, 1888.

Jordan, William George. *The Song and the Soil; or, the Missionary Idea in the Old Testament*. New York: Charles Scribner's, 1913.

Kähler, Martin. *Schriften Zur Christologie Und Mission; Gesamtausgabe Der Schriften Zur Mission*, Theologische Bèucherei Bd. 42. Mèunchen (Munich), Germany: C. Kaiser, 1971.

Kaiser, Walter C. "The Great Commission in the Old Testament." *International Journal of Frontier Missions* 13 (1996) 3–7.

———. "Israel's Missionary Call." In *Perspectives on the World Christian Movement* edited by Ralph D. Winter and Steven C. Hawthorne, 25–33. Pasadena, CA: William Carey, 1992.

———. *Mission in the Old Testament: Israel as a Light to the Nations*. Grand Rapids: Baker, 2000.

———. *Toward Old Testament Ethics*. 1st paperback ed. Grand Rapids: Zondervan, 1983.

Kane, J. Herbert. *Christian Missions in Biblical Perspective*. Grand Rapids: Baker, 1976.

Bibliography

Kanyadago, Peter M. *Evangelizing Polygamous Families: Canonical and African Approaches*, Spearhead 116–118. Eldoret, Kenya: AMECEA Gaba, 1991.

Kanyoro, Rachel Angogo. "Interpreting Old Testament Polygamy through African Eyes." In *The Will to Arise: Women, Tradition, and the Church in Africa*, edited by Mercy Amba Oduyoye and Rachel Angogo Kanyoro, 87–100. Maryknoll, NY: Orbis, 1992.

Kavunkal, Jacob, and F. Hrangkhuma, eds. *Bible and Mission in India Today*. Vol. 1, Foim Series 1. Bandra, Bombay, India: St. Pauls, 1993.

Kearney, Michael. *World View*. Novato, CA: Chandler & Sharp, 1984.

Kirk, J. Andrew. *The Mission of Theology and Theology as Mission*. Valley Forge, PA: Trinity, 1997.

———. *What Is Mission?: Theological Explorations*. Minneapolis, MN: Fortress, 2000.

Kittel, Gerhard, Geoffrey William Bromiley, and Gerhard Friedrich, eds. *Theological Dictionary of the New Testament*. Grand Rapids: Eerdmans, 1964. Logos CD-ROM.

Kiwovele, Judah B. M. "Polygyny as a Problem to the Church in Africa." *Africa Theological Journal* 2 (1969) 7–26.

Klein, William W., Craig L. Blomberg, and Robert L. Hubbard. *Introduction to Biblical Interpretation*. Dallas, TX: Word, 1993. Logos CD-ROM.

Knight, William, Henry Venn, and John Venn. *Memoir of the Rev. H. Venn: The Missionary Secretariat of Henry Venn; Prebendary of St. Paul's, and Honorary Secretary of the Church Missionary Society*. London: Longmans Green, 1880.

Koehler, Ludwig Hugo, Walter Baumgartner, M. E. J. Richardson, and Johann Jakob Stamm, eds. *The Hebrew & Aramaic Lexicon of the Old Testament*. New York: Brill, 1996. Logos CD-ROM.

Köstenberger, Andreas J., and Peter Thomas O'Brien. *Salvation to the Ends of the Earth: A Biblical Theology of Mission*. Vol. 11. Downers Grove, IL: InterVarsity, 2001.

Köstenberger, Andreas J., and Thomas R. Schreiner. *Women in the Church: An Analysis and Application of 1 Timothy 2:9–15*. 2d ed. Grand Rapids: Baker Academic, 2005.

Kraft, Charles H. *Anthropology for Christian Witness*. Maryknoll, NY: Orbis, 1996.

———. *Christianity in Culture: A Study in Dynamic Biblical Christianity in Cross-Cultural Perspective*. Maryknoll, NY: Orbis, 1979.

———. *Christianity with Power: Your Worldview and Your Experience of the Supernatural*. Ann Arbor, MI: Servant, 1989.

———. *Confronting Powerless Christianity: Evangelicals and the Missing Dimension*. Grand Rapids: Chosen, 2002.

———. *Culture, Communication, and Christianity: A Selection of Writings*. Pasadena, CA: William Carey, 2001.

———. "Polygamy and Church Membership." In *Evangelical Dictionary of World Missions*, edited by A. Scott Moreau, Harold A. Netland, Charles E. Van Engen and David Burnett, 1068. Grand Rapids: Baker, 2000.

Kroeger, Richard Clark, and Catherine Clark Kroeger. *I Suffer Not a Woman: Rethinking 1 Timothy 2:11–15 in Light of Ancient Evidence*. Grand Rapids: Baker, 1992.

Ladd, George Eldon. *A Theology of the New Testament*. Edited by Donald A. Hagner. Rev. ed. Grand Rapids: Eerdmans, 1993.

Lapham, Henry Alfred. *The Bible as Missionary Handbook*. Cambridge, UK: W. Heffer & Sons, 1925.

Larkin, William J. "The Role of Biblical-Theological Methods in Missiological Research." Global Missiology, http://www.globalmissiology.org/english/docs_html/research/larkin_biblical_theology_methods.html.

Bibliography

LaSor, William Sanford. "The *Sensus Plenior* and Biblical Interpretation." In *Scripture, Tradition, and Interpretation*, edited by Everett Falconer Harrison, W. Ward Gasque and William Sanford LaSor, 260–77. Grand Rapids: Eerdmans, 1978.

Legrand, Lucien. *The Bible on Culture: Belonging or Dissenting?*, Faith and Cultures Series. Maryknoll, NY: Orbis, 2000.

LeMarquand, Grant. "New Testament Exegesis in (Modern) Africa." In *The Bible in Africa : Transactions, Trajectories, and Trends*, edited by Gerald O. West and Musa W. Dube Shomanah, p 72–102. Boston, MA: Brill Academic, 2000.

Leslie, Charles. *A Letter of Advice to a Friend Upon the Modern Argument of the Lawfulness of Simple Fornication, Half-Adultery and Polygamy*. London: Printed for William Keblewhite, 1696.

Lewis, W. G. *Divine Guidance*. n.p.: W. G. Lewis, [1950].

Lindars, Barnabas, D. A. Carson, and H. G. M. Williamson, eds. *It Is Written: Scripture Citing Scripture: Essays in Honour of Barnabas Lindars, Ssf*. Cambridge, Cambridgeshire, UK; New York, NY: Cambridge University Press, 1988.

Loewen, Jacob A. *The Bible in Cross-Cultural Perspective*. Pasadena, CA: William Carey Library, 2000.

Love, Julian Price. *The Missionary Message of the Bible*. New York: Macmillan, 1941.

Lumen Gentium: Costituzione Dogmatica Sulla Chiesa, Promulgata Dal Concilio Ecumenico Vaticano II. XI ed. Roma: Edizioni Paoline, 1964.

MacArthur, John. *1 Timothy*, The MacArthur New Testament commentary. Chicago: Moody, 1995. Logos CD-ROM.

Maier, Gerhard. *Biblical Hermeneutics*. Translated by Robert W. Yarbrough. 1st ed. Wheaton, IL: Crossway, 1994.

Maillu, David G. *Our Kind of Polygamy*. Nairobi, Kenya: Heinemann Kenya, 1988.

Mann, Pamela S. "Toward a Biblical Understanding of Polygamy." *Missiology* 17 (1989) 11–26.

Marsden, George M. *Fundamentalism and American Culture*. 2nd ed. New York: Oxford University Press, 2006.

Marshall, I. Howard. "Developing a Biblical Hermeneutic for a Developing Theology." Paper presented at the 2002 Institute of Biblical Research (IBR), Regal Constellation Hotel, Toronto, Canada, November 22–23, 2002 2002.

Martin-Achard, Robert. *A Light to the Nations: A Study of the Old Testament Conception of Israel's Mission to the World*. Edinburgh, UK; London: Oliver and Boyd, 1962.

Martin, Hugh. *The Kingdom without Frontiers: The Witness of the Bible to the Missionary Purpose of God*. New and rev. ed. New York: Friendship, 1946.

McCartney, Dan G. "Should We Employ the Hermeneutics of the NT Writers?; or, Can We Reproduce the Exegesis of the New Testament?" Paper presented at the 2002 Annual Meeting of the Evangelical Theological Society (ETS), Regal Constellation Hotel, Toronto, Canada, November 20–22, 2002 2002.

McCartney, Dan G., and Charles Clayton. *Let the Reader Understand: A Guide to Interpreting and Applying the Bible*. 2d ed. Phillipsburg, NJ: Presbyterian and Reformed, 2002.

McGavran, Donald Anderson. "What Says the Word of God?" *Church Growth Bulletin* 5 (1969) 357–59.

McGavran, Donald Anderson, and C. Peter Wagner. *Understanding Church Growth*. 3rd ed. Grand Rapids: Eerdmans, 1990.

McLean, Archibald. *Hand-Book of Missions*. Cleveland, OH: Bethany C.E., 1897.

———. *Where the Book Speaks; or, Mission Studies in the Bible*. New York; Chicago: Revell, 1907.
Metzger, Bruce M., and United Bible Societies. *A Textual Commentary on the Greek New Testament: A Companion Volume to the United Bible Societies' Greek New Testament (Fourth Revised Edition)*. 2 ed. Stuttgart, Germany: Deutsche Bibelgesellschaft, 1994.
Miller, Leo. *John Milton among the Polygamophiles*. New York: Loewenthal Press, 1974.
Mills, Montague Stephen. *Jonah: A Study Guide to the Book of Jonah*. Dallas, TX: 3E Ministries, 1999. Logos CD-ROM.
Montgomery, Helen Barrett. *The Bible and Missions*. West Medford, MA: Central Committee of the United Study of Foreign Missions, 1920.
Moreau, A. Scott, Gary Corwin, and Gary B. McGee. *Introducing World Missions: A Biblical, Historical, and Practical Survey*. Grand Rapids: Baker Academic, 2003.
Mott, John Raleigh. *The Evangelization of the World in This Generation*, Missionary Campaign Library 2. Chicago: Missionary Campaign Library Number Two, 1900.
Mulrain, George M. "Is There a Calypso Exegesis?" In *Voices from the Margin: Interpreting the Bible in the Third World*, edited by R. S. Sugirtharajah. Maryknoll, NY: Orbis, 1995.
Muthengi, Julius K. "Polygamy and the Church in Africa: Biblical, Historical, and Practical Perspectives." *Africa Journal of Evangelical Theology* 14 (1995) 55–79.
Neill, Stephen. *How My Mind Has Changed About Mission*. Three part video series taped at the Overseas Ministries Study Center ed. Atlanta, GA: Southern Baptist Convention, 1984.
Neill, Stephen, Gerald H. Anderson, and John Goodwin. *Concise Dictionary of the Christian World Mission*. Nashville, TN: Abingdon, 1971.
Newbigin, Lesslie. *Foolishness to the Greeks: The Gospel and Western Culture*. Grand Rapids: Eerdmans, 1986.
———. *The Gospel in a Pluralist Society*. Grand Rapids, MI; Geneva, Switzerland: Eerdmans; World Council of Churches, 1989.
———. *The Household of God: Lectures on the Nature of the Church*, Kerr Lectures 1952. New York: Friendship, 1954.
———. *Is Christ Divided? A Plea for Christian Unity in a Revolutionary Age*. Grand Rapids: Eerdmans, 1961.
———. *The Open Secret: An Introduction to the Theory of Mission*. Rev. ed. Grand Rapids: Eerdmans, 1995.
———. *Proper Confidence: Faith, Doubt, and Certainty in Christian Discipleship*. Grand Rapids: Eerdmans, 1995.
———. *Truth to Tell: The Gospel and Public Truth*. Grand Rapids: Eerdmans, 1991.
———. *A Word in Season: Perspectives on Christian World Missions*. Grand Rapids: Eerdmans, 1994.
Newing, Edward G. "Baptism of Polygamous Families: Theory and Practice in an East African Church." *Journal of Religion in Africa* 3 (1970) 130–41.
Nissen, Johannes. *New Testament and Mission: Historical and Hermeneutical Perspectives*. Frankfurt am Main, Germany; New York: Peter Lang, 1999.
———. *New Testament and Mission: Historical and Hermeneutical Perspectives*. 2d ed. Frankfurt am Main, Germany; New York: Peter Lang, 2002.
Nkwoka, Anthony O. "The Church and Polygamy in Africa: The 1988 Lambeth Conference Resolution." *Africa Theological Journal* 19 (1990) 139–54.

Bibliography

Nuñez, Emilio Antonio. *Hacia Una Misionología Evangélica Latinoamericana*. Miami: UNILIT/COMIBAM, 1997.

O'Donnell, Kelly S., ed. *Doing Member Care Well: Perspectives and Practices from around the World*. Pasadena, CA: William Carey, 2002.

Ober, Charles Kellogg. *Bible Studies in Missions: I. Missions in the Old Testament. II. Missions in the Church of Pentecost. Iii. Partnership Privileges*. New York: International Committee of Young Men's Christian Associations, 1899.

Odame, E. R. C. *A Christian Approach to Polygamy*. Ghana: Global Mission, 1988.

Okotie, Chris. *The Last Outcast*. Lagos, Nigeria: Marskeel, 2001.

Okoye, James Chukwuma. *Israel and the Nations: A Mission Theology of the Old Testament*, American Society of Missiology Series 39. Maryknoll, NY: Orbis, 2006.

Okullu, Henry. *Church and Marriage in East Africa*. Nairobi, Kenya: Uzima, 1976.

Oleka, Sam. "Interpreting and Applying the Bible in an African Context." In *Issues in African Christian Theology*, edited by Samuel Ngewa, Mark Shaw and Tite Tiénou, 104–25. Nairobi, Kenya: East African Educational Publishers, 1998.

Omoregbe, Joseph. "Is Polygamy Incompatible with Christianity." *African Ecclesial Review* 21 (1979) 363–72.

Osborne, Grant R. *The Hermeneutical Spiral: A Comprehensive Introduction to Biblical Interpretation*. Downers Grove, IL: InterVarsity, 1991.

Owens, Larry. "Syncretism and the Scriptures." *Evangelical Missions Quarterly* 43 (2007) 74–80.

Padilla, C. René, ed. *Bases Bíblicas de La Misión: Perspectivas Latinoamericanas*. Buenos Aires; Grand Rapids: Nueva Creacion; Eerdmans, 1998.

Park, Eung Chun. *The Mission Discourse in Matthew's Interpretation*, Wissenschaftliche Untersuchungen Zum Neuen Testament 2 Reihe 81. Tübingen, Germany: JCB Mohr, 1995.

Parrinder, Edward Geoffrey. *The Bible and Polygamy: A Study of Hebrew and Christian Teaching*. London: SPCK, 1958.

Peskett, Howard, and Vinoth Ramachandra. *The Message of Mission: The Glory of Christ in All Time and Space*, The Bible Speaks Today. Downers Grove, IL: InterVarsity, 2003.

Peters, George W. *A Biblical Theology of Missions*. Chicago: Moody, 1972.

Phillips, James M., and Robert T. Coote. *Toward the Twenty-First Century in Christian Mission: Essays in Honor of Gerald H. Anderson, Director, Overseas Ministries Study Center, New Haven, Connecticut, Editor, International Bulletin of Missionary Research*. Grand Rapids: Eerdmans, 1993.

Piper, John. *Let the Nations Be Glad!: The Supremacy of God in Missions*. 2d rev. and expanded ed. Grand Rapids: Baker Academic, 2003.

Power, John. *Mission Theology Today*. Dublin, Ireland: Gill and MacMillan, 1970.

Priest, Doug. *Doing Theology with the Maasai*. Pasadena, CA: William Carey, 1990.

The Problem of Polygamy. 2d ed. London: Society for Promoting Christian Knowledge, 1926.

Redford, Shawn B. "Appropriate Hermeneutics." In *Appropriate Christianity*, edited by Charles H. Kraft, 227–53. Pasadena, CA: William Carey, 2005.

———. "The Contextualization and Translation of Christianity in Acts 9, 22, 26." In *Mission in Acts: Ancient Narratives in Contemporary Context*, edited by Robert L. Gallagher and Paul Hertig, 283–96. Maryknoll, NY: Orbis, 2004.

———. "Missiology and the Internet: Facing the Faceless Frontier." In *Footprints of God: A Narrative Theology of Mission*, edited by Charles E. Van Engen, Nancy Thomas and Robert L. Gallagher, 215-24. Monrovia, CA: MARC, 1999.

Ro, Bong Rin, and Ruth Marie Eshenaur. *The Bible & Theology in Asian Contexts: An Evangelical Perspective on Asian Theology*, Asian Evangelical Theological Library. Taichung Taiwan ROC: Asia Theological Association, 1984.

Rowley, Harold Henry. *The Missionary Message of the Old Testament*. London: The Carey Press, 1944.

Sandmel, Samuel. *Anti-Semitism in the New Testament?* Philadelphia: Fortress, 1978.

Schillebeeckx, Edward. *Marriage: Human Reality and Saving Mystery*. New York: Sheed and Ward, 1966.

Schnabel, Eckhard J. *Early Christian Mission: Jesus and the Twelve*. 2 vols. Vol. 1. Downers Grove, IL: InterVarsity; Apollos, 2004.

Scott, James M. "For as Many as Are of Works of the Law Are under a Curse (Galatians 3.10)." In *Paul and the Scriptures of Israel*, edited by Craig A. Evans and James A. Sanders, 187-221. Sheffield, UK: JSOT, 1993.

Senior, Donald, and Carroll Stuhlmueller. *The Biblical Foundations for Mission*. Maryknoll, NY: Orbis, 1983.

Shank, David A. "William Wadé Harris Ca. 1860-1929: God Made His Soul a Soul of Fire." In *Mission Legacies : Biographical Studies of Leaders of the Modern Missionary Movement*, edited by Gerald H. Anderson, Robert T. Coote, Norman A. Horner and James M. Phillips, 155-65. Maryknoll, NY: Orbis, 1994.

Shaw, R. Daniel, and Charles E. Van Engen. *Communicating God's Word in a Complex World: God's Truth or Hocus Pocus?* Lanham, MD: Rowman & Littlefield, 2003.

Shenk, Wilbert R. *Changing Frontiers of Mission*, American Society of Missiology Series 28. Maryknoll, NY: Orbis, 1999.

———. "Developments in the Theology of Mission since 1990." Paper presented at the School of World Mission Faculty Luncheon, Geneva Room, Fuller Theological Seminary, Pasadena, CA, October 31, 2000.

———. "Theology and the Missionary Task." *Missiology* 1 (1973) 295-310.

———. *Write the Vision: The Church Renewed*, Christian Mission and Modern Culture. Valley Forge, PA: Trinity; Gracewing, 1995.

———, ed. *The Transfiguration of Mission: Biblical, Theological & Historical Foundations*. Mission Studies 12. Scottdale, PA: Herald, 1993.

Shipp, Glover Harvey. *Fire in My Bones: Great Missionary Themes from the Bible*. 2 vols. Vol. 1. Winona, MS: J. C. Choate, 1978.

Sjogren, Bob. *Unveiled at Last: Discover God's Hidden Message from Genesis to Revelation*. Seattle, WA: YWAM, 1992.

Skreslet, Stanley. "Doctoral Dissertations on Mission: Ten-Year Update, 1992-2001." *International Bulletin of Missionary Research* 27 (2003) 98-101.

Stamoolis, James J. *Eastern Orthodox Mission Theology Today*, American Society of Missiology Series 10. Maryknoll, NY: Orbis, 1986.

Storr, Vernon Faithfull. *The Missionary Genius of the Bible*. London: Hodder and Stoughton, 1924.

Stott, John R. W. "The Biblical Basis of Missions or Part 2: The Biblical Basis of Declaring God's Glory." Paper presented at the Urbana 1976, Urbana, IL, 1976.

———. *Christian Mission in the Modern World*. Downers Grove, IL: InterVarsity, 1975.

Bibliography

Stronstad, Roger. *The Charismatic Theology of St. Luke*. Peabody, MA: Hendrickson, 1984.
Sugirtharajah, R. S., ed. *Voices from the Margin: Interpreting the Bible in the Third World*. New ed. Maryknoll, NY: Orbis; SPCK, 1995.
Summers, William D. *Marriage; or, the Bible and Polygamy*. n.p.: n.p., 1886.
Sundkler, Bengt. *The World of Mission*. London: Lutterworth, 1965.
Taber, Charles R. "Missiology and the Bible." *Missiology* 11 (1983) 229–45.
Tait, Arthur J. *Christ and the Nations, an Examination of Old and New Testament Teaching*. London: Hodder and Stoughton, 1910.
Tate, W. Randolph. *Biblical Interpretation: An Integrated Approach*. Rev. ed. Peabody, MA: Hendrickson, 1997.
Taylor, John Vernon. *The Growth of the Church in Buganda: An Attempt at Understanding*. London: SCM, 1958.
Teng, Philip. "The Biblical Basis of Missions." Paper presented at the Urbana 1973, Urbana, IL, 1973.
Terry, John Mark, Ebbie C. Smith, and Justice Anderson. *Missiology: An Introduction to the Foundations, History, and Strategies of World Missions*. Nashville: Broadman & Holman, 1998.
Thiselton, Anthony C. *The Two Horizons: New Testament Hermeneutics and Philosophical Description with Special Reference to Heidegger, Bultmann, Gadamer, and Wittgenstein*. 1st US ed. Grand Rapids: Eerdmans, 1980.
Thomas, Robert L. *Evangelical Hermeneutics: The New Versus the Old*. Grand Rapids: Kregel Publications, 2002.
Tiénou, Tite, and Paul G. Hiebert. "Missional Theology." *Missiology* 34 (2006) 219–38.
Tosato, Angelo. "The Law of Leviticus 18:18: A Reexamination." *Catholic Biblical Quarterly* 46 (1984) 199–214.
Travis, Stephen H. "Form Criticism." In *New Testament Interpretation: Essays on Principles and Methods*, edited by I. Howard Marshall, 406. Exeter, UK: Paternoster, 1977. Logos CD-ROM.
Trobisch, Walter. *My Wife Made Me a Polygamist*. 7th ed. Kehl/Rhein, Germany: Editions Trobisch, 1980.
Trowell, H. C. *The Passing of Polygamy: A Discussion of Marriage and of Sex for African Christians*. London: Oxford University Press; G. Cumberlege, 1940.
Turner, Harold W. "Monogamy: A Mark of the Church?" *International Review of Mission* 55 (1966) 313–21.
Tutu, Desmond M. Abp. "Some African Insights and the Old Testament." *Journal of Theology for Southern Africa* 1 (1972) 16–22.
Tyndale House Publishers. *Holy Bible: New Living Translation*. 2d ed. Wheaton, IL: Tyndale House, 2004. Logos CD-ROM.
Urrutia, Francisco J. "Can Polygamy Be Compatible with Christianity." *African Ecclesial Review* 23 (1981) 275–91.
van der Merwe, Christo. *The Lexham Hebrew-English Interlinear Bible*. Bellingham, WA; Johannesburg, South Africa: Logos Research Systems, 2004. Logos CD-ROM.
Van Engen, Charles E. *God's Missionary People: Rethinking the Purpose of the Local Church*. Grand Rapids: Baker, 1991.
———. *Mission on the Way: Issues in Mission Theology*. Grand Rapids: Baker, 1996.

Bibliography

———. "Peter's Conversion: A Culinary Disaster Launches the Gentile Mission." In *Mission in Acts: Ancient Narratives in Contemporary Context*, edited by Robert L. Gallagher and Paul Hertig. Maryknoll, NY: Orbis, 2004.

———. "The Relation of Bible and Mission in Mission Theology." In *The Good News of the Kingdom: Mission Theology for the Third Millennium*, edited by Charles E. Van Engen, Dean S. Gilliland and Paul E. Pierson, 27–36. Maryknoll, NY: Orbis, 1993.

Van Engen, Charles E., Dean S. Gilliland, and Paul E. Pierson, eds. *The Good News of the Kingdom: Mission Theology for the Third Millennium*. Maryknoll, NY: Orbis, 1993.

Van Engen, Charles E., and Shawn B. Redford. "Syllabus." *Biblical Foundations of Mission, MT520/MT620*. Pasadena, CA: Fuller Theological Seminary, School of Intercultural Studies, 2007.

Van Engen, Charles E., Nancy Thomas, and Robert L. Gallagher, eds. *Footprints of God: A Narrative Theology of Mission*. Monrovia, CA: MARC, 1999.

Van Rheenen, Gailyn. *Missions: Biblical Foundations & Contemporary Strategies*. Grand Rapids: Zondervan, 1996.

Verkuyl, Johannes. *Contemporary Missiology: An Introduction*. Grand Rapids: Eerdmans, 1978.

Vollebregt, G. N. *The Bible on Marriage*. Translated by R. A. Downie. De Pere, WI: St. Norbert Abbey Press, 1965.

Wagner, C. Peter. *How to Have a Healing Ministry in Any Church: A Comprehensive Guide*. Ventura, CA: Regal, 1988.

Wagner, J. Ross. *Heralds of the Good News: Isaiah and Paul "in Concert" in the Letter to the Romans*, Supplements to Novum Testamentum 101. Leiden, The Netherlands: Brill, 2002.

Wakefield, Andrew Hollis. *Where to Live: The Hermeneutical Significance of Paul's Citations from Scripture in Galatians 3:1–14*. Boston, MA: Brill, 2003.

Wallace, Daniel B. "The Holy Spirit and Hermeneutics." (1997), http://www.bible.org/docs/soapbox/hermhs.htm.

Walls, Andrew F. *The Missionary Movement in Christian History: Studies in the Transmission of Faith*. Maryknoll, NY: Orbis,1996.

Wambutda, Daniel N. "Monogamy or Polygamy in Africa: A Biblical Investigation." *West African Religion* 18 (1979) 70–91.

Warren, Max Alexander Cunningham. *The Calling of God: Four Essays in Missionary History*. London; Redhill, UK: Lutterworth, 1945.

Welch, Douglas E. "Biblical Perspective on Polygamy." 1977.

Wenham, Gordon J. *Genesis 1–15*, Word Biblical Commentary 1. Dallas, TX: Word, 1998. Logos CD-ROM.

———. *Genesis 16–50*, Word Biblical Commentary 2. Dallas, TX: Word, 1998. Logos CD-ROM.

Wilkins, John R. *The Bible and God's Mission: An Adventure in Study to Rediscover and Rethink Some Biblical Motivations for Christian Mission in Our World Today*. New York: Board of Missions of the Methodist Church, 1962.

Williamson, H. G. M. *Ezra-Nehemiah*, Word Biblical Commentary 16. Dallas, TX: Word, 2002. Logos CD-ROM.

Willis, Avery T. *The Biblical Basis of Missions*. Nashville, TN: Convention, 1984.

Wisdom, Jeffrey. *Blessing for the Nations and the Curse of the Law: Paul's Citation of Genesis and Deuteronomy in Gal 3.8–10*, Wissenschaftliche Untersuchungen Zum Neuen Testament 2 Reihe 133. Tübingen, Germany: Mohr Siebeck, 2001.

Bibliography

Wishard, S. E. *The Divine Law of Marriage; or, the Bible against Polygamy.* Vol. 25. New York: American Tract Society, 1896.

Woodberry, J. Dudley. *Audio Recordings of J. Dudley Woodberry Lectures in Introduction to Islam, Mr550.* Pasadena, CA: n.p., 2005. 29 MP3 files.

———. "Evangelicals, Stereotypes and Diversities." *Mission Frontiers* 25 (2003) 10–11.

———. "Syllabus." *Introduction to Islam, MR550.* Pasadena, CA: Fuller Theological Seminary, School of Intercultural Studies, 2005.

———. "To the Muslim I Became a Muslim?" In *Contextualization and Syncretism: Navigating Cultural Currents*, edited by Gailyn Van Rheenen, 143–57. Pasadena, CA: William Carey, 2006.

Wright, Christopher J. H. "Mission as a Matrix for Hermeneutics and Biblical Theology." In *Out of Egypt: Biblical Theology and Biblical Interpretation*, edited by Craig G. Bartholomew, 102–43. Grand Rapids: Zondervan, 2004.

———. *The Mission of God: Unlocking the Bible's Grand Narrative.* Downers Grove, IL: InterVarsity, 2006.

Wright, G. Ernest. "The Old Testament Basis for the Christian Mission." In *The Theology of the Christian Mission*, edited by Gerald H. Anderson, 17–30. New York: McGraw-Hill, 1961.

Yego, Josphat. "Polygamy and the African Church: A Survey." *East Africa Journal of Evangelical Theology* 3 (1984) 60–84.

Zabatiero, Julio Paulo Tavares. *Liberdade E Paixão: Missiologia Latino-Americana E O Antiguo Testamento.* 1a ed. Londrina: Descoberta Editora, 2000.

Zwemer, Samuel Marinus. *"Into All the World," the Great Commission: A Vindication and an Interpretation.* 2d ed. Grand Rapids: Zondervan, 1943.

Author and Subject Index

Abel, 163
Abendigo, 69
Abimelech, 24, 31, 44, 81, 223
Abraham, 9–21, 23–34, 39–45, 55,
    57, 60–64, 66–68, 72, 81, 174,
    187, 217, 223, 226
Abraham's Chief Servant, 14,
    25–26, 33
Absalom, 163, 204
Achin, 52
Achtemeier, Paul J., 25
Adam, 72, 162–64, 192
Ådna, Jostein, 12
Adutchum, Ofusu A., 138, 140, 175,
    196
Ahinoam, 201
Ai, 24, 52
Aland, Kurt, 249
allegiance, 1, 9, 26, 28, 31, 37, 40,
    43–44, 46, 48–49, 52–54,
    62, 64–65, 69, 72, 77, 79, 83,
    150, 153, 167, 199, 208, 260,
    262–65, 285, 287, 289, 293
Allen, Diogenes, 97, 101, 110, 112,
    116, 122–23, 127, 130
Allen, Roland, 110, 120, 296
American, 92, 137, 180, 255,
    277–78
Amnon, 163, 204
Amstutz, John L., 51–52
Anderson, Gerald H., 261
angel, 17–18, 21–22, 32, 39, 48,
    70–71, 144, 240, 242, 245
animals used by God, 48–49,
    76–78, 236, 240
animism, 47, 49

anthropology, 58, 95–96, 267, 290
Antioch, 244
apartheid, 273
Apollos, 104
apostles, 59, 65, 104
Aramaic, 56, 147
assumptions (bias, pre-existing
    ideas), 2, 13, 48, 52, 54, 61,
    63, 73, 80, 86–87, 90–93, 96,
    98–99, 101, 108–9, 115–16,
    133, 135, 137, 141, 144,
    146–47, 149, 151–52, 163,
    166–67, 171, 182, 184, 190,
    193, 201, 209, 215, 220, 229,
    234, 243, 250, 255–60, 283,
    285, 287–88, 290–91, 296–97
Assyria, 238
Assyrians, 75, 78
Augustine, 126

Babylon, 237
Babylonians, 251
Bailey, Kenneth E., 235, 237–38,
    250–63, 265–66, 271, 280,
    283, 285
Balaam, 9, 37, 46–47, 48–50, 125,
    235–36
Balak, 14, 47–51, 235–36
Bangladesh, 275
Barnabas, 118, 244
Barrett, C. K., 288
Barrett, Lois, 2
barriers, 38, 47, 62, 136, 257
Barth, Karl, 87
Bashford, J. W., 13, 262–63
Bathsheba, 161, 203–5

Author and Subject Index

Bauckham, Richard, 4, 12, 40, 72, 97
Beale, Gregory K., 2, 53, 115
beauty, 16–18
Beeby, H. Daniel, 4, 97, 130, 258
Beersheba, 24, 29
Bengali, 275–76
Berkouwer, G. C., 256
Bethel, 24
Bethsaida, 75
Bevans, Stephen B., 110, 117
Biblical Foundations of Mission (MT520), 3, 16, 53, 99, 123
Biblical Theology of Mission, 1, 3, 12, 58, 85, 89, 94–96, 99, 108–10, 131, 134, 200, 246, 262–63, 283, 296, 299
Bilhah, 167
Blackman, E. C., 12
Blauw, Johannes, 12, 258, 296
Blomberg, Craig L., 5, 72, 82
Blum, William G., 139–40, 152–54, 157, 161, 166–70
Boaz, 46, 168, 174, 208, 223
Boer, Harry R., 181
Book of Mormon, 85
Bosch, David Jacobus, 2–5, 11, 13, 77, 97, 100, 112, 152, 195, 261–62, 294, 296
Briscoe, Jill, 77–78
Brownson, James V., 3, 13, 102, 105, 115, 126
Brunner, Emil, 98
Burnett, David, 12
Burrows, William R., 111
Buthelezi, Manas, 140, 184–85, 196

Caesarea, 240–41, 244
Cain, 163, 166, 169, 192
Caldwell, Larry W., 4–5, 97–98, 106–7, 110, 114–15
Camps, Arnulf, 24
Canaan, 16, 18, 33
Canaanites, 19

Capernaum, 75
Carey, William, 125, 135
Carson, D. A., 3, 260–61
Carver, William Owen, 12, 37
centrifugal, 56, 242
centripetal, 53, 62, 64–65, 149, 281
Chapman, Colin Gilbert, 242, 266, 268–69, 274, 276
children, 19, 24–25, 27–28, 36, 38, 57, 76, 154, 163, 173, 175, 179, 186–87, 193, 199, 201, 206, 212, 218, 221–24, 229, 233–34, 252, 258, 264
Chime, Igwe Kingsley, 140, 148, 175, 185, 187, 190, 197, 209, 211, 213, 216, 226
Christian Missionary Fellowship (CMF), 233, 286
Church of England Mission Theological Advisory Group, 261
Churches Together in Britain and Ireland, 261
circumcision, 27
Clayton, Charles, 97, 99, 101, 103, 113, 116, 122
Colenso, John William, 137, 160, 173, 177, 195–96, 198, 215
colonial mission, 227, 282
command, 17, 21–22, 43, 45, 64, 66, 71, 74, 142, 163, 165, 222, 238
communion (see sacrament), 197, 211–12
communism, 286
community, 1, 2, 12, 58, 70, 80, 84, 88, 90, 92, 94–96, 100, 104–8, 117, 122–24, 126, 128, 131, 134, 160, 172, 191, 207, 221, 237, 252, 254, 260–61, 281, 286, 295, 300
Constantinian mission, 282
conversion, 9, 69, 116, 281
Cook, Edmund F., 12, 20

Coote, Robert T., 4
Cornelius, 117, 237, 240, 242–43
Cotobato Manobo, 106
covenant, 32, 35, 46, 50, 56–58, 65, 76, 169, 192, 206
creation, 118, 152, 157, 159–60, 170
criticism, 92, 94, 114
Culver, Robert Duncan, 13
Currens, Gerald E., 140, 176
curse, 21, 46–51, 235
Cyprus, 244
Cyrene, 244

Damascus, 25–26, 117, 278
Daniel, 9, 69–70, 81, 83, 237
David, 4, 14, 46, 51, 53, 97, 100, 133, 151, 161, 163–64, 167, 172, 174, 187–88, 200–5, 217, 223, 226, 294, 296
de Groot, A., 248
De Ridder, Richard, 12, 64, 296
Dead Sea Scrolls, 252
death, 16–19, 24–25, 50, 75, 143, 162, 181, 189, 199, 204, 245, 271
deceit, 19, 26, 42, 43, 166
Delany, Patrick, 136, 145
Delilah, 168
DeYoung, James B., 2
dialogue, 3, 4, 95, 131, 185, 274, 281
Dietrich, Walter, 5
Dinah, 27, 153
discipline, 93, 113, 132, 149, 211–12, 214, 288, 299
discourse analysis, 91
Dodd, C. H., 2, 59
dogmatism, 2, 58, 133–35, 144, 163–64, 169, 184, 193
Driver, John, 13
drought, 32, 38, 41, 65, 298
du Preez, Ronald A. G., 140–44, 147–48, 151, 157–58, 161, 165, 177, 180, 197, 200–2, 215

DuBose, Francis M., 4, 13

Egypt, 11, 17–18, 22, 24, 29, 38, 40–42, 44, 66, 162, 237, 255
Egyptians, 208
election, 11, 23, 32, 37, 45, 51, 149, 207, 235–36, 256
Eliezer, 25
Elkanah, 174, 223–24
El-Shaddai, 49
Enlightenment, 94
Ephesus, 157, 178–80, 267
Ephron, 44
Esau, 16, 18, 21–22, 33–35, 163, 174
Ethiopian eunuch, 118
ethnocentrism, 5, 60, 107, 114, 137, 211, 238, 267
evangelism, 67, 244, 258, 271, 274, 282
evangelization, 31, 125
Evans, Craig A., 2, 60, 238
Eve, 162–63
extremists, 277

faith, 17, 33, 52, 60–65, 69, 72, 81, 91, 99, 104–6, 110, 122, 128, 131–32, 150, 185, 188, 199, 206, 208, 211, 220, 225–26, 242, 274, 276, 278–80, 300
famine, 16, 18, 22, 31, 38, 42, 56, 298
fear, 16–19, 35, 68, 73, 75, 102, 111, 114, 280, 298
Fee, Gordon D., 86–87, 92, 106, 110, 113–14
Filbeck, David, 11–12
firstborn, 143
foreigner, 16, 18, 22, 25, 28, 29, 46, 106, 188
Fountain, Daniel E., 296
fragmentation, 91, 96, 128
Freedman, David Noel, 189, 241
Frei, Hans W., 89, 103
French, 255

Author and Subject Index

Fuller, Daniel P., 3, 113, 116–17, 224, 266, 288
fundamentalism, 86

Gabriel, 70
Galilee, 56, 255
Gallagher, Robert L., 296
Gaskiyane, I., 140, 175, 203, 213–14, 216, 219
Gasque, W. Ward, 87
genre, 40, 48, 76, 101, 112, 155, 169, 287
Gentile, 10, 54, 59, 62–63, 74, 80, 117, 240, 244, 288
Gerar, 18, 24
German, 86, 255
Gibeonites, 52
Gilliland, Dean S., 12, 187, 227, 296
Gitari, David M. Bp, 174–75, 189, 216
Glasser, Arthur F., 12, 42, 72, 103, 261, 296
Gnanakan, Ken, 5, 12
God, 4, 8–14, 16, 18–26, 28–29, 31–40, 42–45, 47–60, 64–67, 69–72, 74–81, 83–84, 86–87, 89–91, 96, 98–99, 102, 109–13, 116–18, 120–30, 132, 149–50, 153–54, 159–65, 169–70, 172, 174, 179, 181, 185–89, 192–93, 199–200, 202–8, 210, 212–14, 216–18, 220–28, 230, 235–46, 248, 257, 262, 264–66, 268, 275, 278–79, 281, 290, 292–93, 295–98, 300
  Father, 119, 122, 262
  Jesus, 10–11, 36, 56–69, 71–82, 85, 87, 103, 106, 112, 117, 119, 122, 125, 134, 142, 153–60, 163, 172–74, 181–83, 189, 192, 194–95, 197–98, 209–12, 216, 220, 225–26, 230–31, 233, 240– 45, 248–53, 255, 257–60, 262–64, 266–71, 273–82, 285, 292, 300
  Holy Spirit (see Hermeneutics: Spiritual: Holy Spirit)
Goerner, Henry Cornell, 12
Gomer, 208
Gomorrah, 23, 66, 123
Gordon, A. J., 86, 92, 110
grace, 6, 22, 24, 39, 42, 49, 50, 66, 73–75, 77–79, 83, 116, 126, 166, 210, 215–16, 219–20, 223, 236, 238, 245, 254, 268, 280, 289, 292
Great Banquet, The, 258
greed, 26, 48, 81
Guder, Darrell L., 2, 12, 81

Hagar, 59, 187, 224
Hahn, Ferdinand, 13, 286
Hannah, 223–24
hapax legomenon, 147
Haran, 16, 18, 26–27, 29
hardheartedness, 77–78
Harris, R. Laird, 34
Harris, William Wadé, 227–28
Harrison, Everett Falconer, 2
Hartmann, G., 138, 210
Hastings, Adrian, 138–40, 172, 185
Hays, Richard B., 2
Hebrew, 21, 33, 34, 45, 47, 51, 56, 67, 101, 144–49, 252, 283
Hebron, 24, 29
Hedlund, Roger E., 12, 296
Helander, Gunnar, 138–40, 157, 159–60, 173, 175–76, 191, 195, 209–10, 215–16, 219, 221
Hellenists, 244
Hengel, Martin, 288
hermeneutics
  based on inferences, 163, 169, 171, 193, 205, 213, 215, 227
  ethnic, 5, 61, 248

344

hermeneutics (cont.)
  historical-critical, 2, 4, 8–9, 62, 86, 89–94, 99, 105, 107, 110, 112–14, 117, 132, 238, 241, 256–57, 283
  intertextual, 2, 62, 68, 83, 153, 172, 187, 203
  midrashic, 59–61, 248
  missiological, 1–4, 6–8, 12, 42, 46, 52, 58–64, 68–69, 71, 73, 76, 79, 82–84, 107, 110, 119, 133, 135, 182, 197, 200, 203, 206–8, 213–16, 225, 227, 230–31, 246, 248–49, 260, 271, 280, 288, 295, 298–99
    experience, 7, 9, 23, 61, 80, 82, 100–102, 115, 128, 135, 150, 194, 213, 232–33, 237, 247, 271, 273, 275, 278, 280–82, 285, 287, 295, 298
    God's intentions, 9–10, 45, 52, 54, 66, 293
    thematic, 3–5, 11, 13, 15, 17, 44–46, 53, 62, 69, 80, 97–100, 131, 185–87, 190, 205, 217–18, 273, 287
  poor, 62, 73, 149, 155, 171, 201, 227
  spiritual, 1, 79, 113, 119, 298
    dreams and visions, 18, 21, 23, 31, 35, 39–42, 46, 52, 64–68, 70–71, 81, 88, 92, 94, 117, 130, 144, 222, 240, 243, 276, 278, 286
    faithfulness, 66, 110, 125, 128, 131, 164, 169, 179–80, 217–18, 282
    giftedness, 25, 110–11, 121, 125–26, 235–36, 259
    led by Holy Spirit, 54, 57, 60–61, 64, 78, 80–82, 84, 102, 104, 110–13, 115–22, 129, 131, 185, 190, 218, 225–27, 230, 240, 242–45
    meditation, 80, 110, 127, 296
    prayer, 8, 24–26, 46, 53–54, 69–71, 80, 85, 110, 112, 120–24, 131–32, 191, 224, 231, 239–40, 280–82, 290, 296
    Scripture memory, 126–28
    willful distortions, 6, 80, 97, 151, 216
Herod the Great, 175
Hertig, Paul, 296
Hesselgrave, David J., 4, 258
Hiebert, Paul G., 4, 5, 107–8, 113, 175, 183, 195, 216, 248, 286
Hillman, Eugene, 138–40, 158–60, 164, 171, 175–77, 188–89, 195–96, 199–200, 209, 211, 225
Hitchens, Robert J., 140, 152–53, 157–58, 161, 171, 175, 196, 214, 216
Hittite, 25, 44, 187
Hivite, 27, 28
Holst, Robert, 138, 140, 160, 183–85
Holter, Knut, 135
Horan, Hubert, 138
Horton, Robert F., 13, 99, 258, 261–62
Hosea, 77, 125, 208
Howard, David M., 12
Hrangkhuma, F., 13
humor, 49, 77, 252
Hunt, Nancy Rose, 211
Hurty, Sarah, 2
Hutchison, William R., 87

idioms, 145–46, 148
Introduction to Islam (MR550), 267
Isaac, 11–21, 24–26, 28–29, 31–35, 38–39, 43–44, 64, 163

Ishmael, 17, 24–25, 59, 163, 187, 224
Islam, 242, 266–69, 271–72, 274–78, 280–81, 288
Israel, 2, 10–13, 21, 37, 39–40, 47–54, 56, 60, 64–67, 69–70, 72, 77–78, 81, 83, 87, 115, 117–18, 123, 125, 149–50, 152–53, 164, 168–70, 175, 181, 188, 202, 205–8, 222, 235–40, 281, 296

Jackson, Samuel Macauley, 137, 196, 199, 231
Jacob, 9, 11–16, 18–22, 24, 26–29, 31, 33–44, 64, 66, 144, 149, 163, 166–67, 173–74, 223, 226, 238, 250, 253, 255, 257–58, 263
James, 271
Japheth, 208
Jasper, Gerhard, 140
Jehoiada, 188–89
Jerusalem, 56, 69–70, 239, 244, 255
Jew, 10, 54, 56–57, 59, 62–63, 67, 71–75, 77–79, 117, 160, 162, 180–182, 199, 237–45, 250–52, 261–64, 269, 275–76, 280, 288
    "clean" (haberim), 73, 237, 262–265
    "unclean" ('am ha-'arets), 73, 237–238, 262–265
Johnston, James, 137, 196, 199, 231
Jonah, 48, 78–79, 236, 239
Joppa, 239
Jordan, William George, 13
Joseph, 9, 14–15, 18, 22, 26, 28–31, 35, 37, 38–44, 56, 66, 81, 83, 163, 167–68, 208, 237, 269
Josephus, 175
Jubilee, 149–50, 274
Judah, 14, 123
Judea, 239, 244

Kähler, Martin, 112
Kaiser, Walter C., 2, 12–13, 21–22, 37, 117, 140–51, 157, 175, 196, 200–1, 215–16, 286, 296
Kane, J. Herbert, 12–13, 22
Kanyadago, Peter M., 197
Kanyoro, Rachel Angogo, 135, 197
Kavunkal, Jacob, 13
Kearney, Michael, 250
Keturah, 25
king of Sodom, 30, 31
Kirk, J. Andrew, 86–87, 90–91, 94, 104, 109–10, 112, 261
Kiwovele, Judah B. M., 140, 175, 197, 215, 219, 221
Klein, William W., 101
Knight, William, 137, 206
Koehler, Ludwig Hugo, 29, 67, 146–47
Korazin, 74
Köstenberger, Andreas J., 89, 179
Kraft, Charles H., 84–86, 97, 101, 107, 110, 120, 171, 176, 181–82, 184, 191, 194, 217, 285, 291
Kroeger, Catherine Clark, 179
Kroeger, Richard Clark, 179
Kvalbein, Hans, 12

Laban, 22, 25–28, 166
Ladd, George Eldon, 261–62
Lamech, 166, 169, 172, 174, 192, 223
Lapham, Henry Alfred, 12, 32
Larkin, William J., 4, 89
LaSor, William Sanford, 76, 112, 115
Latter Day Saints of the Church of Jesus Christ (LDS), 85–86, 131, 134
leadership, 52, 69, 72–73, 80–81, 150, 172, 175–79, 181–84, 188, 194, 205–6, 214, 217–18, 228, 244, 252, 263, 292

Author and Subject Index

Leah, 27, 144, 149, 166–67, 173, 223
Legrand, Lucien, 16
LeMarquand, Grant, 185
Leslie, Charles, 136
Levi, 27
Levites, 189, 206
Levitical law, 141, 154
Lewis, W. G., 140, 163–64, 166, 202–3, 205–8
Libya, 244
Lindars, Barnabas, 2, 55
Lo-Ammi, 76
Lo-Ruhamah, 76
Lot, 17, 23–24, 30
Love, Julian Price, 13
loyalty, 24–25, 46, 252
Luz, Ulrich, 5, 24

Maasai, 107, 138, 194, 225, 233–34, 249–50, 286–87, 297
MacArthur, John, 179
Mahfouz, Naguib, 280
Maier, Gerhard, 2
Maillu, David G., 140, 175, 195, 197, 216
Mann, Pamela S., 140, 175, 216
marriage, 27, 134, 137, 139, 141, 143–44, 146–47, 149, 152, 157–58, 160–70, 172–74, 179–80, 182–84, 186–87, 189, 191–92, 194–95, 197, 199–207, 209, 212–13, 215–16, 219–24, 228–29
  bigamy, 143, 169
  concubine, 135, 201
  divorce, 104, 137, 139, 142–43, 154, 160, 173–74, 178, 180–81, 183, 186, 192, 196–99, 204–10, 212, 218, 224
  exogamy, 172, 188
  levirate, 137, 166, 168, 186, 189, 195, 197, 205, 222–23

  sororal polygamy, 144, 148–49, 214
Marsden, George M., 92
Marshall, I. Howard, 87, 115
Martin, Hugh, 13
Martin-Achard, Robert, 11–12, 286
Masoretic text, 56
Mazak, Greg, 179
McCartney, Dan G., 97, 99, 101, 103, 113, 115–16, 122
McGavran, Donald Anderson, 48, 175–76, 233
McLean, Archibald, 12, 37, 258
Medina, 269
Melchizedek, 30, 31, 44
mercy, 49, 52, 78, 220, 240
meta-narrative, 91, 238
metaphor, 37–39, 45, 103, 156, 168, 252, 257
Metzger, Bruce M., 249–50
Michal, 201
Middle East, 250–57, 259–60, 263, 265–66, 270, 285
midrash (less obvious meaning of the text), see hermeneutics
midrashic, 60
Miller, Leo, 136
Mills, Montague Stephen, 76
Milton, John, 134, 136
Mischak, 69
missiologists, 48, 95–97, 100–101, 257, 263, 266
mission of God (missio Dei), 9, 23, 72, 74, 78, 258, 293–94
mistrust, 19
Moab, 47–49, 51
modernity, 91–92, 95–96, 100, 107, 133, 214
Montgomery, Helen Barrett, 12, 37, 258, 296
Moravian, 209–10
Moreau, A. Scott, 12, 191
Moses, 13, 123, 145, 173, 199, 226
Mott, John Raleigh, 125

Author and Subject Index

Muhammad, 266, 269, 277
Mulrain, George M., 270
Muslim, 266, 269, 272, 274–75, 277–78, 280–81
Muthengi, Julius K., 139–40, 197

Namaan, 81
Naomi, 46, 154
narrative, 14, 18, 24, 39–40, 44, 46, 49, 78, 89, 93–94, 102–4, 108, 122, 149–54, 157, 185, 188, 191, 193, 208, 218, 230, 238, 240–41, 295
Nebuchadnezzar, 69, 237
Neill, Stephen, 32
New Testament, 2, 6, 8, 10–14, 40, 48, 54, 59, 64–65, 67, 69, 83, 87, 102, 104, 111–12, 115–16, 118–19, 139, 142, 153–57, 160–61, 168–69, 173–76, 180, 182–84, 186, 192, 194–95, 199, 207, 212, 216, 220, 222, 239–40, 248–52, 254–55, 259, 261–62, 264, 269–71, 275–76, 282–83, 285, 288, 292, 296
Newbigin, Lesslie, 13, 42, 58, 86–87, 89, 91, 99, 100–2, 104–6, 109, 111, 116, 118–19, 121–22, 125–27, 129, 250, 258, 261–62, 296
Newing, Edward G., 211
Nicodemus, 74, 116, 267, 276
Nida, Eugene A., 168
Ninevites, 81, 240
Nissen, Johannes, 4, 95, 232, 261, 286, 296
Nkwoka, Anthony O., 140, 175, 191, 197, 216
Noah, 163
Nobel Peace Prize, 280

obedience, 18, 20, 23, 39, 46, 52
Ober, Charles Kellogg, 12

O'Brien, Peter Thomas, 89
O'Donnell, Kelly S., 13
Ockham's-razor, 288
Odame, E. R. C., 140–41, 162, 173, 175, 188, 195, 197, 207, 216, 219–20
Oepke, Albrecht, 180
Ofora, L., 226
Okotie, Chris, 140, 191–93, 197, 219
Okoye, James Chukwuma, 2, 11–12, 54, 296
Okullu, Henry, 138, 191, 197, 211–12, 220–21
Old Testament, 2, 8, 9, 11–14, 21–22, 36, 39–40, 43, 46, 48, 50, 52, 56, 58, 60–71, 75–79, 83, 101, 107, 115, 117–19, 125, 137, 139, 141, 143–45, 147–50, 152–57, 160, 164, 172, 174–75, 187–89, 192, 194–96, 200–208, 212–16, 218–23, 228, 230, 235, 237–41, 245–46, 248, 270, 280–81, 283
Oleka, Sam, 5
Omoregbe, Joseph, 140, 197
Orthodox Church, 123
Osborne, Grant R., 101, 112, 116, 122
Owens, Larry, 280

Pakendorf, P., 138
Palestine, 235, 286
parable, 103, 159, 200, 249, 254–55, 257, 260–63, 265, 270, 280
Park, Eung Chun, 13, 72
Parrinder, Edward Geoffrey, 137, 140, 152–53, 157–58, 171–72, 181, 189, 197–98
Patriarchs, 11, 32
Paul, 2, 4, 9, 12, 14, 20, 36, 46, 55–56, 58–65, 67–68, 72, 74, 81, 117–18, 122–23, 142–43,

Paul (*cont.*)
    153, 156–60, 175–83, 187, 194, 199, 207–8, 216, 218, 234, 248, 259, 266, 271, 278–81, 287, 296
peace, 26, 34, 53–54, 69, 279, 297
Peninnah, 223–24
Pentecost, 56, 228
peshat (plain meaning of the text), 60
Peskett, Howard, 12, 77
Peter, 9, 12, 14, 20, 46, 55–58, 67–68, 72, 80–81, 116–17, 122, 235–47, 250, 271, 275–76, 278
Peters, George W., 12, 262–63, 296
Pharaoh, 18, 31, 40, 44
Pharisees, 59, 267
Philip, 118
Philistia, 22, 24, 29
Phillips, James M., 4
Pierson, Paul E., 259
pioneer missionary, 23
Piper, John, 12
postmodernity, 96
Potiphar, 40, 167
Power, John, 12–13, 30, 120
prayer, 23–25, 66, 70–71, 121, 242
Price, Frederick A., 228
Priest, Doug, 194, 271
Prodigal Son, 259–60
promises
    blessing of growth, 33, 38
    blessing of land, 13, 15, 24–25, 34, 44
    blessing the nations, 6, 11, 13–15, 17–19, 22–23, 32–33, 36, 39–40, 42, 45–46, 71
proof-texting, 80, 97, 151, 216
prophet, false, 48–50, 125, 235–36
protection, 16, 19, 35, 37, 44, 47, 50–51, 53, 124, 235–36, 264, 298

providence, 18–19, 23–24, 39, 43, 64–65

Qur'an, 266, 277, 280

Rachel, 28, 144, 149, 166–67, 223
Ramachandra, Vinoth, 12, 77
rationalism, 93, 110, 129–30
Rebecca, 18, 163
redemption, 27, 68, 258, 278
Redford, Shawn B., 12, 16, 23, 48, 52–53, 65, 81, 85, 97, 101–2, 133, 159, 194, 202, 224
reductionism, 36, 91
relativism, 4
Reuben, 167
Rizpah, 201
Roman, 62, 72, 176–77, 240, 242
Rome, 62, 63, 240, 263, 269
Rowley, Harold Henry, 11, 13, 43
Ruth, 154, 168, 188, 223

sacrament (see communion), 211, 213
Samaria, 266
Samson, 168
Sanders, James A., 2, 238
Sandmel, Samuel, 65
Sarah, 16–17, 24–25, 187, 224
Satan, 80, 276
Saul (NT Apostle), 271
Saul (OT king), 200–202
Sawyerr, Harry, 260–61
Schillebeeckx, Edward, 139, 161, 188, 195–96
Schnabel, Eckhard J., 11, 12, 286
scholars, 2, 9, 11, 22, 36, 39, 48, 60–61, 64, 71, 76, 82, 86, 89, 91, 112, 118, 154, 162, 196, 209, 252, 256, 259, 267
Schreiner, Thomas R., 179
Scott, James M., 70, 279
Sebaste, 241

Author and Subject Index

seed, 12, 19–20, 36, 42, 55, 59–63, 66, 68
Senior, Donald, 12, 296
sensus plenior (fuller sense), 37
Septuagint, 21, 55–56, 147, 156–57, 173
Sermon on the Mount, The, 274
Seventh-Day Adventist (SDA), 141
sexual sins
    adultery, 136, 151, 160–62, 164, 169, 172–74, 185, 189, 200, 202–4, 215, 226–27, 231
    bestiality, 162
    homosexuality, 161
    incest, 148–49, 161
    lust, 137, 161, 167, 205, 222–23
    pederasty, 161
    prostitution, 161–62, 215, 231
Shadrack, 69
Shank, David A., 228
Shaw, R. Daniel, 3, 5, 194
Shechaniah, 206–7
Shechem (person), 27, 31, 153
Shechem (place), 24
Shema, 11, 268
Shenk, Wilbert R., 12, 74, 86, 96, 100, 105–7, 125, 261
Shipp, Glover Harvey, 12
Sidon, 74
Simeon, 27
Sirach, Ben, 255
Sjogren, Bob, 12, 40, 67
Sodom, 23, 30–31, 66, 75, 123
Solomon, 46, 51, 53–54, 75, 158, 174, 187–88, 192, 201, 205, 208, 217, 223
South Africa, 198, 209, 219, 273
sovereignty, 89, 110–11, 116, 204, 223–24
spiritual abuse, 27, 31
Stamoolis, James J., 123
Stephen, 271
Storr, Vernon Faithfull, 12
Stott, John R. W., 68

Stronstad, Roger, 110
Stuhlmueller, Carroll, 12, 296
suffering, 77, 144, 233, 268, 275
Sugirtharajah, R. S., 5, 247, 261
Summers, William D., 151, 166, 172
Sundkler, Bengt, 12
syncretism, 74, 108–9, 138, 182, 214, 219, 244, 246, 280
systematic theology, 5, 8, 257, 286

Taber, Charles R., 4, 247, 258, 273–74, 282
tabernacle, 53, 54, 281
Tait, Arthur J., 11
Tamar, 163, 204
Tate, W. Randolph, 101
Taylor, J. Hudson, 198–99, 231
Taylor, John Vernon, 82
temple, 53–54, 75, 161, 189
Teng, Philip, 37, 38
the poor, 4, 53, 149, 200, 222, 240, 242, 252, 272–74, 282
theft, 16, 28, 165
Thiselton, Anthony C., 3
Thomas, Nancy, 5
Thomas, Robert L., 5
Tiénou, Tite, 4–5, 175, 195, 216, 261, 286
Timnah, 168
Torah, 238–39
Tosato, Angelo, 148–49
Travis, Stephen H., 291
Trobisch, Walter, 139–40, 197, 223
Trowell, H. C., 138, 140
trust, 24, 41, 64, 74, 114, 150, 172, 185, 226, 230, 277
Turner, Harold W., 150, 191
Tutu, Desmond M. Abp, 135
Tyndale House Publishers, 249
Tyre, 74

United Bible Societies, 250
universal, 4, 72, 105, 115, 159, 252
Ur, 11

Uriah, 151, 187, 204–5, 217
Urrutia, Francisco J., 140, 152, 157, 166, 197, 213
USA, 269, 282
USSR, 286

van der Merwe, Christo, 144, 147
Van Engen, Charles E., 3, 5, 12–13, 16, 23, 48, 52–53, 65, 81, 96–97, 101–4, 111, 125, 133, 159, 194, 202, 243, 258, 261, 296
Van Rheenen, Gailyn, 13
Venn, Henry, 137, 206, 208
Vollebregt, G. N., 139–40, 153, 155, 157–58, 160–62, 169–73, 198, 200, 202, 207

Wagner, C. Peter, 48, 120
Wagner, J. Ross, 2, 62
Wakefield, Andrew Hollis, 61
Wallace, Daniel B., 113, 116–17
Walls, Andrew F., 100–101, 115, 258
Wambutda, Daniel N., 140, 175, 197, 216
Warren, Max Alexander Cunningham, 12
weakness, 17, 22, 25, 27, 30, 41, 65, 81, 110, 165, 171, 185, 268, 281–82, 297
Welch, Douglas E., 135, 140, 158, 160–61, 169–70, 172–73, 176, 186, 189, 200–202, 224
Wellhausen theory, 169

wells, 26, 38, 44, 53
Wenham, Gordon J., 27, 30
White, Ellen (SDA prophetess), 141–42
widows, 177–81, 183, 223
Wilkins, John R., 13
Williams, Walter B., 228
Williamson, H. G. M., 207
Willis, Avery T., 13
wisdom, 54, 70, 122, 236
Wisdom, Jeffrey, 11
Wishard, S. E., 137, 157, 165
witness, 22–31, 44, 47–51, 53–54, 64–66, 69–72, 74–75, 79, 116–18, 127, 149–50, 159, 207, 215, 235–37, 241, 260, 268, 275, 278, 281, 300
Woodberry, J. Dudley, 72, 103, 235, 266–81, 285
worldview, 5, 90–92, 95–96, 106, 110, 114–115, 135, 149, 232, 237–38, 242–43, 246, 248, 250–51, 283
worship, 24, 33, 50, 53, 65, 69, 162, 188–89, 266, 280
Wright, Christopher J. H., 5, 296
Wright, G. Ernest, 13

Yego, Josphat, 138–39, 191, 221
YHWH, 11, 18, 20–22, 32, 35, 39, 44, 64, 77, 135, 164, 169

Zechariah (Jehoiada's son), 189
Zwemer, Samuel Marinus, 12, 37

Scripture Index

Genesis

1–11	13
1:26–28	170
1:27	159
1:28	163
2	152, 162–63, 193, 220
2:18–25	154
2:24	141–43, 152–61, 164–65, 173
3	162, 192–93
4:19	169
4:19–24	166
4:23	223
4:23–24	169
4:25	144
8:10	144
8:12	144
9:1	163
9:7	163
9:8–17	163
9:9	36
10:2	208
11	11, 40
11:10–26	208
12	10–11, 18, 24, 29, 35, 44, 57, 65, 187
12–50	10, 13, 16
12:1	28
12:1–3	11, 14, 22, 30, 50, 64, 72, 235–36
12:2	22, 57
12:2–3	13, 16, 21, 53
12:3	6, 8, 10–14, 16, 19–21, 24, 31, 33–37, 39, 41–42, 46–47, 49–51, 53–55, 57–58, 60–61, 68, 84, 238, 240
12:4	25, 43
12:5–6	16
12:7	24–25, 44, 59–60
12:8	24
12:10–20	16–17, 23
12:12	19
12:17–20	44
12:20	24
13:3	24
13:18	24
14	23, 30
14:14	24, 30
14:14–15	30
14:18–20	30
14:21–23	30
14:23	31
15	25, 32–33
15:2	25
16:10–12	25
17	32–33
17:5	21
17:7–8	46
17:10	27
18	23
18:1	24
18:16ff.	52
18:18	8, 10–12, 16–17, 19–21, 34–35, 39, 55, 60, 238
18:18–19	14, 23
18:19	43, 46
19	123
19:5–7	162

Scripture Index

Genesis (cont.)

Reference	Pages
19:29	24
19:30	19
20	24, 187
20:1	24
20:1–18	16, 44
20:3	162
20:3–7	81
20:11–13	19
20:15	24, 44
20:16	16
20:17–18	223
21	17
21:5	25
21:8–21	224
21:12	62
21:13	25
21:18	25
21:20	25
21:22–23	24, 26, 44
21:30–34	24
21:32–34	44
22:7–9	17
22:16–18	14, 17, 46
22:18	8, 10–12, 16–17, 19–20, 34–35, 39, 43, 55, 60
22:19	24
23:1	24
23:1–16	24
23:4	25
23:5	25
23:5–11	44
23:19	24
24	26
24:2	25
24:5–7	32
24:7	14, 25
24:12	25
24:12–15	25
24:19–20	44
24:26	25
24:26–27	25
24:34–48	25
24:40	25
24:48	25
24:52	25
25:5	32
26	18
26:1	24
26:3	29
26:3–5	14
26:4	8, 10–12, 16–21, 34, 39, 55, 207, 238
26:5	172, 187
26:5–6	18, 43
26:7	19
26:10	162
26:11	16, 44
26:14–22	26
26:16	26, 44
26:21–22	144
26:22	26
26:23	24
26:25	24
26:26–31	26
26:28	26
26:28–29	26
26:31	26
26:32	26
27	18
27:29	14, 33
27:36	34
27:38	34
27:46	19
28	21
28:4	14, 34
28:10–22	35
28:13	36
28:14	8, 10–12, 14, 16, 18, 20–21, 34–36, 39, 42, 55, 60
28:16–17	19
28:16–22	43–44
28:18–19	24, 166
29:25	166
29:27	144, 166
29:30	144, 166
29:30–31	166

Scripture Index

Genesis (cont.)

29:31	223
30:1–16	223
30:17–22	223
30:24	144
30:25–35	26
31:2	26
31:19	28
31:32	28
31:34–35	28
32:12	14
32:22–32	21, 37
34	31
34:2–3	27
34:3	153
34:3–4	27
34:11–12	27
34:13–17	27
34:15	27
34:25–29	27
34:29	28
34:30	27
35:1	24
35:1–15	20
35:2	28
35:7	24
35:20	175
35:22	167
37:9	144
37:28	41
38:8–10	189
38:9–10	222
39:4	41
39:5	40
39:7	167
39:14–23	41
40–41	41, 81
41–50	8, 14, 39
41:30–32	18
41:45	208
42	18
42:2	18
45:5–8	14, 43
47:5–6	44
47:5–12	41
47:7	40
47:13–26	31
47:25	31
48:4	14
48:15–16	38
48:22	27
49:5–7	27
49:8–10	14
49:10	37, 46
49:13	38
49:22	37, 39
49:22–26	14
50:20	14, 43

Exodus

6:7	11, 75
15:27	40
20	268
20:14	162
20:15	166
21:7–11	141, 152, 165, 227
21:10	144, 147, 165, 170
21:10–11	167, 212
21:11	186
22:1	165
22:4	144
22:18	162
22:19	162
26:3	145–46
26:6	146
26:17	146
32	123
32:11	52
34:16	188

Leviticus

18	148–49
18:1–17	162
18:7–8	175
18:18	21, 141, 143–49, 151–52, 166–67, 170, 190, 214, 227
18:22	162

Leviticus (cont.)

18:23	162
19:29	162
20:10	162
20:11–12	162
20:13	162
20:14	166, 229
20:15–16	162
21:9	162
23:18	143
25	274
26:11–12	53
26:12	11, 75
27	274
27:20	144

Numbers

5:12–13	162
9:15	53
10:29–32	53
14:24	144
17:7–8	53
22	48, 125
22–24	10, 47–48
22:3–4	50
22:6	49–50
22:23	49
22:25	49
22:27	49
23–24	14, 50, 235
23:13	144
23:23	47
23:27	144
24	10
24:1	48–49
24:9	11, 14, 46–47, 50, 236
24:17	37
25	188
25:6–13	208
36:9	144

Deuteronomy

2:9	50
2:19	50
4:34–39	153
5:18	162
6:4	11, 268
7:3–4	188
17:17	141, 152, 188, 227
21:15	173
21:15–17	141, 143–44, 151–52, 170, 186, 227
22:22	162
23:17	162
25:5	189
25:5–10	187, 222
27–32	70, 207
27:21	162
28:1—30:3	70
29:27	144
31:3–4	52
32:39	153

Joshua

2:8–21	52
4:24	52, 238
6:17	52
6:17–18	52
7:25	52
9–10	52
9:9–15	52
9:24	52
10:1–13	52
23:12–13	188
24:3	61
24:17–18	52

Judges

2:10	144
8:30	223
11:2	144
13:2	168
14:4	168
14:19–20	168
19:22–23	162

Ruth

1:16	208
1:16–17	46
2:8	144
2:22	144
3:10–13	46, 223
4	223
4:9–15	46, 223
4:10	222

1 Samuel

1	223
1:5	223–24
1:10–20	224
5–6	81
8:15	36
10:6	144
12	151
12:7–8	202
14:49	201
14:49–50	201
14:50	201
17:30	144
18:20–27	201
18:27	201
25:39–44	201
25:44	201

2 Samuel

3:2–5	201
3:7	201
5:13	201
11	187
11:27	201
12	133, 161, 164, 174, 200–201, 217
12:1–12	200
12:7–8	141, 152
12:7–14	162
12:8	200–201
12:11	204
12:16	204
16:21–22	204
18:20	144
18:26	144
21:8	201

1 Kings

3:1	188
7:8	188
8:60	153
11	174, 217
11:1–3	201
11:1–8	172, 187–88
11:1–11	188
11:2	158
13:10	144
14:24	162
15:4–5	151
15:5	172, 187–88, 204–5
15:12	162
20:37	144
22:46	162

2 Kings

1:11	144
5	81, 238
7:8	144
12	187, 189
12:3	189
23:7	162

1 Chronicles

2:26	144
3:1–9	201
14:3	201
16:20	144
28:21	53

2 Chronicles

24	187, 189
24:2	172, 187, 189
24:2–3	172, 187, 189
24:15–16	189
24:17–19	189
32:5	144

Scripture Index

Ezra

9–10	188, 206–8
10	206
10:3	206

Nehemiah

13:23–30	172, 187–88

Job

24:15	162
31:8	144
31:10	144

Psalms

16:4	144
22:27	46
23:5	251
47:1	46
49:1	46
51	203
67:2	46
72	10, 46, 52–53, 65
72:1–7	53
72:8–11	54
72:11	46
72:15	54
72:17	11, 46, 51, 53–54
86:9	46
96:3–5	46
102:15	46
105:13	144
109:8	144
113:4	46
117	46

Proverbs

6:32	162
25:9	144

Isaiah

2:2	46
6:9–10	79, 103
25:7	46
28:11	144
29:7–8	46
34:15–16	145
42:1–4	75, 79
42:5–7	53
42:8	144
44:6	153
44:8	153
45:5–6	153
45:14	153
45:18	153
45:21–22	153
46:9	153
48:11	144
49:1–6	53
50:1	181
51:2	61
52:10	46
56:7	46, 53
61:8–9	46
61:9	11
61:11	46
65:15	144
65:22	144
66:18–20	46

Jeremiah

3:1	144
3:6–10	164
3:7–8	181
3:8–9	164
5:7	164
6:12	144
7:1	53
7:9	164
7:23	11, 75
8:8	80
8:8–9	80
8:9–13	80
8:10	204
9:20	145
11:4	11, 75
13:27	164
18:4	144
22:26	144

Jeremiah (cont.)

23:14	164
24:7	11, 75
25:11–12	69
29:10	69
29:23	164
30:22	11, 75
31:1	11, 75
31:31–32	164
31:33	11, 75
32:38	11, 75
36:28	144
36:32	144

Ezekiel

1:9	145–46
1:11	145
1:23	145–46
3:13	145–46
11:20	11, 75
12:3	144
14:11	11, 75
16:4	251
23	164
23:1–43	169
36:28	11, 75
37:23	11, 75
37:26–28	53
37:27	11, 75

Daniel

2:47	81
3–7	8
3:17–18	69
9	122
9–12	6, 10, 69, 71, 84
9:2	69
9:3–20	8
9:20–23	70
9:21–27	8
9:22	70
9:23	8, 70
10:1–2	8

10:12	8
11	70
12	70

Hosea

	77
1:6	76
1:9	76
4	164
4:1–2	164

Joel

1:3	144
2:27	153

Jonah

	76–77, 222, 238
1–4	8
3:4–10	81
4	294
4:2	77–78
4:7	78

Zechariah

2:7	144
7:5	281
7:11	103
8:8	11, 75
11:9	145

Malachi

2:9	80
2:11	188
2:15–16	154

Matthew

1:1–2	72
5	274
5:27–28	162
5:27–32	174
5:31–32	160, 181
5:32	181
5:46–47	101

Scripture Index

Matthew (cont.)

6:16–18	281
8	72
8–12	6, 8, 10, 71–72, 79, 83–84, 292
8:1–4	72
8:10–13	72
8:27	72
8:28–33	72
9:1–8	72
9:9–13	73
9:10–11	73
9:12	73
9:12–13	73
9:13	73
9:37	78
10	74
10:5	74
10:6	74
10:21	74
10:22	74
10:23–24	75
11:4–6	74
12	75–76, 182
12:3	75
12:7	75
12:9–17	75
12:17–21	75
12:22–37	75, 78
12:40	75
12:42	54, 75
13	79
13:2	103
13:11	103
13:12	103
13:13–17	103
13:14–15	79
15:19	162
16	267
16:13–28	272, 274–75, 277
16:14	275
16:16	275
16:21–22	275
16:23	241, 276
19	181
19:3–9	209
19:3–12	181
19:5	153–54, 156–57, 159, 173
19:9	160, 181
19:18	162
21:28–31	249
22:23	189
22:23–33	186, 222
25:1–13	168
26:26–28	103
26:33–35	241
26:61	75
27:40	75

Mark

2	182
2:1–3:6	291
2:18–20	281
4:12	79
4:30–32	79
10:2–12	181
10:7–8	153, 156, 173
10:8	154, 157, 159
10:9	209
10:12	160
10:19	162
10:35–40	241
11:17	53
12:29	11
12:34	276
14:58	75
15:29	75

Luke

2:7	251
2:46	274
3:38	72
4:1–13	80
4:13–34	81
6	182, 274
6:33–34	101
7:46	251

Luke (*cont.*)

10	267
10:2	78
11:5–13	122
15	155, 255, 258–63, 265
15:1–2	262
15:20	255
15:25	155
16:13	162, 171
16:18	160
18:10	281
18:12	281
18:20	162

John

2:19–20	75
3	116, 119, 267
3:1–13	276
3:16	159
4	40, 182, 266–67, 272–73
5:39–40	80
6	40, 57
6:60	103
8:3–4	162
8:44	276
17	122
20:9	81

Acts

1–3	57
1:2	117
1:5	245
2	14, 54, 56, 58, 117, 225
2–3	54, 56, 58, 81
2:5	56
2:6	56
2:7	56
2:36	56
2:38	57
2:38–39	57
2:39	57
2:41	57
3	10
3:1–11	67
3:12–26	67
3:24	56
3:25	11, 14, 20, 55–57
4:36	244
6:1–6	186, 222
7	118
7:44–48	53
7:51	118
7:57—8:1	271
8:14–17	111
8:29	118
8:30–31	118
9	9, 81, 101, 117, 267, 272, 279, 281
9:1–2	271, 280
10	115–17, 122, 237–39, 241–43, 245, 262
10–11	6, 9–10, 80, 84, 236, 244, 246
10:2	242
10:3–6	8
10:4	242
10:4–6	8
10:9	8
10:10–16	8
10:17	243
10:19	117, 243
10:19–20	8
10:20	243
10:22	8, 242
10:28	243
10:30–33	8
10:31	242
10:34–36	117
10:44	117
10:44–48	8, 111
11	242–43, 247
11:1	243
11:2–3	244
11:5	8
11:5–10	8
11:12	8, 243
11:13–14	8

Scripture Index

Acts (*cont.*)

11:14	122
11:15–18	8, 117
11:16	245
11:19–30	244
11:22	244
12:1–2	271
13:2–5	118
14	123
14:19	271
15	101, 115, 118, 182, 267, 288
15:1–5	244
15:5	244
15:7–19	117
15:8	118
15:10–11	225
15:20	182
15:28	118
16:6–7	118
19	267
21:10–11	118
22	101
23:2	280
26	101, 115
28:25	118
28:25–28	118

Romans

1:24–27	161–62
2:22	162
4	10, 54, 62–63, 65, 67
4:11	62
4:11–12	63
4:12	62
4:13	63
4:16	62
6	225
7:2–3	174
7:7	187
9:6–7	62

1 Corinthians

2:12–14	117
5	123
5:1	200
5:1–2	175, 216
5:15	159
6:9	161–62
6:12	161–62
6:15–16	162
6:16	153, 156–58, 160, 173
6:16–17	158
7	139, 199–200, 207–8
7:2–16	174
7:7–8	183
7:15	181
7:17	139, 199
7:17–20	199, 216
7:39	178, 181
9	267
9:19–22	267
12:27	159
13:12	130

2 Corinthians

6:3	281
6:16	11, 75

Galatians

3	67
3–4	10, 54, 58, 62–63, 280
3:2	60–61
3:2–5	61
3:6–16	36, 60, 67
3:8	11, 20, 55–56, 58, 60–61, 67
3:8–10	14
3:10	61
3:14–16	61
3:16	36, 55, 59–60, 62–63
3:19	63
3:23–25	61
3:29	63
4	59–60, 248

Galatians (cont.)

4:21–31	59
5:16	60

Ephesians

1:16–19	122
5	65
5:19	155
5:22–33	174
5:28–33	159
5:31	153, 156–58, 173

Philippians

1:9–11	122

Colossians

1:9–13	122
3:16	155

1 Timothy

1:10	162
2:1–15	232, 234
2:9–10	179
2:10	287
2:15	287
3	216, 218
3:1–2	179
3:1–13	178
3:2	136, 154, 173, 175–81, 183–84, 190, 216–18
3:3	179
3:11	179
3:12	136, 154, 173, 175–78, 180–84, 190, 216–18
5:2	179
5:3–10	178
5:9	154, 177–83
5:9–10	179
5:11–14	179, 181
5:21	179

Titus

	214
1:6	154, 173, 175–77, 180

Hebrews

8:10	11, 75
11:18–19	17

1 Peter

2	246

2 Peter

2:12	162
2:15	48

1 John

2:20	117
2:27	117

Jude

7	161–62
11	48

Revelation

	99
2:22	162
7:9	68
22:15	162

www.ingramcontent.com/pod-product-compliance
Lightning Source LLC
Chambersburg PA
CBHW071145300426
44113CB00009B/1086